In the
Shadow *of the* Enemy

In the Shadow *of the* Enemy

The Civil War Journal of Ida Powell Dulany

Edited by Mary L. Mackall, Stevan F. Meserve,
and Anne Mackall Sasscer

Voices of the Civil War
Peter S. Carmichael, Series Editor

The University of Tennessee Press / Knoxville

 The Voices of the Civil War series makes available a variety of primary source materials that illuminate issues on the battlefield, the home front, and the western front, as well as other aspects of this historic era. The series contextualizes the personal accounts within the framework of the latest scholarship and expands established knowledge by offering new perspectives, new materials, and new voices.

 The Civil War journal of Ida Powell Dulany © 2009 by Charles G. Mackall Jr., Mary L. Mackall, and Anne Mackall Sasscer. Editorial additions (including introductory matter, editorial commentary, and notes) © 2009 by The University of Tennessee Press / Knoxville.

All Rights Reserved. Manufactured in the United States of America.
Cloth: First printing, 2009.
Paper: First printing, 2010.

Frontispiece: Mary Eliza "Ida" Dulany, ca. 1855. Courtesy of the Mackall family.

Library of Congress Cataloging-in-Publication Data
Dulany, Ida Powell, 1836–1897.
In the shadow of the enemy: the Civil War journal of Ida Powell Dulany / edited by Mary L. Mackall, Stevan F. Meserve, and Anne Mackall Sasscer. — 1st ed.
   p. cm. — (Voices of the Civil War)
Includes bibliographical references and index.
ISBN-13: 978-1-57233-761-9
ISBN-10: 1-57233-761-3

   1. Dulany, Ida Powell, 1836–1897—Diaries.
   2. Virginia—History—Civil War, 1861–1865—Personal narratives.
   3. United States—History—Civil War, 1861–1865—Personal narratives, Confederate.
   4. Women—Virginia—Fauquier County—Diaries.
   5. Plantation life—Virginia—Fauquier County—History—19th century.
   6. United States—History—Civil War, 1861–1865—Women.
   7. Fauquier County (Va.)—Biography.
   8. Fauquier County (Va.)—Social conditions—19th century.
   I. Mackall, Mary L.
   II. Meserve, Stevan F.
   III. Sasscer, Anne Mackall.
   IV. Title.

E605.D88 2009
973.7'82092—dc22
2008043581

*We dedicate this book to
the women of the South and of the North,
those free and those enslaved,
in memory of their courage, resolution,
suffering, and endurance.*

Contents

Foreword	xi
Peter S. Carmichael, Series Editor	
Acknowledgments	xv
Introduction	xvii
The Civil War Journal of Ida Powell Dulany	
1861	3
1862	57
1863	157
1864	173
1865	193
Epilogue	195
Appendix A: Statement of John Peyton Dulany	201
Appendix B: The Confiscation Act	205
Appendix C: Major General John Pope's General Orders, Nos. 5, 7, 11, and 19	207
Appendix D: The Death of "Kinloch Tom" Turner	211
Appendix E: Accounts of Mosby's Rangers and Engagement at Oakley	217
Notes	221
Index	261

Illustrations

Figures

Following page 47

Thomas Turner IV, Ida's Maternal Grandfather
Kinloch, Home of Edward Carter Turner, Ida's Uncle
The Hill, Ida's Girlhood Home, ca. 1896
Oakley As It Appeared Shortly After the War
Leven Powell, Ida's Great-Grandfather
George Cuthbert Powell, Ida's Father
Marietta Fauntleroy Turner Powell, Ida's Mother
Modern View of the Rear of Oakley
The Oakley Property, with the Meat House and Guest Cottages
Henry Rozier Dulany, Hal's Father
Henry Grafton "Hal" Dulany, After the War
Welbourne, Home of Colonel Richard H. Dulany
Rebecca Ann Dulany, Hal's Sister
Colonel Richard H. Dulany, Hal's Brother-in-Law
Katherine Powell "Kate" Carter, Ida's Younger Sister
Virginia Powell "Jenny" Minnigerode, Ida's Youngest Sister
Oatlands, Home of George and Kate Powell Carter, ca. 1890
George Carter II on the Porch of Little Oatlands

Following page 150

Ida's Elder Daughter, May
Ida's Younger Daughter, Rebecca
Henry Dulany, Henry Rozier Dulany, and Richard Whiting in Montana, 1880

Major General Christopher C. Augur
Brigadier General John White Geary
Charles Minnigerode and Major General Fitzhugh Lee
Walker K. Armistead, Brother of Brigadier General Lewis Armistead
Colonel John S. Mosby
Crednal, Home of John Armistead Carter
Avenel, Home of Robert Beverley
Ida's Journal

Maps

The Geography of Ida Powell Dulany's Wartime Journal	xxxi
Major Battlefields of Virginia	xxxii

Foreword

The South Carolinian Robert Barnwell Rhett, in eulogizing John C. Calhoun before his state's legislature, observed in 1850: "Our internal life, which is our real life, consists of thoughts, intentions, and emotions. This, no eye can see, no hand can write, but the eye and hand of Omnipotence; and it will only be read at the great day of account." His words are hardly comforting to the historian who seeks the essence of his subject through old letters and dusty documents. Ironically, Rhett, who was renowned for his rhetorical excesses and political extremism, is a source of moderation for those of us who pursue Clio. He asks us to calibrate our expectations against the type and availability of sources, reminding us that words on a paper rarely convey a hard truth. In fact, they often obscure more than what they reveal.

Letter writing during the Civil War era was rarely a private matter. The author often wrote for a larger audience; in some cases, letters were intended for newspaper publication. Thus the public nature of correspondence required a degree of self-censorship by the author. Diaries, on the other hand, were private vaults where the inner world of the author was insulated from nosey intimates and curious onlookers. A diary was the one place where a person could write introspectively about his or her place within the larger society without fear of society's judgment. *In the Shadow of the Enemy: The Civil War Journal of Ida Powell Dulany* contains all of the wonderful advantages of a diary as a historical source. It allows us to feel the raw emotions of the author, to sense the chaotic unpredictability of her daily life, to be aware of the inconsistencies between her thinking and action, and to experience the gnawing uncertainty of life during a time of war.

Too often diaries are as dense as granite with the ordinary matters of life. With *In the Shadow of the Enemy*, however, we find a journal that brings Ida to center stage. She does not hide behind bland descriptions of the weather or skirt controversial matters by commenting on the crops. Dulany expressed her most private feelings without regard to audience. Her private admissions are especially important when juxtaposed with her public behavior. Dulany repeatedly confided to her diary that during times of duress, when her household was suffering some physical or emotional hardship, she pretended to be in high spirits. After a friend expressed in a letter that Ida looked healthy and cheerful, Dulany wrote in her journal that "it shows how well I have succeeded in my efforts to appear cheerful.... But as to my being happy that is utterly impossible. I am lonely and anxious and have an indescribable feeling of pain whenever I look forward to the long year that is to pass before Hal [her husband, who was serving in the army] comes back."

Dulany's admission of deception reveals how Southern women scripted their own public performances until the war effort became so hopeless that their acts of Confederate boosterism were largely ludicrous and ineffectual. Confederate women, moreover, saw it as their duty to wear a mask of contentment as a contribution to the Southern war effort. Of course, not all women were as successful as Dulany in putting on such a convincing show, but even those who could not play the charade well believed that they were responsible for preserving family morale. In taking on this duty, women like Dulany remind us that female political action was more than sewing a Confederate flag, bringing a basket of food to a Southern hospital, or making bandages for the wounded. A Confederate woman believed she had to be more assertive and active in furthering the cause, but her behavior could not violate long-standing rules of gender protocol. We see through Dulany's writings how she crafted a public persona that reaffirmed the notion that women were the emotional caretakers of their family. To perform this task, she was both an actor and director in an effort to get her family to play the "proper" supporting role to the Confederate army.

Dulany's life at her Northern Virginia estate hardly resembled a coherent play, with well-developed characters, a clear-cut conflict, and a tidy resolution. There was a frightening incoherence to her wartime experience, and it is beautifully captured in the diary. There is no single story line that gives purpose to Dulany's experience. Her daily existence was caught in a maelstrom of uncontrollable problems that came at her from all directions. Dizzying arrays of people came in and out of her life. Her husband's departure threw her in an emotional pit from which she could not escape. Slaves, who seemed devoted before the Civil War, were sullen and untrustworthy with Union soldiers in the neighborhood. Fear of Federal cavalry seeking retribution for the guerrilla acts of Confederate John Mosby was always present. And the inability to get accurate news about the war left her groping in a morass of rumor and misinformation. She could never shake the frustration of not knowing what was really happening in the war.

Dulany's entries can best be described as random snapshots, taken at an extraordinary fast shutter speed, spraying light on the many dimensions of life on the Civil War home front. From Dulany's written images we can better understand why women on the Southern home front felt overwhelmed by a world that no longer was ordered or controllable. "It is late at night, all the family are in bed, and I alone sit up because I cannot sleep," Ida scribbled in her diary in 1862, "I trust in God, it is true, and all day long keep cheerful & hopeful, but when night comes and I realize how desolate we are I find it far easier to sit up and write than to lie awake with an anxious ear, wondering what the next day will bring forth."

Dulany's lamentations in the middle of the night should not cause us to pity her, for she and her fellow slaveholders had decided to risk it all in a violent struggle for Southern nationhood, but her suffering and sacrifice deserve our deeper understanding. While we possess a privileged view into Ida's private world, a perspective that Rhett so badly desired when looking at Calhoun, we must not become overconfident. We must not succumb to intellectual arrogance in believing that Dulany's "real life" can be found in *In the Shadow of the Enemy*. Her remarkable diary reveals that human existence, especially during the turmoil of war, can turn into a great masquerade, in which combatants and civilians are always changing masks.

Peter S. Carmichael
West Virginia University

Acknowledgments

In the Shadow of the Enemy is the result of three people working together to edit the journal of Ida Powell Dulany. Two of us, Anne Mackall Sasscer and Mimi Mackall, had been working on the journal for a number of years when, in the fall of 2006, our cousin Ben Dulany discovered that Stevan Meserve was doing the same research. Thanks to Ben, we had the good fortune to meet Steve, a Civil War historian, whose expertise in the military aspects of the war in Fauquier and Loudoun counties complemented our focus on Ida's life at Oakley, her complex family genealogy, and her network of friends and neighbors. In this way, two independent projects came together for the benefit of both.

We three are grateful to have the support of many people. Among these are Michael A. Smith, a Powell descendant; Shelby W. Bonnie, the present owner of Oakley; Nathaniel H. Morison III of Welbourne; Sheila Cochran of The Hill; Robert deT. Lawrence IV, a descendant of the Kinloch Turners; the family of Robert Beverley Herbert of Avenel; Stanley and Anna Dees of Crednal; and Childs F. Burden. We owe special thanks to Ida Powell Dulany's great-grandson Benjamin Weems Dulany.

David Boyce, Elizabeth Simon, and Elizabeth Wall at Oatlands, a National Trust Site, provided help and hospitality. We appreciate the assistance given by the staffs of the Thomas Balch Library in Leesburg, the Kate Waller Barrett Branch of the Alexandria Library, the National Sporting Library in Middleburg, the Virginia Historical Society, and the Afro-American Historical Association of Fauquier County. Our thanks also to Lisa McCown of the Washington and Lee University Leyburn Library and Judith Ledbetter of the Charles City County Center for Local History.

Steve Meserve would like to thank the three wonderful research assistants who helped edit his contributions to the journal: Rebecca Fitzgerald of Amherst, Anne Hughes of the United Kingdom, and Tonia J. "Teej" Smith of Pinehurst, North Carolina. As usual, he owes a debt of gratitude to his wife for being so understanding about his spending so much time with a lady who passed away a century ago.

All of us thank David Woodbury for his outstanding maps, which put Oakley and the Dulany family within the geographic context of the war in Virginia.

Anne Mackall Sasscer and Mimi Mackall would like to thank their husbands, Lansdale Sasscer and Charles Mackall, for their patience and enthusiasm during the years that we researched genealogy and Virginia history and wrote and rewrote the introduction and the epilogue.

Introduction

> The importance of women to the war effort carried over into their domestic lives as well. While acting as the heads of household in their husbands' absences, most wives daily confronted many of life's most difficult and demanding situations. Women were required to make financial, domestic, and other kinds of practical decisions and for the first time enjoyed positions of authority in Southern society.
>
> Wiley Sword, *Southern Invincibility:*
> *A History of the Confederate Heart*

Awaiting the Storm

On Thursday, July 25, 1861, following the Battle of First Manassas, Mary Eliza "Ida" Powell Dulany, 1836–1897, sat down to begin the writing of her journal, "This morning my personal participation in the sad experiences of this dreadful war commenced." That day began the transformation of her life. Her husband, Henry "Hal" Grafton Dulany, 1834–1888, had just left for the Cavalry Camp of Instruction at Ashland, Virginia. Ida remained at Oakley, their 850-acre farm near Upperville in Fauquier County, Virginia, about fifty miles from Washington, and, as the war went on, she struggled to protect her home and property as best she could. Only twenty-five years old, Ida was responsible for a large household that included her three little children, her two younger sisters, her mother, her grandmother, and the many slaves there. Although she had an overseer to run the daily operations of the farm, she became the decision maker, and it was she, the mistress of Oakley, who had to provide food, clothing, and medical care for everyone on the place.

The terrible years that followed changed Ida from the gracious wife of a Virginia aristocrat into a confident, independent woman whose intelligence was respected. She became strong and feisty, attributes admired more in modern women in the twenty-first century than in the slaveholding South, where "women were to be meek, pliant, submissive and dependent."[1] What was it in Ida's background that enabled her to take on great responsibility with success while retaining her feminine persona? She was trained by the devout and conventional women of character in her family to be a traditional wife and mother, but she also had the example of generations of men who were outstanding in public service and successful in their endeavors.

The Powells left Wales for America in 1643. In the fourth generation on American soil, Ida's great-grandfather Lt. Col. Leven Powell, 1737–1810, settled in Loudoun County. After fighting in the Revolutionary War,[2] he served as a member of the Virginia Convention for Ratification of the U.S. Constitution and as a member of Congress. In 1787 it was Colonel Powell who donated the land from his Loudoun holdings for the new town of Middleburg, the midpoint between Alexandria and Winchester. He was a wealthy man, with many projects, including the tract of six thousand acres of western land granted to him by the Virginia legislature in recognition of his service to his country. He also had family ties and business interests in Alexandria, where he continued his long friendship with General Washington. "Leven Powell's descendants and their in-laws dominated regional politics for most of the antebellum years.... [It] was one of the most important political dynasties in nineteenth-century northern Virginia."[3] An able member of the next generation was Ida's great-uncle, Cuthbert Powell[4] of Llangollen near Upperville, of whom Chief Justice John Marshall said, "He is the most talented of that talented family."[5]

Ida's own father George Cuthbert Powell, 1807–1849, of The Hill, Middleburg, was known in the family as a wit and a fine speaker, a skill encouraged by a medal won for oratory from the American Literary Scientific and Military Academy in 1827. He studied law and, following family tradition, went on to serve a term in the Virginia legislature, and it was this body that he was planning to address when he died suddenly at age forty-two in 1849.[6] His daughter Jenny was born a few weeks after his death. His portrait shows a dark-haired man in his thirties with a somber expression on his lean, clever face.

On Ida's mother's side, her grandfather, Major Thomas Turner IV, moved from King George County, where he had served in the Virginia General Assembly, to Kinloch, a 2,252-acre farm in the rolling hills of the Piedmont near The Plains in Fauquier County. He and his wife, Eliza Carter Randolph, were descendants of the powerful and interconnected Tidewater plantation families. As members of this close-knit network of relationships, Eliza and Robert E. Lee were first cousins,[7] so there were strong and affectionate ties at Kinloch to the Lee family.[8] Thomas Turner was a friend and mentor to young Robert E. Lee after the death of his father, Henry "Light Horse Harry" Lee. According to Turner family lore, Lee named his horse Traveller after Thomas Turner's favorite mount, Fancy Traveller. When Lee was growing up, Kinloch was a lively place brimming with visitors, most of whom were related. It was not surprising that in 1831, when Lt. Robert E. Lee married Mary Anne Randolph Custis,[9] also a close cousin of the Turners, two of the Kinloch siblings—Ida's mother,

Marietta,[10] and Thomas Turner[11]—were chosen to be bridesmaid and groomsman at the Arlington wedding. The childhood friendship of Marietta and Mary Custis Lee lasted until Mrs. Lee's death on November 5, 1873.[12] A few weeks later, on December 17, her daughter, Mildred Lee, wrote, "I know dear Cousin Marietta how our grief has been yours too. . . . You were so very near & dear to my blessed Mother, & were so associated with her early days before the shadows commenced to darken her life, that I feel as if you, more than any one else, had the best right to share in our tears. I wish I could see you, to ask you about that dear old life at Arlington—when you were young together."[13]

Marietta and George Cuthbert Powell married in 1831 and raised their children[14] at The Hill, the handsome Georgian house on their 460-acre farm at the edge of Middleburg. For Ida there were many good times at The Hill, her much-loved childhood home, and a lively society in Middleburg, the town founded by her family. Her life, however, was not without its trials. The deaths of two of her brothers, twenty-one-year-old Conrad and three-year-old Thomas, and the death of her father brought sorrow to the Powells. Marietta was left with fewer financial resources, but she held the family together and set high standards for her children. Her granddaughter, Marietta Andrews, wrote, "Discipline, devotion, conscience, over-ruled personal interest and selfish desire at every point."[15]

The loss of her father was particularly hard for Ida, who was very close to him from her earliest childhood. When she was ten, she wrote, "Pa has come home from Leesburg, and brought us [Ida and Kate] a pair of gloves . . . [that] fit us exactly, and are very nice ones. . . . There is to be a very large show in town tomorrow and I want Pa to take us with him if he goes."[16]

This is the background into which Ida was born in 1836, a background where hospitality and obligation to family, church, and community were taken seriously. Although she was guided by these old standards, which were ingrained in her character, she was by nature proactive and energetic. When she heard about the great Charleston fire of 1861, she did not hesitate to invite her uncle Captain Shirley Carter Turner, his wife, and their children to take refuge at Oakley. Fortunately they were out of danger, and the invitation was declined. It is evident from her journal that she was always involved in her own community. In her prewar Jane Austen life of farm and village, the church was a central part of her life. Even in that first grim winter of the war, she took it on herself to seek donations for a Christmas gift for Mr. Kinsolving, the Episcopal minister in Upperville, whose salary was miserly. Later her outreach would be more sorrowful as she nursed and comforted wounded and dying soldiers from both armies.

Ida's adult responsibilities began early. When she married Henry Grafton Dulany in 1855, she was nineteen, and Hal was twenty-one. She was disarmingly pretty, feminine, and spirited, petite in contrast to Hal, who was tall, a fine horseman, and a good shot. If he liked his whiskey, so did many of his peers. His lineage was impeccable,[17] important in that era, and the fact that she had no fortune did not matter.[18] Theirs was, without question, a love match. Generous and hospitable, Hal settled Ida and their first child, Marietta (May), at Oakley, the large farm he bought from his sister and brother-in-law, Rebecca and Richard Dulany of Welbourne, in 1857.[19] By September little Rozier was born, Hal's son and heir, named for his grandfather Dulany, and in 1859 their last child, Rebecca, arrived, named for her aunt Rebecca of Welbourne.[20] Oakley also became the home of Ida's widowed mother, Marietta, who was age forty-nine in 1861, and Ida's two younger sisters, Kate, twenty-two, and Jenny, twelve.[21] In addition to the three Powells, Hal also took in Ida's Kinloch grandmother Eliza Carter Randolph Turner, who at age seventy-nine was frail and required constant attention during her long stays with the Dulanys.

It is fortunate that Oakley was not only a handsome residence but a large one. The house, plaster over brick, was substantial and is described by the Virginia Landmarks Commission as "one of the best examples of Italianate High Victorian architecture in Fauquier County." A long flight of steps led to the front door, sheltered by a gracious portico. One entered through a large hall, square in shape, with a fine graceful stairway curving upwards at the rear. To the right was the parlor, where the portrait of Henry Rozier Dulany of Shuter's Hill in Alexandria hung over the marble mantelpiece. Hal's father was a military man, a West Pointer, resplendent in full dress uniform. To the left was the library with its leather-bound volumes so precious to Ida. The dining room was at the back of the hall, and it was here that Ida began the Oakley tradition of good food and hospitality. Under the handsome paneled stairway were the steps leading to the finished, above-ground rooms of the cellar, where Ida was confronted by abusive Federal troops. The ceilings were fourteen feet high, making the thick-walled house cool in the hot Virginia summers. An unusual feature of the house was the very advanced plumbing system, which included an enormous lead-lined tank in the garret, or attic, to collect rainwater. Although Ida never revealed the secret in her journal, the dark space behind this tank became a hiding place for Hal during raids by Union soldiers.

For the Dulany family, the prewar years at Oakley were tranquil and happy ones, unclouded by death, drought, or fire, the specters that hovered over life on the farm in the nineteenth century. Hal found that the routine of a Virginia planter suited him; he was beginning to make Oakley a success. He bred fine horses in which he took great pride, a Dulany tradition going back to his colonial Maryland ancestors and carried on to this day. By 1857 the Middleburg-Upperville area was well known as prime horse country, "perhaps the best in the State, and better than can be found anywhere else except in Kentucky."[22] He had a responsible overseer, Mr. Kidwell, on whom he could depend and sixty-nine slaves, according to the 1860 U.S. Census, thirty-seven of whom were under the age of fourteen with five ranging in age from sixty-eight to one hundred.[23] The value of the land was listed at $46,240, and Hal's personal property, which included the slaves, was listed at $60,820, a substantial estate for that period. After seeing to his stable and his cattle, sheep, hogs, wheat, corn, and other farm projects, Hal would ride home to an attractive wife and growing children. He did not have the wealth of his brother-in-law, Richard Dulany of Welbourne, who had inherited the great fortune of his wife, Hal's sister, Rebecca,[24] but he lived well. He enjoyed the traditional country pleasure of riding to hounds with the fox hunt organized by Richard Dulany in 1840. In 1904, this Piedmont Hunt was recognized as the oldest hunt in America. In spite of losing one eye in a childhood accident, he was able to hunt quail, wild turkeys, and the other game that were still plentiful.

It was Ida who made Oakley a comfortable and welcoming home. She was well taught by her mother to run a household. "By the 1840s, elite parents, like their poorer neighbors . . . also insisted that their single daughters know how to conduct themselves in the kitchen, garden, sewing room, nursery, and sick room before their marriages."[25] Under Ida's capable direction, there was always delicious food on the Oakley table supplied from the smoke house, or "meat house," where the hams, shoulders, and slabs of bacon were hung. When the hogs were killed in the late fall, well after frost, there was the yearly treat of fresh pork and a new supply of sausage and of the lard so essential for frying and baking. There was the fattening coop for chickens soon destined for Sunday dinner after church, and a henhouse where eggs were gathered for daily use. The chickens, as well as the ducks and turkeys, would be fair game for scavenging Union soldiers. There were fruits in the summer to be made into preserves and jelly, cucumbers to pickle, and grapes from the arbor to be made into the Oakley wine,[26] which, aged in casks, was said to taste like a sherry. Fresh butter was made in the dairy in carefully scalded wooden churns, and clabber, a first cousin of yogurt, was served with heavy cream and sprinkled with brown sugar and nutmeg. In good growing seasons the vegetable garden was bountiful and wild game was plentiful, so no one went hungry in the prewar years.

In comparison to Hal's peacetime routine, Ida's daily life appeared more stressful than his, leaving her little leisure to pursue the reading that she loved, the plays, poetry, novels, history, theology, and astronomy that she taught to two generations of children on starry nights. She taught music and a little French as well. Her endless obligations began at sunrise and ended long after sunset. Since Oakley was always open to family and friends, she never knew when the next guest would appear. This routine, however, was not at all unusual and was expected of wives in well-run households of Virginia planters.

If Ida's daily life was demanding, the life of her domestic slaves was much more physically taxing. The Dulany's open-handed hospitality was well known.

Many guests, often unexpected, made for late hours in the kitchen, extra laundry done by hand, and constant rearranging of bedrooms and relaying of fires. Sometimes sheeting beds and putting down pallets on the floor kept the servants busy long after their bedtime. The kitchen workers rose very early to start the wood-burning stove for the breakfast breads: the cornbread, the beaten biscuits, the buckwheat cakes, and Sally Lunns. The number of guests increased during the war as Confederate officers and soldiers, many of whom were cousins, were made welcome at all hours. Ida's cook and Robert the butler provided late suppers in the dining room, and a groom was roused from sleep to see that the horses were fed, watered, and stabled. A servant was always available to run errands or deliver messages. Ida opened her house and shared her dwindling food supply willingly. For the slaves there was no choice.

They were the framework, the support system on which the family depended for both its social and economic life. The varied domestic skills of the house slaves, the skills of the nurse, the cook, the seamstress, the laundress, the gardener, the butler, and the coachman made the lifestyle of the family comfortable and often elegant. It was the agricultural workers, however, who were essential for the master's income. Their labor included the planting and harvesting of crops, the care of the orchards, the raising of valuable livestock including Hal's prize horses. The good carpenters mended the barns and stables as needed, built gates and fences, and repaired the wagons and farm equipment. The slaves trained as butchers were in charge of slaughtering the hogs in the fall, preparing them for the house slaves who finished the process under Ida's watchful supervision. Slave and master had a vested interest in this ritual, which provided meat in some form for everyone on the farm.

Ida managed a household staff that she referred to as servants, not as slaves. Although Ida was a remarkable and in many ways a modern woman, she accepted slavery as a normal fact of life sanctioned by church and state in the South, and she reflected the Southern prejudices and racist attitudes of her time, which are indefensible today. Custom had so inured her to the slave/master inequality that she could not comprehend the injustice and inhumanity of the system. "Blacks and whites in the old South rarely understood the contours of the other's life—even the significance of some of the most profoundly important aspects of one's existence eluded the comprehension of the other. This expansive cultural gap, and the oppressive social system which held it in place, was a constant source of suspicion, disappointment, and dismissal of the one by the other."[27]

Unlike his distinguished Maryland ancestors, Hal was not driven by ambition or by an interest in politics or the desire to make a great fortune. He had a good heart and a quick wit, and he and Ida shared the same values. He was less intellectual than his well-educated wife, hated to write letters, even to her, and probably did not read a great deal because of his limited sight. Yet the chemistry between them is obvious in her journal. In a house filled with visitors and inhabited by three and often four female members of Ida's family, there was little opportunity for the young Dulanys to be by themselves. They solved this by escaping the gathering in the parlor every Sunday evening to spend time alone. Their love for each other was also apparent from Hal's letters. On a prewar trip north to sell some of his horses, he wrote, "My own darling Ida . . . I have thought of you all the time the first thing in the morning and the last thing at night."[28]

Thunderbolts All Around

The great storm that was about to break over Hal and Ida's well-ordered world would change them both irrevocably and forever in ways unimaginable on their wedding day. By the end of March 1861, seven Southern states, led by South Carolina, had withdrawn from the Union and formed the Confederacy. After the attack at Fort Sumter on April 12, 1861, there was no going back, and the momentum for secession and war built in Virginia, although there were still many doubts. At the Virginia Convention of April 17, the vote to join the other Southern states was eighty-eight to fifty-five. On the local level, Hal's uncle John Armistead Carter of Crednal, one of two delegates from Loudoun County, voted against seceding, and Ida's uncle Edward Carter Turner of Kinloch, an influential citizen, was strongly opposed to the dissolution of the Union. On April 20 Col. Robert E. Lee resigned his commission in the U.S. Army, writing sadly to his sister, Anne Kinloch Lee Marshall, "With all my devotion to the Union, and the feeling of loyalty and duty of an American citizen, I have not been able to make up my mind to raise my hand against my relatives, my children, my home."[29]

As war became inevitable, Hal's duty as a Virginian was clear. He made the honorable choice and signed up for the year of service the new government was asking for at that time. Ida supported his decision, although her early enthusiasm soon turned to a grimmer, more stoic acceptance of the realities of war.

In the early summer, Hal helped his brother-in-law, Richard Henry Dulany, assemble a company of eighty Confederate cavalrymen, called the Dulany Troop, later known as Company A, 6th Virginia Cavalry. In July 1861 Hal went to Richmond to buy arms. He wrote to Ida on July 7, "We have been to see most of the grand people here, and they have promised to do the best they could, but with it all there seemed to be a *blue* chance for getting arms. They are not to be had. General Lee heard I was in town and wanted some letters of introduction [to government officials] and very kindly sent for me and gave me what I wanted. He inquired particularly after Ma and yourself and little Kate, as he called her." In spite of a busy schedule, Hal managed to find time to search, also in vain, "all the book stores for *Very Little Tales for Very Little Children*," and he bought a subscription to the *Richmond Dispatch* newspaper for his mother-in-law.

By July 21 the first major battle of the war was raging along a stream called Bull Run near Manassas, about thirty miles west of Washington and only twenty miles from Oakley. Gen. Irvin McDowell's army, thirty-five thousand strong, marched out of Washington anticipating a victory over General Beauregard's army of twenty-two thousand men, but the rapid reinforcement of Joseph E. Johnston and Thomas J. Jackson from the west enabled the Confederates to achieve victory. The South was jubilant and all of Washington stunned. The war had begun in earnest and on an unprecedented scale.

Two weeks later, Hal was at Ashland, a small town near Richmond, taking part in drilling the Dulany troop in preparation for battle. As an expert horseman, he was well equipped for this task, and Ida was proud of him. Her journal of August 12 referred to a letter from Capt. Richard Dulany in which he praised her husband: "He spoke highly of Hal as a soldier which was very gratifying to me." Pride in the cavalry, however, was not enough to ease the transition from life at home to the rigid discipline and hardships of camp, and Hal like so many soldiers missed his wife and children. In a letter to Ida dated July 29, 1861, he wrote, "For the first day after I started I was so dreadfully home sick that I could not enjoy the novelty of things, but since [then] I have gotten over in some measure bidding you all good bye, I have become more reconciled, and am determined to do my duty as far as I am able."

In the months that followed his departure from Oakley, Hal and Ida learned new duties. Ida had taken over the management of the farm. Hal obviously had confidence in his competent wife; in his letters to her he referred to "your mares," "your cattle," and "your wheat." Meanwhile he had become an experienced soldier, often assigned to be the advance guard on long days of scouting and occasionally skirmishing with Union troops, a position of risk and responsibility. On December 17, 1861, he described an encounter near Manassas, "we left here yesterday morning at 4 o'clock and got back between 4 & 5 in the evening just completely used up. We went about seventeen or eighteen miles down the country under Gen. Stewart [Stuart] with two companies of cavalry and about 100 infantry, and with ten men from our company, [I] was chosen as the advance guard of the Gen. and was ordered to keep from a ¼ to ½ mile ahead and scour the country—a thing hard to do [and] not by any means a very pleasing task. We had heard that the Yankees had for a week or two past been lying in ambush for our men in large force and we determined to catch them. . . . Walker Armistead and I who were ahead saw some Yankee Troops down by the creek just below Ravensworth house.[30] We started with a whoop—I started nine men to the right directly after them and both Walkers[31] with me to the left to head them off which we perfectly succeeded in doing—The Ravensworth house [on] one side has an immense pine thicket which we knew if they got to they would be perfectly safe, that is why we struck off by ourselves as we were both mounted on fleet horses and good jumpers. We took three Yankees."

Ida yearned for these letters, in which Hal shared news and also described life in the cavalry's winter quarters not far from Manassas. The cold weather was unforgiving, and Hal wrote about the mud up to his knees, the poor food, and the monotony of daily life before action came. He felt lonely and depressed ("I have got the blue devils terribly today") and worried about Ida and the children. At home Ida put up a cheerful front to hide her own fears and anxieties about her husband. The only time that she lost control and became hysterical was in mid-December of 1861, the day after she had heard the constant boom of distant guns from the direction of Manassas. At ten o'clock that night, she was upstairs trying to read her book when suddenly she heard the sound of carriage wheels on the driveway approaching the front entrance. In a state of wild agitation and grief, she jumped up and ran downstairs, assuming that it was Confederate officers bringing Hal's body home. Later she was embarrassed by this one loss of composure and called it "her folly."[32]

In a letter from Camp G. W. Smith dated January 5, 1862, Hal worried about her lingering cough.[33] "You can't imagine how uneasy it has made me, and I have no doubt, my darling hard headed little wife, it has been brought on by your own imprudence. If you recollect I was begging you to put on flannel long before you would consent to do it, when if you had have done so, you would have escaped. Do, my darling, take best care of yourself." In the same letter but on a lighter note, Hal, as usual, teased Ida, "We are hard at work on our winter quarters and will have in a short time, by the combined efforts of Plaster, Gibson, Dulany & Co quite a presentable house, *nearly* as good as your old turkey house, pleasant, don't you think so? How do you think you could stand 'love in a cottage' [in] this weather?"

By February 27, 1862, Hal was deeply concerned for the safety of his family. "I feel very uneasy, my darling, about that part of the country about Upperville. If it is over run (and I think there is a strong probability of it) and we have to fall back from here, I may not see you for months. If I knew you were safe I could stand it, as hard as it would be, but it would nearly kill me if there was any doubt of it. Now I want you to see Brother Richard or Uncle John,[34] and get his house up in the mountains, it is the most out of the way place I know of and his family [the Welbourne Dulanys] and you could live up there, I think in safety. If he agrees to let you have it, send all your meat,[35] everything you can possibly want up there and the first intimation you have of the Federal approach, leave, consult Uncle John and Uncle Armistead[36] about this and see what they think of it. Our house is in a most exposed situation, right on the public highway[37] and I know it can't escape them—Think about that, my Darling, if it is only to relieve my fears. I have great confidence in your judgment. Therefore I say to you after thinking about it, do as you think best."

In response to Hal's plea to evacuate Oakley, Ida wrote in her journal on March 4, 1862, "Many families are leaving their houses, unwilling to risk a meeting with the enemy, but I have determined to stand my ground." Ida never wavered after making this decision, although on March 10 she wrote, "Our most anxious personal fears are at last realized."

Hal's own fears were well founded. The location of Oakley on Ashby's Gap Turnpike,[38] the major thoroughfare beginning in Alexandria, passing through Aldie Gap, Middleburg, and Upperville, and winding its way westward to Winchester and the Shenandoah Valley was a critical factor in her wartime experiences. Both Confederate and Union forces frequently moved through and fought to control this important artery. The fertile Shenandoah Valley, the "breadbasket" of the Confederate Army of Northern Virginia, was a way to the north and also to Washington. General Lee followed that route in his invasion north in 1863. Official Washington was always alert to the threat of attack from the Shenandoah Valley, where Gen. "Stonewall" Jackson operated so effectively in 1862.

On the home front at Oakley, Ida could hear the dreaded "dull boom of the guns" from Winchester and points west and from the battles to the east at Manassas in 1861 and 1862 where friends and family fought and died. On June 2, she wrote, "Day after day, one after another, the young and the strong, the good and the lovely fall all around us, and the gloom deepens daily over our poor land." Her closest encounter with battle was from her own balcony at Oakley—fierce cavalry engagements related to General Lee's two northern invasions, Antietam in 1862 and Gettysburg in 1863. Scarcely a day went by without some incident occurring on the Dulany's farm or in Fauquier or nearby Loudoun County. Since both armies lived off the land, the demands on the civilian population were brutal and unrelenting.

In addition to the conventional military operations between Federal and Confederate troops near Oakley, beginning in January 1863, the legendary John Singleton Mosby and his men, officially known as the 43rd Battalion, Virginia Partisan Rangers, waged guerrilla warfare in Ida's area of Virginia, which came to be known as "Mosby's Confederacy." On occasion, the action took place on the Oakley fields. Mosby's daring raids in Fauquier, Loudoun, Prince William, and Fairfax counties inspired awe and fear. Infuriated by his audacity and seeming invincibility, a significant number of Union troops were tied up in pursuing him. In her own estimation of Mosby, Ida saw and feared the consequences of his surprise attacks. On May 1, 1863, she wrote, "The impression in the army seems to be that we are protected from Yankees by [Mosby's men], but I fear it is just the reverse, as every raid Mosby has made has produced a retaliatory raid from the Yankees in which the citizens suffer severely, Mosby having always to get out of their way, as he is invariably out numbered." Still, Ida and Hal opened their home to Mosby's men, who often stayed with them between raids, recovered from wounds in their guest rooms, and, in some cases, died there.

By the summer of 1862, Company A was actively engaged in skirmishes with the enemy, and Hal was doing well as a seasoned officer, when fate dealt him an unexpected blow. An injury to his remaining eye aggravated by unsanitary conditions, long hours in the saddle on picket duty, and encounters with the Federals all conspired against him. As described by his sister-in-law, Kate, in her diary on July 25, "He has been suffering very much with his [good] eye lately and consulted the surgeon of his Regiment, who told him a few more months of such exposed service would have him totally blind. Sometimes after a day's hard march in the sun or rain, at night he would not be able to see a yard before him."[39] Meanwhile Richard Dulany had left the 6th Virginia Cavalry to accept an appointment as lieutenant colonel of the 7th Virginia Cavalry under William E. "Grumble" Jones, leaving a vacancy in the position of captain which was offered to Hal. Hal decided not to accept because of his eyesight. After resigning from the company on July 6, Hal then applied for the less-exposed position of adjutant on Col. Richard Dulany's staff, but he failed to obtain the post, which was not surprising considering his condition. He visited his family doctor, Dr. Gunnell, who confirmed the diagnosis of the military surgeon. Kate continued that Dr. Gunnell had warned Hal "that if he goes back in to the army, even [as] adjutant or quarter master, where he will not be exposed to picket duty, that in three months he may lose his sight altogether. His eye has never been well since he came home from Manassas last winter with it so swollen and inflamed." Hal included with his resignation the certification of the military surgeon,[40] "I have carefully examined the above named officer and find that the sight of his remaining eye is so much impaired that it will be seriously endangered if he remains in service." Hal knew the desperate need for every Confederate officer and soldier, yet if he went blind he could not fight for the South or help his family. He left behind the men of Company A, who would face the risk of death or the prospect of terrible wounds. His year of service was over.

His resignation caused Ida great anxiety and concern. She loved her children, but Hal was the center of her life. She understood the impossible situation in which he found himself as a consequence of his resignation, that of "wandering about without means sufficient, or occupation in his own land."[41]

Hal's return to Oakley brought him neither peace nor security. He may have thought that as a civilian with a medical discharge he would be beyond the reach of the Federal army. He did not know that the war was rapidly turning into a "total war" in which Southern civilians on the home front, like soldiers in the field, were considered enemies. Hal now realized that he would be subjected to the harsh and punitive orders issued by Gen. John Pope in July 1862 requiring noncombatants to sign President Lincoln's amnesty. Any man as young as Hal who refused to sign the oath of allegiance to the Union faced deportation. Once deported he risked death and the confiscation of his estate if he tried to return home. Hal knew that the women of Oakley and his three children would be homeless and destitute if he did not obey. In the early fall of 1862, he gave his "parole" that he would not bear arms against the United States. This decision was difficult for a proud man and a former Confederate officer, and in the end it did not keep him safe or protect his family from invading Union troops. As a wealthy and influential person in the community, Hal was a prime candidate to be taken hostage to ensure good treatment of Union civilians and soldiers in Confederate hands. This was a common practice on both sides. Urged by Ida, he took refuge, camping from time to time in the woods and on the mountains, hiding from the Federals. As late as November 1864, John Peyton Dulany wrote to his son Richard, "Henry Dulany has to leave home, how much better it would be if he had remained in the army."[42] It was ironic that if Hal had gone blind as the doctors predicted, he would have been hailed as a hero of the Confederacy.

Although harassed by frequent Federal raids and the deprivations of war, Ida continued to manage the house and farm as best she could with the slaves who were left. She had learned about the stock, the planting, and the harvesting in Hal's absence and was very much in charge as Hal came and went. Of necessity she had assumed his role, another blow to his self-esteem. Under stress, Hal was drinking more; yet she never criticized him in her wartime journal, and her love for him was constant.

Ida's trials were shared by women of her class all over the South. It was the manner in which she faced the challenges that set her apart. As the months went by, she summoned the courage to endure the ordeal of living each day in the shadow of the enemy. "It is as if I were in a fearful storm and saw friend after friend stricken down by the thunderbolts all around me and knew that at any moment the next bolt might crush me too and that I was powerless to escape."[43]

The Truth Will Be Shown by History

Like most first-time diarists, Ida started her journal with good intentions of making a regular record of her life. At first she made her entries on the unused portion of Hal's old diary. As she explained, "Paper is very scarce these war times so my journal must not be ashamed to find itself in an old day book, which Hal began to keep when we were first married, but of which he soon grew tired."[44] By June of 1862, she was using his old ledger, 6" by 15 ¼", where he recorded some of his stud farm operations and other farm business, including regular payments to slaves for eggs and chickens ("To Aunt Polly for chickens, 25 cents") and many unidentified products or services ("To Simon to bring back butter $1.00"). Ida wrote edge to edge on the paper, sometimes sideways, and sometimes upside down on the page to use every bit of space not already taken up by Hal's accounts. Her large hand-writing tended to become an almost illegible scrawl when she was exhausted, which occurred often during the war. She very rarely crossed out a word and never rewrote a section.

Ida made almost daily entries throughout the second half of 1861; but the gaps between entries became more frequent and longer in 1862 and 1863. The fate of a large section covering July 1863 through November 1864 remains a mystery. No one knows whether she stopped writing for more than a year or whether the missing pages were lost within the family after her journal was divided among her three children following her death. A typewritten transcript was made of the rest of the diary many years ago, and *In the Shadow of the Enemy* consists of this transcript in part and the handwritten journal now on loan to the Virginia Historical Society in Richmond. The transcribed copy of Ida's journal is in the possession of her descendants, the Mackall and Sasscer families, who also own the original. Other transcribed copies have been shared with family members over the years.

Some of the errors contained in these pages may well be early transcription errors; others are obviously Ida's mistakes. For example, she consistently misspelled the names of some officers. She wrote Joseph E. Johnston's name "Johnson," Beverly Robertson's name appears as "Robinson," and Generals Floyd and Rosecrans are always written "Lloyd and Rosencrantz." For the reader's convenience, the consistent misspelling of names has been corrected after their initial appearance. Minor spelling mistakes or variations such as "troup" for "troop" have been corrected throughout the book. Almost all of the dashes Ida used in place of punctuation marks have been replaced, as appropriate, with commas and periods; and long entries have been broken up into paragraphs for ease of reading. The only inclusions in the text are excerpts from Hal's letters that clarify her references to them.

Ida was well educated and interested in events far beyond the boundaries of her Virginia farm. She was an avid newspaper reader who noted her disappointment when the vagaries of war kept her from acquiring the latest issues. Ida recorded what she read about the war in the newspapers, but she was troubled about the accuracy of what she wrote: "I have been looking over my journal today and I find many errors, some gross misstatements as to facts. It would be impossible to correct them all, so I will let all stand. The truth will be shown by history, and my statements that conflict with the truth will serve to show how in these times of trouble we are imposed upon by intentional and unintentional misrepresentation."[45]

Of far more interest than the flawed newspaper stories are Ida's accounts of actual engagements and the portrait in her journal of the society in which she lived, the culture, the role of women, and the treatment of slaves as the microcosm with Oakley at its center was changed forever by the conflict. These pages contain a remarkable history of a war; not of major battles and grand strategy, but of the cost of war on the civilian population, black and white. It is a record of sorrow for the death of loved ones and friends, of hunger and privation, and of anger at the men who visited wanton destruction, suffering, and plunder on the noncombatants of Virginia. At the same time, it is a remarkable testament to the resilience of the human spirit. During the "Great Burning Raid" of 1864, in which Union cavalrymen endeavored to destroy all the barns and crops in western Loudoun and Fauquier counties and kill or run off all the livestock in the area, Ida notes, "I could but remark the cheerfulness with which the devastation was borne by all the inhabitants. I did not see one sad face.... As to our own loss I was only grateful it was no greater."[46]

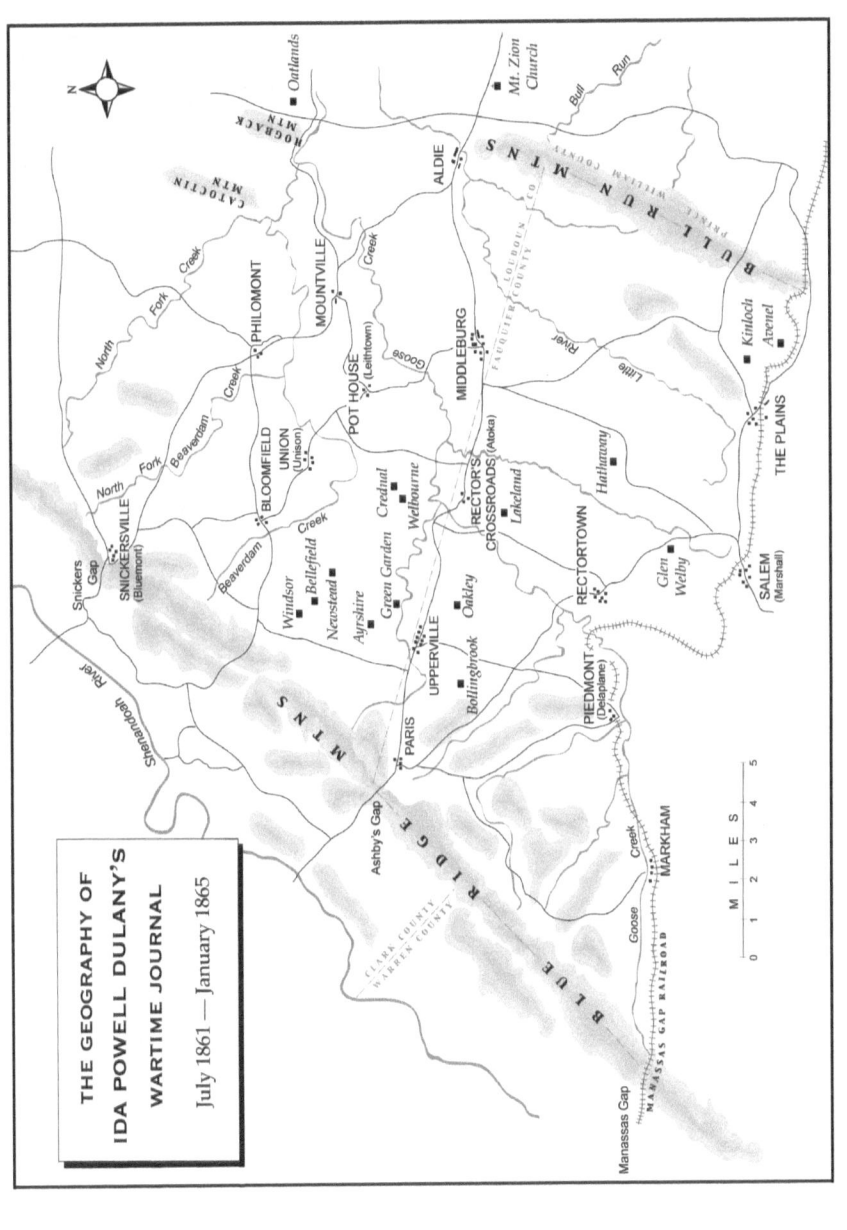

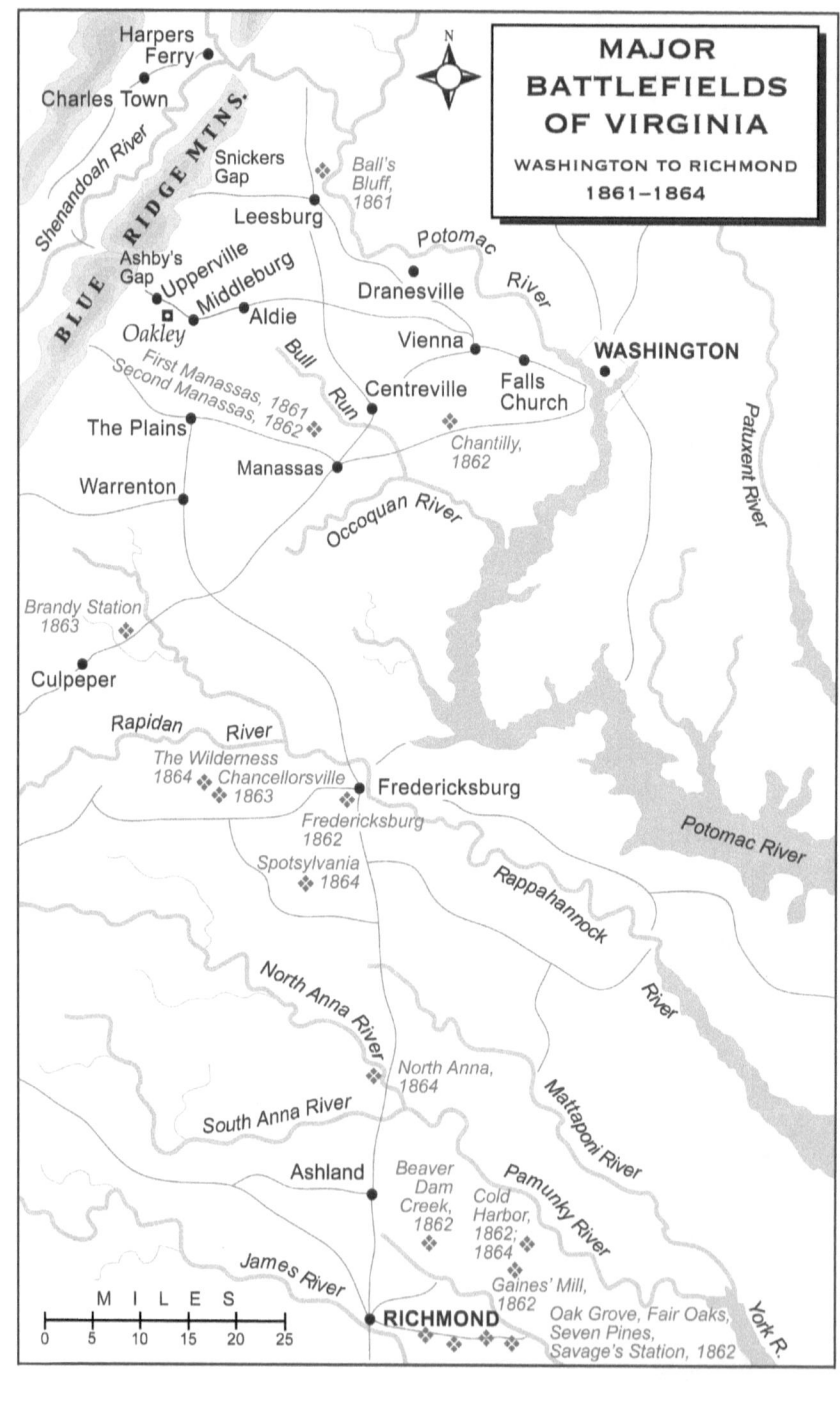

The Civil War Journal of Ida Powell Dulany

1861

July

Four days after Abraham Lincoln was elected president of the United States in November 1860, the South Carolina legislature called for a convention to consider removing the state from the Union. On December 20 they declared, "the people of the State of South Carolina in convention assembled, do declare and ordain . . . that the Union now subsisting between South Carolina and other States, under the name of 'the United States of America,' is hereby dissolved." Mississippi, Florida, Alabama, Georgia, Louisiana, and Texas quickly followed suit. Representatives of all seven states met in Montgomery, Alabama, in February to declare the establishment of the Confederate States of America as a separate nation.

Although it was a Southern, slaveholding state, Virginia was slow to follow suit. Instead Governor John Letcher called for a convention of all the states to meet to resolve the differences between the North and South. Unfortunately passions were too high for moderation and reason to carry the day; and the convention came to naught. Then, on April 12, Confederate batteries surrounding Charleston Harbor began a thirty-six-hour bombardment of Fort Sumter. Two days after the Union garrison surrendered, Lincoln called for 75,000 troops to put down the rebellion. Only two days after that, on April 17, a convention in Richmond adopted an Ordinance of Secession, subject to approval by the state's voters. On May 23, with 124,896 voters favoring the ordinance and only 20,390 opposing it, Virginia officially left the Union. Before dawn the next morning, 13,000 Union troops crossed the Potomac and occupied Alexandria and Arlington. By July 1 Union armies were on the advance in the western counties of Virginia and in the Shenandoah Valley, while yet another army prepared to move against the main Confederate defenses near Manassas.

Events elsewhere in the war are listed in the accompanying timeline.

Timeline of the War

July 5	Union troops under Gen. Franz Sigel are defeated in the Battle of Carthage, Missouri.
July 10	Confederate forces are defeated at Monroe Station, Mississippi.
July 11	Union troops win twin victories in western Virginia when Gen. William S. Rosecrans defeats Col. John Pegram's Confederates at Rich Mountain, while Gen. Thomas Morris bests Gen. Richard Garnett at Laurel Hill.
July 12	Union troops occupy Romney, western Virginia, capturing six hundred Confederate defenders.
July 13	Garnett becomes the first general officer killed in the war when his men are defeated at Carrick's Ford, western Virginia.
July 18	Union and Confederate forces clash at Blackburn's Ford on Bull Run Creek.
July 20	Gen. Joseph E. Johnston's army from Winchester reaches Manassas, having left a screening force to convince Patterson they were still in the Shenandoah Valley.
July 21	The timely arrival of the last of Johnston's men from Winchester allows the Confederate Army of the Potomac to defeat its Union counterpart in the First Battle of Manassas. Almost as disorganized in victory as the Federals are in defeat, the Confederates do not pursue as the enemy streams back to Washington.
July 24	Confederate reverses in western Virginia continue as Gen. Henry Wise abandons Charleston.
July 27	Gen. McDowell is replaced as army commander by Gen. McClellan, who has won a series of victories in western Virginia.

July 25th 1861 [Thursday]
Oakley. This morning my personal participation in the sad experiences of this dreadful war commenced. Hal has gone with the Company of which he is 1st lieutenant & Brother Richard Captain, and to-night I begin my journal, not so much to record my own feelings as to give a simple statement of events as they pass from the time of his leaving till the blessed day of his return. I will however glance over the events of the past fortnight as too striking to be entirely omitted.

    A week ago today, as far as we knew every thing was quiet. We went to bed last Thursday night as usual, but at 2 o'clock in the night I was awakened by the violent barking of our dogs Rollo & Oscar, followed immediately by the tramp of horses' feet and an impatient call for "Henry." I awoke Hal instantly—he went to the window, and soon discovered that it was dear Dan Conrad.[1] We were much surprised, as we thought him with Genl. Johnson's[2] [sic] army near Winchester. He brought Major Botts[3] with him. I listened over the banister, and heard Dan tell Hal that all Johnston's army was at Paris 6 miles off.

We were much excited and begged for news, but all he could tell us was that at one o'clock the day before the order was suddenly issued, to proceed immediately to Piedmont[4] preparatory to reinforcing Beauregard[5] at Manassas Junction, they knew not why. So instantly every thing was stopped, the bread left baking in the oven, the meal boiling over the fire, with no time for adieux, taking such provisions as they had, they left Winchester, the women calling after them with tears and entreaties not to leave them to the mercy of the Northern army, which they expected to attack the town. Dan & Major Botts left the army to spend the night at Paris, and came in to see us. They were tired and we soon fixed a room for them, and were glad to think they had a good night's rest. Early in the morning they left, and we, that is Hal, Kate, the children, and I went down to Piedmont to see them. Before we went John Bolling[6] rode over to see his little sister who was staying with us.

It was sad enough to look at them strong and young and hopeful, somewhat saddened it is true on the uncertainty as to what was before them, and think that the question of life or death might be decided for them in a few hours. The many soldiers at Piedmont scattered about in groups, sleeping, cooking, eating and talking, waiting for the cars to take them to meet the enemy—seemed like sheep gathered for the slaughter and my heart ached to look at them. We talked with our acquaintances among them for some time, and then left—after hearing that at Bull's Run, we had 3 times beaten back the enemy with great slaughter to them and a loss of only 8 killed to us.[7] Capt. William Dulany[8] mortally wounded. For several days our county was constantly excited by the different divisions of the Army passing through.

On Sunday the 21st in the morning Mr. Richards[9] called to say that the McDonald Regt.[10] would be at Upperville that evening, and we must all send provisions. Before going to church[11] I gave the order for preparing everything I could gather, and we took it up to the soldiers in the evening. I saw Col. Ashby[12]—and it made my heart ache to see him. Every glance at his sad face brought so vividly before my mind's eye his noble brother our friend Richard Ashby who had lost his life so gallantly only a few weeks before in the skirmish near Romney.[13] We brought the Chaplain of the Reg. home with us, Mr. Avery[14] of Alabama.

In the night we were aroused by some soldiers looking for Col. McDonald. I listened and heard one tell Hal that a desperate battle was going on between Aldie and the Junction[15] (not more than 15 miles from us) that we had already lost 3,000 men, and would be beaten unless reinforced. I must acknowledge that the shock was so great that I had a violent nervous chill and laid awake for hours, and when I now calmly think of what the consequences of a defeat there would have been to us, I only wonder that I bore it so well. Hal said when he came upstairs again that he felt convinced from the manner of the soldier that he was alarmed and had probably exaggerated the danger, and sure enough the next day we learned that we had gained the great battle of Stone Bridge,[16] for which we owe inexpressible thanks to the Lord of Hosts, and yet when we heard of the numbers killed and wounded, and remembered our many friends engaged in the fight, we felt nothing but the deepest anxiety.

Each day brings the tidings of someone we knew among the killed and wounded, first Holmes and Tucker Conrad,[17] then William Nelson,[18] then Lloyd Powell,[19] and we dread to see the papers not knowing who may be the next. Each day some fresh visitor from the battle field thrills our hearts with horror, by his recount of what he saw, and while our hearts are uplifted in gratitude to God for our deliverance from the hand of our enemy, our eyes drop bitter tears at the thought of the brave young men, dead, dying, wounded, crippled and mangled lying on the bloody field, of the widow and orphan, of the childless, and desolate, the joy of whose life has been crushed out in this great victory, and our thanksgiving is mingled with earnest prayers that this bloody war may cease—oh that it might cease before Hal goes into active service—that is my hope and prayer—for while I said no word to prevent his fighting for his country, God only knows how miserable and desolate I feel tonight in my lonely chamber, haunted by the dread that ere long the tidings of some great victory may be accompanied by the worst news in the world to me.

July 26th [Friday].
After taking my usual morning walk through the garden, and attending to my domestic duties, I came in and cut out all the shirts for the hands then put my work table and drawer to rights. I had hardly finished before Mr. Bolling came bringing Anna and Munzy[20] with him both looking so pretty. He had just returned the evening before from the battle field, and gave us a most graphic and interesting account of all he saw.

He was in fine spirits having found John well and without a scratch. He thinks the victory so decisive that we shall not have much more fighting; but last nights papers state that Lincoln says he is determined to take back every cent's worth of property lost in the fight. He brings sad news about Willie Wilson[21] & Fitzhugh Grayson.[22] The barbarous enemy are said to have murdered all their prisoners not wishing to be troubled with them in their retreat. Several of our men have been found in the adjacent woods manacled, and with their brains blown out. Surely a Holy God will punish such atrocities. Among other preparations for certain victory the Yankees brought with them 20,000 hand cuffs which we took, though I did not hear that we used them in sending our prisoners to Richmond. Mr. Bolling says there has scarcely been in the history of wars such magnificent preparations of every description as the Northerners had with them, besides the 63 brass cannon, and every other description of arms, we captured their baggage wagons numbering 200, $30,000 worth of unwoven clothing, blankets, knapsacks, saddles, ammunition enough to finish the war, and such quantities of provisions that we don't know what to do with them. Among other things Mr. B. mentioned 200 barrels of crackers taken at one depot. Three Congressmen with two daughters of one of them came up to enjoy the spectacle of our defeat. They came in an elegant carriage but the gentlemen had to march back some distance on foot [with] the ladies.

We have had no further tidings. Mr. Kidwell[23] said he thought he could get Bonie's horse for me, but I told him not to have any difficulty with Bishop about it. If Mr. Bishop[24] has it in [his] possession I will not get it, but will get one from Welbourne.[25] Mr. Bolling tells me that I have not much chance of disposing of my cattle and wheat for the present, for which I am sorry, as our property would fare badly if the enemy should get Winchester—of which however there is no danger at present. Mamma and Cousin Sarah[26] are going to Welbourne, I do not feel like visiting, and therefore stay at home. Mr. Bolling has invited us to Bollingbrook tomorrow to spend a sociable day. We declined at first, feeling too sad and anxious about Hal and our other friends, but he insisted saying we would cheer each other, so we consented, but I for one go with a heavy heart. I can never feel safe till Hal is at home again. I can only trust the war will be over before his company is drilled. The children talk about him all the time, Rozier [age 4] particularly. I wonder how much they will have changed before he comes back. I must go and send for the mail; the papers last night were full of triumph. Sunday is appointed as a day of public Thanksgiving. How heartily will all hearts join in the service.

July 29th [Monday].
Three days have passed without my writing. On Saturday we went to Mr. Bolling's to dinner. The day would have been very pleasant but for the heavy weight of anxiety in every heart.

Mr. Bolling kindly offered to be my escort to Ashland,[27] and I have written to Hal to know if I can go down for a day or two. I am so much afraid, he will think I had better stay at home, and it will be a terrible disappointment to me if I cannot go. I know there is a great deal to do at home, but the thought of seeing Hal again before he goes into active service is a perfect gleam of sunshine through the cloud of trouble and anxiety under which we are now passing. Talcott Eliason[28] was here just now; he says Aunt Mary[29] wishes to go to Richmond to see Willie's bride and will be glad to go with me. Poor Willie[30] he is with the forces at Manassas. It must have tried him sorely to leave his bride of two weeks to go immediately into action. God grant no trouble may come to him for her sake as well as his own. Talcott estimates our loss at 3500 killed and wounded, more than double as great as any other estimate I have seen.

I hope he is mistaken.[31] Mamma went to Winchester this morning to stay till Saturday. Uncle Billy[32] took the key of the stable with him so I could not get a bridle to ride to Upperville as I wished this evening, as I want to get a [pair] of shoes for May [age 5] and myself. I will drive up tomorrow morning if nothing prevents. I began regularly with the children's lessons this morning again. They were listless and inattentive. We had an early breakfast this morning so that Mamma could get off before the heat of the day, and my early rising has made me feel badly all day. I will go to bed early to-night as I intend now to rise early every morning. I would like always to get through with my devotions and write in my journal before breakfast, as other duties crowd upon each other so fast later in the day that I have no uninterrupted time.

The wheat stacking is going on just in front of the library window, Mr. Kidwell looking on from his horse. If Hal were only here, what a load would be off my heart. But I think he should be there. Though greatly grieved, I have never murmured at his going to fight for his country, for I know he has done right—nevertheless it is a sad, sad necessity. Holmes Conrad[33] called yesterday. He says the next battle will most probably take place before long on the Banks of the Potomac some miles from Washington.

July 30th [Tuesday].
Rose very early this morning notwithstanding Rebecca's [age 2] being sick almost all night giving us consequently very little sleep. Found the boys very late in getting to their work. So when dressed I went to the barnyard, to enquire into the reason, Mr. Kidwell had gone up into the field after the hogs. Ben was in the stable, Dan hitching the oxen, Simon[34] leaning against the gate. I asked them if they would let me get to my work before them. The wheat was rather wet to stack, they said. I must be careful that time is not wasted. We are already very backward, almost every other farmer has done cutting hay and we have not begun, which does not look right.

I heard yesterday that Ben had been very drunk on Sunday. I spoke to him about it this morning. He denied it, and promised me I should have no trouble with him while his master was away. No mail came yesterday or on Saturday, which is very trying to our patience these stirring times. I feel particularly interested in the proceedings of the force in Missouri;[35] we can get no letter from our friends there, the mails having been stopped, and consequently depend entirely on the papers for news of them. We have not heard from Brother[36] for five months.

As Mamma was unwilling to leave the house without a gentleman, Mr. Weedmeyer[37] [sic] kindly offered to come over to take charge of us. He came last night. Katey and I had taken a walk; we had hardly been out fifteen minutes when a heavy and most unexpected storm of wind and rain came up wetting us thoroughly. Mr. Weidmayer arrived in the same plight, so I had to dress him up in a suit of dear Hal's about four sizes too large for him. He enjoyed the joke immensely and so did we.

July 31st [Wednesday].
This sweet morning while waiting for breakfast, I bring my journal into the West Bay window, and will write here. Kate, Mr. Weidmayer and Willie Turner[38] (who came yesterday) [were] talking in the library. Rebecca kept me awake several hours last night again and so much loss of rest for two consecutive nights made me much too tired to get up by sun rise, so I lost my pleasant morning walk.

Yesterday we drove up to Upperville. Just as we got to the middle gate we saw Uncle John's[39] carriage coming from the woods. He [would] not let us turn back, and I got into his carriage and drove to the village with him. I saw Uncle Armistead.[40] He looks very badly, his anxiety for Web[41] tells on him. He seemed however much cheered up by his escape at the Battle of Stone Bridge, where his danger was so imminent all the time. I suppose also that he is much gratified at his distinguishing himself so much.[42]

No letter yet from Hal; I look for one to-day. There was no news of importance in the papers last night. Willie Turner wishes to join a cavalry company. He has just escaped from Maryland. Mr. Bolling will take him to Manassas to-morrow.

August

Aug. 1st [Thursday]
Again yesterday there was no mail, no papers, no letter from Hal, for aught we know to the contrary another battle may have been won or lost. It is very trying, and, I am afraid, will be the case until the war removes from our part of the country as it is the constant transportation of soldiers from one point to another that prevents the cars making the necessary mail connection. Yesterday I sewed on my new dress all day in my room. Kate, Mr. Weidmayer and Willie Turner [were] entertaining each other in the library. It is not easy to be cheerful and entertaining in the parlor when your heart and mind are so entirely preoccupied by anxiety. I wrote to Hal last night and gave the letter to Willie who will mail it for me at the Junction. When Rozier found I was writing to his papa he told me to tell him to make haste home, and I found great difficulty in getting him to go to bed, as he expected the letter would bring his papa last night and he wished to sit up to see him. Poor child! He little knows how many weary days and months may pass without his seeing him, and it is well for him that he does not know. His devotion to his Father as well as his likeness to him makes me cherish him very dearly now. Rebecca was very [ill] again last night.

> **Timeline of the War**
>
> | | |
> |---|---|
> | August 1 | Confederates declare Arizona and New Mexico Confederate territories. |
> | August 6 | U.S. Congress passes Confiscation Act, declaring all property used to support insurrection, including slaves, shall be forfeit. |
> | August 7 | Confederate general John B. Magruder burns the town of Hampton, Virginia, after hearing Butler plans to use it to house escaped slaves. |
> | August 10 | Gen. Nathaniel Lyon is killed and his army defeated in the Battle of Wilson's Creek, Missouri. |
> | August 24 | James Mason, John Slidell, and Pierre Rost are appointed Confederate commissioners to Britain, France, and Spain. |
> | August 26 | Gen. John B. Floyd mauls the 7th Ohio Infantry in the Battle of Kessler's Cross Lanes, in western Virginia. |
> | August 29 | Confederates manning two forts at Hatteras Inlet, North Carolina, surrender to naval and army forces under Gen. Benjamin Butler. |

Aug. 2nd [Friday].
Yesterday evening a letter came from Hal to my great delight. He was tired and almost broken down with his long march. An amusing circumstance happened to them on the way. The Captain and 1st & 3rd lieutenant went into Fredericksburg, and left 2nd Lieutenant Plaster[43] in command of the Company. He did not know the way and carried them [on] the wrong road, and the Captain was two days looking for his Company before he found them, and Dulany's lost Company became quite a joke. The thing that pleased me most in the letter was the permission to come to Ashland. I feel almost in right good spirits at the prospect of seeing my husband so soon again.

Just as we had fixed a lunch of butter milk and corn bread yesterday, three soldiers rode up; they came to press my wagon and team for the army.[44] I brought them in and gave them lunch for which they seemed grateful. I made no objection to their taking the wagon, though it will make us very backward in our farm work. The wagon I can do better without but we can neither plow nor thrash without horses. However we must do the best we can.

This morning Rozier was so bad, crying when he was dressed, and fretting for Rachel,[45] &c that I took my shoe and administered a good whipping which I think did him great good. No news in the last papers, but numerous extracts of false accounts of the battle from Northern papers.

Hal's letter to Ida, July 29, 1861, Ashland:

I just arrived at Ashland after traveling since last Friday, and I tell you I am pretty well used up. It is just about twice as hot down here as it is in

Fauquier, besides not having very good accommodations to make you as comfortable as the weather will permit, but I suppose as we have taken upon ourselves the calling of soldiers, we will have to get used to all these things.

Some very funny things happened on the way, among them Brother Richard, Cousin Robert [Carter] and myself went to Fredericksburg to buy some things, and left the 2nd Lt. Plaster in command. Plaster carried the company [on] the wrong road and the Capt., Cousin Robert and I went looking for them for nearly two days. I suppose in that time we must have asked about a hundred persons if they had seen anything of them, at last we couldn't ask a man without laughing. One man told us they had gone home. It is a general joke now through that country that Capt. Dulany of Loudoun lost his company consisting of 80 men. . . .

The bugle is sounding for drill and I must go. If you and Cousin Eliza think of coming down for a few days let me know a day or two before hand, so that I may prepare rooms for you at the hotel. Good bye my own darling.

Aug. 3rd [Saturday].
There was nothing passing yesterday worth noticing. I finished my dress, [which] with teaching the children and housekeep[ing] made quite a hard day's work. In the evening we walked over to the stack yard. We have 8 large ricks [of hay] and several small stacks. To-day I will be very busy. I want to finish my mending, and then go to Welbourne.

Aug. 5th [Monday].
Yesterday being Sunday I did not write in my journal. On Saturday evening, just as we were starting to Welbourne, Mr. Kinsolving[46] came, so we gave the visit up. He stayed all night with us. After we were all asleep and the house shut up on Saturday night, the barking of the dogs waked me, and immediately I heard the tramp of horses' feet and voices, one of which I recognized as Holmes Conrad's. I called out of the window to him to come in, but he said he had three friends coming on in a wagon. So I sent for Uncle Billy to take the wagon and horses. And Katey and I dressed as soon as possible and went down. We found with Holmes, Powell Conrad,[47] Mr. Barton[48] and Holmes Boyd.[49] I soon fixed a supper for them, and made Harriet[50] put all the children on the Buffalo robe on my room floor, Mr. Weidmayer being in the little room & Mr. Kinsolving in the nursery, and we put the four young soldiers in Ma's room where the children had been sleeping. They all left yesterday morning for the Junction. The Doctor was here last night to see Lucinda.[51] He was full of the battle scenes having been in the fight.

I want to go to see Cousin Eliza Carter[52] today to know if she will go to Ashland with me. I should greatly prefer having a lady with me. Mary Carter's dear little face looked as bright as possible when I proposed taking Fanny and herself with me to see their Father.[53] I hope he will consent to my taking them.

I should like of all things to take Rozier, he is so anxious to see his papa. But I could not afford to take a servant and I would not know what to do with him without one. Poor little fellow, he misses his papa sadly, half the brightness and life seem to have left him since he left. He was lying quietly on the floor a few days ago and when his mammy asked him what he was thinking about. He would not answer at first, but after a little while he said, "Mammy, I was praying to God just now, I was asking him not to let old Lincoln's soldiers hurt my Pa." An hour or so afterward, he said to me, "Mamma don't you wish you and Pa and all of us were up in Heaven? Cause we wouldn't have all this trouble then." His devotion to his father exceeds any thing I ever saw in a child.

Aug. 6th [Tuesday].
Yesterday I spent the morning after teaching the children & housekeeping, in making a set of [toy] hoops for May, they were nicer than any I could have bought out of the store. In the evening we were going to Welbourne, but a rain storm prevented. The papers last night contained various rumors of McCulloch's[54] having gained a decided victory over Lyon[55] in Missouri, but I am afraid it is only one of the floating rumors that so often deceive us.[56]

Our army is making large preparation for some great move but none except our Great Generals know where or when the army moves. Surely we should be thankful that we are blessed with men at the head of our political and military affairs upon whose judgement and discretion the whole nation can depend. Such is the secrecy with which they plan that the soldiers in the camps have never the least idea of where they are going or what the next move will be till the order comes to move.

Mamma did not come yesterday. I fear she is not well, as she is generally punctual. I wrote yesterday to Aunt Margaret.[57] The letter will go by Adam's Express. There is however but little pleasure in writing when you know that every letter that passes through the Post Office is opened and read, and such is the policy of Lincoln's Yankee Administration. Various rumors are afloat about England's recognizing the Confederacy but none of them tangible. The papers state that the British fleet is in the Gulf of Mexico to protect British Commerce from the Blockade,[58] which is favorable certainly. I wrote to Hal yesterday and hope a letter will come from him today, but he does not love to write, and I don't wish to plague him for letters much as I wish to hear from him. I am very anxious lest the excessive heat should have made him sick, for this is a very trying season to go to the lower country.

Aug. 7th [Wednesday].
We went to Welbourne yesterday evening, took tea and, returned after night. While there William Herbert[59] called me aside to tell me that there was a rumor in the neighborhood that Brother Richard had been thrown from his

horse and much hurt while practicing leaping at Ashland. He had carefully refrained from mentioning it at Welbourne, knowing how anxious it would make them all. I trust in God it may not be so, but I feel inexpressibly anxious. He is so reckless with horses, and I consider Uncle John's not having heard from him as going a long way to confirm the report.

There is also a report that McDonald's command had been cut all to pieces in Western Virginia, and Turner Ashby killed. I do not believe it. I hope we will get some mail to-day, a letter from Hal, and papers that we may know of the truth of these most distressing rumors. Mamma did not [come] home yesterday. I begin to feel uneasy lest some one, either Grandma,[60] Aunt Becca[61] or herself should be sick. I am sure we shall get a letter from her this morning or she will come this evening.

Aug. 8th [Thursday].
Yesterday Mamma came home bringing Sophie[62] with her, which I was very glad of. She had also heard the report of Brother Richard's being hurt, but a letter from Hal written the 4th of Aug. says nothing of it, which makes me hope there is nothing in it. However I should not be surprised if they all kept us purposely ignorant, knowing how anxious we would be. There has yet been no letter from Brother R. Hal tells me to go soon to Ashland, so I am getting ready to go at an early day, but feel some uneasiness about an escort. Mr. Bolling's boys have measles, so I fear he cannot leave home. Uncle [John] has no idea of going, and I heard yesterday that Cousin Eliza could not go. But I will not be discouraged.

Uncle Armistead and Uncle John were both here yesterday. They advise me not to stack the wheat immediately unless I can hear of a sale for it, and the wagon's being away makes it very convenient to follow their advice.

A letter came yesterday from Aunt Julia[63] sent by private hands. They were all well. Brother [Robert Randolph Powell] she said talks of renting a farm till the country was [illegible]. I should prefer his com[ing] to Virginia. She said he was engaged to be married.

Aug. 9th [Friday].
Today we expect to hear news. Yesterday all the cars from Leesburg passed our gate drawn by oxen and mules.[64] They were going to Piedmont for the use of the army, so we look for a speedy movement in the army. Last night a large fire could be seen in the direction of Charles Town [western Virginia], and the servants heard heavy firing of artillery yesterday evening. I am afraid General Banks[65] has begun his boasted work of burning and plunder.

Mr. Weidmayer ordered his horse yesterday to go home, saying he thought we were tired of him and that he would like to stay if he thought we wanted. Of course we told him to stay, and so he did, and I am glad of it, his intelligence and perfect refinement making him a pleasant companion, and then it is always agreeable to have a gentleman staying in the house at such times as this when you are liable to be aroused any night by soldiers coming in for food, information or shelter. I am afraid his oversensitive nature has taken offence at some unintentional oversight in the part of some of us. There was no mail last night, I hope for a letter to-day.

Aug. 10th [Saturday].
No letter yesterday and only old papers, in one paper an account of a skirmish in Kentucky in which we sustained a loss of 40 men to 6 of the enemy. I hope it is a mistake.[66]

Mr. Weidmayer went to Upperville yesterday and brought back intelligence that a letter had come from Brother Richard himself saying he was perfectly well, which relieved our great anxiety for him.[67] Hampton was burned on the 8th by the Federals.[68] All these outrages only make us the more determined to resist, and they show what we may expect from the Northerners should they subjugate us. Such savage enemies could [not] make generous conquerors. This war has fully brought out and developed the peculiar dispositions of both North and South, how poorly does the thieving, burning, murdering Yankee compare with the generous, chivalrous Southerner. While we are caring for and nursing their wounded men, just as we do our own, while their prisoners are being treated with sympathy and kindness, the unhappy men of the South who have fallen into their hands are threatened with murder every day. And on the very day that a Southern soldier sent back to the family of a dead Northern soldier, the watch he had found on his body, a Northern officer sent on to his wife a box of silver he had stolen out of a Virginia house.

I heard from Cousin Eliza yesterday and she certainly cannot go with me. I did not know how much my heart was set in going till I began to find I could not get an escort. I want to take some provisions down to them, and I know their clothes want some repairing, and the longing I have to see my darling Hal no pen or tongue can tell. Little Rebecca has just bitten Oscar's [the dog] ears so that he cried out, and now she is hugging and kissing him to comfort him. It is strange to see how tender he is with her and with Rozier and he is so cross to every other child. He never leaves me for one moment, and for his dear massa's sake he is a privileged character.[69]

Aug. 12th [Monday].
No letter on Saturday from Hal. I was much disappointed—one came from Brother Richard to Uncle John giving permission to the children to go to Ashland with me, and one to Cousin Eliza in which he spoke very highly of Hal as a soldier, which was very gratifying to me. I saw Uncle Armistead yesterday. As he was going to Ashland on Tuesday, I decided to go with him, fearing I might

not find an escort for the time I had appointed. He seemed by no means anxious to take me and almost positively declined taking the children, so when I awoke this morning after a headache and found it raining very hard, as I had gotten yesterday a letter from Mr. Bolling again offering to be my escort, I decided to put off going till Thursday, for many reasons—1st the children could go then and [not] tomorrow, 2nd I could prepare more things to take to Hal, and 3rd Mr. Bolling seemed to want to escort me and Uncle A. seemed not to want us by any means. I do not imply any disobligingness on Uncle A's part. It is an established family fact that he dislikes being bothered with ladies either at his own house or elsewhere. He has been very kind in coming to see me and giving advice about the farm.

Aug. 13th [Tuesday].
Mamma and I drove up to Upperville yesterday to see Aunt Mary [Eliason] and Aunt Armistead[70] who want to send bundles by me to their boys at Ashland. I went also to see Miss Margaret.[71] I saw Uncle Armistead, and told him of the change in my plans at which he seemed a little surprised, and not particularly distressed. It was very well I did change my arrangements, as I have a very bad cold this morning, and it is still raining.

Aug. 14th [Wednesday].
Still raining. It began with the storm last Friday, and has never stopped for more than an hour since. Mr. Bolling came over last night to say that he would go with me to Ashland if Anna was well, but she was threatened with measles. He is to come over to-day to let me know how she is. He offers me Stewart[72] as an escort, if he cannot go, but I cannot let him take the trouble. A good long letter came from Hal last night. Mr. Kidwell came in last night to tell me that Tom had run off from Mr. Laws[73] because he told him he would give him a whipping if he did not do better. I told him to send back and tell him he would whip him if he ran off again. Oh me! What trouble these little darkies [are]. If "Massa Linkums" would only provide comfortably for them what a benefactor he would be to Virginia Masters and Mistresses.

Aug. 15th [Thursday].
Mr. Bolling sent Stewart over yesterday to tell me that Anna was very sick, too sick for him to leave her, and also to offer [Stewart's] services as an escort. I was much obliged by his kindness, but would not think of giving him the expense and trouble of going only as my escort. So now I depend on Mr. Scott[74] but hardly like to give him the trouble of going before his appointed time. Arthur Herbert[75] was up from his camp yesterday. He has been very sick, and got off for a day or two to recover. He tells me that the onward move of our army has actually commenced. God only knows how it will end. I trust

Hal may not have left Ashland when the next Battle begins. Mr. Kidwell tells me he shall have to buy corn. We sold rather too much last spring.

Aug. 16th [Friday].
Yesterday I went to Upperville and saw Mr. Scott. He cannot go to Ashland till Wednesday so I must give up going till then. Mr. Kidwell told me that it was said in Upperville yesterday evening that travel and the carriage of the mail had been forbidden over the railroad. I trust not for I shall then not only be disappointed in my visit, but can get no letters. I went to see Anna Bolling yesterday; she is quite sick and, poor child, must be very lonely in that large house with no other female.[76] The papers last night tell of a certain victory our cause has gained in Missouri.[77] Reports to that effect have often deceived us [so] that we are disposed to discredit this. But I suppose there is no mistake here as the official report to Washington is quoted, giving a list of the killed. Genl. Lyon heads the list, for which every one who has a feeling of humanity must rejoice, either North or South, such brutality as his being shocking even to our bitterest enemy.[78]

Aug. 17th [Saturday].
Yesterday some soldiers came to press the rest of our horses. I did not see them but told Mr. Kidwell to tell them how we were situated, that six horses and two wagons were already in the service, and that we should be obliged to stop farming if they took any more; and as we have nothing but our crops to depend on we should have been in a bad way.

I wish I could know whether there is any hope of my paying my visit to Ashland. I can't feel settled as long as it is undecided. If any travel is allowed, I shall certainly go. It is probable Hal will not leave Ashland for some weeks yet, and I may go down after a week or two.

Aug. 19th [Monday].
Yesterday I went to hear Mr. Kinsolving. He preached an old sermon. He says his mind is so distracted by the war that he can neither study [n]or write. The papers bring the most contradictory accounts of the battle of Springfield, Mo. We have only seen Northern accounts, some exalt over a great victory, and some deplore an overwhelming defeat, but all lament over the death of the bad man by whose orders women and children have been shot down in St. Louis, and whose very name will be detested as a synonym for everything brutal and cruel. The Northern papers acknowledge a loss of 800 men, but some say our loss was 2000.[79] I don't know why the Yankees should have left the field in possession of the enemy and retreated a hundred miles after a great victory.

I saw Mr. Scott yesterday and we decided that he should meet me at The Plains[80] on Thursday morning en route for Ashland, so I trust now my visit will be accomplished without further difficulty. Charley[81] discovered yesterday that his horse had distemper, which we are all sorry for, as I shall have to send him home today by Robert, fearing the disease may be communicated to the other horses on the farm. I saw Uncle Armistead yesterday. He said all were well at Ashland.

Aug. 20th [Tuesday].
Yesterday I rode on horse back to Upperville to have my shoes mended, and then home as fast as I could for fear of rain. But when I got on the farm the rain seemed far enough off for me to ride up to see the cattle, so I went. Some look very well and some not so well; the calves and colts look very well. I paid out $52.00 for corn yesterday. Last night a letter came from Hal. He was uneasy about me, and I am angry with myself for letting him know I had a cold. However I hope to see him on Thursday. On Saturday I gave Wilmouth permission to go to Middleburg with Robert[82] when he went to see his wife, telling her to be sure and come home on Sunday evening. This is Wednesday morning and they have neither of them come home. I don't know what to make of it, and shall have to get Mr. Kidwell to look them up.

Aug. 21st [Wednesday].
I was so engrossed in thinking of my preparations for starting to Ashland at one o'clock to-night that I entirely forgot to write in my journal before breakfast so must do it now before I finish packing. A letter came from my darling last night. He has received my letter telling him why I did not go down [as planned] and is no longer uneasy; says he hopes to be able to come home before long. It excites me so to think I shall see him tomorrow that I cannot sleep to-night. Mary and Fanny and Mr. Scott will come over to-night. I have a box packed with eatables to take to Hal and various packages for the other members of the company. I have just sent Talbot off with a bottle of strawberry juice to Aunt Mary [Eliason] who is very sick. It begins to look again like rain. I know I shall take a good cry if I am again disappointed.

Sophie [Turner] is still with us and just as sweet as she can be. I wish she [could] live with us, but I am afraid Aunt Becca would object to giving her up. She is writing now to Willie Carrere[83] whom I hope to see in Richmond. I have always felt a desire to know poor Marion's[84] husband, for few of my early friends were as dear to me as she, and certainly none more deserving of the warm love of all who knew her. Sophie is like her in some respects. I will take my journal to Ashland that I may write down all I see and hear, for the benefit of home folks when I return.

Ashland. Aug. 24th [Saturday].
We left home at one o'clock Thursday morning and had hardly started when it began to rain, which it did with occasional intermission till about seven o'clock. We waited for the cars an hour and then started for Richmond. The

cars were crowded with soldiers, and had very few ladies or citizen gentlemen on them. We stopped for twenty minutes at The Plains to go through the form of eating breakfast, but the soda biscuit half baked, and chicken broiled with lard were not very inviting so I drank some tea, and contented myself with the top crust of a biscuit, the butter being uneatable. Mary and Fanny did the same. We were soon on the car again. A talkative woman with a baby occupied Mr. Scott's attention pretty closely till we got to the Junction at Manassas, the children went to sleep and I tried to do so but failed.

At the Junction many more soldiers came on the cars, and some Yankee Zouave prisoners. My attention was soon drawn to a couple who came in together: a young private, and his sweetheart. The latter was most grotesquely dressed in a hat with green and pink satin rosettes, and a bright purple tissue veil, which did not hide her face so as to prevent our seeing that she was crying very much. The soldier looked troubled too, a few tears finding their way down his cheek. They talked together for a moment, their distress increasing at every word, and finally the girl threw her arms around his neck and gave him a hearty kiss after which he left her crying bitterly. My sympathy was much excited. I soon noticed however, that she stopped crying and began looking around her, and a biscuit which she took from her pocket seemed to console her no little. Presently a woman came in with a waiter [tray] full of pies, biscuit and chicken, she took half a pie in one hand and a large biscuit with half a chicken on it in the other, and munched away most diligently. I reserved my sympathy and concluded she would not suffer from the separation from her lover, in spite of the assertion I heard her make that she was too busy thinking about him to eat any thing [earlier] that day.

Another party that attracted my attention consisted of two young soldiers and a young girl, their sister. They came in the cars all quietly weeping, the girl with her veil down and her handkerchief to her face, the two men with the tears streaming down their cheeks. One of them was severely wounded in the face, a bullet having gone in one cheek and out the other. The other brother took leave of his brother and sister in a few moments and got off to join the army, leaving them with weeping bitterly. I think there was something more than the parting to affect them so, for the sister and brother who remained in the car seemed perfectly absorbed in their sorrow for the rest of the day, never speaking even to each other except when the sister offered some little attention to her wounded brother. It was very sad to see a great manly fellow as helpless and dependent on the young girl as a little child could have been. He was a very handsome fellow, and they were evidently refined nice people. Someone said they were Mississippians.

When we passed the point nearest the battle field, the stench was sickening, and made a horrible impression upon me.[85] When we got to Richmond which we did about 3 o'clock, we found we could go on to Ashland that night so we hurried to the Depot. The children were very hungry but Mr. Scott said we would not have time to eat anything. He bought us some peaches just as [we] got into the cars, which refreshed us somewhat. [Rutledge] Eliason[86] and Mr. Dick Homer[87] came up in the cars from Richmond with us.

The first man who got into the cars when we arrived at Ashland was Hal. He partly expected me; he is looking unusually well. Brother Richard and Cousin Robert[88] and Tom Goody[89] came to see us not long after we got to the Hotel. Brother Richard looks badly, and seems out of spirits.

After washing and dressing, we went to supper and then to the parlor, where I met Leina and Nannie Brooke,[90] the only persons here that I knew. We stayed in the parlor long enough to hear some very sweet singing from Nannie Brooke and Mrs. Lowe from Maryland and then to bed. Our rooms are very small and badly furnished, and badly cleaned, but we don't mind that very much for the little time we will be here. We will stay about a week and then Hal will take us home, having to purchase a horse for Johnny.[91]

Yesterday morning we arose early that we might breakfast with our soldiers before going to drill. I spent the morning in my room being tired, but took time to look around and see the place. The grounds are prettily laid out and the whole place looks very well, dotted about with the little ornamental cottages that complete the Hotel accommodations of the place. The nights and mornings are very cool and the middle of the day intensely hot. Yesterday evening Hal took me out to see the Cavalry drill. It was very pretty, though there were not men enough to make it at all imposing. Mary has ridden out this evening to see them, and Fan has gone up with Nancy[92] to the camp where her Father and Mary will join her to eat watermelon. This morning I played ten pins with Leina and Nannie Brooke, and some gentlemen, and this evening while Hal and the girls [are] away, I amuse myself with my journal. I have formed an acquaintance with a very sweet person, a Mrs. Lowe from Maryland. She is pretty and ladylike and sings divinely. Cousin Dick Noland[93] is here and goes up this evening to Fredericksburg to see his sweetheart. Leina Brooke has brought me some books so I will stop writing to read.[94]

Aug. 26th [Monday].
Yesterday being Sunday I did not write. We had no preaching, the minister having the toothache. To my great chagrin, Hal was detailed for guard duty directly after breakfast yesterday morning, and kept at the guard house except at meal time till 11 o'clock this morning, the scarcity of officers here making it impossible for him to get a substitute. He looked tired and worn when he came to breakfast this morning. I am expecting him every minute now, and think he will have to sleep all the rest of the day.

On Saturday night we attempted to have some singing from Mrs. Lowe and Nannie Brooke, but an old Mr. Key who was anything but sober insisted upon joining in every song, making the most sentimental perfectly ridiculous and causing every attempt to end in a roar of laughter from singers and listeners. A dance was then proposed and succeeded much better.

This morning, I went to the bowling alley and played two games, after which I took Mary and Fanny in the parlor to practice. Their playing soon attracted some good looking soldiers who at first sat at some distance from the piano to listen and then approached nearer seeming surprised that such little girls should play so. They, however, by no means did justice to their capability, for the instrument is so bad that it puts them out almost every line.

Hal and I will ride this evening. Fan rode this morning and Mary Saturday. I have written one letter home and must write another as soon as I find out whether Hal can return with me or not.

September

Sept. 2nd [Monday, at Oakley].
Many days have passed without my writing, all too busily occupied to spare time for my journal. This morning I got up very early, went to the dairy as I have not been satisfied with the yield of butter from my cows, saw the butter churned, the milk strained,[95] came up, gave out a ham for dinner, read prayers, and now I write. The Col. at Ashland[96] readily gave my dear Hal leave to return with me, so our stay at Ashland was shortened. The evening before we left I was sitting on the front porch looking at the passengers leaving the cars when who should step up but Willie Turner.[97]

Willie Carrere and himself had come up from Richmond to see Hal and myself. I was delighted to see them especially Willie Carrere, poor Marion's husband whom I had wanted to know for so long. He is an elegant looking man, and made a most pleasant impression on me. They went down to Richmond with us next day, and Willie Carrere went shopping with us, and gave us up his room at the Spotswood[98] and in every way was as kind as possible. The night we spent at the Spotswood I saw numberless friends—Cousin Randy Mason,[99] Custis Lee,[100] Cousin Lee Powell,[101] Cousin Llewellyn Powell,[102] and others. We persuaded Willie Turner to come home with us, sorely against his will. He thinks only of rejoining his Regiment, but we do not wish him to do so. Coming up on the cars we are joined by Tom and Wilson Turner from St. Louis.[103] They have come to join the army, & seem to be fine fellows. I only wish Brother was with them, but it would I suppose be very hard for him to leave his sweetheart. The three boys are all here now, and Mamma, Sophie and Kate are busy getting them ready for the army. I am as busy as possible getting Hal ready to go again on Thursday. Yesterday we heard the bad news that the Federals were in possession of Forts Hatteras and Carlysle on the North Carolina coast, and also that they had taken many prisoners. There were only

Timeline of the War

September 3   Gen. Leonidas Polk orders Confederate troops into Kentucky, ending the state's attempt to remain neutral in the war.

September 6   Union troops under Ulysses S. Grant occupy Paducah, Kentucky.

September 10   Maj. Gen. Albert Sidney Johnston is given command of the Confederate Armies of the West.

September 11   Confederate troops commanded by Gen. Robert E. Lee are defeated in the Battle of Rich Mountain, western Virginia.

September 12–20   Confederate general Sterling Price attacks and captures Lexington, Missouri.

September 27   Confederates abandon fortifications on Munson's Hill near Fairfax, pulling out of defensive positions they have held since July.

---

twenty rounds of ammunition in the forts which strikes me as strange negligence on the part of our Government.[104]

Sept. 3rd [Tuesday].
The bad news of the loss of our forts was counter-balanced yesterday by the news of victory gained by Lloyd[105] [sic] in Western Virginia over Col. Tyler[106]—in which the Federals lost 200 killed, our loss not reported.[107]

    Aunt Bena[108] and GrandMamma will come today bringing Lizzie[109] and the two children. We will then have a house full and might be very gay if it were not that my darling Hal leaves on Thursday. Willie Bolling brought us some fine peaches last night, which we all enjoyed very much. I shall be very busy today and tomorrow finishing Hal's coat and fatigue jacket and I fear after all that I shall not get the jacket right.

Sept. 4th [Wednesday].
Yesterday Hal came from Upperville bringing the sad news of his being ordered at once to report at Manassas, also that all the Cavalry about the Country had received the same order. I fear some bold and dangerous attack is to be made or they would not be concentrating the cavalry near Washington and I can know no peace till there is no more danger. I trust our Generals have no intention of storming Arlington Heights. Aunt Bena and Lizzie are here. Grandma did not come.

Sept. 5th [Thursday].
My dear Husband left last night for Ashland to start from there for Manassas on Saturday not knowing to what division of the army he may be ordered,

whether to guard Manassas or to go over into Maryland. Desolate enough will I be till he comes back.

Sept. 6th [Friday].
Yesterday I finished Hal's shirt to send him by Wilson—Mamma and the girls are busy all the time sewing for our three soldiers, Cousins Willie Turner, and Tom and Wilson Turner from St. Louis. I have gotten a partial promise from Willie to come back here immediately if there is no prospect of a speedy engagement. A long and most gladly received letter came last night from Dan Conrad—the first I had gotten from him since he entered the army. He anticipates a speedy engagement.

I have determined this morning to try and be more cheerful. It is very hard to laugh and talk cheerfully and keep up the appearance of good spirits when I do not know what dreadful news may come in a few days. Even now many of our friends may be engaged in battle or lying dead on the field, or wounded and suffering in the hospitals, or worse still in the open fields suffering and dying for [lack of] some few of the luxuries with which [we] are surrounded, and a light laugh or a bright face looks like a mockery, but we will never be strong to do and endure what may be required of us if we yield to our imaginings of evil, and break down in the beginning. I acknowledge to having been culpable in this for the last week. But hearing that Hal was to go at once into such active service when I had expected some months respite, stunned me and I found my usual self control gone. I will however begin this morning to do better. The house is full of young people, and I have, I fear, saddened them with my gloomy face and manner, which I would not willingly do. I would have them be happy while they can.

Sept. 7th [Saturday].
Last night's papers gave accounts of heavy skirmishing near Washington, in one encounter the enemy's loss was one hundred killed and our loss twenty.[110] Many of our friends are in the division of the army nearest Washington and we do not know that some of them may not be among the killed. Thank God Hal will not report till next Tuesday, and I have still a few days respite. What my anxiety will be after that day it is impossible to say. It is a sad, sad thing for months and months to have the same great dread hanging over you. To lie down at night, and fall asleep with a consciousness of a great sorrow that may be right before you in the future, and to rise in the morning with your anxiety only quickened by a little forgetfulness. To find every laugh checked by an inward sense of a coming sorrow; to long for and yet dread any news. Oh it's a weary, weary time, and we will all bless God when it is over. But who can tell what hearts will be broken, or who will be left to rejoice in the peace when it comes.

Sept. 8th [Sunday].
Yesterday Aunt Mary came out early. Anna Bolling and little Anna[111] about one o'clock, Mick[112] soon after dinner, and Aunt Bena late in the evening, so we had a stirring day. Mick is very pretty, very smart but rather bold—she went up to take last night's stage to Winchester. Charley went home last night. No papers came, consequently no news.

    I don't know which of us will go to church. The carriage will not take all. I always feel nervous upon Sunday. It seems the day especially chosen for great battles; and now [that] two immense armies are in sight of each other, it seems almost certain that a terrible engagement must soon take place. I only hope our generals can induce the enemy to accept the challenge of battle and come out from their entrenchments, as they can be much more easily whipped in the open field.

Sept. 9th [Monday].
Yesterday after church the boys asked me to send them to the Depot [The Plains] to see Cousin Robert Beverley[113] about a horse. I did not want them to go on Sunday but they seemed to think it necessary and if I had refused they [would] have thought it was because I did not want them to have the carriage and horses.

    I want to go today to the different houses to see what I can collect towards filling a wagon to send to the hospitals at the Junction. I am going to send provisions to Hal as soon as he lets me know of his arrival, and it would be a good opportunity for getting down a box of delicacies and necessaries for the sick. Mr. Kidwell tells me he can get very good sugar at Salem for 14 cts. so I am going to send today to see about it. I hear that one of my mules has given out that went to the Junction. I cannot spare them another, and have a notion of selling the whole team, wagon and all, to the government.

Sept. 10th [Tuesday].
No letter came last night from Hal. I can't send his horse down or the wagon either till I hear when he will be at Manassas. I met with considerable success in my endeavor to get up a wagon load for the Hospital. I went yesterday to every house and got promises to a considerable amount. I think the wagon will be full.

    A paper came last night but no news—only further glorifications of the Yankees over the taking of Hatteras. They evidently do not expect victories or they would not be so elated at so trifling an advantage. They seem to think Manassas atoned for. I hope before long that their combs will again be cut,[114] and so effectually that they cannot soon lift up their heads again. I tremble when I think of the tremendous importance of the issue of the contest now daily expected on the banks of the Potomac.

Mr. Kidwell has gone to The Plains today to see the government soldier who offers to buy up all the wagons pressed into the service of the army. I have decided to sell mine, as the wagon and team will both be worn out before we get them back, and I shall have no money to buy another.

Wilmouth told me yesterday she was not able to do my washing and milking for another year, so though I dislike such constant changes I am going to give her up, for any thing is better than a dissatisfied unwilling servant.

Sept. 11th [Wednesday].
Yesterday Mr. Kidwell returned from The Plains, saying that he found no officer there—so my wagon was not sold. He found also that no sugar could be bought for less than 20 cts. and I cannot afford to give it to the servants at that price. Uncle John returned from Ashland last night, he saw Ben in Upperville and sent me word by him that he had a letter from Hal in his trunk for me; if he had only opened his trunk and sent it to me how grateful I should have been. I sent to Welbourne for it this morning but the trunk was still in Upperville.

I got a long letter from Uncle Shirley[115] last night thanking me for my letter to him written after the battle of Manassas, and telling me that he had given it up for publication. I do not much like the idea of being in print, but if it gives pleasure to any one, will not object. I cannot send my wagon to the hospitals till I know that Hal is at Manassas, as his horse has to go down the same day.

Sept. 12th [Thursday].
Got a short letter from Hal yesterday saying that they would not leave Ashland till Monday a week, and that he would be able to come home for a few days after he got to Manassas, which is good news for me. The boys and girls have to go to the Depot tomorrow morning so the wagon cannot go to the Junction, and as the contributions I have collected will not keep, I shall have to get Mr. Kidwell to take them down on the cars, which will save his time and the use of the wagon and horses.

I remember a year ago sitting with Hal on the porch and telling him that my life had been so happy for the last two years, no anxiety, no sickness, no death, and every thing I wanted to make me happy, that I was conscious of a feeling of apprehension. Uninterrupted happiness can never long be the lot of any one on earth, and I had had so much to be thankful for that I fear the time must be near when my trouble should come. I little knew that the agitations were then brewing that would cause me the greatest anxiety I could have, and that might result in such trouble that I could never again be happy. It would have been well if before this war had begun, the people who are responsible for it had counted the cost, and compared it with the gain, that seeing how immeasurably the former exceeded the latter, they might wisely have been dissuaded from it.

Sept. 13th [Friday].
Yesterday Uncle John came over; he tells me Hal is very homesick, finding it much harder to bear than before he came home. It is very hard for me to have to stay here and think of him in bad spirits, homesick and enduring privations of every kind. They will not be ordered off as soon as they thought.

I sent off my wagon load to the hospital this morning, it will go down on the cars. Miss Agnes Taylor sent a large box of fruit, Miss Margaret some pickles, stewed tomatoes, some peach syrup, bread and vegetables. Mrs. Stephenson[116] some bread and preserves. I sent a barrel of vegetables, a ham, six dozen eggs, one and a half doz. chickens, two gallons of stewed peaches, books, towels, etc., Mamma buying most of the chickens & eggs. We made also a good deal of bread. Altogether we had a good load and I hope some soldiers may be comforted by it.

The boys and Sophie left this morning, reducing my family no little. The boys will be back in a few days. The cloth for the servants came this morning, and I shall be very busy cutting it out for some time to come.

Sept. 14th [Saturday].
Have just read a letter from Aunt Bettie[117] saying that the fever in Winchester is so prevalent that she wishes to send the girls away. I will write immediately to them to come here, one so hospitable as she is should never be in want of a visiting place for any of her family. Mr. Kidwell has not yet reported the result of his visit to the Junction. We drove into the village yesterday, but could not buy what we wanted; went on to Bollingbrook to call on Miss Mary and Anna Bolling, saw the former but not the latter, as she was out riding. Saw George Carter[118] sitting on Mr. Stephenson's porch. The first time he has been in the neighborhood for nearly a year. I got no letter from Hal yesterday, so don't feel as cheerful this morning as I try to be.

Sept. 15th [Sunday].
A letter came from Hal last night; he is very uneasy about me, and fears I am sick, it shows how wrong I was to give way so when he left. I wrote him that I would keep up now all the time so I hope he won't be anxious any more.

Last night's papers report an advantage that the Federals have gained in Western Virginia,[119] but as we saw only the Northern report we don't know how much confidence to place in it. George Carter was here yesterday with Mittie Stephenson.[120] Aunt Mary Eliason will come out tomorrow to stay. Tom[121] came back last night.

Sept. 16th [Monday].
We went to hear Mr. Kinsolving yesterday, he preached a fine sermon. Heard in Upperville that the fight in Western Virginia was certainly an advantage for

us. There is no dependence to be placed in any Northern reports. Hal's horse came home yesterday not so badly off as I thought he would be from the boys' account of him. I must write to Hal about him this morning. Aunt Mary Eliason is to come out to stay this evening.

Sept. 17th [Tuesday].
Yesterday firing was heard all day in the direction of Leesburg.[122] We look for news from there today, though there has been such frequent fighting across the river with but trifling result that this may turn out to be nothing important. Wrote to Hal yesterday. A letter from Miss Lily[123] says that news from the West of a glorious victory gained by Gen. Lee has reached Winchester. As her letter was dated Saturday I should not be surprised if they had heard the rumor of the engagement between Floyd and Rosencrantz,[124] and if that was what she referred to. Mr. Kidwell took one of the mares to look for a [pair] of oxen, so I could not send for Aunt Mary yesterday, but will send up this morning, though it is raining and I am afraid she cannot come. Tom [Turner] left last night to join the Alexandria [Rifle Regiment].[125]

Sept. 18th [Wednesday].
No letter last night from Hal, and no news in the papers. Aunt Mary came out yesterday morning, but had to go in to Upperville yesterday evening, so I went in with her. As I was getting into the carriage I fell and hurt myself quite badly, and still suffer a good deal of pain though it is nothing serious. I succeeded in getting some very indifferent cotton at 14 cts. and some blue twilled cotton at 20 cts. which was everything in the shape of lining for the people's coats that I could get. I am having a walk laid off from the house to the garden which will I think be an improvement to the yard.

Sept. 18th [later].
I begin to feel very uneasy about Hal as no letter came from him last night. I am so afraid some accident has happened to him in leaping his horse, or that he is sick. I will write to him this morning again, though I wrote yesterday. Last night's papers express no doubt of our having gained a great victory in the West in the fight between Floyd & Rosecrans. Some accounts say that Floyd lost only one man while the enemy lost 400 killed and 1000 wounded, notwithstanding our fighting behind entrenchments, I can scarcely credit such a difference in the loss. If it is true it will be another overwhelming evidence that the Lord is on our side.

The papers contained the sad announcement of the death of J. Augustine Washington[126] the former owner of Mt. Vernon. Such shocks may be looked for every day but they are none the less terrible. It is dreadful to think of the situation of his large family of little motherless, and now fatherless children.

Sept. 19th [Thursday].
Last night a letter came from Hal written in much better spirits than the last, and giving me consequently greater comfort. The hardest thing for me to think of is his being low spirited and homesick with no hope of getting home and nothing in his outward circumstances calculated to comfort him. He thinks it probable that they will be ordered to leave before an answer from me could reach him, and tells me not to write, but I intend to risk a letter.

    Aunt Mary left yesterday, Aunt Armistead being so ill that she did not like to be away from her. I went to the barn yard early this morning; saw Hal's horse which looks better, settled with Mr. Kidwell about threshing out the wheat. He will go out to try and hire horses for the purpose today. He thinks the seeding will be very late, owing to the absence of four of the horses. I want him to get out at least 600 bushels of wheat as that will give us seed wheat for ourselves and leave a good deal to sell to others for seed. The corn crop is very good.

Sept. 20th [Friday].
I went over to Welbourne yesterday to see if Uncle John could lend me 4 horses to thresh wheat for seed, I to give him the same help when he wanted it, but he had gotten out his wheat and could not spare his horses. When I came home I found Mr. Kidwell had seen Mr. Stephenson and found he could get horses from him to be returned when we were done seeding, so we will begin threshing on Tuesday.

    We are making preparations to send down another wagon to the Junction, but I fear we will not get much. Uncle John will give liberally, Uncle A. refused but I think he must have been jesting. I was very glad to find Aunt Betty & Kate[127] here when we got home last night. Aunt Betty has a bad cough, which I hope we can cure.

Sept. 22nd [Sunday].
Have heard no army news since Saturday morning. Saturday evening [Kinloch] Tom came back. He found, when he got to the Junction that there was good reason to believe that he could get a commission from the President, so he left this morning for Richmond.

    Sunday Kinloch [Fauntleroy][128] came. He had just gotten his lieutenancy and was in high spirits. He says there is no prospect of a fight on the Potomac. He left this morning with Tom to return this evening, only going to Avenel. I saw Bowles Armistead[129] yesterday, he had just come from Ashland. Hal is well and they leave for Manassas on Tuesday. How I envy him having just seen Hal.

Sept. 23rd [Monday].
I have not time to write much today. William [Turner of Baltimore] came home last night. He will join Willie Carrere under Genl. Turnball [sic].[130] I am going to

sit up with Aunt Armistead to-night. Miss Margaret and Mrs. Graham[131] dined with me yesterday. No letter from Hal.

Sept. 24th [Tuesday].
Last night I sat up with poor Aunt Armistead. I don't think that she has much longer to suffer. A letter from Hal telling me that he had had his likeness taken for me, and that he would probably be stationed at Fairfax Court House. The papers last night speak of Lee's intended capture as the greatest strategic move of the war; it was frustrated, by [Gen. Henry] Jackson's failure to do his part. No blame is attached to Jackson, his march was obstructed by insurmountable obstacles, roads full of trees etc. We were sorry to learn from a letter from Genl. Johnston to Aunt Bena that a serious misunderstanding had arisen between the General and the President, with respect to the Genl's rank. He has been placed 4th in rank after being second. I hope the difficulty will be adjusted.[132]

Sept. 25th [Wednesday].
We all dine at Miss Margaret Hereford's today, in compliment to Aunt Betty [Conrad]. We will finish threshing today. Tomorrow Hal will be at Manassas. I am troubled about getting things to him, my spring wagon being so much out of order that it cannot be used without mending, and I know no one in the neighborhood of whom I would like to ask the favor to lend me one. There is no spring wagon at Welbourne. Lucinda is again laid up with her leg, and Mary cooking, Robert and Patsey both sick, and Aunt Polly very poorly.

Sept. 27th [Friday].
I could not write yesterday morning owing to my having suffered with one of my bad headaches all the night before.[133] On the 25th all the family except myself spent the day at Miss Margaret's. In the evening thinking a ride might do my head good I ordered my horse, and just as I was starting, Mr. Gibson[134] & Bowles Armistead rode up. Mr. Gibson was to leave next day for the Company, and kindly came to see if I had a letter. He went down on horse back, had he gone by the cars I should have sent Hal a box. I found when I got to Upperville that Armistead Eliason[135] had come, bringing me a very fine likeness of Hal. I have it hung where I can see it the first thing in the morning, and the last at night, and can scarcely keep my eyes from it during the day. The children all knew it instantly, and rejoice over it and kiss it, and Rozier says,"I does love my pa's picture."

Yesterday the day Hal was to arrive at Fairfax Court house we had a dreadful storm of rain and wind all day. The corn is beaten flat, several young trees blown down, and much damage done. I fear Hal must have been out in it all.

The thought made the storm doubly terrible to me. I must see Mr. Kidwell to know if anything can be done for the corn.

Sept. 28th [Saturday].
Yesterday morning Mr. Bolling came over to see if I would go to the mill with him to make an agreement about the flour. I did not go as I had heard that Mr. Dawson[136] and the Miller had had a quarrel.

Just as we were at dinner Rev. Randolph[137] came. After dinner I went out on Cricket to see Cousin Eliza to know if she would unite with me in sending provisions to our Company. She took no interest in it and could not provide a horse for the wagon. I will see some one else tomorrow. In the evening Robert Bolling with three friends from Manassas, Mr. Sterrel,[138] Mr. Carrol,[139] and Mr. Hughes[140] were here. No letter from Hal and no news in the papers.

Sept. 29th [Sunday].
Ben went off yesterday without waiting to see whether we wanted the carriage so Kate, Kate Conrad, Rev. Randolph and I walked up to town. I must confess that I went as much to see Bowles and send messages to Hal as to go to church, for I was so distracted by hearing of an expected battle that I could not think much of the sermon. To my surprise I found Bowles had left early in the morning so my good long letter had to be kept for another opportunity.

I saw Cousin Robert Carter in church. He said they were all well, and would reach Fairfax Station that evening, so it was a false report about their having arrived and been ordered to be ready to move at a moments warning. My uneasiness about the storm was also unnecessary as there was no storm where they were. The Stephensons said they would spend the day here today, and I must ride over to see Cousin Robert Carter this evening.

Sept. 30th [Monday].
Yesterday morning Cousin Robert Carter called to see me. I am to send Hal's horse down when he goes tomorrow. I expected yesterday the Stephensons & Cousins Catherine[141] and Sue[142] to dinner but they all disappointed me. Today Mamma, Aunt Bettie and the two Kates are going to Cousin John Harrison's[143] to dinner. They all want me to go, but I do not care to go to a dinner party, and then I shall be glad of a quiet day at home to set things straight. Last night's papers confirm the intelligence of our Victory at Lexington, Missouri, but the Federal accounts state our loss at 1000 men, which however we do not believe as they acknowledge only 35 killed on their side and yet acknowledge our victory.[144] If the abominable falsifying could be stopped the papers would possess much more interest.

> **Timeline of the War**
>
> October 14   President Lincoln suspends the writ of habeas corpus.
> October 21   The Battle of Ball's Bluff (Leesburg) marks the second major Union defeat in Virginia.
> October 31   Seventy-five-year-old Gen. Winfield Scott, a veteran of the War of 1812 and the Mexican War, resigns as general-in-chief of the U.S. Army. He is replaced the next day by Gen. George B. McClellan.

October

Oct. 2nd [Wednesday].
Yesterday Mamma and Aunt Betty went off early to Mr. Harrison's but just as the girls were ready to start a carriage full came from Middleburg, Cousin Sue, Cousin Cat and Fanny Dudley.[145] The girls stayed to see them for an hour or two and then went off in my carriage. I was very glad to see my relations after so long a time.

While they were here, Mr. Bolling came over bringing two cattle dealers to look at our cattle. They offered me 4 cts. and Mr. Bolling said they would have given more if I had not said so soon that I would be satisfied with that. Mr. Bolling said my grass was yet low and that the sooner I got rid of the cattle the better. I left the matter with him and he is to decide and let me know. I can never cease to be grateful to him for his kindness in taking so much trouble for us.

He told me of poor Aunt Armistead's death. In the evening Mr. Weidmayer and Johnny[146] and Fanny came over and later Mellville [sic] and Tabb Bolling from Elmwood[147] and little Anna from Bollingbrook. My work progresses so slowly that I begin to feel anxious lest I should not be ready for winter. Patsey has been [sick] for some time, Lucinda too sick even to sew, and Mammy sick so that Harriet having all her work to do can do but little sewing, and as for me I cannot sit at my work uninterrupted for one half hour during the day.

I am so troubled at not being able to go to Aunt Armistead's funeral, but I sent one of my horses to the Court House to lead Hal's horse down. I had intended walking up, but it looks so like rain that I am afraid to attempt it. I shall write a note to Cousin Betty[148] explaining to her why I do not go.

Oct. 3rd [Thursday].
I have not yet seen Mr. Bolling and don't know whether the rain prevented his coming or whether they could not conclude the bargain about the cattle. I expect the two Kates home to day (they did not return from Mr. Harrison's on Tuesday). Anna Bolling, Jenny Harrison and the two Stephensons are coming out with them.

Oct. 4th [Friday].
Last night Johnny came up from Fairfax Station for a little furlough and Ben stayed down to wait on his master till John goes back. I got a letter from Hal, all were well. Hal was much pleased with the sale of the cattle, but thought my mare looked so badly that he is a good deal worried about it and tells me that Mr. Kidwell must keep the stable key at night, as he fears they have been ridden. Mr. Bolling wrote me that he had sold the cattle, and every thing is settled. I consider it an admirable sale and feel very grateful to Mr. Bolling for attending to it for me.

> *Hal's letter to Ida, October 2, 1861, Fairfax Station:*
>
> You can't tell how glad I was to hear from you last night through Cousin Robert and Ben, it seems weeks since I heard. I have concluded to send John home on furlough for a short time, he seems so anxious to go and see them all. I suppose his wife Mary will be overjoyed. He is one of the best boys you ever saw and has attached the whole camp to him. When you send the wagon down he can come in it and I will send Ben home.
>
> My dear Ida, what on earth have you been doing with your mares. I thought they looked badly enough when I was up, but the mare Ben rode down is actually very poor. You ought to make one person attend to them, and make him responsible, & let no one ride them unless you send your servant somewhere, and then make him ride the big mare. Send word to Mr. Kidwell to take the key of the stable every night and give it out every morning. I think it more probable from the looks of this mare they have been ridden at night.
>
> I think you did excellently well with your cattle. If there is water in the meadow next to the turnpike have them turned in there the day before they go off and they will go to the scales gently. You had better send over to Henry Arthur Hall or Uncle Armistead or [Uncle] Nathan and get them to carry them to the scales for you, it takes a person of experience or your cattle will lose a great deal [of weight]. I have attended to the wagon and team. I told John Scott he could have my buggy until I come back. I suppose you have no use for it.
>
> Everything here is at a stand still. . . . You hear much more than we do because you see the papers; we don't see or hear anything. President Davis is to have a grand review of the troop today which will be worth seeing. There is no possible chance of your coming to see me, darling, as much as I want to see you. I wouldn't have you here for anything in the world. The call has sounded for drill. Love to all.

Oct. 5th [Saturday].
Rode over [to Welbourne] yesterday evening to see Cousin Eliza [Carter] and Uncle John about sending the wagon. Cousin Eliza said she could contribute butter and pickle & bread—Sarah Carter said she had a box of provisions for Tom Goody [Carter], and Uncle John gave me the promise of two horses. I

found Taylor Scott[149] sick at Welbourne. He had stopped for the night on his way home. I quite envied Fanny having her husband home for an indefinite time even if he was sick. I had the most excruciating headache all during my ride and suffered with it all night—feeling in consequence scarcely able to hold up my head.

Oct. 6th [Sunday].
This morning (Sunday) we will all go to hear Mr. Kinsolving. I did not sleep well last night & feel very badly in consequence. My head still feels unsettled. Cousin Dick [Noland] was here yesterday; he gave me some valuable information with regard to a sick colt, and thinks he will buy my open carriage for which I will be very glad, as I want money more than the carriage.

It is a most lovely day. I miss Hal more on Sunday than any other day in the week, and feel more anxious about him. I cannot bear to think of his Sundays passing without any church or reading. Then our Sunday evenings were always so happily spent. We always felt free to have that time to ourselves no matter who was here, and now Sunday evening seems the loneliest time in the week. He writes me that Bowles tells him I am looking well and happy. It shows how well I have succeeded in my efforts to appear cheerful especially before any one who is to see Hal. But as to my being happy that is utterly impossible. I am lonely and anxious and have an indescribable feeling of pain when ever I look forward to the long year that is to pass before Hal comes back.

Oct. 7th [Monday].
This morning I awaked with a most uncomfortable impression that the farm is not going on as well as it should. The seeding is so very backward, and with all my urging it does not seem to progress as fast as it should. I must send for Mr. Kidwell & talk with him this morning, and if necessary hire more force. I cannot risk losing a wheat crop next year as we have no cattle [to sell]. If I find that we will be so very late seeding I will leave some of the land I had intended sowing in wheat and put it down in oats or rye.

I shall be busy all day preparing a load for the wagon to take to Hal. Walker[150] was in church yesterday and came out after church and spent the day with me. Poor fellow, it is a sad coming home to him after so long an absence, to find his mother dead [Aunt Armistead], and all his companions off to the war. However he is in the same company with most of them. It is a great trial to me to see one and another of the company and know that there is not the least hope of my seeing my husband, either by his coming home, or my going to the camp.

Oct. 7th, at night.
All day yesterday I was as busy as possible getting up a wagon load to send Hal and this morning till 9 o'clock, when I started them, Johnny[151] and Walker

Armistead in charge, and I hope that by this time Hal is enjoying a fine mutton chop. I sent him a cooked saddle of mutton, two chop racks, chickens, ducks, bread, eggs, vegetables etc. and Cousin Eliza sends butter.

This morning, Mr. Kidwell told me the colt was worse. I went to see her this evening and I am too sorry to see her so sick. I am afraid she will die and Hal thinks so much of her. I had her bled in the neck and gave her half a pint of castor oil. I would give a great deal for her to recover. Mr. Bolling (I mean George Jr.) was here this evening, he says he has not begun to cut corn, and I have got a good deal cut so I am encouraged.

Oct. 8th [Tuesday].
Uncle Billy tells me this morning that Mr. Kidwell can not get a buck. We have always gotten one from Welbourne so he says, but this year Uncle John says we cannot have one. I hardly know what to do as it is a matter I cannot well talk to men about myself.[152] However I will not be uneasy—I have found that by carrying all these little troubles before God, I have gotten help sooner than by asking it of any mortal, and my experience since Hal went away has proved more fully than ever the truth that it is better to trust in God than in man even in the most trifling matters.

Oct. 9th [Wednesday].
Ben did not come last night with the wagon so I was disappointed in hearing from Hal and consequently down hearted this morning. The servants heard firing towards Leesburg yesterday evening. I wanted to go over to Welbourne this morning to see Uncle John about the buck but Ben has my carriage harness and it looks too much like rain to go on horse back. I have not heard from the sick colt this morning but don't think from her appearance last night that she can possibly recover. Mr. Kidwell had the hooks[153] as he calls them cut out of her eyes yesterday. I had company at the time and did not know of his intention or I would not have permitted the operation, being advised against it by all the gentlemen. However I am perfectly ignorant on the subject and don't know it may not be the only thing to save her life.

I sent for Uncle Frank[154] yesterday to see Lucinda. He thinks her sore leg so serious a matter that it may cost her an amputation or even her life if she does not follow his prescription. As [the treatment] is both painful and troublesome, I am afraid I shall have some trouble in making her do as he says.

Oct. 10th [Thursday].
Last night the wagon came bringing a letter from Hal. They were all well and delighted to get something good to eat. Poor fellows I am going to be always on the look out for something to send them, and hope to be able to send down every week. Hal sent me $300.00 which he says is to help me along. I don't intend to use it, but will put it away for him when he comes back. He

wrote me word not to let any one touch the colt's eyes—but it was too late. Yesterday she was still better, and I trust will continue to improve. News by yesterday's papers give account of a repulse of the Federals on the Carolina Coast, also of Rosecrans's retreat before Loring.[155]

Hal's letter to Ida, October 9, 1861, Fairfax Station:

Now to business, and answering your numerous questions. First, about Thomas Goody's mare. I suppose you can ride her with the greatest pleasure. Make some of the boys ride her before you get on her. She hasn't been ridden for some time and might be a little foolish. I can't recollect when the note is due in Winchester. I wish you would write to Dr. Dan Conrad. He can tell you. If Mr. Kidwell thinks it necessary to buy another horse you had better buy one.

I will have paid off for the wagons in a few days then I shall let you hear from me. If you can sell the carriage for $200 let it go. Don't let anyone touch Cricket's colt's eyes, if she continues to have that stiffness in her limbs make Mr. Kidwell put her in the stable and blanket her, that she may be kept perfectly warm. If you could have her blistered under the stomach it might do her good.

What do you think of my black horse running off with me regularly? Brother Richard and indeed the whole troop advised me to sell him. I did so and got $350 for him, fifty more than his cost. I will [send] $300 to help you along. Don't think for an instant I was grumbling about the mares. I only spoke to you about them because I thought the servants might impose upon you.

You don't mean to say my picture takes *my place at night,* do you? I flatter myself that you are sensible that you are mistaken. I know that a picture *can't fill your place.* . . . I am going to do my best to get home for a few days as there seems to be no prospect for a fight, but I am afraid it is impossible, it almost sets me wild to think about it.

Tell Katie Conrad I saw Holmes today and he looks as well as possible. . . . He told me that he left Ma in Winchester and that she was well. I sent my shirts back to you to have them washed [and] be returned by the next wagon. . . .

Give best love to the two Kates and Ma. Good by my darling and kiss my dear children for me.

Oct. 14th [Monday].
On Saturday night while we were all sitting around the lamp reading or working, Hal came in upon us, looking bright and well as possible. He had been sent off to look for deserters. I am truly grateful to them for deserting, and hope it will be some time before they can be found. He cannot stay long after finding the men but even this short visit is a great comfort.

He was shocked at the appearance of his little colt, and she does in truth look dreadfully having fallen and skinned herself in the forehead. Hal will see himself to the weighing of the cattle.

Oct. 16th [Wednesday].
Bright and early this morning Hal was up walking up and down in the yard waiting for the man to come to drive the cattle to the scales, not having heard Mr. Bolling say that he would meet them at the scales. As soon as I woke I called to him and told him that he must not wait for the man, so he started the cattle immediately, and was much annoyed at being half an hour later than the time laid down in the agreement. I hope however that it will occasion no difficulty.

All day yesterday we were visiting or receiving visitors. In the morning, I rode up to Upperville with Hal; when we came back, in a few moments Edith[156] and Sophie Carter[157] were here and after dinner Melville [and] Tabb from Petersburg and Bollingbrook Anna Bolling[158] all came—later Mr. Bolling, Mr. Stephenson, Mr. Harrison & Mr. Weidmayer. Today we dine at Mr. Bolling's. Sophie and Lizzie Turner[159] will be here this morning. Edith and Sophie Carter left yesterday evening. Hal will stay till Saturday, and then my loneliness will be worse than ever. At times I have an indescribable feeling of rebellion against this wicked cruel war and cannot get reconciled to a whole year's separation from my dear husband.

Oct. 17th [Thursday].
Hal had the cattle weighed yesterday but the purchaser did not show himself; they weighed 1432 lbs., a very heavy weight, and even at 4 cts. will average $57.28. We all dined at Mr. Bolling's yesterday. He was much annoyed at the failure on the part of Tavenner[160] to fulfill his contract and told me to be sure it would all be made right. Tabb looked unusually handsome, she will be a great beauty at eighteen.[161] Hal was at Piedmont all day but rode over to Bollingbrook in the evening just in time to come home with us.

Oct. 18th [Friday].
Last night just as we were at supper Sophie, Lizzie, Willie & Wilson all arrived from Avenel. They go home today. Yesterday morning Davy having been impertinent to Mr. Kidwell and threatened by him with punishment ran off, and has not yet come back. I am afraid it will give me trouble. At any rate this first act of insubordination must not pass unnoticed. My dear Hal goes tomorrow.

Oct. 19th [Saturday] at night.
I did not write this morning because I was getting Hal ready to start. Poor fellow! He went off and a pouring rain caught him before he got more than a

mile off. So he had to drive all the rest of the way with all his clothes wet. Mr. McDonald[162] was with him, having spent last night here. Mary and Fanny are here. They were caught in a pouring rain and wet to the skin.

Oct. 21st [Monday].
Yesterday I went on horseback to church, heard a good sermon, text, "cast thy care on Him for He careth for thee." Talcott Eliason, who had gotten a few hours leave, told me that he met Hal on Saturday, and that he did not get wet. Davy came back on Friday night, and Hal took no further notice of his conduct than to order him to apologize to Mr. Kidwell, and to threaten him with severe punishment if he heard of any further bad conduct. I am afraid it was a mistake, as he positively refuses to apologize to Mr. Kidwell, and is, Mr. Kidwell says, very surly & disagreeable in his manner. I am afraid I shall have great trouble with him yet. I have ordered him to apologize and if he does not he will in all [*Here the diary breaks off, not to be resumed until November 30. Evidently, these pages were lost.*]

> *On the morning of October 21, 1861, a small body of Union troops, part of the command of Brig. Gen. Charles P. Stone, crossed the Potomac River into Virginia near the town of Leesburg to conduct a raid. They soon found themselves engaged with the forces of Confederate colonel Nathan "Shanks" Evans. The ensuing battle, known as the Battle of Leesburg, or the Battle of Ball's Bluff, eventually involved some 1,700 men on each side, and resulted in yet another defeat and blow to the morale of the Union Army. In addition Col. Edward D. Baker, senator from Oregon and good friend of President Lincoln, was killed. Following this battle, Evans moved his forces back to Oatlands, where he made the home of George Carter his headquarters through mid-December, at which time he was relieved by Gen. D. H. Hill, promoted to brigadier general, and transferred to command the First Military District of South Carolina.*
>
> *Ida received two letters from Hal in early November, both written from Camp Letcher, near Centreville.*

November 1, 1861
Camp Letcher

Bruce Gibson's boy goes home tomorrow and I am glad to have the opportunity of answering your most welcome letter. I should have done so before but have been waiting for this boy and some ink which is a scarce article in this part of the world, however I have the promise of some tomorrow. For the present if you can read pencil writing you must put up with this.

We have been worked to death lately on picket and reviews. The reviews were the most magnificent thing of the kind I ever saw. Yesterday morning

Gov. Letcher reviewed the Cavalry and in the afternoon the infantry Regiment (Virginia) He made a fine speech and presented the different infantry regiments with flags. Some of the Colonels made some very pretty speeches in return; altogether, the whole thing passed off very handsomely. There were about 20,000 Va. Troops present, and you would have thought that Gov. Letcher was the greatest man of his day which I have no doubt he thought at that moment.

I wish you could see some of the views around Centreville. They are the most beautiful I ever saw—from one point you can see some twenty different regiments. Their white tents cover the whole country and give it the most picturesque appearance.

What do you mean by William Eliason's being sick? I saw him not long ago and never saw him looking better. I suppose he must have taken one of those miserable camp fevers. We are most fortunate our regiment is as healthy as possible, as most of the cavalry through out the country are. I see these poor devils in the infantry throwing up fortifications and cutting wood—Turner [Thomas "Kinloch Tom" Turner, 17th Virginia Infantry] with two others detailed to cut wood six hours a day. The cavalry have nothing of that kind to do. Wilson missed it when he went into that business. I sent some dirty clothes up to you, very few, which you can send down by first opportunity....

November 5, 1861
Camp Letcher

More fortunate than when I last wrote, I have found some ink—I have also just returned from picket duty, which I have been on for the last twenty four hours, and tho' rather tired, knowing that you are a great grumbler about writing, I have determined to commence a letter, whether I finish it or not.

Since I last wrote the enemy have certainly advanced, not so much as to interfere with our pickets, but near enough to hear their drums and to get firing much more distinctly. I went this morning about a mile below the Court House which I suppose is the nearest outpost to the enemy, and you could almost imagine that you could hear the commands, they seemed so near to us. Their cars were running all last night to Vienna, about four miles from the Court House. They were supposed to be running up troops, and munitions of war—I hope they may. Let us fight, if it must be so and have it over—I think they will get enough of it by the next time.

On Sunday last I went over the battlefield of Manassas, and I suppose it must have been the last hard rains—but hundreds of dead bodies (Yankees) are washed up. They were only buried in gullies for convenience, and they were put by hundreds in one pit. The sight is perfectly disgusting, and I for one shall not forget it for some time to come. I saw Web's [Welby Carter of Crednal] horse and those of his company that were killed....

Did you receive my letter by Bruce Gibson's boy? If you did, I suppose it was as much as you could do to make it out; no matter, there was nothing in it. You can write one letter here and it will do for the whole season for it is the same old routine day after day....

November

Nov. 30th [Saturday].
Paper is very scarce these war times so my journal must not be ashamed to find itself in an old day book, which Hal began to keep when we were first married, but of which he soon grew tired. I was much disappointed at not receiving a letter from Hal by mail this morning. The papers contain no news this morning, except that the Northerners hold [our] captured commissioners as hostages, to be hung in retaliation for the lives of the officers threatened by Jeff Davis in case our privateersmen are hung by the North.[163] This system of retaliatory murder that will date its commencement from the hanging of the privateersmen will be to my mind the most horrid feature in this most horrid and unnatural and unnecessary war.

Timeline of the War

November 1	Gen. George B. McClellan officially assumes command of all Union armies.
November 6	Jefferson Davis, previously serving as provisional president of the Confederate States, is elected to a six-year term as president with Alexander Stephens as vice president.
November 7	Port Royal, South Carolina, falls to Union naval and land forces, further tightening the blockade of the Southern coastline. Union forces under Gen. Grant are defeated at Belmont, Missouri.
November 8	Confederate commissioners Mason and Slidell are removed from the British mail packet *Trent* by Capt. Charles Wilkes of the U.S.S. *San Jacinto*.
November 29	Confederate Navy Department orders the conversion of the U.S.S. *Merrimac* into an ironclad renamed the C.S.S *Virginia*.
November 30	Lord Lyons, British envoy in Washington, demands the release of Mason and Slidell and asks for a formal apology from the Lincoln government.

December

Dec. 9th [Monday].
I can scarcely believe that more than a week has elapsed since I wrote last in my journal, so busy have I been, so happy, and so sad, so sick and again well that it seems at least a month. I must try and give as well as I can some account of all that has happened. On Sunday we went to Church and I was surprised to find Lucy Kinsolving[164] there. She came out to Oakley with her husband and baby to spend the night with me. After Church I went to the P. Office and got a long sweet letter from Hal which made me long to see him ten times more than before. Alex Grayson[165] came over to dinner from Uncle Nathan's;[166] he had spent the day and night before with us. He looks very well considering his past illness and he and Anna are so happy together it makes me almost happy to see them.

I had a bad headache on Sunday night, and went upstairs in Lucy Kinsolving's room while she was with her baby. She was playing with the baby and I leaning my aching head on the bed when the door opened quietly and there stood my dear husband. My headache troubled me no more for that evening, and I enjoyed the prospect of having him for a whole week so much that I could think at first of nothing but happiness, but before many days the thought that in one short week I will again be alone would intrude and marred my otherwise great happiness. Hal looked so well and so very handsome and seemed so glad to be at home with his wife and little folks once more, and Rozier's happiness at being again able to trot about after his papa knew no bounds, and even little Becca looked radiantly triumphant when she [could] say, "me pa's 'tome 'ome," while May played her best pieces on the piano for him, and all tried to make his visit as pleasant as possible.

Alex & Anna have been together almost all the week and it does me good to see how happy they are, she placid and quiet, every feature expressing her

Timeline of the War

December 4	Britain announces an embargo on all exports to the United States.
December 9	The U.S. Senate approves the establishment of the Joint Congressional Committee on the Conduct of the War.
December 11	Charleston, South Carolina, is ravaged by a fire that destroys 575 homes, churches, and businesses.
December 14	Prince Albert, consort of Queen Victoria, dies at Windsor Castle.
December 30	Commissioners Mason and Slidell are handed over to Lord Lyons, who immediately puts them on a ship for England.

great content, while he looked so handsome and manly that I did not wonder at her being so much in love.

On Thursday I killed some pork and on Friday while Hal dined with Alex Grayson I attended to my lard. But Friday morning I awoke feeling very badly and was forced at dinner time to leave Bob Powell[167] who had come in the morning to Anna and my lard to Mamma and lie down. I dressed later in the evening to meet Hal when he came, but I soon had to go to bed, and when he came back, I had high fever. In the morning however I was better to my great delight for I could not bear to see how sad Hal looked at the idea of leaving me sick.

On Saturday Mamma went to Middleburg—Uncle Billy having said he wished to be hired out, I got her to see if Mr. Kinsolving would not take him, and also if I could get Mrs. Knap's[168] servant to put in his place. She could only tell me on her return that the matter was under consideration. How strange it is that the most indulged servants should almost invariably prove the least faithful. No servant on the place has been so indulged as Uncle Billy and he of all has chosen this time when from his age and intelligence he might be a comfort to me to wish to leave because he is tired of being dining room servant and thinks he would like the farm. . . . I do not regret the change as though a comfort in some respects, I do not think his example was good. He has been allowed to do too much as he pleased.

On Saturday in the day Hal came in from Upperville and with some light excuse said he must go back to camp at once, as he had rather be many hours too soon than one too late. I knew at once that he had heard there was a prospect of a battle but I made no to do about it as I knew Hal did not wish to see me distressed, and I do not place any great confidence in any report that comes. He started off as soon as he could get something to eat. I felt sad and lonely enough all the evening, and indulged after he left in the tears I restrained while he was here. At nine o'clock the door opened, and he came in again. [He] had found out in Middleburg that it was a false alarm and he determined to spend another night with us.

But early the next morning he left, not to return, I fear, for many, many, days to come. I do not complain but I cannot get reconciled to my husband's absence. It is something so unnatural to be without him, my anxiety for him is so great, my responsibility so heavy that sometimes I involuntarily shrink from a long continuance of the present state of affairs and my courage, patriotism, and faith all seem failing together. I can only pray, and hope, and especially need all the consolation that both prayer and hope can give such nights as this, when I miss my dear husband the more from just having seen him. Tom Turner is here. Today I rode to Upperville but got there too late to attend to my business.

Dec. 10th [Tuesday].
The first thing this morning, I was awaked by Mamma's telling me that they were killing the hogs. It was as warm as a summer's day and close and damp. I was much annoyed at my having neglected to tell Mr. Kidwell not to kill but really I thought he had better sense.[169] I was not pleased with his conduct when I sent for him and told him not to kill any more. He was very angry and not very respectful showing for the first time a disposition to resist the authority vested in me by my husband in his absence. I was firm however thinking it better that Mr. Kidwell should have some trouble for nothing than that 10,000 lbs of pork should be needlessly risked.

Anna and Tom and I drove out today. I have been trying to get $60.00 as a Christmas gift for Mr. Kinsolving from the congregation. At first I was very successful getting more than I expected from many of the members, but some from whom I expected, most disappointed me, Mr. & Mrs. Scott not giving anything and Mr. Bolling only $2.00. This is a strange world. I cannot understand how people who profess to be devoted to their minister can withhold from his necessity a few dollars out of their abundance.

Dec. 14th [Saturday].
I can hardly believe that five days have passed without my writing, but the mornings are so short that I have to hurry to breakfast and at night I am often too tired to write any thing more than my letters to Hal one of which is always on hand for as soon I as I finish one I begin another.

Yesterday I had another lot of pork to put away, and again had a bad headache to attend to it with. I stood the smoke and grease all the morning but broke down completely in the evening, and had to go to bed suffering very much.

No letter has come from Hal. I look for one every day. The papers have no news of any importance. Alex Grayson has been over a great deal, he will leave for camp on Monday, so I have given Anna and himself the parlor that they may see as much of each other as possible before he leaves.

Dec. 16th [Monday].
All day yesterday we heard heavy firing in the direction of Centreville which makes me very anxious, though Mr. Grayson said he thought it was only exercising the men. Anna Bolling and Rebecca [the two little girls] are both very sick today in consequence of eating fresh pork. I have sent Mr. Kidwell to Paris this morning to buy leather having heard that it was sold there for 40 cts. pr. lb. while here we give 75cts. I want to get enough for the plantation shoes for next summer.

My servant women are all hired but two, some boys are to be hired, and Uncle Billy. I must go to Upperville this evening to see about their homes.[170]

I am perfectly at a loss who to put in Uncle Billy's place, and am not willing to keep him when he has shown himself so unfaithful as to wish to leave the family just now when the services of a faithful servant are so much needed. No letter from Hal yet. I could have cried from disappointment yesterday when none came, so certainly did I expect one.

Dec. 18th [Wednesday].
Having written a long letter to Hal and made a collar for Anna, and Ben not yet having brought the mail, I will write while waiting for him. I have been busy all day preparing a wagon load of provisions for Hal, and Mr. Kidwell will start with them for Centreville tomorrow. I have not heard one word from Hal since he left, and I have become very uneasy. I know he does not like to write, but still he knows my anxiety and has never let so long a time pass without writing before. I hardly think he can be sick for Talcott Eliason who saw him on Saturday says he is perfectly well, but I cannot understand his not writing, especially as he knows I am waiting to hear from him before transacting some business of considerable importance to me. All this evening we have heard heavy guns firing in quick succession at Centreville, but since the constant firing on Sunday turned out to be only trying to bring down a Federal balloon,[171] I do not feel so uneasy. But I must not omit to record my folly on Monday night.

All day long I had been thinking of the firing the day before, and every time the door opened I had started fearing it was someone coming with bad news. Mamma and I had gone up into her room leaving Anna and Mr. Grayson in the parlor.

The clock had struck ten and I was reading when I heard carriage wheels on the road. In an instant it flashed upon me that someone was bringing Hal home either killed or wounded. Wild with terror, I did not stop to find out the truth of my fears, but downstairs I rushed, and saw on looking out of the passage window a long black carriage slowly driving up. To my excited imagination it could be nothing but an ambulance and I was confirmed in my fears without opening the front door. I rushed into the parlor entirely speechless and frightening Anna and Mr. Grayson half to death by my terror stricken countenance. I only stayed in long enough to let them know something was the matter, and then went out to face my terror. Just as I opened the door a stranger came up the steps, without waiting to see who it was I grasped his arm with both hands, and implored him to tell me what he came for and who was in the carriage? "My dear Madam," said he, "my name is Turner, Tom Turner[172] of Baltimore, nothing is the matter! No one is in the carriage. I hope I have not alarmed you."

It was some time before I could believe him and then it required all the firmness I could summon to keep me from going into hysterics, so great was the revulsion of feeling. In the meantime Alex Grayson wished to follow me out but Anna thinking the Federals had come or the Contrabands[173] risen, and thinking Alex would be shot, seized him, and too agitated to notice where she held him [until she] saw him gasping for breath and found she had him by the throat. She was soon brought to by seeing Alex reach his hand for a glass of water to throw in her face, the very idea of the cold water acting as a restorer. All this time poor Tom stood in abject amazement thinking doubtless that he had landed in a Bedlam.[174]

The whole scene seems perfectly absurd to look back upon but it was no joke at the time. I never in all my life had such a feeling of horror, and it is the first time in my life that I was ever speechless from terror. Now I am shocked at the bare idea of my having so little self possession, and am mortified to think of how much worse I should have made matters had any thing really been the matter. But at the time I had but one thought and that one of unutterable horror. Tom has left for The Post.[175] Again to-night the mail has come and no letter from Hal. I am really uneasy and truly glad that Mr. Kidwell is going down tomorrow, as I must hear something now on Friday.

Dec. 19th [Thursday].
The wagon started this morning two hours before I was up. I took the trouble yesterday to inform my neighbors that I would send down this morning and charged them to send what they wished last night. They did not do it however and this morning I shall have the trouble of sending back bundles sent out a few moments ago.

So yesterday Mamma and I drove up to Upperville to see Cousin Willie and Aunt Mary [Eliason]. While at Cousin Willie's Mittie Stephenson brought me in $10.00 George Carter had given toward our Christmas gift for Mr. Kinsolving, so that I have now $65.00 to send him by Mamma today when she goes for Jenny.[176] I am so glad we undertook to get it for it will be a great help to him these hard times. My horse is lame so no more carriage drives till Hal sends my big horse home.

Dec. 21st [Saturday].
Yesterday I got a long letter from Hal and last night another by the wagon.[177] He thinks my scold rather unjust as he wrote me a long letter by Mr. Moss[178] which I did not get besides the two I got yesterday. He has formed a new mess[179] and wants a good many things for it so I shall send down another wagon load after Christmas. All England is alive with indignation over the Capture of Mason & Slidell. I wonder what will be the result. I think that Lincoln will apologize and give them up, saying he had no idea their capture would be offensive to the English government, but I cannot help hoping that with their usual pigheadedness and Yankee conceit they will brave John Bull's wrath, trusting in the omnipotence of the Universal Nation [the Union]. I feel

very anxious to hear from my Uncle Shirley Turner of Charleston. I wrote to him as soon as I heard of the fire in Charleston offering him a home for as many of his family as my house can accommodate if he should be one of the sufferers.[180]

Hal's letter to Ida, December 17, 1861, Camp Letcher:

Walker [Armistead] sent you in my pouch a fine looking orange [an exotic treat] given to him by a gentleman from Georgia. I hope that you and Ma will enjoy it.

Send me down as soon as possible a wagon load of things. Lt. Plaster and myself have opened a Mess. I have just left Mr. Bolling and son and nephew. I should have had my letter ready for today's mail, as it is I shall have to put off sending it until tomorrow. In opening a mess we will have to supply ourselves again with plates etc. . . . I shall enclose you an order for them to Mr. Thomblin who will send them to you and you can send them down by the wagon. I wish you would send me a list of the things you send down, and see that the things sent [including] a half dozen of each. I forgot to say cups & saucers, in other words a full complement. [In addition to the cutlery, plates and cups, Hal also ordered "2 small shallow dishes, 2 small deep dishes, 1 tin coffee pot, 1 tea kettle."]

Tell Ma I saw Allan Randolph and he told me that he had heard through a friend from Ranny [Ida's brother Robert Randolph Powell from St. Louis] and that he was capt. of a cavalry company in the Confederate Service and that he was well & [illegible]. So she need make no change in her will. He is all right. [Hal is joking about Ranny's tardiness in enlisting, a source of concern at Oakley. He teases that his patriotic mother-in-law might leave her only son out of her will.] . . . if there is a chance of my seeing you I will be there. . . .

Dec. 25th [Wednesday].
Christmas day—and the little folks as happy as cakes, candy, nuts and toys ever made them, and day as bright and joyous looking as if there was no cruel war to make a day of festivity a mere mockery to many anxious hearts. To me it is sadder than any day has been for a long time, for I miss so much that [which] has made many Christmas days happy to me. When I was first married every Christmas was spent at Welbourne where all the members of the family old and young would be collected, Katey [Ida's sister] always there, and Hal and Sister [Rebecca Dulany], and we had everything to make the day pass happily.

The contrast today strikes me very forcibly, Hal is at the war, Kate away, and my darling sister dead. Brother Richard sick at Centreville, and my dear little ones at Welbourne without Father or Mother have but little to make the day a merry one. Brother R. was to have been at home but is detained at Centreville by sickness. Uncle Armistead sent me a short note from Hal this morning, telling me nothing but that he is well.

Since I last wrote a considerable battle has taken place at Dranesville, which the Federals will certainly claim as a victory but which is said by some to be a drawn battle and by others to be a victory on the Confederate side, as more Yankees were killed than Confederates. The truth being, I believe, that both sides were pretty badly handled and that neither knew how badly the other was served.[181]

Dec. 29th [Sunday].
Christmas day all the Bolling young men called, and the day after we dined at Bollingbrook; Fitzhugh Grayson and George Carter called in the morning just as we were starting. Anna did not come back with us as she was to leave for Petersburg the next day with her Uncle.

What a week of disagreeables this has been. All the hirelings [who have been working elsewhere in the neighborhood] are at home; consequently, the whole place seems topsy turvy, and of course the house servants join in the general distraction. Letty when I told her she must live with Mrs. Lunceford[182] was very impertinent, refusing positively to stay with her. I reprimanded her severely at the time for impertinence is an offence I never pass by. Yesterday she came to see me and made a humble apology. Hal hired Uncle Billy to Genl. Bonham,[183] and when I told the old man of it, he expressed great unwillingness to go and said he did not wish to leave me, only thought a little change from the house to the farm would be pleasant. I think finding that no objection was made to his leaving will do him good, I have decided to take two little boys home and send one of the grown hands to Hal.

I heard yesterday that some cattle were to be had in the hollow. I sent Mr. Kidwell up this morning but when he got there he found they had all been sold, which was a great disappointment to me. I can get some potatoes for seed from Mr. Harrison. I sent Hal down a good wagon load of provisions by Mott Ball[184] this morning, also his horse. A good long letter came from him tonight. Poor fellow a sad Christmas he must have had. He complained of suffering from cold while writing. It makes me almost hate my comfortable room to think of what he has to endure. He wrote me that he wanted me to send him Ben for a cook. My judgment was against his taking him, and I wrote Hal fully my reasons for thinking he had better take some one else. I am sorry I did for I am afraid he did not understand my motives, and may have thought indifference to his comfort made me object, which was far from the case, my chief reason being that I do not think he can be trusted, and another reason being that I did not think Hal could afford to provide all the servants for the mess. He says now that the other members of the mess will pay part of his hire.

We have not received one paper for two nights, but the last contained two items of bad news, first the Federal Government has decided to give up Mason and Slidell to avert a war with England, which is a sad disappointment to us—as the aid [of] England's Navy was all we wanted to make our speedy success beyond the possibility of a doubt. Then there were Northern accounts of a great victory gained by the Federals over Price in Missouri,[185] which I do not fully credit, but which makes me uneasy. It is utterly impossible to believe anything we see from the North. The Father of lies is Senior Editor of every paper.

Rebecca has a cold which makes me a little uneasy, and Rachel a stubborn cough that I have been for some time doctoring in vain. I have had the blues pretty badly lately, I think in consequence of having so much on my hands and being often puzzled in my ignorance how to act, which together with my missing Hal and being anxious about him, and fearing too that I had annoyed him somewhat by writing about Ben, altogether depresses me, but I must not forget my unfailing friend, from whom I have often received comfort and guidance and whom alone is my hope.

Little Katey Noland[186] came home with Jenny for Christmas, she is a lovely child. Brother Richard has spent one day with me since he came up; his back gave him great pain all day. Willie Carrere and William Turner spent the night before Christmas here but went on to The Post Xmas morning.

Hal's letter to Ida, December 26, 1861, Camp Letcher:

> I received your most welcome letter last night, and heard from some one in the 8th Regiment that Alex Grayson has another, he has gone on picket and I won't be able to get it until he returns which worries me considerably. I hope that you have spent a more happy Xmas than I did, for of all gloomy, miserable days I think it took the lead.
>
> I suppose you received a little note from me by Uncle Armistead in regards to Billy and Ma's boy. Tell Ma when she gets me to hire her boy again she will not disappoint me in letting him come, it has put me in rather an awkward situation as I positively hired the boy to Capt Young for 20$ per month. I shall go over and see him today, however, and tell him that Mrs. Powell, not hearing from me, concluded that she had better get him a home before the 1st of Jan. (Confound it, my fingers are so stiff and cold that I can't use them.)
>
> How very stupid in my not sending you the tax bills. I spoke to Dick [Noland] about them and would have sent you a statement but it takes so much writing that I concluded to let him explain it when he came up. You did not think for an instant that I was going to furnish a servant for Lieut. Plaster and Gibson; if Ben cooks for them they will pay me $20 per month for him— that is their portion of it. I thought that if you wanted another servant you

could get a better one than Ben for less money but you can do as you think best. . . .

I wish you would ride up [to] Upperville some good day and see that Latham [the family lawyer] in regard to that land. They are making us pay for it and Richard [Dulany] does the same thing. When you go to see him carry up the deed and get him to have it registered at Warrenton.

I don't think you need be alarmed about the horses, corn will be very high about Spring and will pay you just as well. If you are not in need of money [now] I think prices won't go down but you had better consult Uncle Armistead or John about it and do as both of them advise, both of them are very sage men.

I am glad to hear you got in a good humor with me before Xmas day. As you acknowledge that you were rather hard [from my not writing], I shall forgive you, but don't be down on me in that way if I'm innocent. I think I told you once before that writing before a warm fire and writing in the frozen air are two very different things. I don't think there is much chance of my getting home for a long time. They won't give over 24 hours now. I can ride home in 5 & back in 5, that would leave me 14 hours for your society—*would you really like to see me?* Because if you would, I think I will try some of these fine days to get up. . . .

Thomas Turner IV of Kinloch, Ida's maternal grandfather. Courtesy of the Mackall family.

Kinloch, home of Ida's uncle Edward Carter "Ned" Turner. Courtesy of the Mackall family.

The Hill, Ida's girlhood home, ca. 1896. Courtesy of Sheila Cochran.

Oakley as it appeared shortly after the war. Courtesy of the Mackall family.

Leven Powell, Ida's great-grandfather, was a friend of George Washington and the founder of Middleburg. Courtesy of Michael A. Smith.

George Cuthbert Powell of the Hill, Ida's father. Courtesy of Anne Mackall Sasscer.

Marietta Fauntleroy Turner Powell of Kinloch, Ida's mother. Courtesy of Michael A. Smith.

Modern view of the rear of Oakley. Courtesy of the Mackall family.

Modern view of the rear of the Oakley property, showing the meat house on the left and postwar guest cottages on the right. Photograph by Stevan Meserve.

Henry Rozier Dulany, Hal's father. Courtesy of the Mackall family.

Henry Grafton "Hal" Dulany after the war. Sketched by Marietta Minnigerode Andrews. Courtesy of the Mackall and Sasscer families.

Modern view of Welbourne, home of Colonel Richard H. Dulany. Photograph by Stevan Meserve.

Rebecca Ann Dulany, Hal's sister and wife of Col. Richard Dulany. Courtesy of Nathaniel H. Morison III.

Hal's brother-in-law, Colonel Richard H. Dulany of the 7th Virginia Cavalry. Courtesy of Nathaniel H. Morison III.

Katherine Powell "Kate" Carter, Ida's younger sister and wife of George Carter of Oatlands. Painted by Marietta Minnigerode Andrews. Courtesy of Oatlands, a National Trust Site.

Virginia Powell "Jenny" Minnigerode, Ida's youngest sister. Courtesy of Oatlands, a National Trust Site.

Oatlands, home of George and Kate Powell Carter, ca. 1890. Courtesy of Oatlands, a National Trust Site.

George Carter II, Ida's brother-in-law, and his dog, Trilby, on the porch of Little Oatlands. Courtesy of Oatlands, a National Trust Site.

1862

January

Jan. 1st, 1862 [Wednesday].

I began my New Year badly. I was obliged to leave home early this morning to see Brother Richard about some business before he left for Centreville; consequently, some of my home duties were neglected, and when I came home at one o'clock I found several of the servants not gone to their homes, Mammy who took herself off on Sunday without leave, not returned, and Uncle Billy in Upperville, no fire in the library and no preparation for dinner. I soon sent all the servants home. When Uncle Billy came, [I] reprimanded him for not being in place, and have a lecture in store for Mammy that she will either remember as long as she lives here, or will find her stay with me very much shortened.

I sent yesterday for Mr. Latham[1] and consulted with him as to what was best to be done with the unrecorded deeds I have, and got the necessary information from him regarding the transfer of the land Brother Richard bought from Hal.[2] I also found the paper containing the statement of the former settlement between Brother R. & Hal, and having made a close calculation of the amount of taxes that Hal had paid for Brother R. owing to his not having had the land transferred. I got the whole business perfectly clear to my own mind so as to give Brother R. as little trouble as possible, and with the papers all nicely arranged went off to Welbourne where I had a satisfactory talk with him, was paid for the taxes, and got from him a promise to settle with Hal about the boundaries of the land, and let me know at once that I may make the deed out and have the transfer made.

When I returned from Welbourne on Monday where I had been dining, I found Willie Carrere, Willie & Tom Turner, Sophie and Lizzie [the Baltimore Turners], and after supper Powell Conrad and Archie Fauntleroy[3] came, so the house was full. Archie and Powell left the next morning, the others this morning. I enjoyed their visit very much and was sorry to part with them. Today Mr. Kidwell told me that Mrs. Chichester's[4] servants had been in my woods cutting up large trees. I gave her permission to pick up the down wood & brush, and I cannot easily excuse her abusing the permit. I have hired out all the

> **Timeline of the War**
>
> | | |
> |---|---|
> | January 3 | "Stonewall" Jackson leaves winter quarters in Winchester and begins a campaign into western Virginia. |
> | January 13 | Lincoln appoints Edwin Stanton secretary of war. |
> | January 19 | Confederate general Felix Kirk Zollicoffer is killed in battle at Mill Spring, Kentucky, and his men are routed from the field. |
> | January 27 | Frustrated by the inactivity of Union armies, Lincoln issues General War Order No. 1, ordering a "general movement of the naval and land forces of the United States against the insurgent forces" on February 22. |

servants except two boys, and think of apprenticing one to a black smith, and letting Mr. Newlon[5] have the other.

Jan. 3rd [Friday].
Yesterday morning tho' feeling very badly from my cold having heard that Patsey's child was very sick, I walked up to Uncle Dan's to see it. The morning was bitter cold, and I was so very unwell after my walk as to be entirely unfit for anything else the whole day. This morning I still felt so badly that Mamma has done all my house keeping, and tonight in consequence of nursing myself up a little I am much better.

At last this morning Mott Ball sent my wagon home, and with it a long letter from my dearest husband. Mott lost my nice baskets which I am very sorry for as I cannot get them replaced easily. After writing a long letter to Hal and letters to Aunt Margaret and Mrs. Pinkney,[6] I heard Rozier his spelling lesson and May her music, then read till dinner some old English dramas, and this evening cut out nine [pairs] of pants for the out hands.[7] Tonight I knit on many sleeves and fixed Rachel's knitting then made a stew for my cold; now I write and when I've done writing will read till half past ten o'clock, then to bed.

A long letter from Katey tonight, in which she tells of the departure of all of Jackson's division to the mountains near Romney. She writes gloomily and speaks of her pain at parting from different soldier acquaintances whom she names but says not one word of Mr. Barton which looks strange as we hear he has been more attentive to her than any one else.

Mason and Slidell have been given up by the Lincoln government to the demands of England—so I suppose all prospect of war between Great Britain and the United States is at an end. Prince Albert is dead.[8] I wonder if the Queen will grieve like other wives, or if her greatness will deny her the indulgence or afford her consolation extraordinary!

Jan. 4th [Saturday].

The second snow we have had this winter fell last night, about two inches deep. My cold is not much better, but no worse. Mr. Hotchkiss[9] came up from camp today and reports all well. The papers today say that the Federals have been driven back into their boats by the South Carolinians which is good news.[10] All the Northern papers speak of a simultaneous advance movement that is to be made by their army at every point in a few weeks, but such programs have been so often laid down that I do not place much confidence in them now. Mr. Kinsolving preaches tomorrow but I fear I shall not be well enough to go to hear him.

> *Hal's letter to Ida, January 5, 1862, Camp G. W. Smith:*
>
> I received two letters from you my darling Ida nearly together, one brought by Brother R, and the other through the mail in answer to the one sent by Baltimore—Brother R told me you were looking so well, and nearly before I received the good news your other letter tells me that you have the same old cough. You can't imagine how uneasy it has made me. . . .
>
> They all tell you are doing so well and so much, they think it would be best for all parties if I staid away all together, and I have no doubt you think with them, as long as you a house full of handsome young men to help you to make out your accounts. [Hal is teasing Ida about her houseful of cousins]. . . . Well never mind, there are plenty of handsome girls down here, and if I don't hear good reports (d— the farm) I shall take French leave and look up some one else. So don't let me hear any more about book keeping, unless it is solo.
>
> Well, I have gotten through grumbling—and shall proceed to give you what items of news there are down here which is mighty little. I suppose you have received the New York Herald I sent you a day or two ago, it was the latest northern news that has been received about here (Dec. 30th it was). I got it from *Miss* Smith down below Burke's Station, and at the same time a nice glass of eggnog and cake. She told me the day before, that there had been about 1000 Yankees up at the Station reconnoitering, after staying up there a few hours went off, without doing any damage, except to some turkeys.
>
> Now that England has been gratified in her demands by the delivery of Slidell & Mason, every one down here confidently expect a battle. They must fight or back down entirely, and that soon. I don't know what they will do for a General, McClellan is bent on "playing possum," and I can't imagine who they have to take his place. Well if they do risk a fight and come here, they will be whipped worse than they even were before but they are too smart for that, they will attack, down at Evansport, and advance towards Winchester, and possibly make a feint here, while all that is going on, they will find a match in Genl. Beauregard, Johnson and Smith. . . .

Tell Ma I don't think I can hire her boy by the year at that price—but if he is on her hands and she will send him down, I will see what can be done, there is no difficulty in hiring him by the month. Best love to her and the children. My fingers are about 0, and my paper is run out. . . .

Jan. 6th [Monday].
I did not go to church yesterday and it was well I did not, for my cold is very bad, worse I think than it has been, and yesterday was very cold. Mr. Kinsolving called here this morning.

I got a note from Mrs. Pettit[11] this morning telling me that Beck had been so insufferably insolent to her that she must insist upon sending her home immediately. I hired her to her for the year and [in] the bond I expressly stipulated that she should not be returned to me during the year. I have no place to put her and nothing for her to do, so think I ought to insist upon Mrs. Pettit's keeping her and so abiding by her bond, but her being a soldier's widow makes me very reluctant to disoblige her if I can help it. I will see what I can do however, if the cold weather and my indisposition will allow of my going out tomorrow.

Mr. Kidwell complained to me today that Maria for two days past had cooked no dinner for the hands, giving as an excuse for not doing it that she had butter to beat [churn] for me. I sent for her and gave her [the] choice and one month to decide whether she would do her duty or be hired out. She answered respectfully that she would do her best.

My cold and cough keep me awake so at night that I feel depressed and indolent all day. I have been reading several old English plays from a large volume Uncle John lent me, and have enjoyed them very much—Home's old play of "Douglass" is [a] delight, and Howe's "Fair Penitent" and "Jane Shore" are very pretty and some comedies have amused me no little especially "The Devil to Pay."

Jan. 8th [Wednesday].
To begin at the beginning yesterday morning directly after breakfast Mr. Bolling sent over an immense basket full of toys—presents from Anna to the children, and great was their delight thereat. I had hardly put them all away and was sitting here copying a letter for Mamma when the door opened and in walked my dearest Husband, looking so well and so happy to be at home. But early this morning he left again and I feel very blue tonight, but still am very, very thankful to have seen him even this little. There is a rumor of fighting in Berkeley but nothing certain.[12]

Jan. 21st [Tuesday].
For an unusually long time has my journal been neglected, but I have been very busy in many ways—and a good deal has happened for me to record

tonight. Hal left me on Wednesday the 8th. My cold kept me a prisoner till Monday.

In the meantime Mamma had heard the rumor of fighting in Berkeley and wrote for Katey to come home [from Winchester] immediately instead of going by Clarke [County] as she had intended. So on Monday we went to Upperville to meet her, and finding that the stage did not come in till late in the evening paid some bills, made a few purchases and went with Ma to see Aunt Mary and Miss Margaret who were both sick, and we came home and sent the carriage back for Kate.

I had not been at home an hour before to my surprise and delight Hal walked in, bringing Lt. Waldhoem[13] with him. They had been given two days leave. [They] being half starved, I soon got them a dinner and while they were eating Katey arrived, looking well and prettier than I had seen her for a long time, in fine spirits and well pleased to get home, and not displeased at finding a young soldier ready to do his best to make up for her separation from Jackson's Brigade.

The gentlemen staid till Wednesday and left in a driving sleet. Hal [was] very unwell when he started but I have heard from him repeatedly since. The Lt's. horse was sick so I loaned him one of the carriage horses to go down on, and the next day Hal sent him back by Johnny, and wrote me word to send Dan down the next day which I did. Johnny has been very ill ever since he came with camp fever.[14] I have not been able to see him as the incessant rain has made me afraid to go out with my cold. Dr. Bronaugh[15] visits him regularly and I send his prescriptions from the house.

On Friday Lt. Grey[16] and Willie Wilson came up to see Kate and spent the day and in the evening George Carter and Richard Grayson[17] called. Mr. Carter brought her a beautiful bouquet from his green house. At night Walker Armistead came. He stayed all night and left for Camp in the morning. That day we heard that the Yankees had retreated precipitately from Romney leaving all their stores ammunition etc. in our possession. We hold the town at present.

The great Burnside expedition was reported a few days ago to have started on its mission.[18] We heard yesterday heavy firing from Evansport[19] and fear that an attack may have been made there.

Last week I bought a work horse from Dawson for $85.00 and yesterday Hal sent me one from the army so that we now have enough to plough for corn. I bought 16 pigs last week, very good sized ones, at $6.00 a piece—a high price. I was offered on Saturday $4.00 for corn and 50 cts. a hundred for straw by a government agent. I will sell 60 barrels of corn and three ricks of straw.

Lt. Gray was here again yesterday. William Turner spent last night here, and left this morning for Warrenton where Willie Carrere is ill with typhoid fever. I hope sincerely it may be a slight attack. Katey has a sick headache today, and is now in bed.

The children's education goes on very regularly now, May making the most astonishing progress in music and doing well in her other lessons which her Grandma teaches her while Rozier and I fight along over ba ba's and be be's. I have finished reading the British Drama and Miss Austen, and have begun Robertson's Charles Vth preparatory to reading Phillip the Second by Prescott. The servants are at work on the summer clothes for servants and children while I am busy cutting out and fixing them.

February

Feb. 13th [Thursday].
Nearly a month has passed since I wrote before in my journal, and how much has happened in this one month. Hal has been at home very sick for two weeks, and has gone away again. Poor Johnny came home ill with camp fever and died in a week.

The whole face of military affairs has changed. First a great defeat at Somerset Kentucky,[20] cast a gloom over the whole South, and in the last week disaster has followed disaster till our cause, to the despondent seems almost hopeless—The Federals have taken Roanoke Island where 3000 of our men under Wise were ordered to remain and offer resistance to the Burnside Fleet. Poor fellows they fought nobly, but could not hold out against 15,000, and were all except 50, killed, wounded or captured. Jennings Wise was desperately wounded, and when being carried off on a blanket he broke his sword and threw it at the Yankees, upon which he was instantly murdered.[21] His company composed of the young men of Richmond were all killed or wounded except six who were sick—

Every one looks gloomy and the old men prophesy ruin, and desolation, but I will not despair. The Lord God Omnipotent reigneth, and it may please him to do us good even by these reverses. Our Authorities have seemed to be negligent of late and this may be needed to stir them up. Norfolk and Richmond are immediately threatened in Va. and in Tennessee the capture of Fort Henry[22] gives the Federal an advantage that it will be hard for us to over come. The future is dark enough and the end to our troubles seems hopelessly distant, but the deepest gloom is often followed by days of great brightness and God grant it may be so with our beloved country now.

Feb. 14th [Friday].
Today's paper gives more encouraging accounts from Roanoke. The "Examiner" says only one hundred of our men were killed, and the "Dispatch" puts our loss at only 45, while they both state the Federal loss to be between 1000 and 1500. I fear they are mistaken, time and history will tell, but such is the spirit of deceit and falsehood abroad in our land that we cannot credit half the

> ### Timeline of the War
> | | |
> |---|---|
> | February 6 | Fort Henry surrenders to Union gunboats. |
> | February 8 | Confederate garrison of Roanoke Island, North Carolina, surrenders to superior Union force commanded by Ambrose Burnside. |
> | February 16 | Fort Donelson surrenders, ensuring the loss of Kentucky and Tennessee to the Confederacy. |
> | February 21 | Confederate general Henry Sibley wins a victory at Fort Craig, New Mexico. |
> | February 22 | Jefferson Davis is inaugurated as president of the Confederate States of America. |
> | February 24 | Union troops under Gen. Don Carlos Buell occupy Nashville, Tennessee. |
> | February 28 | Jefferson Davis proclaims a national day of fasting and prayer for the success of the Confederate cause. |

intelligence gleaned from the papers. A long letter came from Hal today. He says the men are reenlisting very rapidly.[23]

> *Hal's letter to Ida, February 12, 1862, Camp G. W. Smith:*
> I received your letter my dear wife last night just as I came off a scouting party of which as usual I had the honor of being the advance guard, rode some thirty odd miles and used ourselves and horses nearly to death, without seeing any Yankees. I received my keys by Thomas the Good [Thomas Goody Carter] just in time to get my coat out for duty. Our adjutant has gone off for a few days and I am acting in his place, an office the business of which I know very little about. I find it hard work, but as it is only for a short time I reckon I can survive it. . . .
>
> About Ma's boy, I shall go down and see Gen. Ewell about him, but will not take him, of course on Ma's terms, viz without paying for him. . . . I have not been able as yet to send off your letter to St. Louis—It is against Gen. [Stuart's] orders and I will have to see him first, and explain the contents. When I do that I shall send it by first opportunity.
>
> The men are re-enlisting very fast. They are giving them $50 and thirty days furlough, to commence the day they arrive at home, and to have their expenses paid to and from home. I tell you it has brought a quantity of them in. The officers fare worst of all, of course, they can't leave their companies, and they have to take it out in recruiting, which they generally do in their own neighborhoods. . . .

Thank goodness the ground has at last frozen up so that a man can step outside of his door without being in mud over his knees, it is now passable down here. . . . Hams, Turkeys and hominy all came to hand safe [sent by Ida]. I can't say as much for the cooking. I boiled the hominy six hours, and it came out as black as the Devil. I boiled the ham six hours and it came out all to pieces. Even the bones were boiled out. I must say your receipt is a d—d humbug. I shall try another today on my own hook. Well, considering that I said I would not write to you again (and, tho I have a fire, my fingers are confoundedly cold) I think this will do very well. . . .

Take good care of yourself my own darling and write soon to your devoted husband.

Feb. 18th [Tuesday].
A fearful fight is going on at Fort Donelson, the final result of which we have not heard. For three days Feb. 13th, 14th, and 15th the Confederates have repulsed the Federals with great slaughter, but the Federals have been largely reinforced and the Confederates were expecting another attack on the 16th. We await the issue with great anxiety. The fort is the key to Tennessee and its capture will leave the whole state as well as Memphis exposed and Nashville in great danger.

> *Hal's letter to Ida, February 14, 1862, Camp G. W. Smith:*
> I wrote to you yesterday enclosing a check from Brother Richard. I thought then that he would not go home for some time, but the order came to this office a few moments afterwards for him to leave on recruiting service, and he left today. Therefore if you have not received the check per mail, you can see him about it, and arrange it immediately, before the check has time to be used. . . .
>
> It is just possible that in a month or two I may be able to get off on recruiting service myself but I shall be among the last, as I have been home since all the other officers of the company, and it is nothing more than fair that they should have a chance before me.
>
> What do you think of the news from Europe, about England and France recognizing the Southern Confederacy? They say it is certainly so. If that is the case it will more than counterbalance the defeat at Roanoke Island, which after all I think is more for us, than against us. Men never fought better and the Yankees must see from that specimen what Southern, and especially Virginia soldiers are made of. It is also reported here today that Gen. Price has gained a great victory out in Missouri, but that needs confirmation. I hope it may be so.
>
> I sent your letter [to St. Louis] below the lines this morning to Capt. Boyd Smith with the request that he would send it if possible, if not return it to me.

The Yankees have gotten very strict lately, and have been taking up all doubtful persons, they have also gotten very impudent, and have been taking, and running in some of our Cavalry pickets. I think we will put a stop to that before long. They are such a confounded set of cowards that they never come without an overwhelming force and the only way we can catch them is to wait in ambush with a large body of infantry and have the Cavalry in readiness to charge them when thrown into confusion.

[Hal jokes about Kate's beaux]. I have not had the pleasure of seeing him since I returned and suppose he has gone South, to look out for oranges and sweet potatoes. It is a d— good thing to have a good looking unmarried sister, I shall keep her single as long as possible for my own special benefit. Have you heard anything of George Carter [the main contender for Kate's hand] since he left for North Carolina? I wonder that he could leave for such a distance, his perfection of loveliness and amiability. . . . Never mind, there is some consolation in having a little husband [George was short], you can make him behave himself, although I know a small woman [Ida] that does that with one that weighs 185 lbs. *The Lord help and protect poor little George.*

Up to this time I have had no return of sore throat or eyes and hope that I have had my share of sickness for the winter. Our camp is miserably muddy but otherwise we are as comfortably fixed as could be expected so don't make yourself uneasy on my account, it is entirely unnecessary. I do feel uneasy about you tho, my darling, the way you go about that wet farm land and stand while they are milking the cows, I am afraid it will bring back your cough and, it may be, lay you up for the winter. Do, Ida, for my sake take good care of your health, and if not for that, to preserve your good looks. You have no idea how much prettier you are fat than thin.

Well, I sat down here to write about three lines and have written about three pages. All quiet down in this section, best love to all. . . .

Feb. 19th [Wednesday].
The truly disheartening news of the capture of Fort Donelson by the Federals came today.[24] There was only the "Dispatch" stating the fact, and no particulars except that the Confederates yielded only to a reinforcement of 50,000 men from Cairo [Illinois], and that after having repulsed the enemy four times with great slaughter. Our fortunes seem now on the decline. Four successive disasters such as those of Dranesville, Fort Henry and Roanoke and Fort Donelson are enough to discourage and alarm a people fighting for every thing that makes existence endurable. It is terrible to have such immense interest depending on events that will probably be concluded in a few short weeks.

As long as we were always successful we believed God was on our side and feared for nothing. Can it be that the kind Providence that blessed so signally our struggle for Independence in its commencement will forsake us now? Or have we in our presumptuous confidence forsaken the God who was our only hope at first and depended too much on our arm of flesh. God grant this may be a lesson to bring us back to our trust in Him, and that His face may again shine upon us as it did at first. The bare idea of subjugation by Yankees is enough to freeze the hottest blood that ever bounded through Southern veins.

Feb. 22nd [Saturday].
Jefferson Davis was inaugurated our first President today.[25] Our Government begins under a cloud. The disaster at Fort Donelson can scarcely be estimated. Various accounts estimate our loss in killed wounded and prisoners at from 2000 to 15,000.[26] Our forces have made a stand at Nashville. The next fight will probably be there. There one whispers of treachery and cowardice as the cause of our disasters. It is rumored today that the Federals have captured Savannah, and that they are marching on Winchester with 60,000 men.[27] Our men and women have need now of all their courage and endurance and I trust will be found equal to the emergency.

These are times to try and prove men. The President issues in today's papers a beautiful proclamation for fasting and prayer for next Friday.

Feb. 24th [Monday].
This morning we had a terrible wind storm which blew open my French windows and broke them all to pieces, which is a great worry as the immense panes cannot be replaced till the war is over and wooden panels will look very badly in the front windows. There is no further news except various accounts both Northern and Southern of the taking of Fort Donelson. The children on the farm are ill with typhoid fever. I have not heard from Hal for several days and begin to be restless for a letter. Poor fellow. I wonder where he was in this terrible storm. The children get along very well with their lessons. May's playing astonishes every one and Rozier begins to read quite well for him.

March

On February 24, 1862, Union colonel John W. Geary and the 28th Pennsylvania Infantry, Knap's Battery, and a squadron of the 1st Michigan Cavalry crossed the Potomac River from Harpers Ferry, becoming the first Union troops to occupy Loudoun County. Geary made his headquarters in Lovettsville, where he oversaw the protection of the Baltimore and Ohio Railroad against Confederate raids. By March 6, D. H. Hill was ordered to move his men out of Loudoun toward Richmond, leaving the county open to Union occupation. Before leaving, though, Hill ordered his men to burn all nonportable supplies in an attempt to keep them out of the hands of the Union army.

Timeline of the War	
March 4	General Robert E. Lee is recalled from South Carolina to become military adviser to President Davis.
March 6	Confederate troops abandon Leesburg, Virginia, leaving Loudoun County open to Union occupation.
March 8	The Battle of Pea Ridge, Arkansas, begins with Confederate troops winning, only to wind up defeated two days later.
March 9	U.S.S. *Monitor* and C.S.A. *Virginia* clash in the first battle between ironclad naval vessels.
March 11	McClellan is removed as general in chief, retaining command only of the Army of the Potomac.
March 23	Jackson's Shenandoah Valley Campaign begins with a defeat in the Battle of Kernstown, and he withdraws up the valley toward Woodstock.
March 28	The Confederate campaign in New Mexico ends in defeat at Glorieta Pass.

Mar. 4th [Tuesday].
The whole country seems depressed. Winchester is evacuated by our troops, and the next thing we hear will be that the Yankees are in possession of it. A letter from Hal last night expressed such uneasiness at the idea of this country being overrun by the Yankees that it troubles me to think he should have this anxiety added to his separation from his family. There is strong talk of our army falling back from Centreville, I do not know why—and also a talk of an advance upon our fortifications by the Yankees that will lead to a great battle, and people all talk constantly of it and say it will be the bloodiest battle ever fought. The very expression makes my blood run cold and those who used it so thoughtlessly surely forget that it is human blood that will flow and that [it is] the blood of the best and noblest of the land, the blood of husbands and sons and fathers, that for every head that falls the destiny of an immortal soul is decided, and the earthly happiness of some once happy home forever blighted. The enumeration of thousands among the slain, makes my heart sicken, and cry out "How long, Oh lord! How long?"

Many families are leaving their homes, unwilling to risk a meeting with the enemy, but I have determined to stand my ground.

Hal's letter to Ida, February 27, 1862, Camp G. W. Smith:
I received your most affectionate letter, my own darling, last night just as I was returned off picket where we had, I think, the most disagreeable time we have ever had, never in all my life saw the wind blow as hard and even at Oakley where I thought it blew harder than anywhere else. We had to pass

through a large body of woods on the way to the "out post" and the wind tore up the largest trees around us as if they had been seeds. One about as large around as my body came within an ace of catching me, nothing but the activity of my horse saved me, it coming so near to him that top limbs as they broke flew entirely under him. I don't think I was ever half so frightened in my life and in the same minute so grateful to Providence.

The Yankees are *nearer* us now than they have ever been before since I have been here. We could distinctly hear their drums and sounds of music and almost distinguish the tunes they were playing. I went down to Captain Smith's to carry a letter to *Miss Lucy* and to get some news but found they had not received a newspaper for a week or more, and were expecting to be arrested every day. I gave them a considerable fright, they took me and my two men for Federals, and were very relieved when they found out their mistake....

I should have gone down towards Springfield where, they say, the enemy is in large force to reconnoiter, but my old horse struck lame, and I could hardly get him back to our picket. Rather a bad fix I should have been in if the Yankees had made their appearance.

They are speaking very strongly here now of the probabilities of a fight and are moving the sick and heavy baggage back to Manassas, but I know the roads are in such condition that it is impossible for the enemy to advance, and I must say if they did, we are not as strong as we have been to meet them, owing entirely to this furlough system which I think is the most miserable and suicidal policy a government ever [conceived of]. In speaking to old Gen. Ewell the other day on the subject, he told me that there were 50,000 men now absent from the Army of the Potomac and that there were about 75,000 men present, so if we are whipped the legislature and Congress can blame themselves for it.

I feel very uneasy, my darling, about that part of the country about Upperville. If it is over run (and I think there is a strong probability of it) and we have to fall back from here, I may not see you for months. If I knew you were safe I could stand it, as hard as it would be, but it would nearly kill me if there was any doubt of it. [Hal urges Ida to take refuge at Richard Dulany's house in the mountains.] . . . Think about that, my Darling, if it is only to relieve my fears, I have great confidence in your judgment....

If you could possibly sell your wheat, do so, better sell low than have it burnt. Pay no more [cash] at present, save your money to move your family at the shortest notice. I am due two months pay and if I can get it which seems impossible at present, I will send you [the pay], one more drop in the bucket which may help out in a pinch. But no more grumbling, we are not whipped yet, and God willing [won't be], though they may make us fall back a little by superior numbers. Every man here seems to be determined to do or die, and when that is the case it is pretty hard work to conquer us.

Henry A. Hall [brother-in-law of Robert Carter of Company A] was down here yesterday [to] see Bruce Gibson [who] tells me [he is] offering a thousand dollars for a substitute. What do you think of that? Money seems to be an aspect but I hope . . . after he gets his substitute, he will be subject to draft himself . . . it is just the way all such fellows ought to be served. . . . Give my best love to the gentlemen [Ida's visiting cousins] and tell them I hope they will have a good time. . . .

The Col. received a letter from Brother R. yesterday saying that he had gone to the mountains to recruit. . . . I shall write to him by the same mail that you receive this, on business connected with the Company. If he is not there and you see Uncle John, direct him to forward the letter. Tell him I am getting d—d tired of playing Capt. Well, I have written you a long letter for *me* and as I have accounts to write and some pay notes to make out for the Company, I must close. My best love to all. Good bye my own darling wife and take the best care of yourself for the sake of your truly devoted husband.

[*This is the last known letter Hal wrote Ida during his year of active service.*]

March 10th [Monday].

It is late at night, all the family are in bed, and I alone sit up because I cannot sleep. I trust in God, it is true, and all day long keep cheerful & hopeful, but when night comes and I realize how desolate we are I find it far easier to sit up and write than to lie awake with an anxious heavy heart, wondering what the next day will bring forth. All day I have been busy packing my silver, which Uncle Billy buried this evening—making arrangements to secrete my meat and getting my horses ready to start for our army in the morning, and tonight I wrote to Hal the last letter I fear that he will get from me for many days.

Our most anxious personal fears are at last realized. For weeks we have been hearing that our army would probably fall back, and leave this country to be over run by the enemy, and now it has actually taken place. The whole [Confederate] Army of the Potomac[28] is falling back, having left the fortifications at Centreville and are moving off, in what direction we do not know.[29] I have not heard from Hal for some time and do not know when another letter from him will reach here. We have no longer any mails. The railroad is broken up, the bridges being all burnt.

Our army has left Winchester and in all probability the enemy are in possession of the town. They already have Leesburg[30] and are extending their pickets nearer to us every day. We will soon be completely within the Federal lines, and cut off from all communication with our friends. I am surprised to find how little alarm I feel. I heard tonight that there was great excitement in the village owing to the Yankees being in ten miles of us, but I do not share in the feeling. I am deeply grieved that our soil should be desecrated by the presence of an invading foe, but I trust in God for protection and feel no fear.

Doubtless we shall lose many of our men servants who will be made to go off whether they wish it or no, and our crops and stock will be taken off but God will provide, and I look to Him for all things. A feeling of intense sadness comes over me at the idea of our men being obliged like criminals to skulk about their own homes, or to flee before the enemy. Many peaceable citizens have been arrested in Leesburg. The greatest trial of all to me is to be separated entirely from my dear husband, not even knowing where he is, and with no idea of when we shall meet again.

March 13th [Thursday].
On Tuesday morning Davy and Richard ran off and Otway and Ralph positively refused to take the horses so if Ben had not been more faithful they would have had to stay for the Yankees. However Mr. Kidwell with Ben and the two little boys went off to Warrenton with the horses. It seems the men have been told that they were to be sent off to be sold and that accounts for their refusing to go.

March 15th [Saturday].
Yesterday evening about 5 o'clock Aunt Bena drove up with Grandma. Uncle John [Dr. Fauntleroy] insisted upon their leaving "The Post," so at a moment's warning the whole family packed up and started for Front Royal, from which place Grandma and Aunt Bena started to come here. They were met just before they got here by a man who was fleeing from Upperville who told them that the Yankees were in Upperville numbering about 300 men.[31] A few moments after they got here Uncle Nathan called to tell me the same thing. Aunt Bena left at day break this morning to rejoin her family at Front Royal and our poor old Grandmother is added to our household—four women, with not a man within reach of us and a Yankee army one mile off. Still I do not feel afraid. All day we have been expecting to see some of them but a kind Providence has kept them away; and I trust to that Providence for further protection. My greatest fear is that Grandma may be frightened, she is already very apprehensive. I hear the army has quartered itself on the different inhabitants of the village.

March 17th [Monday].
Since yesterday morning I have been constantly annoyed by visits from Yankee soldiers. At first they were civil saying they did not intend interfering in any way with our slaves or other property. The first two that came went by the house to Mr. Kidwell's where they breakfasted, even offering to pay him for what they [ate]. Others came and only passed by the house but in the evening one came in and sent for something to eat. Uncle Billy[32] gave him something to eat, and he asked for the ladies, expressing himself much offended at our not going down to see him.

This morning early, Mr. Weidmayer kindly came over to see us, and not long afterwards Uncle Frank came. I took him to see the sick and felt encouraged by what he said of them. In a little while both left, Mr. Weidmayer going over to Mr. Bolling's and Uncle Frank going home. Mr. Weidmayer promised to call when he left Bollingbrook.

He had scarcely left before the soldiers visits began again. The one who was out yesterday evening came and another with him. They have eaten up everything I had in the house, and the one who has been out twice was very impertinent, sending me word that if I did not give him everything he wanted he would come upstairs and see if he could not make me do so. Very soon a party of Cavalry came out and took off my wagon and four horses and Otway, in spite of Mr. Weidmayer's remonstrance who got back just in time to see them. The one who sent me the impudent message spoke most brutally of Mr. Weidmayer, saying "his horse was far too good for him" that "it just suited to hunt secessionists on," and that "if Mr. W. did not take care he would find himself with a rope around his neck before he knew it."

At Mr. Bolling's they have behaved shamefully, insulting him, and treating him so that he is almost deranged from indignation. They have taken from him every horse, all his provender, and some of his servants, and they stand at his door and abuse him violently. They went to Welbourne and searched the house at 12 o'clock at night. Three of them spent the whole evening in my kitchen.

I sent Mr. Kidwell to Upperville with a written remonstrance to the Colonel. Mr. K. said he gave my note to him but that he said he had not time to read it. He told him he would have the men who had come here arrested, as it was against orders for them to interfere with private families; but he could get no satisfaction about the wagon.

To-night Mr. Kidwell came in to tell me that Richard was in the kitchen with two soldiers. I sent for Uncle Billy and told him how surprised I was at his allowing such a thing. He was disposed to be disrespectful, and perhaps it was expecting too much of him to inform on his own son.[33] But altogether this is the most miserable, disagreeable, worrying time that ever I passed through. How long? Oh lord! How long?

March 18th [Tuesday].
The first thing this morning I was told that Uncle Billy had gone off to the Yankees. It is no great loss but I was surprised at his leaving.

After breakfast I went to see the sick, and then was in the garden pruning grape vines when Mamma called to me that the Yankees were coming with wagons. I collected the children and went into the house. Soon eight soldiers with three wagons were at the gate, the men armed with guns and swords. Two of them came to the house and from the nursery window I heard one say to Mimi, "tell your Mistress to have a dinner ready for us by the time we come from the barn and that we are going to break open her corn house." Provoked by the insolence of his manner I determined that they should have nothing to eat, and told Mimi to tell them "I had no dinner for them." They sent her back to say that if it was not ready when they came they would break wide the house and take what they wanted. I did not believe the cowardly threat, but was only made more determined by it that [men] who behaved so should not eat of my bread. So I told the servants to give them nothing, and fastened the doors and barred the windows securely. They soon came back with their wagons loaded with corn, and again demanded their dinner. When told that they were not to have any they stormed about, said they would break open the meat house, came up on the porch, and struck on the doors and windows with their guns.

I watched them from an upstairs window with no little amusement, as I saw by their irresolution that they did not dare to commit any actual outrage but were only trying to frighten me into giving them what they wanted. Finding they could not get in they walked off saying they would get an axe to break into the meat house, but finally they all left without dinner, and no locks broken.

In a few moments afterwards we heard reports of a gun and I found another party were shooting my cattle. They shot about forty times and finally ran the whole drove off the place. Then I heard firing in another direction and found they were shooting my turkeys. They are by no means good shots as with all their firing they only killed four steers and two turkeys. The whole party soon came in the yard, two of them looked like gentlemen but the others were horrid looking. Mr. Kidwell talked with them; they insisted they had a right to everything they wanted because Hal was in arms for the South.

Mr. Weidmayer came to see us again today. He turned white with anger when he found how we had been treated, and will go with me tomorrow to see Col. Geary[34] to protest against such conduct. He was soon hurried off by the approach of two more soldiers fearing they would take his horse, Lady May. These two came on a bridle stealing expedition, they searched the harness-room and finding no bridles contented themselves with taking the stirrups off of a saddle. We ate our dinner in Mamma's room fearing to be interrupted if we were downstairs. Poor Grandma is terrified nearly to death and Mamma becomes very much excited and so does Kate, but I am determined to keep cool. After dinner Stewart and Munzy Bolling rode over to drive home my cattle which had strayed to Bollingbrook. It was very kind, and I was gratified at it. Their visit would have been a decidedly pleasant incident of the day had not Grandma persisted in asking them after their mother, and as their own mother was dead and their step mother divorced from their father, it was decidedly awkward!

After they left I walked out to see what damage the Yankees had done. Many of the cattle were bleeding from wounds from random shots, besides those that were killed. All the evening heavy firing has been heard from the direction of Strasburg.[35] The Yankees said today they had lost Jackson, so I trust by the firing that he has found them and is making them feel where he is. I must not forget to mention that my cellar store room was opened last night and potatoes and flour taken out. God grant this thralldom may not be for long.

March 19th [Wednesday].
This morning while I was at breakfast a soldier sent in for something to eat and as he asked civilly I sent him some breakfast. Uncle Nathan came while we were at the table, and a few moments afterwards Mr. Weidmayer. I appreciated most highly the kindness shown us by our gentlemen friends, especially Mr. Weidmayer, who comes over every day. This morning he brought a buggy to drive me to Upperville to see the Col. I was soon ready to start but was detained for a few moments by Mr. Brown[36] who came to pay me some money. We were not stopped till we got to the top of the Vineyard Hill though we passed two cavalry pickets just beyond Brown's. At the top of the hill two foot soldiers stopped us. Old Mr. Bishop's carriage was just behind us. We enquired why we were stopped going in and were told it was the order. The men were civil, and one of them went to the village to see his Capt. who was officer of the day to know from him if we could not pass. He came back in a few moments saying he was sorry to detain us, but the Capt. was mounting a guard and could not leave for half an hour. While we were waiting Mr. Bishop talked to the men.

They laid the blame of the war on the South and said we were doing more to free the Negroes than the North, and other Yankee sayings. After about half an hour a squad of infantry with an officer came up and asked why we were detained, "Orders" was the reply. The officer wished to know our errand and when we told him, one of the men said all persons wishing to see the Col. could pass. The officer asked if any depredations had been committed by the soldiers, & when Mr. Weidmayer told him all, he was very indignant and said the army was disgraced by such conduct and it would not be allowed. We were then suffered to pass with a soldier to guard us to the Col. The soldier talked with Mr. Weidmayer and said he would shoot a soldier who insulted a lady as soon as he would a dog, for he did not deserve to be called a man.

When we reached Mr. Stephenson's, the Headquarters of the Col., we were told to wait in the passage as the Col. was busy. I soon found it was Mr. Bolling who was engaging his attention. I do not know what satisfaction he got, but he came out and seeing me introduced me very kindly to "Col. Geary, ex-governor of Kansas." The ruffianly countenance of the man was anything but encouraging, but his Adjutant and the Officer of the day were gentlemanly looking, decidedly. I made my statement to the Col. as briefly as possible; he seemed excessively annoyed at my report of the disorderly conduct of the soldiers on my place and gave most peremptory orders that any man found beyond the lines without a pass should be shot. His tone and manner to the quiet gentlemanly Adjutant was almost insulting in its rudeness. He gave me no satisfaction with regard to my team, but referred me to the Quarter master for settlement for the corn and cattle. Then saying good morning to me, he turned abruptly to his Adjutant and said "now for Heaven's sake don't bother me with any more such business," with which polite speech he walked off.

The Adjutant wrote us a pass, and told me with rather a peculiar smile that I would be given an order on the Treasury of the U.S. as payment for my property. The thought of the improbability of my ever being paid and of the certainty of his knowing the smallness of the chances was amusing to me, contrasted with the formality of the assurances of my being satisfied. I went in to see the Stephenson family on leaving the parlor, but my lamp is going out and their experience must be reserved for another night.

March 20th [Thursday].
Federal wagons have just passed to get corn. I feared they were coming here but to my relief they went by, I suppose to Uncle Nathan's. I feel sorry for him. His family is so large to be stripped of everything.[37] But to return to the Stephensons. I will not write all they told me for I have not time, but only note the most striking incidents. The federal Commander Col. Geary as soon as he reached the town took possession of the parlors and best bed rooms of the house confining the family to the attic and the cellar rooms. The day after his arrival Col. Geary missed his pistol off the table in the parlor where he had laid it. He became enraged instantly and going into the passage said the family had stolen it. The three girls Josephine, Mittie and Nannie were in the passage. He drew his sword on them, called out, "Guards, advance and arrest these women," then seizing Mittie by the shoulder and pushing her before him while the low bred vermin he calls guards seized the other two. They were locked in one room. The guards then pushed Mrs. Stephenson in the basement room the family were using and locked her up there while the brave Col. seized old Mr. Stephenson and told him his house should be burnt to the ground in ten minutes if the pistol was not instantly produced. Just as he got through with imprisoning the whole family his own son[38] handed him the pistol which he had misplaced. One would suppose any man would have made some apology for such conduct but his only notice of acquittal was to say "Guards, release those women." One of his Staff made the best apology he could for him.

To annoy the family they constantly have the servant women in their rooms drinking and eating cake and bonbons with them and a few days ago while Mittie was in the kitchen one of them came in and put his arm around the cook and pinched her cheek. The guards jump from behind the doors and *boo* at the girls as they pass.

As soon as I came home I was told that wagons had been again for corn, and in about an hour two more came. With the last two came the officer I met on the Vineyard Hill. He came in the house and asked to see me. When I went down he assured me he would see that no more depredations were committed on my property, and said also that he would represent the number of servants to be fed here and try and prevent my corn being taken any more. I believe he was sincere for he seemed gentlemanly, and then the corn wagons passing me by this morning looks like it, but I am afraid he cannot do much in the way of protecting me from depredations as while he was in the house talking to me, his men were robbing the henhouses. We have not been molested since that party left.

Amid all this worry I had the one comfort yesterday of seeing Robert[39] and Uncle Joshua come, two faithful servants whom I think I can rely on. Lucinda is sick so Robert came straight in the house, and I already feel the comfort of having about me a willing efficient man. I wrote this far this morning, and have not much to add tonight. Good Mr. Weidmayer came over again today in all the rain to see after us. He thinks I had better go tomorrow to protest against their taking all of my corn. Another load was carried off today, and I have the prospect staring me in the face of seeing all my servants suffering for food. I am taking what precautions I can, having all hands shelling the corn to conceal it, but I have no place to put enough to feed all my family [and servants].

I am now more than ever convinced that I should have burnt it when our army fell back from Centreville. I allowed myself to be persuaded against my judgment, and now my substance is fattening the enemy of my country. What deterred me was the fear that in suffering my servants would reproach me as the cause, and that I might reproach myself for having voluntarily reduced them to want. The reason was a plausible one, but I am not satisfied that I was right.

Mr. Kidwell went up to see if there was any chance of my being paid for the corn and cattle. The message I received from the Quarter Master was that he "would settle with Mr. Dulany for the corn and cattle and would keep the wagon and team as a present for Uncle Sam." Oh, for one sight of our own beloved Army! Oh, that I might but be with my own dear husband!

March 21st [Friday].
Yesterday soldiers came out and shot more of my cattle. They came down to the house and drove off the children's pet steers. I sent to tell them they were the children's and to ask them to kill some others, but they said if I did not want them killed I ought not to have been for secession and drove them off. I was so angry that for the first time in my life my heart was filled [with] cursing.

I am afraid I sinned greatly, and today I found that tho' the soldiers drove the steers off, they did not shoot them, so I am all the more penitent for my inordinate anger.

Mr. Bolling came to see us yesterday and today Mr. Scott and Mr. Weidmayer. We have gained a great victory in Missouri, so rumor says, killing 10,000 and capturing 12,000 of the enemy, but we lost 6,000 killed and among them Ben McCulloch.[40] The enemy have taken Newborn [New Bern] and Evansport.[41] I am busily secreting corn and wheat.

March 23rd [Sunday].
Sunday morning and no service, our little church[42] being taken as quarters for the Yankee soldiers, and there where we have worshipped God for so long they eat and sleep, fiddle and dance, gamble and sing obscene songs. Our Minister does not even show his face among them, for his flock is scattered, and his church desecrated.

This morning I saw six cavalry in the field shooting the cattle and went over to Mr. Kidwell's to send him up to take note of how many were killed; while there I saw four come to the house and drive off my young Alderney bull and the children's steers. I have prayed for protection and for help. It has pleased God to try me severely and now seeing it is His will, I should endure and pray only for patience, trusting that in God's own time we may triumph over our enemies, and on this Sunday morning I will endeavor to begin to run with patience the race that is set before me, looking ever unto Him from whom it is just and right that I should receive evil as well as good. We are told in the Bible to hate sin, and the Devil, Oh! God show me if it is wrong to hate these wretches whose life is sin, and whose actions are so sinful, even as I hate the Devil whose children they are.

March 25th [Tuesday].
Yesterday morning I [ordered] killed the pretty white steer to keep the Yankees from getting it, and found after an hour or so I might have let it live; about 12 o'clock Mr. Bolling came in, and his first words were "Madam, they have gone, I have just seen the last Yankee leave the village en route for Aldie,[43] where they rendezvous to march on Gordonsville." They had gone it is true but Geary was ordered to go back by Snickersville[44] [to] Winchester, and he is tonight at the [Shenandoah] river. Our sense of relief at the loosening of the chain was intense, but with me there is still the sad consciousness that even the absence of the enemy brings me no nearer to my husband. We are still within the Yankee lines, and likely to remain so for some time.

I immediately gave orders for wheat and corn to be sent to the mill, and for every advantage to be taken of the space allowed by their temporary absence. My farming is I fear completely put a stop to, as the Yankees took all my horses except two that are completely broken down. I have lost since they came four grown men servants, 15 cattle, 50 barrels of corn and my wagon and team. I sent Mr. Kidwell to Aldie this morning hoping to recover the latter but he met with no success.

Last night while we were at supper Walker Armistead came in. He was the first Southern soldier we had seen since the Yankees came, and he was most cordially welcomed. He had left our army at Warrenton Junction. Hal was well but had been sleeping on the ground without tents, and with only one blanket all those cold nights. It was a comfort to be able to send him a message. Walker left at 9 o'clock to walk to Lt. Gibson's.

This morning I planted my hot bed, saw the beef cut up, and passed the rest of the morning with Mr. Kinsolving who came in to see us. After dinner Katey and I walked up to Upperville across the fields. We stopped first at Miss Margaret's where we found Cousin Mittie[45] & Mr. Weidmayer. From there we went to see our poor little church. And such desecration as we saw! My barnyard is as clean. The filthy odor in the yard took away our breath and as to the interior! I could scarcely believe my eyes. Mud two inches deep all over the floor—the altar covered with scraps of bread, and fat meat; the reading desk having been taken for a pillow, filthy and torn, and every thing about the building polluted or ruined.

Sick with indignation, I went to Aunt Mary's—and now comes the event of the day. While each was recounting her wrongs and congratulating the other upon our regained freedom, Harriet put her head in the door and said, "Mrs. Eliason, the Southern Army is marching into town."

We rushed to the porch, every lady was at her door, every man on the street, and sure enough right before us, with the blue flag of Virginia waving over them, a portion of our own beloved army was marching through the town. Our delight and enthusiasm completely overcame us! We shouted, clapped our hands, waved our handkerchiefs, and hailed them with every possible demonstration of welcome, while tears of joy stood in almost every eye. They seemed surprised at the excess of our enthusiasm, but soon responded with hearty huzzahs. They did not know all we had suffered from the invader they were come to repel. In less than fifteen minutes, all along the street, tables with waiters full of provisions were placed, and the women were soon busy carving for the soldiers, while the officers handed the bread and meat to the men.

They brought no news. Only that there had been fighting yesterday and the report was that Jackson had fallen back after suffering heavy loss.[46] We staid a good while helping to carve for them, and then hurried home to send up what provisions I had cooked in the house. Just as the provisions were ready to send, a soldier came with a wagon for some corn. I cheerfully had it loaded for him, and made him come in and get his supper while the servants loaded the wagon.

Mr. Kinsolving came back to spend the night with us. I could but notice on the street this evening two of the men of the town well known to us all who absolutely scowled on the soldiers. God grant it may not be in their power to do them harm.

March 26th [Wednesday].
This morning early Mr. Bolling came over. He evidently wanted sympathy in his joy at finding himself again surrounded by his own people, but he had the misfortune to think they were Federals on his place till after sun rise this morning, and passed, consequently, a sleepless night. Our men left us this morning to go we know not where, and I heard to-night that more Yankees would be in Upperville before morning. Our happiness is destined to be short lived. Uncle Ned[47] came up this morning to settle about Grandma and it is decided she is to stay here until circumstances make it necessary for her to leave.

The effect of all the excitement I have gone through lately is a feeling of mental exhaustion. I cannot even think, and seem conscious of but one idea, and that is anxiety for our cause in general and especially for my dear husband. Uncle Ned told us that he had heard from a reliable source that Jackson's army had cut Banks' men all to pieces. I trust it is so but am almost afraid to hope it. Firing was again heard today from the direction of Winchester.

April

No events of any importance have transpired during the last three or four days. The Yankees have been at Middleburg and have passed from there to The Plains, Geary having been ordered back from Winchester. We have heard that Jackson was entirely victorious in the Battle of Kernstown near Winchester killing from 1500 to 1700 of the enemy and losing only 300,[48] and who of all our many friends in his command may be among those 300 we cannot know, as we have had no communication with our own people since the boat was burnt at the ferry.[49]

Dan came home from the army the day before yesterday having run off. He was left at Culpeper Ct. House in charge of his master's baggage and his excuse for leaving is that he was sick, overworked and half starved, had not seen his master for a month, and had been told that he was at home, and thought he had better come home too. If I could rely on what he says I should be uneasy about Hal as he says he had been away from the Regt. for more than a week, and he heard every one wondering where he was. I try to keep from being more anxious than usual, by supposing him on Picket duty, and by making allowances for Dan's ignorance.

We were just speaking of Dick Ashby. I always remember his death with a fresh regret. Three years ago he was here with Mr. Armstrong[50] and Mr.

Timeline of the War

April 4	McClellan's Peninsula Campaign begins with a skirmish at Big Bethel.
April 6–7	The bloodiest battle of the war to date is fought near Shiloh Church on the banks of the Tennessee River, ending in Union victory after the death of Confederate commander Albert Sidney Johnston.
April 8	Union general John Pope captures Island No. 10, assuring federal control of the Upper Mississippi.
April 16	Lincoln signs a bill outlawing slavery in the District of Columbia.
April 25	New Orleans surrenders to the Union Navy.

Ashton Marshall[51]—now all three are dead, but how different the manner of their deaths, and how different the feeling with which they are remembered by those who knew them. Mr. Armstrong and Dick Ashby, admired and beloved by all, while living, each fell at his post, nobly fighting in a noble cause, their names to be recorded with distinction on the pages of the history of the greatest revolution the world has ever known, and to be forever gratefully enshrined in the hearts of the people for whom they died, while all who loved and knew them living feel proud to say of either "he was my friend." And Ashton Marshall lived a drunkard's life and died of manuaportu.[52]

There are times when I feel my loneliness more than at others, and tonight is one of them. I do not know where Hal is. I only know that his Regt. is employed in advance scouting, that they have no tents, no baggage, none of the common necessaries of life. The weather has been unusually inclement lately and my anxiety for my husband is very great. I can only pray to my Heavenly Father to shield him. I seriously entertain the idea of starting out to learn something of him, tho' all my friends speak of it as madness; but I cannot hear from him, and the uncertainty is harrowing in the extreme.

April 5th [Saturday].
Truly we live in stirring times. Our country is full of Yankees, in every direction except one and Mumford's[53] cavalry still scout there. Rumors of several successful encounters with the enemy have reached us. We hear that Jackson's advance guard has decoyed Bank's army back to a place where his whole command was most advantageously situated and has cut the Yankees all to pieces.

Then again Ashby posted his cannon[54] in the streets of Woodstock, and as the enemy entered the town mowed then down by hundreds. Again reports reach us of great victories in Tennessee and Missouri. Our county is kept in constant excitement by the skirmishing between Geary's command and

White's Guerilla cavalry.[55] We went to Middleburg on Thursday to bring Jenny home for a day or two, and there heard many more anecdotes of our invaders, some shocking in the extreme and many very amusing.

The slaves in Middleburg behaved admirably, much better than in this neighborhood, where they generally sided with the enemies of their masters. Many in Middleburg resist[ed] large bribes offered to induce then to leave their masters, [and] by their firmness and fidelity contributed greatly to the protection of the property of the different families to which they belonged. Some of the women were allowed by their owners to cook for the Yankees at night, and some hoping to make a little money sat up all night to bake biscuits, but these true Yankees went off in the morning without paying them a cent. One black woman who washed for them was paid with a "Mustang liniment" note.[56] In Mr. Noland's kitchen some soldiers were questioning the servants as to their sentiments. They asked one what opinions she held. She held—she said secession—and another made the same answer. They then asked old Polly the cook what she was? "Nothin 't all but Polly Geams" was the curt reply. They were bragging very considerably to the same old woman another day, telling her they had but to blow a trumpet and millions more would flock to them, her reply was "Humph! Your women folks must have children then like rabbits."

I was told of an instance of their barbarity so shocking that it is hard to believe, and yet I know it to be true. Mrs. John Rogers, who is staying at Genl. Rogers'[57] in Middleburg, lost recently two little girls, her oldest children. She had collected all their clothes and placing them in a camp chest, had put them in Genl. Roger's garret for safety. The Yankees came at two o'clock at night to search Genl. Rogers' house, and going into the garret were about to break open the chest containing the clothes, when the Genl. told them its contents and begged then not to distress his daughter by disturbing them. They insisted however upon opening it. In some way the poor mother heard what was going on and rushing to the garret insisted that her dead children's clothes should not be touched. They paid no attention to her remonstrances, and she had to stand and see little dresses and aprons that her darlings had worn tossed rudely about by the ruffianly soldiers. She bore it in silence till the sight of a half worn little shoe held up by one of them proving more than she could bear. With a loud shriek she fell senseless to the floor, while the wretches who had thus outraged her feelings walked off laughing at the whole affair as a good joke.

About 25 of White's men were met by 40 Yankees about three miles above Middleburg. White dared them to fight, but finding [that] they persisted in declining combat, he called out loudly, "Charge! White's Cavalry!" Then all the brave Yankees tore off as fast as their horses could carry them. They dashed furiously through the village calling out "they are coming, coming." A Capt. who stood at a street corner, halted one by threatening to shoot him if he did not stop long enough to tell him the matter. "Elizah [sic] White" whispered the soldier—"Where?" said the Capt—"Coming" replied the soldier—The Capt. waited for nothing more, but mounting his horse he fled as fast as the men. In the meantime Elijah White with nine of his men rode into the village amid shouts of "Hurrah for White!" and "down with the Yankees!" He was however stopped opportunely by one of the citizens who told him that the enemy occupied the other end of the village 1500 strong, so that to remain would be certain death to him and his men. Hearing that, he turned his horse and leisurely rode back again. In about half an hour, the whole column of Yankees marched up the street with their cannon and forming in line of battle began to look for the enemy who were so small that they could not see him, but they contented themselves by firing four balls and two shells in the direction where they had gone. That evening one of the Yankee officers observed to Lilly Powell,[58] "The Secesh ran as usual." "Yes," said Lilly significantly, "as usual." The Adjutant of one of the regts. shot himself accidentally a few days ago. Col. Geary sent 10 men to Salem for a coffin, but the indefatigable White was there. He captured 8 of the men and shot the other two who were spies. Fifteen Yankee officers near Warrenton went into the woods for a council of war, but their sitting was disturbed by a party of Confederates who captured the council.

Mr. Bolling brought Anna over this evening and left her to spend the night with Jenny. After he left, I walked out to see Mr. Kidwell to tell him to have some wheat made into superfine flour for the hands. The scarcity of corn [is] making it necessary to economize on that article as much as possible. I also gave some orders about the change of the fencing.

It is Saturday night, and tomorrow our little church will be open for the first time since its desecration. I sent a letter to my husband the day I was in Middleburg but do not know when or how to expect an answer.

April 15th [Tuesday].
More than [a] week has passed since I last wrote, my journal being mislaid. A week so full of events that it is perhaps fortunate for my readers (if such ever exist) that this book could not be at hand to have spun out over many of its pages daily accounts of circumstances which will now be concisely related in the short space of time elapsing between ten o'clock and bed time.

On Sunday week we went to church and there heard of the death of Buddy Powell[59] brought on by the violent excitement produced by the visit of the Yankees to Middleburg. He was attacked by brain fever and was perfectly delirious during the three days of his illness, yet even in his delirium his last words were a beautiful and earnest prayer for the success of our cause, and for God's mercy to himself. It was a singular circumstance in a boy of 15 years who had never before shown feeling on the subject of religion. I heard also at church that a battle had been fought near Fredericksburg. I felt miserably anxious knowing that if it was true Hal must have been engaged in it.

On Monday morning I was giving May her music lesson when I heard a servant say "Master Henry's coming." I could not believe my ears, but felt all my blood rush to my face at the hope. Running to the yard I saw Rutledge Eliason standing on the grass and heard Hal's step on the back porch. His anxiety overcame his prudence, and he had determined to risk seeing me. He looks perfectly well and seemed in fine spirits, bringing most encouraging accounts of the condition of our army. The President and Genl. Johnston are in fine spirits, he said.

Our first step was to caution all the servants not to mention his having come, and a violent snow storm which lasted the entire three days of his visit favored his concealment. We sent out watchers every day to enquire [about] the movements of the enemy and were satisfied that he might remain with safety unless purposely betrayed. The day of his arrival I found out that it was known in Upperville that he was here and then I became anxious and wanted him to go back to the army. I could not have borne seeing him dragged off as a prisoner.

On Wednesday night at eleven o'clock Hal received a note from Talcott Eliason telling him that a large body of Yankees were at Salem en route for Upperville, so the necessity for his going immediately was imperative. He got a few hours sleep, and left at 3 o'clock in the morning, the storm having ceased during the night. Anxious as I was till I knew of his safe arrival in camp, I cannot express the happiness his visit gave me. I do not feel now so entirely cut off from him, and amid all the worries and troubles we have been enduring for months past it is delightful to have the sad retrospect broken by one circumstance that gave great pleasure to us all.

I need scarcely say that there was no fight at Fredericksburg. I had hardly time to miss my darling husband before I had cause to rejoice in his timely departure. Suffering intensely with [a migraine] head-ache I heard some one say "the Yankees are coming"—In a few moments I heard a servant say, "three soldiers say they must have something to eat." Mamma gave the order that they should be fed. I thought it best to dress my self, not wishing to be caught in bed in case they should come to search for Hal. The soldiers could be seen coming to the house in every direction. I gave them all something to eat till one of them stole a knife he was eating with, and then I determined to feed no more. It is too late to write more, I must defer the completion of my second Yankee experience to another night.

April 16th [Wednesday].
Late in the evening three more came out and when I refused to feed them they broke into my meat house and took some pieces of meat. Night came and I thought we would have some peace, but after nine o'clock I heard a bustle in the hall and loud talking, and going down found four Dutch ruffians[60] clam-

mering [sic] for food and a warm room to sleep in. I never saw such horrid looking men before. I determined at once to be firm with them and to prevent their staying here if I could. I looked them full in the face and told them firmly they could not stay here. At first they persisted but I was equally persistent and at last by shaming them for such cowardly conduct induced them to go down to the basement.[61] I did not like the idea of sleeping so near such men, but could not help myself. Afterwards Mr. Kidwell came and took them to his house. The Sergeant told Mr. Kidwell that it was fortunate he was with the men, that their object was plunder and that but for his authority they would have sacked the house. It was the mercy and goodness of God that protected me, and I hope I will be grateful.

Many houses of the poor were completely sacked and almost every horse in the whole country stolen. Brother Richard sent an express to Uncle John to tell him that we had gained a glorious victory in Tennessee,[62] and had taken Fort Craig, with 5000 prisoners, many guns, small arms, etc.[63] Yesterday I sent Mr. Kidwell to Piedmont to make another effort to recover my team, but Col. Geary had left there.

Today Uncle Ned came and to our astonishment and delight Uncle Henry[64] with him. Uncle Henry left St. Louis as soon as he learned that the Yankee lines extended to us. He brings the news that the Virginia has captured 6 more vessels, and is a terror to the northern fleet.[65] He says the impression in Washington is that two tremendous battles will be fought very soon, one at Yorktown and another on the Rappahannock. God grant that the victory may be to our men. Yesterday two very fine horses belonging to Geary strayed in to the farm. My first idea was to keep them in place of those Geary had taken from me, but then I decided that I would not care to keep them for myself, and wished to send them to our army. But as soon as Uncle Henry and Uncle Ned came they insisted so upon my sending them to Col. Geary that I decided to do so, at the same time feeling very reluctant to doing any thing like aiding the Yankees.

I told Mr. Kidwell to try and recover my team. He has not yet come back and I fear has gotten into some trouble as he had only to go to Rectortown and could have gotten back long before this.

Ralph ran off the morning after the Yankees came, making the seventh servant we have lost in the same way. I amuse myself reading the "Dutch Republic" when I have any leisure. My sewing for the spring will soon be finished, as the impossibility of procuring raw material makes our wardrobes very small.

April 17th [Thursday].
Mr. Kidwell's errand to Col. Geary was entirely fruitless. The only message I received being that I could not get my team unless I would avow myself for the Union. So there ends that matter and good bye to my wagon and team.

About ten o'clock this morning I saw a train of eight wagons with a small company of cavalry as escort go into Uncle Nathan's farm.[66] I knew they would all be here in little time, for they have taken nothing from him of any consequence, and sure enough I soon saw the whole party approaching the house, wagons empty. My heart sank for to have filled all those wagons at my corn house [would] have left me very little.

As soon as I found that they intended filling here, I determined to send for the Officer commanding the party and to tell him how much I had already lost, and see if I could not save what I had, at the same time determining to improve the opportunity to infuse them as much as was in my power [with] a doubt of the justice of the cause in which they had enlisted. My tongue being my only weapon, I determined when I came in contact with the enemy to use it in the service of my beloved country.

They drove the wagons to the hay stacks, but the officers, a Lieutenant and Sergeant, rode to the house before giving the order to fill. After representing to these men how little I had to lose and how unjust it would be to take from me more than I could spare without suffering to my family, & finding they were gentlemanly I very calmly talked treason to them while they stayed.

I non plussed the Lieutenant completely, a shallow little fellow, but found the Sergeant a more difficult subject. I hope however that what I said was not lost upon the men who accompanied them, and who listened attentively to what was going on. I gave them [something] to eat as they asked it, but talked to them all the time. At any rate if my secession talk had no other effect, it induced them to go back as they came with empty wagons.

One thing was quite amusing. The flippant lieutenant was quite incredulous of the possibility of Col. Geary's men having committed any depredations upon my property that were not authorized, and the Sergeant assured me that whatever might have been the case before I need feel no fear of his men. No sooner had they left the hall then Robert sent me word that while the officers were talking to me, the men had broken open my cellar store room. I instantly sent for the Lieutenant, and when he came, without comment showed him the broken lock, at the same time unable to repress a laugh at his expense. He seemed much annoyed and vowed vengeance on the man who was guilty of the deed, but the servants could not identify him. After they left, I found they had broken both hen house locks and killed two turkeys and two hens. My head aches badly tonight.

Sunday, April 20th.
For the last two or three days we have been unmolested. Mr. Bolling has been over, and when he told us of how he was treated by the Dutch robbers the Yankees call an army, I can only feel thankful to the mercy of God for His goodness in protecting us, females alone, a mile from the village. We were entirely exposed but suffered less from the Dutch than any family in the neighbor-

hood, except Uncle Nathan who always gets off well, being fortunate in having his house very much out of sight from the two public roads.

Within the memory of living men there has never been so backward a spring. This day the 20th of April, vegetation is no further advanced than is often the case in February. Not a tree in leaf, no farming or gardening of consequence done and the ground in such a condition from the constant rain that it will be a week before we can do anything at either. No church today.

We are all invited to spend tomorrow at Mr. Bolling's in honor of Anna's birthday, [although] the pouring rain now falling will probably cause us a disappointment. Mr. Bolling's kindness has been unvarying ever since Hal left, and I shall always feel grateful to him and his family. Mr. Weidmayer has also been a faithful friend. These are the times that try men, and we find many wanting in whom we had relied while God has raised us up friends where we had no right to expect them.

April 23rd [Wednesday].
There has been another visitation of Yankees to this neighborhood but they did not come here. They rode through the streets of Upperville about thirty in number, insolently ordering the gentlemen on the streets to go to their houses and attend to their business. Uncle Nathan was arrested but soon released. I walked to Upperville this morning and there learned that the Dutch soldiers under Blenken[67] had stripped Mr. Addison Carter[68] of every thing he had on earth, leaving nothing in his house but one sheet, no food, no furniture, no anything. He could badly afford to be treated so. They have gone over to Mr. Harrison's to stay,[69] being deprived of the necessaries of life at their own home. Surely a judgment from God will fall on such creatures. Genl. J. Johnston has gone to Yorktown to reinforce Lee with 60,000 men, and unless McClellan declines the combat a fearful battle will take place there. The Lord help us and put our foes to flight! I hired Mimi today to Mr. Wheat.[70] Mr. Bolling was over this evening.

April 24th [Thursday].
Went to Bollingbrook today, we were all invited but the Stephensons came out and Ma and Katey staid with them while I went to Bollingbrook with the children. We encountered a troop of about 70 Yankees. They had been to Welbourne and took off both Uncle John's carriage horses, so now he has no horse to ride or drive. Fanny Scott and Sophie wrote letters which they sent us by Alick.[71] He brought also a letter to me from Willie Carrere which had been left with them.

April 27th [Sunday].
Not one line have I received from Hal since he left. I am very anxious. This morning Uncle John sent me word that Brother Richard with his Company

had gone to Yorktown. I am truly sorry. It was some comfort to know Hal was near me even if I could not see him. Then the next battle will probably be there. There is no service any where today our churches all being closed. I cannot take my usual interest in my affairs. It is impossible to occupy my mind with comparative trifles when such vast interests are daily at stake.

Nannie Grayson[72] kindly sent us some papers today. They contain such conflicting accounts of every circumstance noticed that it is impossible to know what to believe. In the very same column the battle of Corinth is claimed as a victory by both sides.[73] Our knowledge of Yankee lying of course inclines us to credit the Southern account. Official reports from each of the contending Generals to his respective Governments giving glowing descriptions of victory are published. We cannot be blamed for partiality in crediting Beauregard before Grant.

The only feeling I am conscious of today is intense weariness. Weary of it all and yet with only a distant hope of relief, distant, it may be years, certainly months, and nothing to look forward to in that time but insult and robbery and anxiety and total ignorance of passing events. We might as well be caged, so far as our intercourse with our own people is concerned. Living in the country, our horses and our neighbors' horses all taken, any social intercourse even with our fellow sufferers is next to impossible. We have however no right to complain. Many mercies are still granted us that our friends are denied but we have much to be thankful for. Still I know that I do not deserve more than others, and when I hear of fresh outrages to our neighbors I have always the fear that my turn may come next. I am afraid I write rather gloomily today from being influenced by the total bad news of Hal's being sent to Yorktown. So I will write no more for fear of leaving to my children an impression that their mother was unwilling to bear her share of the sacrifice necessary to accomplish our independence. This is far from the case. I so rarely indulge in these despondencies that every one wonders at my cheerfulness.

April 29th [Tuesday].
Event follows event, all alike calculated to intensify the hatred always sufficiently strong towards the savage invader of our soil. Yesterday morning Mr. Kidwell came in to tell me that a squad of Yankees had gone into old Mr. Hutchinson's[74] house and shot him dead, and had arrested Mr. Johnson[75] and Mr. Stephenson. I could scarcely believe my ears. That so atrocious a murder of an old man with hair as white as snow who had never borne arms against the United States should be committed without any chance of redress will give some idea of the reasons we have [no] desire [for] Union with such a people. I hear they spoke of the matter afterwards as an accident saying they halted him and he refused to stop, but the eye witnesses say the halt and fire were simultaneous.

The same day they went to Welbourne and took all the meat, pulling down the chimney of the roof where it was secreted. They also took some silver but how much I have not heard. They sold one of the children's cups for $6.00. They also took off the last horses that were left on the place. The Captain of the foray said in Upperville that he intended coming out here today or tomorrow to take my meat. He will probably fulfill his threat tomorrow.

It would be impossible to describe the effect of all this upon me. My nature seems changed entirely from having at all times a disposition not easily roused to anger. I find such feelings of deep indignation at and utter detestation of these foul practices and even such a constant desire that the time of vengeance may be near that I scarcely recognize my own identity. In place of my usual energy I find my interest in my accustomed avocations entirely gone, [although I am] far, very far, from hopeless, I am yet utterly listless and weary—weary beyond expression. I do not sew because then I must think, and my thoughts become too easily anxious, so I read, study, practice my music, teach the children, fix work for the servants, and attend a little to my garden. I do not know when I can get clothing for the extra servants who are returned on my hands [after being hired out]. If my meat is taken I fear they will have to scatter over the country and work out for a living.

The impossibility of hearing from Hal preys upon me. Shut up as closely as if in a cage, surrounded only by Yankees, we have no earthly means of communication with the world out side the Yankee lines, and no hope of hearing the truth about any thing, for the wit most in vogue among the Yankees is to tell immense lies to depress and cow the spirits of the secessionists.

May

May 1st [Thursday].
Last night Mr. Weidmayer came over to see us, and gave us a full account of all the outrages of the Yankees at Welbourne.

It makes my blood boil to think that my venerable Uncle whose dignity and goodness have made him respected and beloved for so many years by the whole community should be insulted and reviled in his old age by a little squirt of a Yankee Captain with a band of robbers to support him in the outrage. Capt. McCabe[76] (I write his name that my children even may know & detest him) first put Uncle under arrest in his chamber and then in his presence the party ransacked his room taking what they wanted. They then demanded his keys, and the keys of the whole house, and going into every room they stole everything they could find, clothes, groceries, trunks, some pieces of silver, all the wine and whiskey, a gold watch and snuff box, etc., and completed the outrage by opening the chest containing my dear dead sister's clothes, and taking some of them. Poor Brother Richard, how little he knows what is going on at his

Timeline of the War

May 3	Confederates abandon Yorktown and fall back toward Richmond.
May 8	Jackson wins the first of a series of victories in the Shenandoah Valley when he defeats Milroy and Schenck at McDowell.
May 15	Gen. Butler, commanding occupied New Orleans, issues his General Orders no. 28, threatening to treat as prostitutes all women who insult Union soldiers.
May 23	Jackson defeats Union troops at Front Royal.
May 25	Jackson defeats Banks at Winchester and pursues him to the Potomac River.
May 31	Forty thousand Union troops who otherwise would have supported McClellan's drive on Richmond are now in or converging on the Shenandoah Valley to deal with Jackson's sixteen thousand men. In the Battle of Fair Oaks on the peninsula, Gen. Joseph E. Johnston is seriously wounded. Command of the Confederate forces defending Richmond and the Shenandoah Valley passes to Gen. Robert E. Lee.

house. Cousin Mittie gave this brave captain such a piece of her mind that he threatened to send her a prisoner to Washington, a threat which only amused her, but in order to alarm her he ordered his men to fire on the house, taking good care however not to go quite so far as to enforce obedience to his order.

Mr. Bolling was here tonight. He tells us of an exactly similar scene at his house, indeed, two such, one when he was at home, and one when he was absent. He says his home is literally naked. He has been to Winchester and reports our friends all well, has also seen some Federal papers from which he learns the passage of the Confiscation Bill. So if we lose our cause I will be thrown upon my own resources for a support, an alternative that does not occasion me much uneasiness, for two reasons: 1st that our cause will in my belief surely succeed, and 2nd because let my circumstances be what they may, I can never have to labour so hard for my self and children as I have done here for all my slaves, and certainly never with so poor a reward.

I am far more anxious from the fear that my darling may try to come home to see me thereby endangering his life and liberty. He is at Gordonsville still, and I can almost wish that he had gone to Yorktown, as from there he could not get home.

May 5th [Monday].
Yesterday being Sunday, Katey and I walked up to Upperville, our little church being opened for the first time for many a long day. We heard after church that Mr. R. E. Scott[77] had been brutally murdered on his own farm by the Yankees. If this is true it will ring far and wide, for he has long been considered one of the first men of Va.

When I came home I received intelligence that my dear husband was well, in fine spirits and on the eve of a battle. The source of the information I cannot mention even in my journal, as it is considered a crime now to hold intercourse with the Southern army in any way. My anxiety for Hal is very great, so great that I can speak of it to no one. My fears for our cause, my anxiety lest a battle should go against us I can speak of, but when ever I think of danger to Hal I cannot speak, and I suppose that the family sometimes wonder why I do not oftener express anxiety for him—I cannot speak of it, and find it inexpressibly painful even to write my fears. I can only pray for him and trust in God.

I saw yesterday a letter from Sallie Conrad[78] to Lilly Powell. She says she watched from the roof of her father's house the battle of Newtown,[79] saw the enemy constantly reinforce, knew that Jackson had but 5200 men and that the enemy had 15,000, knew that her brother and many, many friends were with Jackson, and yet had to look on and could do nothing. She says our victory was brilliant, for though Jackson at last retreated in admirable order, upon the enemy's being largely reinforced, he killed 1000 Yankees, and wounded 1200, losing himself only 85 killed, and 150 wounded. She knows the truth of what she says being on the spot both during and after the battle. When they left Winchester the Yankees left 800 of their wounded in the town.

I am still reading the "Dutch Republic" and am much interested in it, but its scenes of bloodshed and horrors of all kind make me nervous. We learned today that Aunt Ann,[80] in addition to the death of her daughter, has to bear the entire destruction of her property by the Yankees. The Yankee women stole every thing of value from her house.

May 8th [Thursday].
I drove to Upperville today in Grandma's carriage with old Charley, our only dependence for a carriage horse. I heard there that the Yankees had boasted at Piedmont the day before that they had gained a great victory at Yorktown.[81] My heart sickens at the bare idea though I cannot place confidence in any thing the Yankees say of the events of battle. It surely cannot be that Yorktown will fall—we are a sinful people and deserve all we suffer but I trust and hope that our Heavenly Father will in mercy stay his hand and deliver us from this savage enemy, and I fear the fall of Yorktown would rivet the chain indefinitely. Oh for deliverance and help!

Spring has come and the beauty of earth and sky seem to mock our misery. I walk out morning and evening, and if in my daily occupation of gardening and looking after the place the loveliness of nature tempts me to forget our bondage for an instant, the hated whistle of the Yankee locomotive transporting troops to murder our nearest and dearest, the boastful beat of their drums sounding over the quiet green fields or the roar of artillery, fired in honor of some real or pretended victory, sounding like a death knell to our hopes, soon recalls me to all we must endure. We feel the bitterness of our capture in every way. Of all that nearly concerns us we speak only in whispers, not knowing who is a spy to report our every word, all visiting necessarily ceases when we know not at what hour our homes will be invaded by a band of robbers who would sack or destroy every thing within their reach. The stagnation of trade, the cowed look of the men, the arrogant triumphant insolence of the slaves all daily remind us of our bondage.

God has mercifully spared me from an attack lately. It may be His will that I escape without further injury, but I cannot hope to be more blessed than my neighbors. I find my natural cheerfulness giving way to a great extent under the long continuance of the evil. The entire separation from and uncertainty about Hal preys upon me constantly, and I must acknowledge that I am often weak and nervous from the constant pressure of an anxiety that I cannot speak of. My courage and hope, thank God, have not failed me yet, but my interest in every thing except the events of the war and what concerns my absent friends is gone. Even the children's education lags sadly. I can only pray for strength and trust and hope on.

May 10th [Saturday].
Ma and Kate have gone to Middleburg to spend the night—the children are off to bed; Grandma has just gone up terribly discomposed at the idea of sleeping without Mamma in her room, and I am downstairs alone to write and read my "Dutch Republic" till I think the children in my room are asleep.

I went [to] Welbourne yesterday having had an offer for my cattle and wishing to know whether Uncle John wanted me to sell brother Richard's with them. He advised my selling everything I could, and I will take his advice.

The rumor of Mr. Scott's death is only too true. He went with another man by the name of Matthews[82] to try and capture some Yankee deserters who had hidden in the mountain and had been ravaging the country all around them for weeks. Hearing they were in a house not far from him, Mr. Scott determined if possible to free the country from them. They succeeded in capturing one, but one from the interior of the house fired and killed simultaneously Mr. Scott and Mr. Matthews. The crowd around the house enraged at the death of their friends, instantly killed their prisoner while the actual murderer within the house escaped unharmed. The wretch little knew that his murderous ball had pierced the noblest and strongest brain in Virginia.[83]

I heard at Welbourne that my dearest husband had been re-elected Lieut. of his company and Brother R. Captain.

I saw a late paper yesterday giving a full description of a brilliant victory gained over us by the Yankees at Williamsburg,[84] while the same paper publishes most desponding dispatches from Genl. McClellan, so I have no doubt but that we have whipped them soundly. I sold two cows this morning for $55.00 not a very good price but this is better than that Col. Geary should get them. I have not been well lately, suffering from strange attacks of weakness such as I never had before.

May 11th [Sunday].
Yorktown is surrendered to the enemy. What I dreaded so much has come, but in such a form as to comfort rather than depress me. [General] Lee & [President] Davis visited the place and ordered our army to fall back and remain out of reach of the enemy's gun-boats thereby entirely disconcerting McClellan and depriving [him] of his greatest and indeed only advantage over us.

Dicky[85] is here with the children. I am glad to have him and wish we could see more of all the little ones from Welbourne.

May 11th, evening.
Mr. Scott sent me a "Baltimore Sun" today. It claims a great victory at Williamsburg for the Yankees—says Ewell's Brigade or rather Division was engaged and that seven men of the 6th Va. Cav. were captured. I know that but little reliance can be placed in any thing from the Northern papers, but this seems very explicit and Genl. McClellan's private letter to his wife is published claiming a brilliant victory. At any rate to know that Ewell's[86] Division was engaged gives me intense anxiety till I can know that my husband is safe. I cannot feel that anything has happened to Hal, it seems so utterly impossible that I could be for days entirely unconscious of any trouble to him. Surely I would know it in some way.

I had scarcely written the above when my little Becca ran up to me from the midst of a violent romp of all the children and looking into my face said with momentary gravity, "modder my Faders dead"—what could make her say it just then I cannot imagine. I am afraid I am very nervous to let a thoughtless speech of a little child shock me so.

May 14th [Wednesday].
I have been quite sick since day before yesterday evening, with [a] violent headache, a good dose of opium relieved me last night, but this morning I again suffered very much—tonight am better.

On Monday morning I found that Horace had gone off to the Yankees, taking my horse and cart with him. Mr. Kidwell tracked the cart to Rectortown where he recovered it, Mr. Cridler[87] having recognized it and saved it for me.

Aunt Louise who has always been one of the most respectful servants on the place was quite impertinent yesterday morning. Poor fools! I am afraid that in any event they are destined to suffer severely for their folly. As far as I can judge Harriet still seems perfectly loyal, she expressed to me today great disapprobation of all that is going on around us. I am having the floors stained this week. A fine rain has refreshed every thing today. The fourth colt was born today, two of them are beautiful. I can but think what pleasure Hal would take in them. Poor fellow! What would I not give to see or even hear from him. I have seen no paper lately so have no news.

May 15th [Thursday].
Mr. Scott sent me a paper today containing accounts of various Federal victories, not one of which do I believe. I went to Welbourne to pay Uncle John some money, and from there to Upperville where I heard the first good news that has gladdened my ears for many a day. The Yankees themselves say that France and England have both recognized the Confederacy. Ten chances to one it is a Yankee lie, but their habit is not to fabricate rumors to their disadvantage.

Mr. Wheat came up from Alexandria on Tuesday. He says the Yankees there acknowledge a serious defeat at Fredericksburg, and that Banks had been repulsed. If this be true it is good news. Brother Richard's company has had a successful skirmish killing ten of the enemy and capturing seventeen.[88] They lost not a man. This is the only certain news I have had from my dear husband for some time.

Mr. A[yre][89] came over this morning to ask me to give him a written statement of the manner in which I had been treated by Geary and his men. His object is to collect all the evidence of Geary's misconduct to report him at Washington. I made out my statement and took my oath to its correctness but Mamma is so opposed to my sending it that I have decided not to do tho' sorely against my will.

May 16th [Friday].
The gentleman who is to take the papers to Washington called this morning. I gave him mine and he was to ask Uncle John's advice about sending it.

I went to Upperville this evening for Katey (who stayed last night with the Stephensons) and carried May and Rebecca. They behaved very sweetly and the girls admired Rebecca prodigiously.

The Fredericksburg battle turns out to be only a skirmish. The Confederacy is not yet recognized [by France and England], but it is speedily expected. All accounts from the Williamsburg fight proclaim it in our favor notwithstanding the efforts of the Yankees to conceal the fact. I was truly sorry to see among the names of the killed on our side Eugene Fairfax[90] and Winston Carter.[91] I hear Cousin Richard[92] has resigned and come home, but hardly credit it. Mr.

Gibson[93] told me he had heard that Brother Richard's Company had been terribly cut to pieces in the recent skirmish. I do not believe it, but still am anxious, more than I can tell. The entire uncertainty as to the fate of those so dear to me is insupportable, and while I go about my duties almost as usual and try to be cheerful, I carry with me always a weight of anxiety—no, I may say anguish—such as I never even dreamed of before.

May 17th [Saturday].
I have great cause for gratitude to God for his goodness. I heard from Hal today, he was at Cousin R. DeB[utts]'s[94] on Thursday, and well. Brother R. was with him. So Mr. Gibson's story is utterly without foundation.

May 18th. Sunday—
All have gone to church, no one being here but little Becca and I. I should like to have gone but we do not think it safe to leave the house entirely unoccupied in these lawless times. Some one (most probably a run-a-way negro) took Brother R's fine mare Celeste out of the field, and she can no where be found. Mr. Loughborough's fine riding mare was stolen from his stable a night or two ago. I cannot describe the relief I feel at having heard from Hal. I did not know how anxious I had been until I felt the inexpressible relief. Brother R's company captured fourteen Yankees on Thursday, and killed one without the loss of a man killed or wounded. This is the second affair of the kind they have had lately. It makes me anxious for fear some of them should be hurt in these encounters, and Ma is anxious lest Genl. Geary[95] should wreak vengeance on their families, but I would not have our men to let any such probability hamper them in their efforts for our cause for the world, and on the contrary I cannot avoid a feeling of appreciation of the justice of the fact that the men whose families have suffered so severely should be the ones chosen by the authorities to punish their oppressors. It is tantalizing to know that Hal was so near me as Linden and that I could not see him.

May 20th [Tuesday]
Uncle Nathan came this morning to tell me that Jackson had driven Banks out of Strasburg, and that a small band of Guerrillas had gone into Rectortown and captured five Yankees within a mile of Geary's headquarters. I have shrewd suspicions as to who the Guerillas were. The federal gun-boats have been repulsed, seven miles below Richmond on James River.[96]

May 22nd [Thursday].
Josephine Stephenson[97] is staying with us, and the two girls enliven the house no little. The day before yesterday Ben arrived here having run off from his master. His proving [to be] like all the others is a disappointment to me. It

speaks badly for our men that not one of them will consent to share with their kind master the hardships of war. I consider his coming as a prelude to his going to the Yankees. A party of Yankees drove off Brother R's whole drove of cattle this morning. They also took some more meat from Welbourne. I heard today that Geary was to be removed from his post at Rectortown. We were so delighted that we cheered, shouted and sang with delight, and finally burnt a Roman candle to celebrate our release from his bondage. I hope it may not be premature.

May 24th [Saturday].
Yesterday morning Mr. McA.[98] rode up and when he came in he had a letter from my dearest husband. I could scarcely keep from crying with joy at seeing his dear hand writing again. I am going to send his horse to him next week and will have an opportunity to write. I have twelve pages already written for him and my letter is not finished yet.

I went to Welbourne today. The Yankees have paid them another visit taking off almost all the meat and twelve steers. All day long heavy firing has been heard from over the [Blue] Ridge. We do not know what it is; only fearing another battle.[99] Every report of the cannon makes me shudder.

How many, many immortal ones are to he ushered into eternity? How many young, buoyant, brave hearts to be stilled forever before this unholy [war] ceases? We hear that Geary has actually struck his tents. Anna Noland[100] came home with Jenny. She is very sweet. So many young girls enliven the house very much.

May 26th [Monday].
Bless the Lord, oh my soul, and all that is within me, Bless His Holy Name! Little did I know when shuddering at the reports of the cannon what a deliverance they were working for us. Glorious old Jackson! He for three days has driven the enemy before him routing them with great slaughter. It is said he is at Winchester now having sent Master Banks running for dear life towards Martinsburg. And as for the redoubtable Genl. Geary, he did not wait to learn the result of the fight but no sooner was he informed that it was taking place than he turned his face and started his feet as rapidly as possible towards Manassas, instead of going in the other direction, where had he been as brave as he is boastful he might with his three thousand men have turned the tide of battle against us. He went off in such a hurry that he left 1,000 men, (so our soldiers say) 600 (his men say) who were captured at Front Royal without striking a blow. There is now not one Yankee soldier in our rescued valley.

The crowning blessing to me is that my darling husband and Brother R. were in the battle and came out unhurt. Can I ever be grateful enough to God for this? The colored friends look rather down cast, I think, but excepting them, all nature seems to rejoice. Even the poor horses and cows seem to know something good has happened for them and I am I sure I can sympathize in the general joy.

I heard, but it seems too good to be true that Beauregard had whipped them at Corinth and that Johnson had captured Rosecrans.[101] God grant it may be confirmed. I am expecting Hal every moment. Some reports of cannon were heard yesterday, we suppose that Genl. Ewell has fallen in with Banks. I cannot yet really realize the new sense of freedom. Mamma has taken the children to Middleburg to glean further news. Poor John Fletcher[102] was killed and Mrs. Brook's[103] screams of agony when told of the death of her only boy saddened the most exultant spirits.

I hear that Arthur H.[104] was wounded at Williamsburg. I trust it is not so. I already dread to see the list of killed and wounded thinking it scarcely possible that when so many friends were engaged in the fight, no familiar name will meet my eye. Tom and Wilson [Turner from St. Louis] have both been in battles since we heard from them, also Holmes Conrad and Willie Carrere and William Turner [of Baltimore] possibly. We rejoice at first setting aside anxiety, fearing lest a few days may develop cause for great sorrow. But it seems selfishness itself to do any thing but rejoice at the great national good.

May 28th [Wednesday].
Josephine and I rode up to the village today. Every one is exalting, Aunt Mary E[liason] had just received a paper telling all the good news so we collected in her room to hear it read. Banks has been driven out of Winchester with great slaughter, has retreated across the Potomac, our forces it is said pursuing them into Maryland. It was Milroy and Schenck[105] who were whipped out in Western Virginia. All their baggage train was captured. Banks has lost all his men except 4,000. He had 20,000. I have just written a long letter to Hal which I hope to send him.

On Saturday Mrs. Stephenson's women all came in and told her they were going off to Geary, that he was to send three wagons for them. The wagons did not come, and when the news of our victory arrived the whole party came in crying and sobbing, begging forgiveness and expressing everlasting hate to Yankees; of course the family knew what confidence to place in their professions [of loyalty].

May 29th [Thursday].
Yesterday evening Katey and I drove up to Upperville for Aunt Mary. There we heard the sad, sad news of Lucy Kinsolving's death. It was a great shock to me. Soon after we came home Lieut. Gibson rode up to give me certain intelligence of my dear husband's well being. It was truly kind of him. Mamma and I started very early this morning to go to Middleburg to dear Lucy's funeral,

but we met Mr. Fletcher[106] coming up from there who told us that 600 Yankees were just below Middleburg—so we thought it best to turn back. We went on to Upperville for a little while and then came home.

    I was lying down reading when Mamma called me to say that the Yankees were in the fields driving off my horses. I looked out and the field was literally covered with Yankee Cavalry. They looked at my horses, but did not take any. Later in the day some came for corn. I sent word to them I had none, but one came to the house and asked to speak to me. He was a rather good looking but perfectly common soldier, said he was sorry to be under the necessity of taking the corn and also of pressing my ox cart to haul it. I said what I could to prevent it but could not have any effect. He said their horses were starving. Another came on the same errand. I spoke civilly to him as he seemed much disposed to behave himself. He confessed (which surprised me somewhat) that he was sick of all this and would like to go home. I said what I could to induce him to do so. He said it was impossible now, that he was in for it and would not be allowed to resign. He went away without taking any thing from us.

    Mr. Bolling has come home and says that Genl. Kirbey [sic] Smith is in pursuit of these men with a large force.[107]

May 30th [Friday].

This has been quite a day of adventure. Just as I got up from the breakfast table I saw Yankees driving up my horses; in a very little while they started off leading the beautiful Cleveland colt, Orphan Girl. I was so sorry to lose her that without waiting to consider the propriety of the proceeding, I ordered hastily old Cricket from the field and asked Mr. Kidwell to get his horse. Almost before the Yankees were off the farm I was mounted, and in pursuit. I thought the Yankees were in Upperville, but to my dismay found the Colonel had started on his way to the river several hours before. As my object was to see him, I was much disappointed, but determined to let Mr. Kidwell try to overtake them. I heard that the party with the colt had only five minutes start of us in leaving the town.

    After Mr. Kidwell started, I determined not to leave it to him but to go myself in spite of the many disagreeable obstacles in my doing so. I rode rapidly alone trying to overtake Mr. Kidwell, but old Cricket was just off grass and had not been ridden for some time, and I was afraid of injuring her. So meeting a boy on a good horse I asked him to ride on before me and stop Mr. Kidwell. He did so and I caught up with him just in sight of all the Yankees.

    I soon espied the white horse ridden by one of the men who took the colt. I rode leisurely through them all, I suppose about 200 in number. They were sitting, lying down and walking up and down and were stretched along the road for about 200 yards. I kept my veil closely down but at the same time watched closely for my colt. I could see nothing of her, but when I got about half way through them I heard a voice say, "Here's your colt." I turned, but could see nothing of her, and so rode on till I came to the last man. I stopped at him and asked him if he could show me the Officer in Command. He pointed to a small man under a tree. I rode up to him, and asked him if he was the Commanding Officer of the troops I saw. "I am, Madam," he said. I told him a favorite unbroken colt had been taken from me an hour before by a man in his command, and that I had come to recover it. "I will see about it Madam," he said, and mounting a horse near him rode rapidly off. I stood under the tree waiting for his return, and though closely veiled saw I was an object of considerable curiosity to the soldiers standing around.

In about five minutes the Major[108] returned, and following behind him at a little distance a man came leading the colt. The Major said, "I find a colt here such as you describe. If you can prove him yours, you can take him." The fact needed no proof for no sooner did the colt see us than she exhibited the greatest pleasure—neighed, and held up her head and tried hard to get to old Cricket. I found no difficulty in establishing my claim to her and was soon ready to start home with her. The Major told the soldier who took her to lead her home and get his own horse that had been left here this morning. He said, sullenly enough, that his horse was worth nothing and that he had sooner walk, so it was arranged that the colt should follow us home and the Yankee horse is here to be cared for till called for.

As we repassed the soldiers, many jeers and jokes were cast at the discomfited horse stealer. The Major accompanied me some distance and then told a Capt. to escort me out of his lines, which he did, talking along very amicably as we rode. He expressed great horror of the Confiscation Bill, and also much desire for peace. After the Capt. left, Mr. Kidwell and I rode on followed by the colt. Soon I heard horse's feet behind us and looking back saw a soldier following us. The colt instantly quickened her pace till she got before us, and she maintained her position till the Yankee left us. No sooner did the soldier come up with us than he began to talk of the war, and to my surprise expressed a perfect horror of it all, did not blame the South at all but laid all the blame on the Abolitionists and Republicans, and wound up by saying that he intended to desert the first opportunity he had. He left us at the Piedmont road.

There was quite a Jubilee in Upperville when I entered with the colt. When I got home I found Mr. Weidmayer here. He looks well and describes every thing in Washington as in a great state of panic. He saw Uncle Billy in Alexandria. He looked miserably, and skulked away before Mr. W. had an opportunity to speak to him.

In the evening I saw two Yankees walking across the fields. I was not surprised as I had seen the long train of their wagons going to Upperville before dinner. The two men went to Rosetta's room and staid for some time, and then came towards the kitchen. I was determined they should not sit there, so I went down and stopped them just as they were going up the steps. I will give our conversation exactly as it passed.

Mrs. D.	Good evening. What do you want?
1st Yankee	We have come to buy meat. Can't you sell us a ham?
Mrs. D.	I have no hams to spare.
1st Yankee	Oh I know you have plenty of meat.
Mrs. D.	I have meat but no more than I want. I cannot sell you any.
2nd Yankee	Do let us have a ham, I will pay you in gold or silver.
Mrs. D.	I have none to spare.
1st Yankee	Oh I know better—if you have none in your meat house you have it in the garret.
Mrs. D.	I am not accustomed to have my assertion doubted. You can get no meat, and as to the garret, when you are sent here with authority to search my house I will take you there and you can see for yourself.
2nd Yankee	Well, can't you let us have a pound of butter?
Mrs. D.	No—I cannot.
2nd Yankee	Is this Captain Dulany's house?
Mrs. D.	No.
1st Yankee	Are you his wife?
Mrs. D.	No, his wife is dead.
1st Yankee	Capt. Dulany is a very bad man. He murdered our prisoners in cold blood after they laid down their arms.
Mrs. D.	You say what is untrue, and what is more you shall say nothing against him before me.
1st Yankee	Why not?
Mrs. D.	Because you are on my place, and I don't choose it.
1st Yankee	I don't care whether you like it or not.
Mrs. D.	You may go now Sir—I do not care to talk to men who don't know how to behave themselves.
2nd Yankee	We belong to Genl. Geary and if he knew this was Capt. Dulany's house it would be bad for you all here.
Mrs. D.	This is not Capt. Dulany's house.
2nd Yankee	Well it's Lieut. Dulany's then.

I turned then and went into the house. They walked off, and muttered as they went that McCabe should come and burn the house to the ground, and many other threats, but principally against Brother R.[109]

Mr. Bolling called this evening, but did not stay long as Mr. Kidwell came in and told us that Geary's men were all encamped in Mc[Artor]'s woods. Of course it was not safe for him to be away from home. I have as yet heard nothing from the boy who took my letter to Hal.

June

June 2nd [Monday].

Sad, sad news has come to us this morning of the death of Powell Conrad—poor fellow! Poor fellow! It seems but yesterday that he was here well and as likely to live as any one. I cannot bear to think of Aunt Betty's sorrow. We have heard no particulars of his death but know that he was not at home. If ever a boy had a praying mother, he had, and how hard it is with our weak faith to see why he should be suddenly cut off in his youth.[110] If her prayer was unanswered, what right have I who am so far behind her in every Christian attainment presume to be secure in my darling's safety? Yet Oh my God! Thou hast spared him thus far, in mercy spare him still.

Poor Marshall Barton[111] was killed and left a young wife and little child. A letter came from Mr. Kinsolving. He seems broken hearted for the loss of his lovely young wife.[112] There seems no end to the death and desolation all around us. Day after day, one after another, the young and the strong, the good and the lovely fall around us, and the gloom deepens daily over our poor land. Tom Turner of Kinloch was wounded at Front Royal, how, we have not heard.

Yesterday was Sunday and we were reading the service in Mamma's room when my attention was distracted by seeing the wheat field almost alive with Yankees riding some towards the house, some towards the upper end of the farm, trampling the wheat in every direction. Then I saw another party escorting a long train of wagons through the wheat towards the house. Of course I knew they were coming for corn. So I put on my hat and Mamma and I went down to the barnyard to be ready for them. I planted my back against the

---

Timeline of the War

June 3	Union troops in Mississippi, having taken Corinth, advance on Memphis, Tennessee.
June 6	Jackson's cavalry commander, Turner Ashby, is killed in a skirmish near Harrisonburg.
June 8	Gen. Richard Ewell defeats Gen. John C. Fremont at Cross Keys.
June 9	Jackson defeats Shields at Port Republic; Union armies give up pursuit of Jackson and adopt strictly defensive positions.
June 12	Brig. Gen. J. E. B. Stuart begins his first raid around McClellan's army.
June 15	Lee orders Jackson to move his troops as quickly as possible from the Shenandoah Valley to join the army at Richmond.
June 26	Fighting in the Seven Days Campaign begins near Richmond when Lee attacks an isolated Union corps at Mechanicsville.

corn house door, determined to resist their taking the little left me to the last. Soon they came riding in. I asked for the Officer, one said he had gone over to the adjoining farm. I was struck at once with the fact that these were more respectable looking men than any I had seen before. With huge exceptions, I should judge that they were well born and educated. In talking to them I told them positively that I had no corn to spare and that I had already lost so much by the Yankees that no man with any conscience would wish to take more from me. These men had recently joined Geary's command and were a part of Col. Carter's Regt.,[113] the same from whom I recovered my colt.

After waiting a while one who had not come near to where I stood called out that they were wasting time and might as well begin filling the wagons. Another near me said they should not take a grain till the Officer came. After talking a little longer, two of the best looking said they would take nothing from me and gave the order for the wagons to go on. There was almost a quarrel when the order was heard, some saying it was folly to go farther when they had the corn right by them, and the two good looking ones remaining firm to their determination. I saw the wagons turn towards Mr. Kidwell's and then stop. I decided to wait, and it was well I did for immediately they all turned and drove back into the barnyard close to the corn house. In a few minutes one of my advocates rode up and told me the officer had returned and countermanded his order.

I waited till the officer came up, and then asked him simply if it was possible that he, an armed man, would insist upon plundering a woman of the last corn she had. He looked a little ashamed, and said arms had nothing to do with it, that my husband was a rebel, and they were suffering for the corn and must have it. I told him then, "Very well, you have the power and if you will take it, I cannot prevent you. I have done my duty in exerting myself to the utmost to preserve it, now if my people suffer I shall not have myself to reproach. You will be responsible, and must answer for it at the bar of God—"

"Madam," he said, "what am I to do?" I said, "I do not pretend to know what you are to do, but one thing I know—if you have in you anything of the man or the gentleman you will not take this corn." Much more passed between us, till from arguing we got to talking amicably, one said they would not feel so to the South if the Southern soldiers did not commit such atrocities. I begged him not to believe all the falsehoods told only to inflame them. He said Jackson had gotten their men completely in his power and had then murdered them in cold blood. I told him I knew it was not so.

Just then, a very fine looking young man, neatly dressed, and very handsome rode up, and hearing what was said rebuked the speaker very sternly, asking him why he could not tell the truth and say that Jackson did every thing in his power to induce them to surrender, and that not till they positively refused to do so, was the order given that proved so fatal to them. Some rode off then but the last comer and the two who had from the first seemed friendly lingered as if they liked to talk, and when they did go the impression was left upon my mind that their hearts were for the South. They drove off taking no corn.

Even while I write, the heavy dull boom of the cannon falls on my ear. For three hours we have heard them in such quick succession that I fear a terrible battle is going on, the sound from the direction of Winchester or Front Royal.[114] My heart sinks at the sound, such immense reinforcements have been pouring up the valley for Banks that I dread lest our little army should be cut to pieces. I heard yesterday that Banks had been severely repulsed at Harpers Ferry but no rumor is reliable now.

June 2nd [continued].
This evening while [I was] lying down, Mamma told me the Yankees were after the horses again. I looked out and saw two who were here yesterday, the ill looking ones. I called after one and asked him if he was sent for the horse? (It was Cousin Robert Carter's colt). "No," he said. I asked him if he knew it was against regulations—yes, he did, but didn't care. I said, "Do you not know that a soldier should be brave and honest and it is neither brave nor honest to steal a horse from a lady?" "I know that," he said, "but can't help it," so off he rode. I called to him "Catch him if you can," feeling pretty sure it would be more than he could do. The colt ran and they ran. They caught it, and it broke from them, and all the while a terrible storm was coming up. Soon the storm became so violent that they had to ride off without the colt. So thanks to the colt and the storm I was again victorious. Mittie Stephenson came home with Kate.

June 4th [Wednesday].
Last night Aunt Mary sent us a paper. It was full of bad news. Boasting in a decided victory at Richmond[115]—stating that the Confederates had been driven from Front Royal with considerable loss, and that Beauregard had evacuated Corinth and was retreating southwards. Also that Ewell and Jackson had again fallen back to Strasburg, leaving the Yankees once more in possession of the Valley. The last two items I fear are true, indeed I know them to be so. But for the two former, thanks to the general want of veracity in Yankee news, we may doubt till we hear it confirmed from Southern sources. It is comfort to know that the battles of Williamsburg and Pittsburg Landing[116] were claimed at first as great victories for them. I had the good fortune to learn through Mr. A[yre] that Hal was well on Sunday. He saw him as rear guard to Jackson's army en route for Strasburg.

June 5th [Thursday].
Today notwithstanding the rain, just before dinner, two Yankees came into the field near the house and took poor old Charley, Grandma's horse, off. I sent

Mr. Kidwell after them to try and recover him but they refused to give him up, saying that all the horses in the country were claimed by widows, and so the old fellow is gone. In about an hour afterwards I looked out and saw a troop of cavalry approaching the house. I was afraid I should have some trouble and so secreted the little silver we are using and the money I have in the house. Two of them came to the house, while the others remained on their horses at the fence. The two who came in sent for me, so I went down and met them in the parlor. One a Capt. Orl[117] (so his name sounded), I saw to be a gentleman at a glance. The other I was doubtful of for his manner was not very respectful. The Capt. asked if I had any meat? I told him promptly yes—but not more than I needed for my family. The Lieut. insinuated that I would have said as much even if I had it, said he was always told there was none to spare and had often on searching found a great deal. I told [him] simply that I was not accustomed to saying what was not so.

Mamma talked with the Capt. while I had rather a spicy conversation with the Lieut. He began abusing Brother Richard, saying he had no more heart than a stone etc., etc. I told him I had refused to listen to such abuse before and would not listen to it now. He went on to excuse McCabe for his atrocious conduct at Welbourne. I stopped him at that by telling him I knew all the circumstances of his conduct, and that I was really surprised to find that even in the Yankee army there was one other man enough like McCabe to attempt to excuse him. I flatly contradicted what he told us of Brother R., and by one or two side slaps at disrespect to ladies and at the insult to them of abusing their friends in their presence, succeeding in bringing the pert Lieut. so far to a sense of what was proper that he said before leaving that he had no doubt but that Captain Dulany was everything I represented, and that he might have been misinformed. They did not take my meat, but I am by no means sure that it will not be taken yet for they are evidently entirely out of provisions.

It is impossible to describe our utter feeling of insecurity, our house at any moment subject to intrusion and search, our property to plunder, and I fear ourselves often saved from personal insult only by the presence of some officer who may not chance to be with the next party that comes. But even this is nothing compared with my anxiety for my dear husband. Entirely cut off even from all communication with him, and always conscious that his life is in peril, I do not think that for one moment that this consciousness leaves me. It is as if I was in a fearful storm and saw friend after friend stricken down by the thunder bolts all around me, and knew that at any moment the next bolt might crush me and that I was powerless to escape. And with it all I feel thankful that I have been spared thus far, and am conscious too that the storm may blow over at last, and I may not be stricken.

June 6th [Friday].
Our wedding day, the seventh anniversary, and it has been a day of deepest anxiety, also one of thanksgiving. Early this morning we heard that McClellan had been driven back five miles into the swamps of the Chickahominy, but the report is not perfectly reliable. God grant it may be true. I tremble when I think of the immense importance to us of the issue of this great battle before Richmond.

The same report said the battle had raged for three days and was still going on. Another report says that Jackson was intercepted in falling back to Strasburg and that he fought his way through, completely getting the better of the Yankees and making good his own retreat with but little loss. Another rumor, coming from a Yankee, says he was completely caught, most of his men captured, and all terribly cut to pieces. That there has been a severe fight we knew, for many car-loads of the dead and wounded Yankees have passed through Rectortown. When I think that Hal was in that fierce struggle, I am nearly wild with fear lest he should have been hurt, yet here I am, shut up in a cage, ignorant even of his present position and without the faintest possibility of my hearing from him. The anxiety is almost insupportable. I can only hope, and pray, and trust in the goodness of God to spare him and me.

June 8th [Sunday].
Yesterday morning I was so fortunate as to see Mr. Ayre for a few minutes. He saw Hal on Sunday, and says that from his position then, he is certain that he could not have been in last Monday's fight. I am truly thankful to be relieved from my great anxiety regarding him.

The news from Richmond seems upon investigation to be reliable and it certainly looks encouraging for us, that the newspapers (Northern) have been suppressed since last Saturday.

Last night I could not get to sleep till way in the night. I became so excited, thinking of passing events. Mr. Bolling called yesterday evening. Mamma started yesterday morning to Leesburg to try and make some arrangements by which we may preserve our property in case of the passage of the Confiscation Act.[118]

Uncle Nathan called yesterday to tell us that a party of Yankees had been to his house for meat, had cursed him and threatened him, and had behaved in every way outrageously. They did not get his meat however, as he refused to show them where it was concealed, and they had no authority to search the house. I was surprised to learn that they were Carter's men. Here they have behaved like a different order of beings from Geary's men.

It is Sunday and I have just finished reading the service with the family, and that with Sunday School makes me feel very tired.

June 9th [Monday].
This morning I sent for Dr. Gunnell[119] to see poor Margaret. He says she has only a few weeks to live, her lungs being almost destroyed.[120] It is very sad. He told us that our loss at Richmond was 20,000.[121] I can but hope that he may have received a false estimate. I fear though, that it is a dear bought victory.

Kate received a letter from Sophie Carter [of Glen Welby] today. Among other items of news, she mentions that Cousin Mary Lee and two of her daughters have been captured by the Yankees and are held as hostages for two Federal Officers.[122] I can scarcely believe in the outrage. She also mentions that the Confiscation bill has passed the Senate in its worst form; so I may look out for squalls. Two men from Fairfax were here today. I sold them some sheep at a great sacrifice, having been advised by Uncle John to sell at any price, but I shall hate to see them go. Mamma did not return tonight.

June 10th [Tuesday].
As a step [in] preparation for the Confiscation, I sold this morning four of my little heifers and an old cow. Of course I did not get a full price for them, but anything is better than having them taken from me by the Yankees.

Mr. Kidwell told me this morning that he had seen a man from the Valley who told him that the fight of last Monday was a terrific one, and that we were completely successful, Ashby having contrived to capture the Yankee pickets, thereby preventing any information of Jackson's approach being given. I would give anything in reason to get some Southern papers, but have no hope of seeing any for a long time. The pouring rain has prevented any visitors coming today, so I have nothing new to relate. Mr. Kidwell told me today that he thought Simon had made up his mind to run off. It does not trouble me much.

June 11th [Wednesday].
Early this morning while trimming my grape vines in the garden, I saw a Yankee walking along at the foot of the garden. He came to the house and I saw he was the one who had stolen my colt. He had come for his horse, he said, and then he expressed his penitence for taking my colt. I talked to him as long as he stayed, trying, as usual, when I had an opportunity, to make some impression on him.

Mamma returned this morning from Leesburg, and brought the sad, sad news that Brother R. was wounded badly in the thigh.[123] It was a great shock to me, making their constant danger seem so real, and making me so anxious for him. Poor fellow.

I went to Welbourne to see Uncle John this evening and found that he had only heard a rumor that he did not credit. He was mightily distressed, but seemed to take comfort in the hope that it was not a severe wound. I am anxious to go to Brother R. at once, and if I go Mr. Weidmayer will go with me. I will take two chances, try if I can get a pass from the authorities and if not, will start secretly and attempt to cross the lines between the Pickets. I long to go, we will be so anxious here, and then I shall be near Hal, without being either useless or burdensome. I cannot for one moment believe that Brother R. will die. It would be such a hard, hard thing to his father and dear little children. I feel about him as I do about my own darling, that God will surely hear our prayers.

Poor Willie Gray[124] was killed. General Johnston [was] badly wounded[125] at Richmond. Our victory was decided. Hearing that the Yankees were putting Union people in all the unoccupied houses, I ordered Aunt Polly and Patsey to move to the one at the lower end of the farm. Aunt Polly objected, but Patsey positively refused to go. I told Mr. Kidwell to go tomorrow morning and move them without saying a word to them. I fancy they think themselves free already.

June 13th [Friday].
Yesterday morning directly after breakfast, Mr. Ayres called to tell me he had been to examine the lines to see if I could get out. He reports it an entire impossibility. I am troubled very much to hear it, but still hope I may be able to get a pass. Mr. Weidmayer has given up all idea of going and Uncle John has sent Edward Carr,[126] thinking he stands a better chance of getting through the lines. I know our anxiety will be almost insupportable till he returns.

Today Mr. Ayres came again bringing a Richmond "Dispatch" with him, in which I was terribly shocked to see an advertisement for the body of "Clarence Whiting," supposed to have been killed in Saturday's battle before Richmond, with an exact description of his person.[127] Poor fellow. It seems but yesterday that I saw his bright handsome face. His mother's idol and the pride and hope of his large and already afflicted family. I cannot bear to think of the agony of grief his death will cause. His unusual intelligence, his piety, and his attractiveness both of manner and appearance make him conspicuous among the victims of this fearful desolating war. I have determined not to tell Uncle John till there can be no doubt of the truth of his death. I fear this news coming so soon after his hearing of Brother Richard's wound would be more than he could bear.

As each fresh shock comes I wonder if that will not be the last to us, and yet every one makes me realize more fully the danger to all, and I feel the impulse each hour stronger to go where I can hear constantly from Hal and can get to him at a moments warning. It would be an unspeakable comfort to me to go to Brother Richard, and I have by no means given it up, though every one advises me to wait till Edward returns, and then only to go if I am needed, but I cannot bear to wait. And yet if I go I can not tell what the consequences will be. Yet every day almost, my presence is absolutely required to protect the property. If I pretend to keep the farm, the only way to do so is positively and firmly to resist the foragers when they come, or the place would soon be stripped of everything that we could subsist on.

Yesterday a party of soldiers with a wagon came after my meat again. I met them at the door and saw directly that they were men from whom I must expect no good feeling. The wagon-master told me he wanted meat. I told him I had none to spare. He said I must show him what I had. I got the meat house key and led the way for him. When I opened the door I showed him where the Dutch had broken in, he asked if that was all I had. I told him no, that I had some in the garret. He wanted to know how much. I told him I did not know exactly, but no more than I wanted. He said he would go to the overseer and see if he had some. I told him the overseer had no more than he wanted for he was a poor man with a large family.[128] He said he must see him and so walked off. The men with him stayed in the yard waiting for him. They seemed disposed to talk, but I did not like their looks and so came in the house.

The wagon master, on going to Mr. Kidwell's, said he must see his meat. Mr. Kidwell opened the meat house and told them that there it was, they might take it if they chose, but that he should follow their army with his whole family if they did. They looked at all the children around the door, and thinking, I suppose, that they would be rather troublesome camp followers, decided not to take the meat. He came back to the house and ordered two of his men to search the garret and see how such meat I had there. I looked at them and seeing that a boy about seventeen years of age was the least ill looking of the party, I told him he might come in the house, but that I could not let any other of the men come in. He hesitated for a moment. I told him he need not be afraid, that there were no men in the house. He said Oh no, he was not afraid and afterwards in coming up the steps he said he hated very much to do it but was ordered and could not help himself. His youth, and his air of reluctance prevented my feeling the intense indignation I should otherwise have felt.

I piloted him up to the linen closet and showed him the shelves and the trap door, up and through which he would enter the garret. He showed no intention of making the attempt to mount, but said I could not have gotten meat up there. I assured him I had and insisted upon his going up to see, as I did not wish any other of the men to come in the house. He laughed a little and said I need not be afraid for that; I could not get any of them to go up that place. It had not occurred to me till then that he was actually afraid to trust himself up without his arms, which he could not have retained in climbing up the shelves. I could not help laughing heartily at the idea. He laughed too, and said he thought if I had gotten it up there I had earned it, and so down he went. I don't know what he told the wagon master, but they all went off with their wagon empty.

The papers which we saw today report General Ashby as killed in the last engagement in the Valley.[129] I do not believe it but still feel uneasy. Every day I find myself less and less cheerful. My anxiety for Hal is so great, and to feel that I cannot get to him makes it ten times worse. I hardly know what to do. I only know that should Hal be wounded and suffer for want of attention I should never forgive myself for not going to him in spite of every obstacle.

June 14th [Saturday].
This morning Mr. Weidmayer came over to tell me that Mr. Haley[130] had seen a man directly from Jackson's army who reported Brother Richard as wounded with a sabre slightly in the thigh. It gives us great comfort.

No light has yet been thrown on poor Clarence's fate, and there seems more and more probability of the truth of the report of General Ashby's death. We heard also today that Arthur Rogers[131] was among [those] killed at Richmond. I hope it is not so, but fear its truth very much, for bad new flies so rapidly and surely that it does not often require contradiction, while good news seems to gather its wings chiefly from our hopes, and is followed often by disappointment.

The "News Sheet" today gives an account of another battle on last Sunday in which Jackson was completely victorious over Shields'[132] advance guard. Mr. Bolling drove Miss Mary[133] and Anna and Sammy [to Oakley].[134] He has received two letters from Willie[135] and both his boys were safe after the two first battles in the Valley. He does not believe that there is any purpose to take every thing from this place as they are doing from Captain Fletcher's [to avoid confiscation by Union soldiers].

Sunday, June 15th.
This morning Mamma and Katey went to church. I stayed at home because I do not think it's safe to leave the place with no one to protect it should the Yankees come. Mamma and Kate brought back much news with them. Report gives us another great victory at Richmond, and it is certain this time that Jackson whipped Fremont[136] and Shields terribly on last Monday.[137]

Last night at twelve o'clock, G[eorge] C[arter] and R[ichard] G[rayson] arrived at the home of the former, bringing the news that yesterday again had Jackson severely beating his Yankee foes and was still pursuing them towards Winchester when they left. They say he has notified the women and children that they must leave Winchester as he intends shelling the Yankees out.

The boys do not believe that Ashby is killed. They say they saw him after Monday's fight. They saw Hal after Monday's fight, but of course could tell nothing of him after yesterday's.

In spite of the news of victory my heart is heavy as lead from apprehension of harm to him. I have never felt so anxious before. Brother Richard's wound and poor Clarence's death make me realize the danger so fully. I fear I won't find rejoicing for victory in my heart if it costs harm to my husband, and yet I know I love our cause most devotedly. Arthur Rogers was not killed at Richmond, but escaped unhurt.

Sunday night.
This evening I walked out, and before I got back, was told the Yankees were coming. As usual, I hid money, silver, etc. but this time it was unnecessary. I soon saw that Mr. Weidmayer was with them and so was not alarmed. Mr. W. came to the house while the soldiers waited at the gate. He told us they were a Colonel Anisansel[138] and a Lieutenant, who were sent to see him by his Consul (the Colonel being also a Swiss), to offer him his protection. The Colonel, who has very recently joined Geary, was so shocked at what Mr. Weidmayer told him of our treatment that he determined to do what he could to put a stop to such proceedings. I told him unreservedly what treatment I had met with. He did not seem to understand it; said such things were so entirely against orders that he was sure Geary could know nothing of if. He gave me a safe guard for my place and property, and told me that if I wanted a pass to go to the Southern Army, he would ensure me one. They got up to leave just as supper was ready and as they had come with such kind intentions, and behaved-themselves so well, and had a long ride to take, I felt it incumbent upon me to offer them something to eat, but I did terribly dislike eating with them; however, they did me such good service, taking a load off of my mind about getting to Hal, that I ought not to begrudge them the little they ate as pay for it.[139]

They told me, but I do not fully credit it, that they had captured 800 of our men over the [Blue] Ridge. I do not think much of it, yet it makes me uneasy. I never felt so anxious for Hal as I have done today. Every now and then I find myself regarding my anxiety as a presentiment. Oh! If I could only hear from him. He has already escaped in four or five battles. God preserved him in them all.

These men report Ashby is certainly killed, but I did not think that the Colonel seemed to believe it fully, for he said several times as if inadvertently, "If he is killed." It is very late, but I do not feel like sleeping, so anxious am I for Hal.

June 16th [Monday].
Mr. Bolling came in for a few minutes this morning to tell us he had been to see Geary and was just from his camp, and though he was there by invitation from General Geary with a promise from him that his mules should be delivered to him, he was treated by these courtly gentlemen with every indignity, rudely refused his horses, and ordered out by the General's turning to the

officer of the day and telling him at his peril to tell no more "ever to come into his office to annoy him with their requests for horses." Mr. Bolling saw Colonel Anisansel. He was much pleased with his courtesy and told him that from the interest he expressed in us he thought I need fear no harm it was in the power of Colonel Anisansel to prevent.

I must say that this is some comfort to me, though I do not like being under any obligation to one of the enemy, but this man is a foreigner, and a gentleman, and I know my own dear husband would feel it a privilege under similar circumstances to protect in like manner the wife of this gentleman, so I am very thankful to him for his kindness, and try to forget that he is in the Yankee Army, especially as he told me plainly he wished he were out of the scrape as he was heartily tired of the whole affair.

I have been annoyed today by Mr. Kidwell's telling me that Sarah Carter had sent word that my servants must be moved from the white house at once, as the house has been kept vacant the whole spring and summer waiting for her to move into it, and the servants were only put there two days ago (taking a whole day to move them) in order to keep the Yankees from taking it. I have written to her that I cannot stop any plough to move them out again, especially as her brother-in-law's house, not a quarter of a mile off is vacant and will be preserved by her moving in it.

June 18th [Wednesday].
Brother's wedding day, and not one of his family present.[140] I hope he will be able before long to bring Annie to see us. Ma and Kate went to Middleburg yesterday to engage a man to take some wheat from me and exchange it in Alexandria for goods and groceries. To such shifts are we reduced.

They bring word that two men from our lines report Ashby as certainly dead, and say that they saw him buried in Charlottesville, and that his grave was literally filled with flowers by the ladies of the place.[141] In contradiction to this, old Mr. Fletcher told me this morning that two men had come near here who had seen him well and hearty since he was [reported] killed by the Yankee papers. I cannot feel as if he were dead.

Last night quite late Uncle Henry[142] from Cousin Mary Welby Carter[143] brought a note saying she had heard my place had been stripped of every thing and that the Yankees were going today to her place to sack it. I was very glad to be able to relieve her fears by telling her how false the threat had been as far as I was concerned, and that I believed it would prove equally so in her case. I referred her to Colonel Anisansel, in case she had any trouble, as the most gentlemanly of the Yankee Army near us.

Again yesterday two of Colonel A's men were here fulfilling his promise to assure himself that I sustained no further injury. I feel much more serene since his visit.

Heavy cannonading was heard all yesterday in the direction of Winchester, and two Yankee deserters report Jackson in possession of the town.[144] I would give anything on earth I have to hear from Hal. Thank God I do not feel such a terrible weight of anxiety as I did on Sunday, having more faith today in God's mercy in hearing and answering prayer.

June 19th [Thursday].
Today's papers acknowledge a decided defeat [of the Union forces] by Jackson on last Saturday, for which I thank God, but Oh! How much more thankful I should be could I know that my dearest husband was safe.

General Ashby is certainly dead and General Robinson[145] is appointed in his place. Poor fellow. He will be sadly missed, not only by the army but by many loving warm friends. The lives of those two brothers, if written, would form a brilliant romance—each disappointed in the dearest object of his life, and each dying so nobly the very death of all others their brave spirits would have chosen had they been given their choice. At the head of their command and in the face of the foe, with only this difference, that with one his military career was very short, and he fell in an unsuccessful skirmish, while the other was the successful hero of scores of battles and fell at last at the very moment when his command had achieved a brilliant victory.

[Illegible] and I walked to Upperville this evening but could get no news.

June 20th [Friday].
This morning early Mr. Ayre came over to tell me that he had bought [for me] 30 pounds of sugar, a great accommodation, as I had not more than a pound, in the house. He also told me that Edward [Carr] had come back from our army, bringing intelligence of Brother Richard. I had intended going to Welbourne this evening, but Uncle Joshua being sick, also Uncle Dan, I had no one to go with me, not liking to take off Robert, the only man left about the house. However, it proved well I did not go, as Mr. Weidmayer arrived shortly after dinner bringing us a pocket full of papers and the much desired news of Brother R. He was very severely wounded in the thigh, the bone being shattered by the ball, but thank God, is now out of danger and doing well, though he will not be able to leave his bed for four weeks longer.

He was wounded as follows: In the retreat of Jackson's army they saw at a distance a squad of soldiers. Not knowing whether they were friends or foes, as is usual under the circumstances, Brother R. rode forward to find which side they belonged, expecting that an officer from the squad would advance to meet him. He was however disappointed in this for no one advanced. Still he called out, "Who are you?" They gave no answer save a repetition of the question to him. He answered, "Southern," and instantly the whole squad discharged every weapon, pistol and carbine at him. Only one ball struck him. Through the Mercy of God, his life was spared, but his severe wound gave him such pain that on reaching his company he had to be taken from his horse. Cousin Eliza and Cousin Robert Carter[146] are with him. He is now at James Hall's in Amherst County. Uncle John got a long letter from him in which he says he is well. If I could only hear that [Hal] had escaped unhurt in the last battle how happy I should be.

A Southern paper Mr. W[eidmayer] brought contains the most beautiful description of the battle of Port Republic. The hero of the day was General Taylor,[147] commanding the Louisiana Brigade. They charged upon and took a battery of eight[148] guns, thereby deciding the day in our favor. The guns were immediately presented to General Taylor and his men by General Jackson, the presentation being accompanied by a handsome compliment.

I saw tonight a letter from G[eorge]C[arter] to Kate urging upon her a decisive answer to the question he has asked so often. I do not know what she will do, as I do not think she is prepared either to give him up entirely or to accept him positively.

June 21st [Saturday].
This morning Mr. Bolling came over early, having called at Mr. Fletcher's on his way to inquire what news his son's letter brought, but Mr. Fletcher was [away] from home.[149] He told us he would send Sammy over at twelve o'clock to take Katey to Bollingbrook to meet the Stephensons. I was glad, very glad for her to go for her life here is dreary enough for a young girl. Shortly after Mr. Bolling left Uncle John came. It did me good to see him. He had cheered up since receiving good news of Brother Richard. Thank Heaven! He told me Hal was certainly well after Saturday's battle. Oh! Can I ever be thankful enough to a merciful God for thus preserving my darling amid so many dangers.

This evening Mr. Weidmayer came and with [him], to my surprise, Colonel Anisansel in citizen clothes, and unattended by any escort. He came to express unreservedly his horror of General Geary's proceedings, saying he felt constrained on Sunday by the presence of the Lieutenant who was but slightly known to him. He really seems a gentleman and a good man, and I think his sympathy for the South is so great that he does not enjoy fighting against us. Indeed he told me this evening plainly, that he did not think he would fight any more except to protect us. He cordially detests the whole system of plunder and oppression, and heartily wishes himself rid of the business. His purpose is evidently through kindness of heart to atone to us all as far as [it is] in his power by his position and [to offer] effectual protection for the future for what we have suffered in the past. Oh! If this war had only been carried on in this spirit by all, how much sooner might it have terminated, but unfortunately for one Colonel Anisansel you find one hundred Geary's.

Uncle John says Colonel Anisansel is the only gentleman he has seen in the Yankee Army. I can realize now more fully how forlornly unprotected we were, since I feel the intense relief occasioned by Colonel Anisansel's interference. I told him this evening (for I wished him distinctly to understand that it was not in his official character that I converse with him in my house) that while many persons in our neighborhood had been changed from Unionists to Secessionists by General Geary's treatment, I had been from the moment I saw Lincoln's war proclamation a Secessionist from the bottom of my heart, and that though I had to look terrible calamities, confiscation, poverty, want and death to the nearest and dearest I had in the face, I would not shrink from it could I only see our glorious cause advancing. He said he could sympathize with my enthusiasm, though his flowed in another direction, and finally left, assuring me again of protection, and offering any assistance in his power. How I wish Hal could know of this. It would prevent many hours of uneasiness to him.

June 22nd [Sunday].
This morning early Uncle Nathan and Cousin John Harrison[150] called at the door for a moment to tell me that on Tuesday last when we heard such distinct firing, Jackson had again severely whipped Fremont, almost annihilating his army. He said that Mr. Bitzer,[151] who had just come from the battle field, reports all the neighborhood people as well, another crowning mercy to me, for Hal's name is too familiar to him to be over looked if he was hurt.

I got a note from Katey in Upperville telling me that I must send for her this evening. The violent storm has prevented till now, when it is so late that I fear the carriage can hardly be gotten up in time, especially as Uncle Joshua instead of going after the horse himself, has sent those utterly trifling boys Richard and George, who are capering about the fields making scarcely an effort to accomplish what they were sent for. I am afraid Hal will be obliged to sell all four of these fourteen year old boys when he comes back, for they are the torment of the place.

Katey suggests that I put away some supper tonight, and Cousin John Harrison told me if I heard a knock tonight not to let a servant go to the door but to go myself, from which I infer that G... C... is coming.[152] How hard it seems that our friends should have to skulk about their own homes like criminals, and cannot even visit a friend except under cover of night and after taking every precaution to secure secrecy. Poor G, I wish I could hope he would be repaid for his risk and trouble by finding his suit successful after he gets here, but I think there is but small chance of it, for it seems to me that Katey can never let any lover approach within a certain distance. Surely if constancy and devotion should ever make a man succeed, it should in his case, for five years of a young man's life is a long time to devote hopelessly to one woman. I have heard however, that he says he had rather love her hopelessly than be loved by any other woman, though [she] may be the greatest beauty on the earth.

June 23rd [Monday].
Last night after the girls, Kate, Nannie and Josephine arrived I hurried supper so that Grandma and the children might get to bed and the servants be all out of the house in time for our expected visitors. The girls dressed themselves very nicely hoping that all four of the Confederates were to come.

I sent out for Mary to put Grandma to bed, and hear the children their prayers, so that every thing might be ready, but to our dismay, Grandma insisted that she would sit up an hour later in honor of the girls. It was in vain we tried to get her to bed, go she would not. I thought I would try reading prayers to see if strong habit would not make her retire as usual when we arose from our knees.

I had hardly commenced reading the psalm when I heard Oscar barking violently. Fearing a servant would go to the door, I stopped reading and went myself as soon as I heard a faint knock. There was no one but G[eorge]C[arter] who had stronger motives than the others for venturing out such a stormy night. As he came in Mary was standing on the stairway, and I hope, poor fellow, for his sake, that she will not prove as faithless as most of her race have shown themselves.

It was not long before we contrived to give Katey and G. the West Parlor to themselves and there they sat till I wondered what they could find to talk about so long. Ma got sleepy and went to bed. Josephine soon followed her, and Nannie and I were left to keep watch for propriety's sake in the library. In spite of our interest in the success of George's suit, our eyes got very heavy long before there was any flagging in their conversation, and three o'clock in the morning came before they moved. At last they walked out just as Nannie and I were settling ourselves for a nap which we prophesied would, from present appearances, last till morning. We did not think it safe for G. to stay till daylight, so off he started in the pitch dark to look for his horse, which he had left in the field, saying that he should come back and wait till daylight if it had strayed off. However, we soon heard the whistle which was the signal agreed on if it was where he tied it, so off he went.

Just now Mr. Kidwell came by the house to say that he had seen a troop of soldiers with fourteen wagons go down the Green Garden road, and feared my horses might be taken out of Loudoun, so he has gone to see about them.

June 24th [Tuesday]. Night.
Ben went down in Loudoun this morning on the Confederate horse to get me some cabbage plants, and had not come back when Mr. Kidwell left. Late this evening, I saw him walking to the house with an empty basket. I called to know where his horse was. "Gone, Yankees done take him. General Geary and all his men gone to Harpers Ferry, and they took the horse away from me."

It was good news to know Geary was gone, but the loss of the only sound horse on the place is an annoying accompanying circumstance.

June 26th [Thursday].
All day yesterday I was expecting to see Mr. Kidwell come home, but night came and still to my no little alarm, there was no sign of him.

In the evening the girls walked out and, meeting Mr. Ayre, w[ere] told by him that George Carter, Ben Carter[153] and a Mr. McArty[154] would be here after dark. They came back as quickly as possible to dress up nicely for the Confederates, gladly, poor things, of another excuse to put on pretty dresses and flowers in their hair. They had scarcely gone upstairs before Mr. Weidmayer came in to tell me that the fine Cleveland colt I had rescued once before from the Yankees, had been taken from the farm where I had put it for safety. I was exceedingly sorry, for the creature had grown so beautiful that it had become a favorite wish with me to preserve it for Hal, knowing the pleasure he would take in it. So Mr. Weidmayer and I planned a trip for today in search of it. Having discovered that Colonel Anisansel was still at Alex Grayson's farm,[155] we decided to start by light, I with a servant from here, to meet Mr. Weidmayer at the school house between Bellefield[156] and Welbourne and go from there to see the Colonel, hoping that some of his men had taken it, and knowing he would give it up.

When we told Mr. Weidmayer the boys were coming, he was very indignant, insisting that it was inconsiderate towards me, and trifling etc., in them, to be going about so. He would not stay to meet them.

About ten o'clock they came. Knowing that I had to rise very early the next day, I thought I would take a nap in the library while the young people sat in the west parlor, but soon the others came out, leaving Kate and George to themselves in the parlor, so my nap was a failure.

It was decided they were to stay till just before day, and then go to Mr. Ayres before light, so we brought down the Buffalo robe and some blankets and at one o'clock, left them to their short repose. I told the servants to wake me by light and have the horses, Cricket and old Martha, ready in time. I had hardly, it seemed to me, gotten to sleep, [before I] was awakened again to start for the camp. Every thing was ready and I in the saddle just as the sun rose, with Robert for an escort.

The morning was beautiful, the fresh breeze just strong enough to waken me completely and make me forget, in the enjoyment of the ride, the fact that I had slept only three hours out of the last twenty-four. I went to the school house hill and not seeing Mr. Weidmayer, went on to Welbourne, finding he had left there some time before. I decided that we had misunderstood each other as to the rendezvous, there being two school houses on the same road about a mile from each other. I rode forward very rapidly, not fancying having lost too much time, and not wishing to keep my kind friend waiting. It was as I thought, for on approaching the [other] school house, I saw him sitting on a stone. He had been there an hour. He was naturally somewhat irritated and rather discouraged from the enterprise by his long sitting in the cold morning air. He said he thought it would prove a wild goose chase. Trusting to the Colonel's kindness I differed from him in opinion and we decided to go on, and I tried by lively talk to divert him in a bright humor, taking at the same time very meekly the scolding he gave me for being so little practical as not to have noticed particularly where we should meet.

We rode on till we came to the Pickets, who told us Colonel Anisansel was at Newstead.[157] We rode on till we came upon a party of the encampment. An officer told us he was sick at Mr. Harrison's. We turned back and went at once to Windsor.[158] We met with a cordial reception from Cousin John and Mrs. Harrison,[159] and the Colonel soon came down. He looked badly and I hesitated at troubling him, but while I talked with a Captain Higgins,[160] Mr. Weidmayer told our errand to the Colonel. He told me, when he had thought some time about it, that he feared he could not do much to help me, though he had every inclination to do so. He said if my colt was in his command I should certainly have it, but he knew that the work horse must have been taken by Geary's men, in which case he would have no influence in recovering it. But he told me he had left a very fine work horse of his own at The Plains, which he begged me to accept. I could not consent to take it as a gift,[161] so he gave it to Mr. Weidmayer, telling him to leave it with me as long as I wanted it. As soon as we had finished breakfast we mounted our horses and accompanied by the Colonel and Captain Higgins, we went to the camp. I had quite a lively discussion on politics with the Captain, who rode up by my side. After a while, Mr. Weidmayer called me aside to tell me that Colonel Anisansel had just heard that Geary had issued an order to press all horses, so it would be useless to go further than his camp in search of mine. He also brought me a hint from the Colonel not to be too communicative to the captain, as he did not trust him fully.

As we approached the encampment, I was very struck with the picturesque effect of the white conical tents against the dark green background of the woods, while the large troops of Cavalry drawn up in regular array in front completed the picture.

"You see Mrs. Dulany, I received you with the honors of war," said the Colonel. The object was that I might see every horse in his command. I looked in vain for my colt. At last I saw a young colt that looked like mine. It was brought up for me to see, but I soon found I was mistaken. At last a soldier said that a stray colt had been turned in a field of Mrs. Carter's[162] by a soldier, so the Colonel proposed we should go to see it. I feel uneasy about taking them to the farm, fearing Mrs. Carter might lose her horses in consequence.

As an orderly accompanied the Colonel, Mrs. Carter received me very kindly and sent immediately for the colt.

While waiting, Colonel Anisansel paid Mrs. Carter for some bacon that one of his men had taken the day before. She showed him her pictures and was very kind.

When the colt came I was again disappointed. The Colonel seemed very sorry, and the orderly told us he had offered $100.00 reward to any of his soldiers who would recover it for me. When I went out to mount my horse, I found a beautiful new bridle on her. Robert said one of the soldiers had put it on. Mr. Weidmayer said it was from the Colonel. I hardly liked to take it, but he asked me not to wound his feelings by refusing him so small a favor. He had been so kind and had taken so much trouble for me that I felt I would not be excusable in refusing.

We parted in the Bellefield yard, shaking hands and with expressions of kindness; I thanked him for his kindness, telling him I was a Southern woman and would not forget. While riding to Mrs. Carter's, he showed me the likenesses of his wife and boy and made me describe Hal accurately to him, saying he never wanted to harm him even if they met on the field of battle. I was glad enough to start homewards from Bellefield, leaving Mr. Weidmayer to go to Welbourne and get Cousin Mittie to come over to dinner, while I came home through Upperville with Robert, to seek for news. I heard none, but met with Mr. Bolling and Uncle Nathan, who came home with me, but I was so tired that [I] don't remember one word they said except that Ashby's Cavalry was at Front Royal. When they left, I went up and, undressing, threw myself perfectly exhausted on the bed where I slept for two hours.

I was waked by Mary coming in to tell me that George Carter and Robert Grey[163] were here. I began to dress, but before I got through, Mr. Weidmayer and Cousin Mittie came and the dinner bell rang.

When I came down, I found that the boys were going off to the army directly, and would take a letter from me, so I wrote one very hurriedly, for they were waiting; the first time he has had one from me for many a day.

Geary will cross the river at Snickersville early tomorrow, as our houses are again our own, for how long we do not know.

This evening I heard that Geary has taken poor Mr. Kidwell a prisoner. I am afraid he is alarmed, but think he will be released when the army had crossed the river. And now to bed as fast as I can for I am almost worn out.

June 28th [Saturday].
This morning I walked towards the barn to see what the hands were doing. Simon and Ben were plowing, and all five of the boys in the lower garden chasing Maria's children over the corn instead of hoeing it as they were told. I gave each of them a separate task, telling them to come to me when they had

finished. I then set them to cleaning the road and raking up the grass Uncle Joshua and Robert had cut in the circle. About ten o'clock Henry Arthur[164] called to bring me the keys of the barn yard from poor Mr. Kidwell, that miserable Geary having released all his prisoners except him. I firmly believe he carried him with his army over the river only to annoy me.

Not hoping to see him shortly, I thought it necessary to start out this evening to engage harvest hands. I succeeded in getting all I shall want and what is more than all, a white man to take the management. As Henry Arthur came over also to offer me Cousin Robert Carter's horses for the reaper, I feel as if Providence had interposed, especially in my behalf.

Mr. Bolling was over yesterday and told us that the Federals had been severely repressed at Fort Darling and also at Charleston.[165] The paper today tells of a severe skirmish across the Chickahominy[166] in which they say they lost 200 men and that the enemy's (that is the Confederates) loss must be equal. Another victory for us, no doubt. Their notes of triumph would have been much louder had we been really defeated.

June 29th [Sunday].
This morning I looked out and saw a servant riding Hal's black horse towards the house. Henry Arthur had been so kind as to send down into Loudoun for it, and it [was] his man who brought it to me. I learned from him that my big mare and colt were also safe.

Mr. Gallaher[167] called to tell me that he was one of the men confined with Mr. Kidwell. He had seen Colonel Anisansel, who asked him to tell me no effort on his part should be wanting to obtain Mr. Kidwell's release. Mr. Gallaher thinks it probable that Mr. Kidwell followed them voluntarily, hoping thereby to recover my horses, both of which were in Geary's camp.

Uncle Nathan was here this morning, but brought no news.

July

July 1st [Tuesday].
Yesterday, I went down to Welbourne and stayed there while I sent Robert down into Loudoun to get the carriage mare and colt. I learned there that Mr. Kidwell had been sent on to Washington, upon what pretext it is impossible to imagine.

Maria is sick this morning, besides Uncle Reed, Uncle Dan, Rosetta, Patsy and Beck. Really a fine beginning for harvest. I am so sick myself from headache this morning that I am scarcely able to go about.

Cricket broke her bridle while I was at Welbourne and paced off home leaving me to get back as best I could. Fortunately, Dr. Gunnell met her in Clifton Lane and expecting to pick me out of some fence corner, brought her

Timeline of the War	
July 1	Fighting at Malvern Hill ends the Seven Days Campaign with Richmond no longer threatened by the enemy.
July 11	Maj. Gen. Henry W. "Old Brains" Halleck is appointed general in chief of the U.S. armies.
July 21	Jackson reaches Gordonsville, ready to oppose Union general John Pope's Army of Virginia while McClellan sits idle on the banks of the James River.

back to Welbourne as soon as possible, for which I am much obliged to him, as I had begun to despair of getting back at all that night. The doctor rode home [with me] to the [Oakley] gate. We met old Mr. Glasscock[168] near his house and I could but be struck with the kindness of his manner in speaking to us. I was gratified by Dr. Gunnell's telling me that he had been often struck with the respect and even affection with which all the men in this neighborhood spoke of us.

In spite of my headache this morning, I felt it necessary to get up and come down tho' I did not do so till breakfast was ready. The servants had all to be given their week's allowance of corn meal and flour, to be given their work, etc., etc., and then I had to see that every thing was ready for harvest.

[July 1st] Night.
I rode to Upperville this evening and got the paper. There was a brisk skirmish before Richmond in which the Sickles Brigade[169] was very badly cut up. Also a full account of the battle of James Island in which the Yankees are said to have lost 1113 men, and we 175.[170] The papers are filled with extracts from English papers expressing the utter abhorrence felt by all Europe at Butler's infamous proclamation with regards to the women of New Orleans.[171] There is also a beautiful and eloquent appeal from the daughters of New Orleans to the men of the whole South, calling upon them for help, and imploring them to burn their cities to the ground and plunge their dagger into the breast of every woman sooner than give over to their merciless foes. Surely the judgment of an outraged God will visit the wretch who deliberately gave over the women of a whole city to the outrages of the common soldiery.

July 3rd [Thursday].
I began harvest this morning under very disadvantageous circumstances, Maria, Rosetta, Wilmouth, Uncle Dan, Uncle Reed, besides Margaret, Patsey and Beck all sick. I fear my wheat will most of it fall before it can be cut. Dr.

Gunnell has just come, bringing a rumor that we have whipped McClellan at Richmond, so that he was obliged to fall back twenty-eight miles. If true, I shall not fret over the loss of one or two hundred bushels of wheat.

I sent Tolbert out to catch Cricket about two hours ago, as it is important I would go to Upperville on business. He has been racing and charging up and down the field ever since and the horse is no nearer caught than before, yet I have no one else to send. It will wind up in my walking after all. These are trying times, but they cannot last for ever, and I must remember how many have been left worse off than I. I heard a few days ago that Hal was safe. That is blessing enough for one week.

July 3rd. Night.
I rode up for the paper this evening and the first thing I saw in it was that the "ministers of two leading powers in Europe had notified that hostilities must immediately cease." Can it be true that the long expected intervention of France and England has come at last? If so, and if effectual, millions of hearts from Maine to New Orleans will pray a "Vive l'Empereur" and "God save the Queen" as fervently as ever uttered in Paris or London. The whole of the front sheet of the paper was taken up with the "Great Battle of Richmond," and what does it tell? Heart chilling tales of streams of blood and heaps of dead, of shrieks and groans, of mowing men down like heads of wheat, of onslaught and repulse, and after three days of fighting, from Thursday the 26th of June in the evening till eleven o'clock on Sunday the 29th, the battle still undecided, only McClellan has moved back his headquarters seven miles, and has removed from the White House all his stores and all the gunboats from the York and Pamunkey Rivers, from which, as well as from the accounts of the battle itself, [we can tell Lee has won a great victory, though the Northern papers] hide it as best they may.

We discover without much difficulty that the advantage is all on our side. Our forces were commanded by Lee, Beauregard, Jackson, Hill, Anderson,[172] Branch,[173] Longstreet, and others. The success enjoyed on each side immense, and the losses necessarily enormous. Oh! How my heart sickens at the thought, and could they weep at all, my eyes might shed drops of blood at the fearful record. Oh! That a merciful God would spare his people, while there are any left to bless His goodness.

I cannot tell even which of my friends were in the fight, much less which of them have fallen. I can only pray my Father in Heaven to spare those who are near and dear to me.

I have reason to hope that Hal is still in the Valley, but the uncertainty makes me miserable. Mr. Bolling starts for our lines tomorrow, taking Hal's horse to him. No news as yet of poor Mr. Kidwell.

July 4th [Friday].

Mr. Weidmayer came over this evening bringing Mary and Fanny and Johnny with him. The two girls [are] to stay with Jenny. He had seen today's paper, having gotten it from Union. The battle raged all day Monday and ended by McClellan's falling back seventeen miles. We captured all his heavy artillery, and so many prisoners that every little boy in Richmond was kept busy carrying off the arms taken from them. Rumor says the Confederates lost 25,000 and the Federals 70,000. I do not credit the rumors as any correct estimate is as yet impossible.[174]

General Bonham is in Washington and confesses that he does not know where his brigade is. He says it was sent off from him by Jackson, a most remarkable account for a General to give of his command.[175]

A rumor has come that Webb Carter is killed, but I do not believe it. We heard also this evening that Geary had re-crossed the river at Snickersville to again take possession of the railroad. I have heard heavy firing of cannon today and yesterday, and believe Geary is running from Ewell. I only wish he had been caught.

One of my servants, Mimi, behaved shamefully today, provoking me so that I was determined to have her whipped, which she found out. Indeed, I told her of my intentions, in consequence of which she watched her opportunity and ran off. I sincerely hope I have seen the last of her, for she has been a constant worry to me for years.

July 5th [Saturday].

This morning when I went before breakfast to the barn yard I saw by the surly manner of all the servants that something was the matter. Soon Mrs. Kidwell[176] came down and told me that Mimi had gone to each one with a long story of my having abused them and said I wished the Yankees had them all, mentioning them by name, and that I should never [want to] see the face of one of them again. Ben and Selina, she said, I had aroused especially. I told them what [Mimi] had said what was false, but am by no means sure they believed me.

Mrs. Kidwell went over this morning to a Mr. Blakeley's[177] to enquire for Mr. Kidwell. Mr. Blakeley was arrested with Mr. Kidwell. He said that Mr. Kidwell told General Geary when he was undergoing his examination, that my wheat was ready to cut and my corn suffering for attention. Geary said if that was so he should take him on, and the others were all released and he detained. It is a petty meanness, so low that I can hardly credit it of any one, though I have been told by Mr. Bolling and others that there was no doubt of the fact that he had an especial dislike of me. If he knew the opinion I have of him, it is probable his dislike would be anything but softened.

Bartlett Bolling brought Anna over this morning to stay with the other little girls, and a merry time they have had of it. Uncle John called today for a moment to tell me that he had heard from Hal through Mr. Stephenson and he was well three days ago and at Harrisonburg. This is the first definite intelligence of his whereabouts I have had for some time. Uncle John also heard that Brother Richard was still in bed, though mending surely.

For at least two hours this morning I heard heavy cannonading in the direction of Manassas. I can form no conjecture as [to] its cause, as I did not suppose we had any troops near there.

On account of yesterday being the fourth of July, we will have no paper tonight, but Katey has ridden to Upperville with Bartlett to enquire for news. Mamma is quite sick, so all the housekeeping and dining room cleaning falls to my lot, with Tolbert's assistance, and some help from Katey whenever she is not otherwise occupied. The women are still sick, only Mammy, Lucinda, Harriet and Aunt Louise being up to do all the farm and house work, where the usual number is twelve.

July 5th [continued].
Contrary to our expectation, a paper came this evening. There is not much news [other] than a repetition in several forms of yesterday's news, only that the summary states that after seven days of hard fighting General McClellan has fallen back seventeen miles, having saved out of his large army only 40,000 men and some of his guns. They acknowledge a loss of 20,000 men, and we may fairly double the number and yet fall below the mark. The Confederate loss they estimate at 30,000. I put it at half the number, for so the Yankees count. The paper also states as quoted from a Richmond "Dispatch" that Stonewall Jackson is dead. If this be so, the victory we have so certainly gained is a costly one, and not even the loss of seven Generals[178] (one killed and six put hors de combat) can compensate for it. I trust it is only a consolation story.

July 9th [Wednesday].
On Sunday the 6th, I went to Upperville expecting to hear Mr. Kinsolving preach, but he had gone to Richmond to try and have General Rogers exchanged,[179] and Tudor[180] gave us a sermon. The first news I heard when I got out of the carriage was that Richard Grayson was killed. I was truly sorry, for he was a fine young man and a darling with his two sisters. We heard also that McClellan was then in such a position that he had been ordered to surrender by our Generals, and having asked five days to consider, was given two hours.

On Monday, Kate and I went to Middleburg, Bartlett Bolling kindly taking us down in his Father's carriage. I there saw the Southern papers. They state our loss as enormous, but our victory almost complete, and at the same time give McClellan great credit for Generalship. The only names I recognized among the killed were Wood McDonald,[181] George Adie and Richard Grayson.[182] I learned from Uncle Ned that our Cousins, except St. Louis Tom [Turner] (who is my favorite) were not in the fight. The report of Jackson's being killed is, I am thankful to say, untrue. His loss added to Ashby's would have been hard to bear. General Griffith of Mississippi[183] was killed and also General Elsy [sic].[184]

Mrs. George Carter sent me a letter from George in which he sends me word that my dear husband was well on the 19th of June and between Staunton and Harrisonburg. I only wish I could know where and how he [is] in this oppressive weather. He was not in the Richmond fight. Now that the way is open, I should certainly go to see him if I knew where to go. I cannot help hoping to see him before long.

I was glad enough yesterday to see Mr. Kidwell coming by the house. He had been arrested without any charge, except suspicion that I had sent him to gain information to send to the Southern Army, and was released without any trial or acquittal.

My harvest progresses so slowly that I fear I shall lose most of my wheat before it can be cut.

Mr. Kidwell brings good news indeed, if it can be relied on. He states that a man named Jackson who rode home with him, having been released at the same time, told him that while he was in the office of the Provost Marshall in Winchester, a soldier came in and told the Provost that McClellan had surrendered with 60,000 men. I do not fully credit it. I copy here some verses written on Ashby's death. They show the love felt for him and express very truly the sorrow felt by the whole country for his loss.

A Dirge for Ashby

Heard ye that thrilling word?
Accent of dread!
Flash like thunder bolt
Bowing each head.
Crash through the battle drum.
Over the booming gun
Ashby our bravest one.
Ashby is dead.

Saw ye the Veterans,
Hearts that might have known
Never a quail of fear,
Never a groan,
Sob mid the fight they win,
Tears their stern eyes within?
Ashby our Paladin,
Ashby is gone.

Dash, dash the tear away,
Crush down the pain.
Dulce et ducus be
Fittest refrain.
Why should the dreary pall
Round him be flung at all?
Did not a hero fall
Gallantly slain?

Catch the last word of cheer
Dropped from his tongue.
Over the volley's din
Loud be it rung.
Follow me! Follow me!
Soldier! Oh could there be
Paean or dirge for thee
Loftier sung?
Bold as the "Lion Heart,"
Dauntless and brave,
Knightly as knightliest
Bayard could crave.
Sweet with all Sidney's grace
Tender as Hampden's face
Who! Who! Shall fill the space
Void by his grave?
'Tis not one broken heart,
Wild with dismay,
Crazed with the agony
Weeps o'er his clay.
Ah! From a thousand eyes
Flows the proud tears that rise,
Widowed Virginia lies,
Stricken today.
Yet charge as gallantly
Ye whom he led.
Jackson, the victor still
Stands at your head.
Heroes! Be battle done
Chevaliers every one
Nerved by the thought alone,
Ashby is dead.[185]

Not two years ago this brave and lamented hero, a modest unpretending young man visited us frequently, and won us by his gentle courtesy, to love him as a friend. He had not even had a military education, and it was not till later that the company was raised in which as Captain, he commenced his brief and brilliant military career. Who could then have foreseen that in two short years a nation would grieve at his death? Two years! Two centuries rather, so much have we lived and known and suffered in that little time.

July 14th [Monday].
There has been such perfect quiet since the week of battles that I have had nothing to write, and have only to say here that though each day saw a victory for us, they were dearly bought with the blood of thousands of our best and bravest.

On Saturday I started out alone to go to Wurnel's[186] [to make] purchases, but meeting Bartlett Bolling, he kindly escorted me there and back. I was very glad to have him with me for he is very entertaining and the road so lonely. I did not much like the idea of going alone.

I was sick all day yesterday and have been in bed all day today. Uncle John came over to see me and when he went home, sent me some ice, which is very grateful to my parched mouth. Anna Noland, Nannie Taylor and Fannie Powell are all here, and this evening Stewart and Anna Bolling rode over. I hope the young people will have a merry visit in spite of the war.

July 16th [Wednesday].
All day yesterday I was very sick, but towards night became better. In the night I heard Mamma calling at my door, and then her voice saying Hal had come. I was up in a minute and sure enough, there he was, looking thin and very brown as a soldier should, but well and hearty. He has resigned his Captaincy, having heard that Brother Richard is made Colonel[187] and wishing to get the Adjutancy of his Regiment. He has suffered so with his eyes that his Physician told him he might lose his sight entirely by continued exposure, so he thought it best to try a change.[188]

The girls are still here, also a Mr. Dowdell[189] who came with Hal. I was amused at May just now. She said to me in a low voice, "Mamma, my Pa is heaps good lookinger than Tom Dowdy, ain't he?"

July 18th [Friday].
Yesterday morning Uncle John came over to see Hal. He drove old Kate and brought Lewis[190] with him, and when he ordered his buggy, the child found some difficulty in collecting the reins, and in an instant the horse started, and running off, threw the child with such force against the ground [that] the blood gushed from his ear and nose and caused violent concussion of the

brain. He lay all day motionless, except every now and then when be roused to vomit blood violently. For hours I thought he must die, but this morning he has waked in his right mind and the doctor pronounced him out of danger, unless inflammation ensues.

Grandma received a very sweet letter from Annie, Brother's wife. It came through Alexandria.

July 21st [Monday].
This morning was the day appointed for a picnic for the girls. The Bollings and the Stephensons came over early. It looked so rainy that I hardly thought they would come, and tried to persuade them to stay here, but they seemed unwilling to give it up, and so went. I was sorry not to go with them, but Hal's fine horse was taken very sick and so Bartlett, who was to have ridden, was thrown out of a seat as he had given up his horse to put in my carriage, and I gave him my seat.

We have news of several victories, one West, the greatest of which is the capture of Curtis and his army,[191] and a victory at Murfreesborough,[192] where we captured 2,500 men. Rumors come thick of further fighting at Richmond and of stirs in the valley and it is said that our pickets are at Millwood and a portion of our army in Winchester.

July 24th [Thursday].
The girls all left yesterday. Last night's paper, though containing no news, was interesting from its general tone of despondency. It contained extracts from all the leading Northern papers, severely blaming their administration, both Civil and Military. McClellan's evacuation of the Peninsula was hinted at as by no means improbable, the volunteering for the new three hundred thousand men pronounced lamentably slow, and the National debt contracted during the war said to be so enormous that the energies of every baby in its cradle will be mortgaged to pay the interest off.

Morgan's "raids" as the Yankees call them, still continue. Cincinnati is in a great state of excitement, expecting to be taken by him any day and Newbury in Indiana is already in his possession, forming the first instance of aggressive war on our part. Nashville is threatened by the Confederates and the Union folks there in a delightful state of alarm. General Pope is to begin operations at once in the valley, and the Yankees expect great things from him. He has commenced his course by giving his men permission to plunder the inhabitants at pleasure, and his orders are that horses and men shall subsist upon the people.[193] A sweet time we shall have if he succeeds in bringing his men this far.

A servant reports the Yankees still in possession there. Hal complains very much of rheumatism since his return. His hard campaign tells on him.

July 27th [Sunday].

There was no news of importance in the paper last night, except that a Naval battle had been fought near Vicksburg in which the single Confederate ram Arkansas had succeeded in passing the whole Federal fleet after disabling several vessels and sinking one, and had arrived safely under the guns of Vicksburg.[194] The noble city still holds out against the whole attacking force, and will do so to the last, the sad fate of New Orleans having taught such a lesson that every Southern city has formed the resolution to surrender to our savage foe only in ashes.

General Pope sends a dispatch to the War Department headed "A Brilliant Cavalry Expedition," and winds up by saying that he does not know the name of the fortunate Commanding Officer. This thoughtless acknowledgement of the brave Dispatcher makes a big hole in the mill stone through which we can all see.

Yesterday morning a man came to lay claim to the horse given me by Colonel Anisansel. He says it was stolen from his father-in-law, and that the Colonel refused to deliver it up unless he would take the oath of allegiance to the Lincoln Government. It is really astonishing that not one honest man can be found in that disgraceful army. I believed in Colonel Anisansel. He seemed so much better than others, but here he is proven in a deception, for he told me he had paid for this horse with his own money.

July 31st [Thursday].

On Monday Hal wrote me from Upperville that he had heard Means'[195] men were coming to this neighborhood to administer the oath [of allegiance to the Union] to all the citizens, and that as G[eorge] Ayre was going across the lines, he would go with him. I accordingly prepared all his clothes, but when he came home, he had hurt his foot so badly that he could not go till this morning, when he left me for an indefinite time, his return depending entirely upon the course of events.

Pope's iniquitous proclamation enforcing the oath upon all male inhabitants and empowering his soldiers to punish suspected communicants with the Confederates with death, without trial, make it impossible for any man to remain in this country with honor and safety both, should the country be occupied as before by Federals. In that case, of course he cannot come home, still the doctor says he is entirely unfit for service and I should be miserable if he were again in the army, but do not know that it is any worse than his wandering about without means sufficient, or occupation. I am more anxious for him now than I have ever been and must continue so, as I cannot hear from him. Still I hope and pray that a kind Heavenly Father who has watched over and protected him this far will still guide him to do what is wisest and best.

All the men are in great trouble. All resolved not to take the oath, yet all naturally anxious and troubled at the prospect of having to start off at a moment's warning, leaving families to fare as best they can, many with no earthly provision to take with them, not knowing where they are to go. If our men will only be firm and united in their refusal to take the oath, the very severity of the order will defeat its object, as it would be impossible to banish or punish with death or imprisonment a whole community.

Mr. Bolling returned on Monday and came over early this morning to see Hal before he left. He brings very encouraging accounts from Richmond and gave us an amusing account of General Hatch's skirmish in Mr. Leigh's[196] place, in which a body of one hundred and fifty Cavalry under General Hatch[197] was completely routed and driven across the Rapidan by a party of forty Confederates. The most amusing part of the story is that General Hatch rode up to Mr. Leigh's door and ordered Miss Leigh to have one hundred and fifty pounds of bacon and bread in proportion cooked instantly for his men. She, thinking it safest to comply, gave orders accordingly, but before the provisions were half ready, the expected supper eaters were in full retreat, and doubtless Miss Leigh's abundant preparations proved very apropos to our brave Yankee drivers when they returned weary from their chase.

My head aches tonight for which I was very sorry as I have to rise early to ride to Wurnel's with the ox cart to deliver some wheat. Our last two men, Simon and Ben, ran off on Sunday night. Simon having volunteered to tell his master a week ago that he would never leave him and Ben having started on the pretence of getting some medicine for his little baby who was very ill, and taking with him a pair of shoes and a pair of pants belonging to his master. Poor Selina, his wife, is much distressed, not only at Ben's going, but at his leaving without letting her know anything about it, and that too when their only child was not expected to live. I went to see her this evening and fear she will lose her pretty little yellow baby.

August

August 1st [Friday].
Today's paper contains much encouraging matter for us. Brilliant moves by Morgan, seven pieces against the North from English papers, and a notice from the West that commander Farragut[198] had sent a flag of truce to General Candom,[199] asking permission to pass the batteries at Vicksburg, and offering to evacuate the Mississippi and New Orleans. A skirmish is described at Malvern Hill in which the enemy attacking were repulsed. Our loss was one killed, six wounded, and that one killed was Julian Carter,[200] my bright handsome girlhood friend. It seems but yesterday I heard his merry laugh in this

> **Timeline of the War**
>
> | | |
> |---|---|
> | August 3 | Halleck orders McClellan to move the Army of the Potomac from Harrison's Landing to Alexandria to reinforce Pope's Army of Virginia. |
> | August 5 | Gen. John C. Breckenridge attacks Baton Rouge, Louisiana. Capt. Alexander Todd, Lincoln's brother-in-law, is killed fighting for the Confederacy. |
> | August 9 | Jackson narrowly defeats Pope's army at Cedar Mountain. |
> | August 26 | Jackson seizes Pope's supply depot at Manassas Junction and destroys what he cannot carry away. |
> | August 28 | Jackson initiates the fighting at Second Manassas when he attacks Pope's troops marching past Groveton; fighting continues until August 30, when Pope retreats to the defenses of Washington. |

very room, and the sound of his voice yet rings in my ear saying, "Cousin, I love my country, and I know I am no coward and relish a good fight, but I am not ready for killing just yet."

August 2nd [Saturday].
I have been somewhat perplexed within the last few days by finding out unmistakably that old Maria and Mary have planned going off with their children to the Yankees. I think they are taking advantage of Hal's absence. As to their loss I care very little, but for the sake of example I should like to capture them in the act and so offered today $500.00 to any one who would undertake to carry them South for me, but no one could be found with energy enough to undertake it.[201] I have taken what precautions I could to prevent their taking much plunder.

The news in tonight's paper, if true, is most gratifying, viz., that a fleet of ten iron clad gunboats made in England for the Confederacy, have arrived at Mobile and opened the blockade. If so, we can get supplies of ammunition etc., without further difficulty.

August 5th [Tuesday].
Today's paper has no confirmation of the report of the blockade's being opened at Mobile. I have had a message from Hal. He has gotten safely through to our lines. Mr. Weidmayer was here this morning. He called to tell me the Yankees, about sixty strong, were in Upperville and said that more were coming. I immediately sent Mr. Kidwell off with the best horses and the colts to a secure place in the mountain where Hal told me to hide them in case of another in-

vasion. My heart sinks within me when I look forward to having another Yankee visitation. I fear this set will leave but little behind them. There is one consolation I have now, very little [is] left for them to take. Thank Heaven Hal is beyond their reach. It is supposed they have come to administer the oath to the inhabitants. I only hope our men may have the firmness to resist to the death. Exile, confiscation, even death before perjury and disgrace.

August 8th [Friday].
We have found out the object of the Yankee visitation. A servant who came from Leesburg to bring Josephine Stephenson some money informed the Yankees on his return that her brothers were in Upperville, so they sent off this party to capture them. An express was sent to the boys to warn them, so they left Upperville the evening before the Yankees arrived, and their friends were congratulating themselves on their escape. The girls were told the Yankees were returning through the village and on looking out, poor Josephine saw the first thing her youngest brother Johnny, brought in a prisoner by them. He had been captured at the river, some traitor having betrayed where he would wait for his comrades.

The papers today state that the Yankee fleet has ruined the siege of Vicksburg, acknowledging a disastrous failure. Glorious little town! She deserves a white place in history and will have it. For months she has withstood and baffled all the attempts of the mighty gunboats that took Columbus and Island Number 10, and has come off gloriously victorious at last.

The summary of news reports Richmond as evacuating on account of a pestilence, but I don't believe it.[202]

Washington is in considerable agitation, expecting the Confederate army to attack it. Since the tables have turned there is not even boasting in the Northern journals, so the depression must be complete.

A skirmish is mentioned in which General Robertson[203] is said to have been driven out of Orange Court House with a loss of twenty-three killed and forty-three wounded and prisoners. Many of my friends were with Robertson so I shall feel anxious till I hear from them. My daily anxiety is for Hal. The capture of young Stephenson shows plainly the impropriety of his staying at home, yet what he is to do without money and without employment I do not know.

August 9th [Saturday].
The paper last night boasted of a successful fight against the Confederates in which Jeff Thompson's men were routed with great slaughter.[204] We shall hear another version of the story before long. They report that our Guerillas have captured seventy-five of their men, and all their camp equipment, ammunition, etc. in North Alabama. To counterbalance this, they claim to have retaken

Malvern Hills near Richmond, and report that the Confederates in large force are advancing upon McClellan. God send us the victory if it be true.

No news as yet of Hal. Mr. Throckmorton[205] came yesterday for the Anisansel horse. He told me many hard tales of my Yankee protector. It seems he made a decided exception to his general side in my favor.

August 10th [Sunday].
I have been looking over my journal today and I find many errors, some gross misstatements as to facts. It would be impossible to correct them all, so I will let all stand. The truth will be shown by history, and my statements that conflict with the truth will serve to show how in these times of trouble we are imposed upon by intentional and unintentional misrepresentation. I am also struck with the great change these times have effected in my own character and feelings. Familiarity with hardships and annoyances and difficulties of every kind have accustomed me to thinking with less distress of the deprivations of the same kind endured by our soldiers and a constant repetition of descriptions of death and suffering have hardened me, and I hear now of acres of dead and cities full of wounded with less sensibility than was at first occasioned by hearing of the loss of half a dozen men in skirmish. As blow after blow falls and our hearts are in a measure seared by the constant touch of the fire, we grow graver and older and take a great shock more quietly than we would a year ago have taken a trifling annoyance.

Pope is driving peaceable men before him in his progress by his odious test oath. We do not know how soon he may be here, and there is not a man of any respectability who will remain to take the oath. We will then be given up entirely to Yankees and negroes. I am looking anxiously in every paper to see that Pope's haughty spirit has had its fill in the shape of a whipping from Jackson. This is our only hope.

My poor husband! I am utterly at a loss to conjecture what he will do and long, yes really long, for a time when wars may cease to put asunder what God has joined together. That the duty of man and wife should actually lead them into such entirely separate paths cannot be in accordance with God's will.

August 11th [Monday].
Tonight's paper gives rather a different version of the fight at Orange Court House. The Yankees now acknowledge that they lost a good many men and were pursued by the Confederates for some distance, still these victory makers claim a decided advantage, and call it a brilliant affair.

All west Tennessee is reported as entirely over run by Confederates, and the Yankee Army fear that their communication with the North will be cut off.

Mr. Weidmayer brought Mary over today and I persuaded him to leave her with us. Stewart Bolling brought my sheep over this evening, his father having most kindly taken care of them for me as long as there was any danger to them from the Yankees.

I heard from Hal today that he was well and in Richmond. George Carter sent Katey some Southern papers, but there is not much in them.

August 13th [Wednesday]
Yesterday morning Mamma and Katey went to Middleburg. They had scarcely left before Mr. Kidwell handed me the paper containing an account of a bloody battle near Culpeper Court House at Cedar Mountain, by Federals under Pope, Banks, and Geary and others, and the Confederates, all under Ewell and Jackson.[206] From their own accounts (all we have seen) we have whipped them badly. They acknowledge having been completely surprised, having thought we had 15,000 when we had 50,000 (so they say). They tell of a panic and rapid retreat. They give a list of officers killed and wounded, long enough to discourage the most sanguine, and say they have lost 3,000 others. To counterbalance this, they tell of our General Winder's death,[207] say they recovered the ground and that [Jackson] had requested permission to bury our dead. Our arch enemy Geary has lost an arm, by far too good a fate for such a fiend incarnate.[208]

I feel deep anxiety to see the next paper. The battle was only considered suspended for a time while each side rested, and before this, one or the other has probably been completely routed. All our friends were engaged. Brother Richard's company was there.

Mr. Bolling drove me to Welbourne to see Uncle John (who is sick) this morning. He is miserable about Willie.[209] Poor Tom of St. Louis on Ewell's staff was, of course, there. I don't know why but I have had always a sad presentiment about him. It may be because I am particularly fond of him, and consequently more anxious. I am sure though that he would rather seek than shun posts of danger. I thank God Hal was at Charlottesville.

On several occasions in the West the Guerrillas have surprised, captured or routed squads of Federals and have taken some town of minor importance and very many stores.

Mamma and Katey heard in Middleburg that the Yankees were completely routed, and Pope with four thousand men captured, but as it is only a rumor, we cannot take much comfort. One circumstance favoring the truth of the report is that the cannonading that was heard for two days after the fight is approaching us nearer and nearer, which looks as if the Yankees were being pursued, as our troops would not retreat in this direction.

August 15th [Friday].
Today we learn from the papers that the battle has not been renewed since Saturday, both armies keeping quiet. The Yankees in some instances acknowledging a severe defeat and in others claiming actually to have routed the

Confederates, but the editorials clearly indicate that we need not feel any uneasiness as to the actual result. No further mention is made of General Winder's death.

Our forces in Missouri have taken possession of Independence, Missouri, on the Mississippi [River north] of Baton Rouge, and in East Tennessee, they claim to have captured after a severe defeat General Morgan (the Yankee) and his command of 5,000 men.[210] This, I fear, needs confirmation to be fully credited. Surely our star is in the ascendant.

As yet we have heard no Southern account of the battle in the attack upon Baton Rouge. After the attack upon Baton Rouge, the ram Arkansas became entangled among some Federal gunboats and her machinery being out of order, she was blown up, her crew and Captain escaping.[211]

General Pope's proclamation has drawn a counter proclamation from [President] Davis holding all officers of his command that may fall into our hands as personally responsible for the lives of any men who may suffer by Pope's order Number 11.[212] The officers captured at Culpeper will help us in this no little. No further news from Hal.

August 19th [Tuesday].
Yesterday morning Uncle Ned and Janey[213] came up to take our poor old Grandmother to Kinloch. She had been miserable for a month because she could not get there, and when the time came for her to go, she was bitterly opposed to leaving us, and I was sorry to see her go, for I am afraid it will be impossible for Aunt Sarah[214] with all she has to do to pay her the constant attention she has been accustomed to from Mamma.

Mr. Bolling brought his carriage to take me to Middleburg this morning. We started, but before we got near there, met several persons coming back who told us that the merchant whose goods we were going to buy had not been able to come out of Alexandria, so we turned back. Before starting I walked to Maria's to tell her that I had hired her to Mr. Yerby. She was violently opposed to being hired out and was rather disrespectful in manner.

This evening I took the children and followed Uncle Dan with the body of Beck's baby to the grave yard, where I read the funeral service over the little grave, not liking that the child should not have Christian burial. Afterwards I went to the cabin to see poor Margaret whose days I fear are fast drawing to a close. On returning to the house I met two nice looking men, who were going on horseback towards Mr. Bolling's. Ma told me when I got to the house that she had talked with them and learned that they were Messrs Bruin and Jennings from Alexandria trying to escape from the Yankees. They say Jackson has whipped the Yankees again most severely.[215] Tomorrow's paper will probably mention it. However, we have less chance than ever of learning the truth, for the "News Sheet" (the only paper that dared tell the truth) has been suppressed and we must depend upon "The [Baltimore] Sun" for information.

Uncle Joshua has come back bringing word that Aunt Bena is returning home.

August 20th [Wednesday].
This morning I got up very early, having had a head ache all night and thinking an early ride would do me good, started to Upperville to get some medicine from the Doctor for Margaret. I took Rozier behind me on Cricket. Finding the Doctor still in bed I went to Doctor Williams[216] to pay him for pulling Mary's tooth, and then back to Doctor Gunnell's to wait till he came downstairs. He had just come down when Mr. Carr[217] put his head in the door and said in the most distracted manner, "Mrs. Dulany, Mrs. Dulany, the Yankees are coming, coming fast, you had better, better, you had better—"'I had better secure my horse and will thank you to lead her into the back yard if you please sir"I said. This he kindly hastened to do, but the Doctor was before him and Cricket was hardly out of sight when the Yankees came racing and tearing through the village.

They pulled up just before the Doctor's, and soon every kitchen in town was full of them calling for breakfast, and the stables were broken into and provender taken to feed their horses. I trembled for Oakley, knowing they must have seen the gate. On the whole they behaved tolerably decently for Yankees, taking only horses and some goods from Gibson's[218] store. They took Cricket, but the Doctor recovered her but lost his own good horse. While I sat at the window with the blind closed, one opened the blind and stared at me, but when I turned my back, walked off. They only stayed in town to get breakfast, and then returned [by] the road [on which] they came. They were some Maryland Companies and Means' company,[219] one hundred and thirty-six in number, and were looking for droves of cattle they heard were in the neighborhood.

When I got home I found that they had not been here at all. Stewart Bolling escorted me home. The paper contained no news. The late battles of Cumberland Gap, Baton Rouge and Slaughter Mountain were all represented as Federal victories, and our having twenty-seven of his officers in close confinement has so cut General Pope's comb that he has published a proclamation so modifying his infamous order Number nine, that he might as well have cancelled it entirely. No [Union] soldier is now at liberty to enter a private house under the severest penalties.

August 24th [Sunday]. Morning.
Yesterday I heard that Rutty Eliason was at home and I mounted Cricket straightway to go to see him to enquire if had any news, message or letter from Hal. He had none, not having seen him since he left here.[220] I could not help feeling very much disappointed. He tells us he left Stuart's Cavalry at Warrenton and says we have at least one hundred thousand men along the Rapidan and Rappahannock Rivers, with almost all our great Generals in command,

Lee included. A great battle is anticipated. Just opposite from our forces across the river Pope's army composed of sixty thousand men [is] drawn up awaiting the arrival of McClellan's grand army from the Peninsula. This junction is the object of our Generals to prevent and of theirs to accomplish. On the event great issues hang. God help us, and confound our enemies!

Rutty says we lost in killed only one hundred and fifty at Cedar or Slaughter's mountain, and gained a decided victory.[221] I have been endeavoring to hire out some of the women, but the number of children with them seems an insuperable objection.

August 24th. Noon.
I cannot doubt but that the great battle has commenced. Since ten o'clock there has been one incessant roar of Artillery in the direction of the hostile armies. Each instant as I write a solemn boom of cannon falls on my ears, and my heart sickens at the thought that for every such sound I hear come, it may be many of those fighting for our homes and liberties are stricken down by the awful cannon. I have many friends and acquaintances there, and my mind's eye sees them killed and mangled and dying, and we can know nothing and hear nothing but this distant roar which makes me shudder to my heart's core. Oh! God of battles and hope of the oppressed! Deliver us this day from the hands of our enemies! Put wisdom in the heads of our Generals, courage in the hearts of our soldiers, and strength in their hands, and turn to confusion the counsel of our enemies and achieve for us this day such a victory as that the whole world may ring with it and that the very Heavens may resound with the shouts of thanksgiving that will go up from one end to the other of this beautiful Southern land that Thou hast given us; and to Thy great name, Oh God, will we render thanks and praise and glory forever and ever. Amen.

August 24th. Afternoon
The firing slackened after one o'clock and had ceased altogether by three, and now we shall have, most probably, days to wait to hear the issue, and then it will come to us so misrepresented through the Northern papers that it may be weeks before we hear the exact truth, and this fighting cannot be more than twenty-five or thirty miles off. I think if I were a man in a whole community, and one so intensely interested, [the community] should not remain long in ignorance of what has occurred, but it will never enter the head of any one of these stay-at-home gentlemen to get on his horse and ride in the direction of the firing.

August 24th. At night.
I was mistaken in supposing the firing had ceased. A strong north wind prevented our hearing it. As soon as the wind lulled, we heard it again, constantly

till after the sun went down. At times it seemed more distant, but that may have been the difference in the size of the guns.

August 26th [Tuesday].
Nothing certain has been heard from the firing, though various rumors are afloat, the most reliable seems to be that it was an artillery fight between the two armies across the river.[222]

A few moments after I got up this morning, I heard Uncle Nathan's voice calling me in the yard, and saying he was in a great hurry. I threw a shawl around me and went to the window. He was so excited that his voice had an unnatural sound as he told me that Jackson with forty thousand men was at Salem, and on route for Manassas, it was supposed. Our own dear General, our own beloved army within ten miles of us once more. I could well sympathize with his excitement and had any one been here to go with me, I think I would have ridden all day to cheer my eyes with the blessed sight. He had sent word to the people around to send all the provisions they could, as he was making a forced march and carried nothing with him, so I immediately sent word to Mr. Kidwell to get the spring wagon and my two old mares (all the Yankees left me) and soon he was under way with corn, hams, tomatoes and a barrel of flour, as much as the wagon would hold.

It seems that while Lee was amusing the Yankees with a feint of crossing the river in one place, Jackson and his army were actually crossing much higher up, and here they are in the enemy's rear while they suppose him before them across the river baffled and disappointed. Many conjectures are afloat as to the result of the move, but I will wait for facts, and paper is too scarce in these days to conjecture with pen and ink, but we wonder all the day what we shall hear next and have high hope of Glorious old "Stone Wall." I expect Mr. Kidwell back from The Plains, where we thought he would arrive just in time to meet the whole army.

August 29th [Friday].
I hardly know where to begin my story this morning. I have so much to tell, and yet of this new and great move of our army, know really nothing except the actual fact.[223]

Mr. Kidwell came back very late at night from The Plains. I did not see him till the next day when he came in bringing me to my no little mortification, money for the provisions I had sent to the army [as a gift]. He got to The Plains too late to see the main body of the army, which by that time was far on its way to the Junction. Shortly after he left the house Mr. Bolling came with Cousin Addison Carter,[224] Jenny Harrison, Stewart and Anna. Mr. Bolling had been to The Plains, had seen all our boys, Tom, Willie, Bev,[225] and all were well. Every one [was] in jubilation at the move, expecting great things. It is evidently some grand simultaneous move in which every division of our immense army has its part to play. Thus far it is completely successful. The passage of the river having been accomplished and Jackson actually at the Junction before the enemy missed him from the opposite side of the Rappahannock. At the Junction our troops captured eight hundred prisoners and forty car loads of commissary stores. Jackson sent for instant reinforcements and Longstreet with sixty thousand men has been sent. Today we heard he had had another engagement in which he captured three thousand more prisoners.

A note from Cousin Mittie today tells that General Ewell has been wounded[226] and also one of our Turner cousins, she does not say which.

Clarence Whiting is at Welbourne. Yesterday we went to Middleburg and just before entering the town caught up with a long train of our army wagons going to Jackson. Our poor soldiers looked so dirty and tired I longed for something to give them, and thought with regret of the milk, eggs etc., at home that they would have enjoyed so much. They were received with the greatest enthusiasm by the ladies of the town. Plates of provisions were handed from every house, and every demonstration of welcome shown them.

At Cousin Cat's we heard the sad news of Charley Powell's[227] and Cousin Randy Mason's[228] death. Charley Powell I did not know, but can feel sincerely for his parents, whose only son he was, but Cousin Randy was one of the best loved friends of my girlhood, and it is with a feeling of keen regret that I think I shall never see him again.

This evening I heard the clank of a sword on the porch, and knew instantly a soldier had come. It was Walker Armistead.[229] Cousin Lewis' Brigade is at Salem. He told us of a little skirmish at Thoroughfare [Gap] in which Longstreet had driven off the Yankees. Hal, he tells me, is in Halifax County on a visit to Dr. Carrington.[230] I am very much afraid he will miss this chance of coming home. Not-with-standing the buoyancy of our soldiers, I can not help feeling very anxious for our army. They say we have the whole Yankee army in a pen from which there is no retreat, but theirs is an immense army, and desperate circumstances sometimes make cowards fight like brave men. I am a little afraid lest we should have caught a tartar. The suspense is almost intolerable, and our means of information is so scanty, that my patience is very much tried, but I must hope and trust and pray.

August 30th [Saturday].
This morning after attending to my household duties and teaching the children, I mounted Cricket and with Rozier behind went to Upperville to learn the news. There I heard that General Ewell had lost his leg, for which all seem sincerely sorry for he is a gallant officer. I feel particularly sorry for he was so kind a friend to St. Louis Tom that I shall feel greater uneasiness about him now than ever.[231]

Bev. Turner has been severely wounded. Many wounded soldiers are being brought to Middleburg, and it is said some will come to Upperville, but I fear it is too far to bring them. Dr. Williams[232] sent to me for aid in sending them a wagon load of provisions tomorrow. I only wish I lived near enough to the hospitals to assist in nursing.

Dear old fellow Walker Armistead is with us. It looks like good old times to see him sitting in our circle once more. His health does not admit of his being in the service now.

I saw Brother Richard in Upperville this morning.

September

September 1st [Monday].
Yesterday having heard that a great battle was fought the evening before near Manassas in spite of its being Sunday and raining a little,[233] I mounted Cricket and with Uncle Joshua as an escort, started for Middleburg thinking I could gain information and wishing to tell Kate who is there to look out for people going to the battlefield, so we might hear from our boys as soon as possible in case of their being wounded.[234] I met a good many of our soldiers on the way, and had an adventure in the way of being thrown over Cricket's head in the dust from her falling with me. Fortunately I was not hurt.

Timeline of the War

September 1	Jackson and Pope clash in a heavy thunderstorm in the Battle of Ox Hill (Chantilly).
September 2	Pope is relieved of command and his army given to McClellan.
September 5	Lee begins his first invasion of the North by way of Leesburg.
September 14	Elements of the Army of Northern Virginia and the Army of the Potomac fight all day for control of the South Mountain gaps, with the outnumbered Confederates eventually retiring toward Sharpsburg.
September 15	Federal garrison in Harpers Ferry surrenders to Jackson, who then immediately marches to Lee's support at Sharpsburg.
September 17	In the bloodiest single day's fighting of the war, more than twenty thousand men are killed or wounded fighting along Antietam Creek.
	Braxton Bragg accepts the surrender of Munfordville, Kentucky.
September 19	Lee's army returns to Virginia.
September 22	Lincoln issues preliminary Emancipation Proclamation, freeing slaves in all rebellious territory as of January 1, 1863.

In Middleburg I saw Cousin Burr [Powell Noland] and Willie Wilson who had come home the day before. Everybody looked so happy that I could hardly believe it to be the same country it was two weeks ago. Brother Richard and Mr. Weidmayer were at Cousin Burr's. I rode up behind their carriage and found when I got home that Hal had come in my absence, so now my satisfaction is complete.

The news brought to Middleburg of Saturday evening's fight was that after a severe battle the Yankees were in full retreat, the loss being heavy on both sides.

September 3rd [Wednesday].
Yesterday morning Uncle Nathan came over to tell us of dear Wilson's[235] death. He was killed in the battle of Saturday. Poor fellow, it is very, very hard to bear. We had so hoped that those two would have been spared. God only knows who will be left when this fearful struggle is over. Mr. Bolling came over later in the day. Hal had started to the battle field to see about Willie's body, but Mr. Bolling having just come up from there told him that he was buried, the place marked and that Uncle Ned had gone down to remove him to Kinloch.[236] I hate to think of the grief of his parents when they learn that the bright, happy, hopeful boy who left there a year ago is to return to them no more. And he was such a fine fellow, so universally beloved and promising. Every such sacrifice only intensifies my detestation of the wicked Government that has caused all this needless suffering, and increases my love for the cause daily becoming more and more hallowed by the dearest and noblest blood of our land.

September 11th [Thursday].
Everything is so completely changed I can scarcely believe myself in the same land. Every day we see our soldiers. Where the Yankee army is I do not even know. Our own army is in Maryland. [It] is said, but has not been positively confirmed, that Baltimore invited General Lee to come in and take possession, the whole city being one bonfire. We hear also that Jackson is en route for Pennsylvania, that all the Government papers have been moved from Washington, Lincoln, Seward and Company following suit. We can learn nothing positive, but believe in the perfect success of General Lee's great move.

Willie Carrere and Willie Turner have been here, but left in a perfect glee to go home to Maryland. The two Toms and Walker Armistead are here now. We have a hospital full of wounded soldiers for whom we are very busy providing food and clothing, and in Middleburg there are fifteen hundred.

September 28th [Sunday].
I cannot write regularly now. The house is crowded from day to day with our soldiers. Most of them, I am sorry to say, stragglers from the army who

had better be at their posts. Some of them though (and those I am always delighted to see) weary marchers calling for a meal and night's lodging, and many of them prove to be nice gentlemen whose acquaintance it is a pleasure to have made.

Our own boys, the Turners, are here, some of them all the time. Last night even the floors were covered with mattresses. Much of importance is occurring every day. Our army after severe fighting in Maryland,[237] has re-crossed the river. In spite of our hopes of a general rise of the Marylanders to our assistance, we were forced by the stern reality to the conclusion that there is but little enthusiasm for our cause in the State.

In the battle of Sharpsburg both sides claim the victory, and with equal pretensions to it. I believe it to have been a drawn battle. In two other engagements in Maryland our troops were worsted, so that the invasion may safely be termed disastrous to our cause.[238]

The Yankees in quite large force made a raid through this neighborhood last week. They did no damage except paroling some of our wounded in Middleburg, and killing one man and wounding four in an engagement with the Sixth Cavalry above Upperville. A good many gentlemen were staying here who might all have been captured very easily, as the first intimation we had of their being within fifty miles of us was the reports of musketry from the skirmish.

Provisions are getting low with us. My sugar is all gone. We have no coffee, and the corn is alarmingly low in the granary.

The churches being all occupied as hospitals, we have no service. In Middleburg upwards of one hundred men have died; in Upperville, two. We again realize all the horrors of war when our own men suffer and die all around us. As long as we knew only of the enemy's suffering it did not trouble us so, but my heart bleeds to its very core for the poor fellows who are fighting for my home, dying away from friends among total strangers in hospitals, out in yards under trees with no comforts, all to be buried together with only an inscription on a plank to mark their separate graves.[239] Some talk of peace, but I can see no hope of it. One little advantage elates our enemies so that they forget all previous defeats and talk of the rebellion being crushed as fiercely as they did before the battle of Bull Run.

Not much was happening in the war during the month of October 1862, when Ida did not write in her journal. The Army of Northern Virginia spent the month in the Shenandoah Valley, while the Army of the Potomac rested in camp in Maryland. On October 9, Jeb Stuart took several hundred cavalrymen on his second ride around McClellan's army, crossing the Potomac near Clear Springs, Maryland, and returning to Virginia by way of White's Ford in Loudoun County. He brought with him more than a thousand horses taken from farms in Maryland and Pennsylvania. In the West Bragg's invasion of Kentucky ended at the Battle of Perryville on October 8.

Lincoln spent the month writing to McClellan urging him to attack Lee as soon as possible. McClellan finally crossed the river into Virginia on October 26, but it was too little, too late. As soon as the mid-term congressional elections were over, Lincoln replaced him as army commander.

A series of cavalry battles began in the Loudoun Valley on October 29 and continued through November 5 as the Confederate cavalry slowly withdrew through Loudoun and Fauquier counties to screen the southward movement of Lee's army in the Shenandoah Valley.

November

November 2nd [Sunday].
Nearly two months have passed since I last wrote. Battles have been lost and won, friends have come and gone, our country has been occupied by our troops generally, but occasional Yankee raids have produced temporary excitement in the neighborhood. On two occasions we have had the mortification to see our Cavalry retreat before an equal or superior force of the enemy. At Perryville[240] under Bragg we have been victorious and under Van Dorn defeated at Corinth.[241] For the last ten days there has been much excitement amongst us. First, Walker's[242] division of two Brigades, and then Hill's[243] whole division

Timeline of the War

November 1	The first Loudoun Valley Campaign continues with a fight between Union and Confederate cavalry at Philomont. Fighting continues at Bloomfield, Union, Aldie, and Upperville for the next four days.
November 2	Grant begins his Vicksburg Campaign, moving along the railroad from Memphis into Mississippi.
November 7	McClellan, now nearing Culpeper, is replaced by Maj. Gen. Ambrose Burnside as commander of the Army of the Potomac.
November 17	The first elements of the Union army reach Falmouth, across the Rappahannock from Fredericksburg, which is only lightly defended, but do not cross the river because their pontoon bridges have not arrived.
November 30	Jackson's corps, the last of Lee's army to arrive, reaches Fredericksburg, bringing Confederate strength in the city to eighty thousand men.

have been encamped about Upperville. Stuart's famous Cavalry have been in the neighborhood. The day before yesterday they sent in sixty prisoners captured near Union.[244] Yesterday Hal was present at an artillery skirmish near the same place.[245]

This morning we all went to church but were hardly seated before Hal came in to say that General Hill recommended the removal of women and children from the village as the enemy were advancing. We came rapidly home, meeting the infantry pickets and wagon train. Since then, we have been listening to the artillery. Just now it has ceased, but Hill's whole division is drawn up in line of battle on Vineyard Hill, and we expect a general engagement every moment, unless as was the case yesterday, the enemy falls back tonight to renew the attack tomorrow.

Not only have we had the horrors of war to contend with, but disease has been carrying off numbers in our midst. For weeks I have been alternately with Mamma, helping to nurse Uncle Nathan's little children. Of his six daughters, four are dead from diphtheria, and many other children are dying and dead in the neighborhood. Cecil Gray and Mr. Fletcher, our kind old friend, have died in the last week and the week before, Lizzie Powell and Katey Taylor both died.

As I sit in the balcony and write, the road seems alive with stragglers and Hal has just brought in a sick soldier who is put to bed in the little room. Four Cavalrymen are coming up to the door.

Eleven o'clock at night.
The house has been crowded with poor hungry, tired soldiers since I stopped writing before. General Stuart's Cavalry fell back slowly before the enemy, disputing every inch of the way, the enemy occupying the ground as he retreated. I sat on the balcony of my room and watched the battle which became very distinct from the flashes of the artillery as night came on. With the aid of a spy glass, we could see many movements of our men, the enemy being entirely concealed by the woods. The firing at one time was just over Welbourne, and one of our batteries was placed on Venus Hill.[246] It is a strange sight to us in our withered quiet country to hear the roar and see the flash of artillery, to watch the movements of an army and feed at night dozens of soldiers wearied with a hard day's fight.

November 4th [Tuesday].
Yesterday was a day of days. Just as we sat down to breakfast, a courier rode up to say the Yankees were advancing. Soon after breakfast the soldiers in the house began preparing to leave. With a sad heart we took leave of Brother Richard and Tom and all the rest. Then they went off to inquire the news. Soon Tom came riding back to say our army was falling back towards Piedmont and had no intention of giving battle to the enemy. Stuart's Cavalry continued to

dispute the way with the Yankees. We could see from the location of the batteries [as] they approached us each change of position. First they were [at] Fletchers, then in the woods below our house, and so on, the Yankees regularly occupying in advancing the position our men had left.

About eleven o'clock Hal rode up with Welby [Carter], Rutty [Eliason] and Captain Rogers.[247] I hastily prepared lunch for them and then we all together watched the skirmishing, our field being entirely covered with Videttes, and our pickets at Number Six;[248] then the Videttes going across the fields towards Upperville. The soldiers here and Hal with them rode at this time away. A few moments after they started, I saw them start off their horses in a gallop and looking to the right I saw our Videttes coming in more rapidly; then looking to the hills beyond Number Six, I saw them covered with Yankees and soon the field in front of our house was filled with their sharpshooters. They fired frequently at our retreating Videttes, the firing being occasionally returned, no one being struck on either side. In a few moments a Yankee rode before the others about fifty yards and took deliberate aim at our men and fired and missing them rode rapidly back.

The next thing we saw was a battery on Cousin Robert Carter's hill just in front of our house, which soon began to stay on our men. Soon there were no more Southerners in sight and the house was surrounded by Yankees. For about an hour, we watched the battery pouring out shells against our battery, which was planted in the vineyard. The shells from both batteries burst in full sight of us, frightening the servants nearly to death. I was forcibly reminded of their startled exclamation on the 19th of April in Baltimore[249]—"Fore God. Dey gwine t' shoot!"

After a while the Yankee battery, followed by a large body of Cavalry, moved across the field just in front of the house. In passing, a soldier rode in and dismounting rang at the bell. I went to the door, received a polite bow and was asked whose house it was. On answering I was asked if I had forgotten the soldier who returned me my filly last summer. I then recognized Major Chapman[250] who had really been very kind, but so sad did I feel at seeing our men go and the Yankees take possession that my reception was rather chilling. He seemed to feel it, for he stayed a very few moments only, saying that he had always promised himself the pleasure of calling on me if it was ever in his power. I had soon cause to regret not having taken advantage of the incident of obtaining a protection. Soon after he left the house, I looked out and saw Hal coming to the house between two soldiers. He came in and told me that he attempted to return home the Piedmont way, but when by Uncle Dan's the Yankees began firing at him very rapidly. He waved his handkerchief for a white flag, and rode up to them.

He was carried to Major Chapman who on finding out who he was, introduced himself and told Hal he must consider himself under arrest. Hal told them very well. He wanted to know if Hal was in the army. Hal told him no, but that he had been and had given them the devil while he was there. Hal gave his parole and was released. He soon became sick and lay down, and hardly had he fallen asleep before our troubles began.

I first saw them taking off the turkeys, then the bridles, then the chickens, and fearing every thing would go, I awakened Hal. He went out and succeeded in rescuing nine hens with their heads off. He contended with them till eleven o'clock and then, worn out, went to bed. When we awoke this morning there was not a turkey on the place, only two ducks, and about a dozen out of two hundred chickens. The first thing I saw was men in my yard chasing and throwing [rocks] at the chickens. Before many minutes four officers came up to see if they could get breakfast. Hal told them they could, but they must pay for it. I hated to touch their money, but knew it was best to do so, as we should have been annoyed to death if we gave to all that asked, and to refuse them entirely would prevent our obtaining the protection we needed from them.

While those men were in the house, I saw others with dogs chasing the sheep. I called one of the officers who instantly put a stop to it, so our sheep were saved that time, but five were killed the night before, also some hogs. Directly after breakfast, Hal went with the officers to see General Wilcox,[251] and was fortunate enough to obtain a guard since when we have lost nothing. About twelve o'clock two men came to take our horses, but the guard prevented it. Last night our guard was changed, and I rather think it was fortunate for us that it was so, for the first party kept up such a terrible grumbling that I am sure they would soon have connived at the plundering [rather] than preventing it, had they been sure of escaping detection.

November 5th [Wednesday].
Early this morning Harriet sent in word that the guard was going off. Hal went down to see the officer who told him that this division of the army was to move off this morning and the guard had to go with them but he thought we might get another guard by going to the General, as he was sure that some of the troops were to be left behind. Hal has gone to the camp to try to get some protection, if he cannot get [a] guard.

Yesterday evening Mrs. Loughborough came over to ask us what we were doing to protect ourselves. She was in the greatest distress, every sheep, every fowl of every kind, almost every hog, every horse and colt had been taken and then they were threatening to break into her meat house. Uncle Nathan had been here this morning and left here to go in pursuit of his horses and colts.

Later.
Hal could not succeed in getting another guard, consequently the depredations have recommenced. They are all over the place threatening to carry off

first one thing and then another. They have broken into the corn house and taken off as much corn as their horses could carry, and are insolent and overbearing in manner.

We are told that the army has moved off but the fields are alive with men and Vineyard Hill white with their tents. The Cavalrymen are going by the window now with horses laden with our hay. The three horses that are worth anything are locked up in the meat house and Mr. Kidwell is watching the others in his yard. Hal is guarding the hog pen while Katey and I keep alternate watch over the sheep. I fear that by tonight another division will be here primed for fresh plunder. It seems like a dream that only a few days ago our own men were here, and we [were] entirely safe from evil of every kind under their protection.

November 9th [Sunday].
Several days have passed since I wrote. Not one moment of time could be spared from contending with plunderers that have surrounded us day and night [reminding] me [more] of ravening wolves than anything else.

The night our guard was removed at least one hundred [men] were here all night, and when morning came, of our large flock of improved sheep only fifteen could be found, while from one end of the field to the other their skins were dotted about over the ground. They killed several hogs more, every shoat and took most of the cabbage out of the garden. We had to butcher four of the sheep that were found badly wounded. The night before last Hal came in bringing a guard. Another division, fortunately the rear guard, was in the neighborhood and he did not wait to feel the need of a guard before he obtained one. The night before he had brought home a Chaplain of the Regiment nearest us, thinking his presence would be some protection. He was a wordy old fellow named Van Dryen[252] who thought the loss of chickens, turkeys, sheep, etc. a small matter when thought of in connection with the great question of the integrity of the Union, and so doubtless it was to him as they were my chickens, etc., and not his, but I could but observe the spirit with which he described the trouble he had and the indignation he felt when some undiscerning thief treated his old grey mare with as little respect as if he had been the most obstinate rebel and left him in the same condition that most of our gentlemen are [in], namely afoot.

Hal learned from a Yankee officer yesterday that Stuart has re-crossed the mountain unexpectedly and come up in the rear of the Federals and cut off an entire wagon train. If true, Hurrah! for old Jeb.

I have been much struck with the difference in the servants' conduct during this invasion. Last spring they were all more or less disposed to take advantage of the times, but as far as I can see now, their indignation equals ours. This time these last invaders are no respecters of persons, and made way with their chickens and other little matters as unscrupulously as if they had been the original secessionists, and when you interfere with a darkey's "things," you touch him to the quick.

The old Chaplain called Rozier to him and said in the blandest manner, "Well, little boy, what do you think of the Yankees?" "I thinks they is nasty, stinking devils," quoth good master Rozier. "Ah, my boy," said the chaplain, "you will find when you go to school that among your playmates, there will be some boys who play truant and rob orchards and strawberry beds, etc. etc." "I dun know what you talking 'bout," was all the answer vouchsafed by Rozier, so the old man let him alone.

Evening.
Hal just came in from Welbourne, bringing the first intelligence from the family that we have had since the invasion. Both at Crednal and Welbourne they were stripped of everything.

A straggler spreads the report that Jackson having attacked Washington, McClellan is called there with his whole army. Of course we do not rely upon the information. Heavy firing has been heard today from Snickers Gap, which being in the rear of the enemy puzzles us.[253]

November 12th [Wednesday].
We do not get any very reliable intelligence from the army, both Confederate and Yankee soldiers tell us that a battle has been fought at Chester's Gap,[254] resulting in victory to us, but they give no particulars. Yesterday four Yankees delivered their arms up to Hal; he directed them to Captain Gibson who was at Paris, but kept their arms to make sure of them. This morning four Confederates came for the guns. We saw immense camp fires towards The Plains. We hear again that the Confederacy is recognized by England, France and Russia, but we do not know whether or not to believe it.

I find it impossible to get clothes for my servants. As to myself, I get on with little or nothing, but my great perplexity is to keep Hal covered. The children had a supply laid up. Shoes are a great difficulty. My feet are literally on the ground and I have not the least hope of getting another pair.

November 14th [Friday].
Yesterday evening, having heard that the Widow Fletcher[255] had sent into Loudoun for groceries, I determined to ride down to inquire what chance there was of my getting some and so was off the farm for the first time since the Yankees came in. The whole country is a vast common, not a rail fence is to be seen for miles around and the stone fences are so pulled down to permit the army to pass that they do not serve as enclosures. When we got to Mrs. Fletcher's we found that her wagon had been expected for some hours [but]

had not arrived, so we determined to wait to learn the result of her effort before we went.

Her son told us some of their Yankee experiences. He showed us where the shells had burst in the yard and struck the house, the plaster was broken in several places and a window broken. In the front of the house where I did not see, a shell entered the window of Mrs. Fletcher's chamber a few moments after she had left it and bursting in the room tore everything to pieces. A General made the house his headquarters and had with him a Miss Chaste,[256] who took off with her, when she left, the brushes and combs, bed linen and towels and Miss Fletcher's side saddle, etc., etc. They killed 60 hogs and 40 sheep, 8 head of cattle and most of her poultry.

Every one I met told the same sad story and many poor men in this neighborhood are left without a mouthful of meat for their families. Heavy firing was heard yesterday, but we have no chance of learning the issue!

November 16th [Sunday].
Yesterday evening Brother Richard sent his butler to me to send him some cold meat and bread. His whole regiment was in Upperville. Mrs. Loughborough was here and told me to send the boy to her house for some nice corned beef she had while I got ready what I had in the house. The boy mistook my order and went directly to camp from Mrs. Loughborough's, leaving what I had prepared behind him, so I had to make Robert take a bucket full of apples, walnuts, bread, meat and butter up to the headquarters after dark.

Hal returned from his foraging expedition into Loudoun last night with 16 pounds of coffee at 50 cts, 24 pounds of brown sugar at 20 cts and 25 pounds of white sugar at 31 cts, 1 pound of tea at $2.50 and a little soda tacks,[257] etc. The store-keeper, an old Quaker, promised to get him a large supply of all kinds of groceries in a few weeks. Hal has been away all day and I can't imagine what keeps him. Talcott Eliason was here today. He wished to purchase Hal's horses, especially his bay mare. I would greatly prefer Hal's taking her to some safe place as she is too fine an animal to sacrifice.

November 23rd [Sunday].
This is Sunday. I have a sore throat and cannot go to church. We have had no preaching for six weeks, every service being prevented or interrupted by Yankee movements.

We heard last night from Kinloch and Avenel. Dr. McIlhaney,[258] just from the neighborhood, gave us a full account of the outrages of the enemy. At Avenel they treated Aunt Jane[259] so outrageously that she became deranged from terror for half a day. They destroyed every thing they could. Shot 900 sheep, took poultry, hogs, etc., and on one occasion broke down the front door before breakfast and twelve of them went into old Mrs. Beverley's[260] room before she was dressed, broke open her wardrobe and trunks, taking what they wanted, and behaving in every way outrageously. At Kinloch they acted very much in the same way with the additional outrage of taking Uncle Ned and [his son] Tom prisoners, and after carrying them to the Thoroughfare, confining them there for some time in a dirty henhouse.[261]

Last summer some of Geary's men brutally murdered Mr. R. E. Scott. This fall the soldiers went to his place and literally left his family without one mouthful to eat. Every grain of corn and wheat, every pound of meat, everything that lived except the human beings, who they left to starve, was carried off to add to their abundance and when General Burnside[262] was applied to for something to keep her family from starving by Mrs. Scott, his only reply was that he could not help her, that if she suffered she must remember the South brought it on her. I do not ask for any retaliation on the part of man, but am contented to wait for the judgment of the Almighty, who in His own good time will show to the world and especially to those who trust Him, that the people who call upon His name shall be avenged upon their merciless destroyers.

December

December 1st [Monday].
I scarcely know why it is, but I can barely find time to write in my journal now. The days are so short, and when night comes we are all together in the Library, sewing, knitting, talking, playing chess etc., and from the failure of Hal's sight, and his consequently not being able to read at night, he goes to bed very early, and as he always likes me to go with him, I can rarely find a leisure hour to devote to writing.

Last Monday I went to Loudoun and engaged a good supply of groceries at enormous prices, but food is worth far more than money in these times. I should hardly like to have my choice between a barrel of sugar and a barrel of paper money, I am almost sure my love of sweet things would make me decide for the sugar.

On Thursday late at night, on coming out of the dining room, I saw shadows on the window panes around the front door. I told Hal of it, and on taking his gun and going out he found Cousin Robert and Eliza[263] Beverley. We were delighted to see them, to learn the truth of all the reports in circulation about their sufferings; there had been no exaggeration except that the henhouse episode in Uncle Ned's captivity was a mistake. That morning Hal had been fortunate enough to kill a wild turkey and as it was the only one we were likely to have we asked Uncle Nathan and Mr. Bolling over to help us eat it. The country is full of game, and Hal is a very good shot, so if we can only get ammunition I shall consider it an especial provision of Providence, fully equal

> ### Timeline of the War
>
> | | |
> |---|---|
> | December 4 | Winchester is reoccupied by Union troops. |
> | December 7 | Union general James G. Blunt defeats Confederate general T. C. Hindman at Prairie Grove, Arkansas. |
> | December 11–13 | Burnside suffers a disastrous defeat in the Battle of Fredericksburg, losing more than ten thousand men. |
> | December 20 | Grant's first Vicksburg campaign comes to an end when his supply base at Holly Spring, Mississippi, is destroyed by Confederate cavalry. |
> | December 31 | Bragg and Rosecrans meet in battle at Murfreesboro (Stone's River), Tennessee. |
> | | Jeb Stuart makes a momentous decision when he gives John Mosby permission to remain in Northern Virginia to conduct independent operations when the Confederate cavalry returns to their winter camp from a raid. |

to the supply of manna and quails given to the Israelites, by which reparation is made to us for the loss of all our domestic fowls.

We sent for Jenny[264] on Friday. She was detained by a Brigade of Yankees stopping her at the Cross Roads. Jenny's tears lie shallow, so when she found that her assertion that she was only a little girl going to see her mother had no effect, she began to cry, while Lena Noland, who was with her, tried to move the soldiers by earnest entreaties, accompanied by vehement complaints of cold to let them pass, but all in vain, for possessed with an idea that Jackson's men occupied the gap, they would consent to let no one go up the turnpike before them. At last after they had rested and fed their horses, the children were permitted to start, preceded by about eighty Cavalrymen. The children got home safely, but another party of travelers were not so fortunate. Miss Brown and Miss Edmonds were riding both on the same horse just above Upperville. The Yankees came up behind them. Two of our soldiers were some hundred yards before them on a hill. The Yankees fired and both ladies dropped from their horse, Miss Brown severely wounded, both bones of her leg being broken above the ankle, and Miss Edmonds severely bruised.[265]

The next day a man named Johnson, a good but timid Southerner, approached Upperville from Piedmont with a wagon and team, intending to go to Loudoun for groceries. At McKinster's Hill he met McKinster[266] who told him the Yankees occupied the village. On entering the town he was met by two of our soldiers who halted him. He called out "I am an Englishman and favor the North." The soldiers called to him to advance and deliver himself up with both hands raised. Instead of doing this, the man turned to his wagon and began filling his pockets. He was again ordered to surrender. He, thinking the soldiers were Yankees, still refused, and being taken for a Yankee Sutler[267] and supposed to be looking for his pistol, he was fired at and instantly killed. Such scenes are terrible and the insecurity of the lives of peaceable citizens not the least horrible feature of this fearful war.

George Carter returned on Friday from Fort McKinley[268] having been released some time ago. He came over yesterday and brought the children some tracts sent them by Aunt Margaret.[269] She did not write but sent me a message begging me not to write to her about the times. I am afraid she will be offended when she gets a letter I sent her last week by young Brown in which I gave a full account of all we had gone through, taking care, however, to say nothing which could lead to a suspicion that she sympathized with us in any but our private sufferings. I must write again explaining. George represents the tyranny in Baltimore as insupportable. He brought us a paper containing some interesting items from Europe, particularly the offered intervention of France in our affairs which being rejected by England raised conjecture as to whether France will interfere alone, or in conjunction with Russia or not at all. For my part I am heartily sick of this question of the long promised ever deferred intervention. Infamous Butler[270] has confiscated the entire property of whole districts in Louisiana.

December 28th [Sunday].
We are in the midst of all the disagreeables of Christmas week. The poor children have had a dry time of it; no toys, no bonbons, no parties, and as to me I have had but one idea for weeks, and that is finding homes for all the servants, so that none may be left to sit in idleness at home for the coming year, helping to consume the scanty supplies laid in for the family. All have found homes but Patsey, who is as hard to get rid of as a counterfeit shilling, and in fact not much more useful.

Great events are taking place every day. Our great victory at Fredericksburg,[271] the backward move of the Yankees towards Washington, successes in North Carolina[272] and Tennessee,[273] the dissolution of the Lincoln Cabinet,[274] Jeff Davis' severe but admirable order retaliatory upon Butler,[275] combined with our own relief from the presence of our barbarous foe, all combine to excite our hopes and cheer our spirits.

My little Mary and Fanny are staying with us, and Jenny too, Jenny looking prettier than I ever saw her, bidding fair to eclipse her older sisters before very long.

On January 1, 1863, Lincoln's Emancipation Proclamation took effect, changing the entire complexion of the war. Militarily, the winter, for the most part, passed quietly in the East, with cavalry raids and skirmishes providing most of the action. Burnside's sole attempt to renew combat along the Rappahannock line in January dissolved in a sea of mud as torrential rains made roads impassible. On January 25, Lincoln replaced Burnside with Maj. Gen. Joseph Hooker as army commander. Hooker spent the months of February, March, and April reorganizing and reequipping his army in preparation for the spring campaign. One of his most important changes is gathering cavalry regiments that had been assigned by companies to various infantry units into a unified Cavalry Corps that will operate as a true separate arm of the service.

In February the U.S. Congress passed the first Conscription Act to fill the depleted ranks of the army.

On March 8, Mosby became a nationally known figure when he led twenty-nine men into the Union encampment at Fairfax in the middle of the night and rode out with Brig. Gen. Edwin H. Stoughton and ninety men as prisoners without firing a shot. A little more than a week later, the federal cavalry launched their first offensive of the war when William Averill crossed the Rappahannock River at Kelly's Ford to attack the camp of Fitzhugh Lee's brigade. One of the Confederate dead was Maj. John Pelham, commander of Stuart's horse artillery.

In the West Grant successfully crossed the Mississippi River and began operations against Vicksburg by land, even as Hooker prepared the Army of the Potomac to take the offensive once again along the Rappahannock.

Ida's and Hal's elder daughter, May. Courtesy of the Mackall family.

Ida and Hal's younger daughter, Rebecca. Courtesy of the Mackall family.

From left to right: Richard Dulany's son, Henry; Ida and Hal's son, Henry Rozier Dulany; and Richard Whiting, photographed on a hunting trip in Montana in 1880. Courtesy of the Mackall family.

Maj. Gen. Christopher C. Augur, commander of the XXII Corps and the Department of Washington from 1863 until the end of the war. Library of Congress.

Brig. Gen. John White Geary commanded the Military District of the Upper Potomac in 1862. U.S. Army Military History Institute (USAMHI).

Charles Minnigerode and Maj. Gen. Fitzhugh Lee, on whose staff he served. Stevan F. Meserve's collection.

Walker K. Armistead, brother of Brig. Gen. Lewis Armistead, sketched by Marietta Minnigerode Andrews. Courtesy of the Mackall family.

Colonel John S. Mosby, whose men often stayed with the Dulanys, fought on their land, and, in at least one case, died in their parlor. Stevan Meserve collection.

Crednal, home of John Armistead Carter, Ida's "Uncle Armistead." Photograph by Stevan Meserve.

Modern view of Avenel, home of Robert Beverley and where Gen. Robert E. Lee spent the night before Second Manassas. Photograph by Stevan Meserve.

Ida's journal is on loan to the Virginia Historical Society in Richmond. Photograph by Anne Hughes.

1863

May

May 1st 1863 [Friday].
The winter has passed away, the dreariest, coldest, wettest, saddest winter followed by the latest spring within the memory of man. This first of May is here and not one tree is to be seen in leaf, the garden not even cleaned up. Every one dressed in winter clothes, curtains up and carpets down.[1] No corn in the ground and very little grass on the fields. At last we have a bright day, but from the middle of January till now, we have never had three days of continuous good weather. The unusual lateness of vegetation and farming operation causes serious uneasiness as to the coming crops and has caused our President to issue a beautiful proclamation urging upon the people of the whole South to turn all their energies to producing food, and to think more of supplying the army and people with provisions than of their individual gain, to give up cotton and tobacco, cultivate corn and wheat and raise livestock.

The two armies have been during the winter principally in status quo, but we hear at last that Hooker has crossed the Rappahannock and a bloody battle is anticipated almost immediately. In our own neighborhood we have no lack of excitement. General Fitz Lee[2] has been not far off, and Major Mosby with his one hundred and twenty-five Partisan Rangers occupies the country immediately around Upperville, the village itself being the rendezvous when a raid is in contemplation.[3] The men live upon the citizens, consequently there is scarcely a house where they are not quartered, and as a change of residence generally takes place after every raid, we have strangers every day or two. The impression in the army seems to be that we are protected from Yankees by them, but I fear it is just the reverse, as every raid Mosby has made has produced a retaliatory raid from the Yankees in which the citizens suffer severely, Mosby having always to get out of their way, as he is invariably out numbered. The broken bridge on the turnpike has protected us till this time but the people of Middleburg and the vicinity have suffered severely. Mr. Barnes,[4] a young Marylander and many others of the men stay here, Mr. Barnes all the time and the others coming and going. It is a comfort to have our own soldiers

> **Timeline of the War**
>
> | May 1–3 | The Battle of Chancellorsville takes place; Stonewall Jackson is mortally wounded. |
> |---|---|
> | May 14 | Grant's army takes Jackson, Mississippi, forcing Pemberton's Confederates back toward the fortifications of Vicksburg. |
> | May 18 | The Siege of Vicksburg begins. |

around us and a pleasure to administer to their wants, but the utter breaking up of all family privacy is very much to be lamented. I now fully realize the inconveniences of living in a roadside tavern.

I have been on a trip to Baltimore and succeeded in getting clothes for the family and the servants, but could get no groceries. I sent Henson[5] to Harpers Ferry and he succeeded in getting me some brown sugar, which we are drinking in tea, coffee having given out. The blockade is very strict now. Nothing can be gotten across the river and we begin seriously to feel the pinch of the times. For months we have had nothing but salt pork on the table, potatoes and rice being equally unobtainable, and hominy consequently our only vegetable, varied occasionally by fried mush and carrots. A dish of asparagus today was a real treat, but the family is so large that it will take days to collect enough for another dish. The prices in Richmond are almost fabulous, $75.00 a cord for wood, $18.00 for a small turkey, $3.00 per yard for cotton and calico, $30.00 a pair for ladies shoes and every thing else in proportion.

We hope and pray for peace, but see no signs of [it] and the horrors of this evil war increase upon us every day. Only last week Kinloch Tom left us bright with hope and enthusiasm and glowing with youth and health and manly beauty. The day he left he went on a scout for Mosby and was shot through the lungs by a party of Yankees in ambush. Fortunately he was near enough Kinloch to be carried there in a litter. The wound was pronounced mortal, but his end was hastened by the Yankees who came to the house and insisted in taking him off. He died a few moments after they left his room.[6]

Mosby left to go on another raid yesterday, his object being to burn some bridges. It is a very hazardous business and I feel anxious for the result.

While I was in Baltimore Katey engaged herself to George Carter, and will be married in October, but for this war her prospects for happiness would be very great, but these times of death and terror cast a gloom over every thing.

May 7th [Thursday].
A few days ago Major Mosby started on a raid towards Dranesville, his object being to surprise a Yankee camp. This he accomplished most successfully, capturing with his little band a whole regiment of cavalry. Just as the men were

remounting, some bringing off prisoners, and more collecting plunder, an alarm was given and Lo! a whole Brigade was immediately upon them. His prisoners were of necessity released, most of the plunder relinquished, and the whole party had to scamper for their lives, with loss in killed, wounded, and prisoners variously estimated at from seven to twenty.[7]

Yesterday was appointed as a rendezvous for the company in Upperville. Mr. Buchannon[8] and Mr. Barnes left us in the morning expecting a possible raid. About one o'clock Mr. Barnes rode hastily up saying he had heard that sixty Yankees were down the Union road and a party headed by young Turner of The Plains[9] had volunteered to go in pursuit of them. He soon armed himself and went off. Just before dinner Hal came in with Mr. Elzey. Robert Grey had borrowed Mr. Elzey's horse to join the scout. We were just done dinner when I saw Mr. Barnes ride rapidly up. I went to the door to meet him. On looking through the door window at him I thought he looked strangely, and opening the door involuntarily exclaimed "What is the matter?" "Upperville is full of Yankees," he said. "We ran right into them and Buchanan is shot."[10] Inexpressibly shocked, I made him give me the details, and learned that Mr. Buchanan, from the loss of blood, was left at Brown's,[11] unable to come farther. Instantly everything was confusion, horses had to be hurried off, meat concealed, silver, jewelry etc., secured, fowls put in the cellar, and every preparation made to escape the rapacity of our enemy, and all the time my mind's eye never for a moment lost sight of the poor fellow bleeding and suffering, who had left us a few hours before as well as any of the others. It rained such torrents that we could not send for him that evening, but Hal went over to see him and thence to Upperville to try and get a Doctor, but the place was alive with "Blue Devils" and no doctor could be found, so I had to be content with sending Robert to stay all night with him with minute directions as to dressing his wound. This morning the Yankees left and this evening Hal took six men with an ambulance litter and brought him home. He is badly wounded in the leg, but no bones broken. He bears it very well, but occasionally suffers a good deal.

Mr. Barnes, Mr. Grey[12] and Mr. Elzey[13] are still among the missing, but I expect they will return in the night tonight.

May 10th [Sunday].
After another-week's spell of cold rain, at last a bright, beautiful spring day, bringing out rapidly the poor, cramped, weary vegetation, pale with its long confinement and longing for encouragement to burst its prison bounds, and with the glorious beauty of the spring day comes the soul gladdening tidings of a great victory over Hooker on the Rappahannock, a greater victory that we have ever had before says Lee's official dispatch, for which our hearts ascend spontaneously in warm thanksgiving to the Lord God of Hosts, the Giver of all victory.[14]

Seventeen thousand prisoners are reported to have been captured. The Yankees themselves estimate their loss at twenty thousand men killed, wounded and missing. What our loss is I have not even heard conjectured, but fear it is heavy enough [to] make many, many sad hearts and check the rejoicing for victory in many a truly patriotic breast. The list is headed by the severe wounding of Stonewall Jackson who has lost one arm and been wounded in another.[15] Could he know (and perhaps he may) how beloved he is by every Southern man, woman and child, he would feel richly repaid for all he might suffer.

Mr. Buchanan is doing very well, poor fellow. I hate to see him shut up in his little room while all the others are riding, walking and enjoying in every way the loveliness of this sweet day. He is as bright and cheerful as possible, and seems well content to be where he is.

May 11th [Monday].
Fresh rumors continue to pour in from [the] Rappahannock, various and conflicting as possible, but it is perfectly useless to record them, as in all probability long before any one thinks it worth while to read my journal, history will have placed it in the power of every half grown boy and girl to contradict what I say.

Again today a report came that the Yankees were advancing on us in large force from Snickersville, and all around me I saw people removing their horses, etc. to hide them in the woods and mountains, but we determined not to stop the all-important corn planting unnecessarily, so Hal rode out to reconnoiter and everything was to remain in status-quo till his return. As he was long in coming back I made myself easy, not the least evil of these troublesome times is the constant agitation produced by reports of approaching Yankees. We have so little left us that we cannot venture to risk what we have, so upon every rumor we have all the meat taken from the meat house and concealed, the stock all run off to a safe place, the silver, money, arms, etc., concealed, and generally it amounts to nothing, for we have not even seen a Yankee for months and with our greatly reduced [labor] force, this extra trouble is no trifle.

Mr. Buchanan is not so well today. Dr. Gunnell saw him this morning, and expressed some uneasiness from the nearness of the wound to the main artery.

The Stephensons walked out this evening to see Kate who is quite unwell.

May 22nd [Friday].
Tonight for the first time since January we are a family circle in the library, Mr. Barnes who has been with us so long having left for Richmond this morning and Mr. Buchanan still confined to his room by his wound. I hope I am not inhospitable, but I do sincerely enjoy this little return of our old privacy.

Since I last wrote we have had two Yankee invasions. I was in the garden pruning my grapes when a trampling of rapidly approaching horses feet attracted my attention, and lo! the enemy was upon us. I trembled for Mr. Buchanan, the others having gone to the mountains the night before, the horses were all in the same place of safety, so we lost nothing, as Cavalry could not carry off meat, poultry, etc.

A few mornings later I was awakened by Uncle Dan's voice in the passage, an unusual sound which soon alarmed me. I heard him say "the Yankees are coming," but so often had the alarm proved false that I prepared leisurely to dress, but thought I would make one reconnaissance from the front balcony, and to my surprise, there just before the house was a squad of Blue Devils coolly surveying three of the horses. Hal sprang from bed like a flash. Mr. Barnes and William [Elzey] rushed into boots, pants and coats, utterly regardless of collars, cravats etc. and in less than five minutes Mr. Barnes' long legs and William's short ones were striding and double quicking it over the ploughed field, their bodies bent nearly double to approach as near as possible to invisibility, the Yankees being in front of the house at the very moment, they were retreating from the back.

Hal, with trembling eagerness, made arrangements for running off the few fine horses we have left, and then with admirable composure, strolled toward the three in the field then undergoing the Yankee investigation. With strategic ingenuity, worthy of Lee or Jeb Stuart, he parleyed with the enemy, holding them in check till everything was safe and convincing them in spite of their eyes that the horses they examined were not worth carrying off. He finally returned to the house completely victorious, the enemy slowly retreating without any trophy towards Upperville.

My meat is still secreted in different places. It is already alarmingly diminished in quantity and to go shares with the Yankees would utterly ruin us. An unusually long spell of dry weather speeds the corn planting which will be finished tomorrow, and then every energy will be directed towards getting in a good supply of potatoes. My garden is looking beautifully, every vegetable being far before my neighbors. My spring needle work is nearly over, and my quiet summer holiday beginning. The constant succession of visitors, gardening season, clothes making, etc., have kept me so constantly employed that I am as thin as a lath, and I must acknowledge some times very weak, and even painfully weary, but I anticipate now a glorious recouperating [sic] time of pleasant reading, cooling baths and refreshing naps, all having a tendency to fatten me like a pig, however *nous verrons*,[16] there's many a slip etc.,[17] and tomorrow may bring forth some new duty to disappoint my expectations of ease and rest.

May 27th [Wednesday].
Perfect quiet for the last two or three days, scarcely a visitor, no positive news, and but for a few rumors. Mamma had gone to Middleburg and Kinloch. From

the former place she wrote us that Johnston had fallen back across the Big Black and the Yankee papers claim in consequence to have taken Vicksburg.[18] I believe no bad news till positively confirmed. I mention here a little incident as indicative of our miserable state of insecurity. Uncle Ned, having provided himself with accommodations for them, was prepared to start south with his most valuable stock and a large family of Negroes when, the night before he expected to leave, a squad of Yankees appeared with a wagon and team and carried off the family of Negroes, thereby rendering abortive the whole scheme.

I have been much interested today in getting in a large planting of potatoes. Owing to our large family, meat is very scarce, and vegetables have become all important. Mr. Buchanan is down on his crutches today for the first time. I took Uncle John over my garden today. It is in beautiful order, and I received warm commendation from him for my good management. The poultry thus far prospers finely. I cannot help being surprised at my interest in such matters when a Yankee raid may any day deprive me of the fruit of all my labors. Poor little chicks and ducks, I should hate them to fatten Yanks! A duck was born today with four legs. The servants shake their heads and say "Humphs, that's a sign of something sure nough." And I suppose any event of importance that occurs for the next month will be laid to the charge of my poor little duckling.

To our great regret Mr. Bolling has sold Bollingbrook to Lursnes [sic],[19] the lumber merchant.

May 28th [Thursday].
Another alarm of coming Yankees this morning. They were in Upperville, but we were so fortunate as not to have a call from them. I have been planting tomatoes this evening and was obliged to water the plants copiously as everything is suffering from a three week's drought. Tonight a Kind Providence promises rain, which every thing in the vegetable world pleads for with dry and thirsty leaves.

May 31st [Sunday].
Yesterday I dined at the Bolling's, taking May and Rozier with me. Master Rozier disgraced himself by crying for his dinner when he found there was no seat for him at the table.

We saw a Yankee paper, again claiming the capture of Vicksburg. I hope it is not so, for the loss of Richmond would be scarcely a severer blow to our struggling Confederacy. Another report of the approach of Yankees has just reached us. I am too accustomed to them now to feel any agitation. Just saw in the paper the death of young Hill Carter of Shirley.[20] Death after death, friend after friend, till soon none will be left. Happy [are] those whose nearest and dearest are spared and whose tears are those of sympathy and not of heart-breaking sorrow.

June

June 21st [Sunday].
For some days and even weeks after my last entry, affairs remained to all appearance in status quo. We had a few rumors and among others, one to the effect that Lee's army was preparing for a forward movement. Still nothing was definite. Then first came the news of Stuart's Cavalry fight at Brandy,[21] then without any warning or preparation, rapid and heavy firing from over the mountain told us more surely and more rapidly than courier or telegram that operations had commenced in the [Shenandoah] Valley.

Hal listened to the firing till his anxiety could stand it no longer and then on mounting his horse, he told us to put his supper away for him, and he would inquire from the nearest picket the last news. He did not return till the next night and then it was to tell me that Ewell had captured Winchester with nine thousand Yankees, untold quantities of government stores, ammunition, arms etc., Milroy only escaping with seven hundred men.[22] The miserable brute, guilty to his heart's core of every species of outrage upon the defenseless citizens, telegraphed from Harpers Ferry to General Early[23] (prompted doubtless by the warnings of an uneasy conscience) to demand that his prisoners should be

Timeline of the War

June 3	Lee's army begins to move westward from Fredericksburg, heading toward the second Confederate invasion of the North.
June 9	One of the largest cavalry battles in American history takes place at Brandy Station. It is a tactical draw, but the newfound fighting ability of the Union cavalry bodes ill for the future of Stuart's corps.
June 13–15	Jubal Early destroys Milroy's army in Winchester, opening the Shenandoah Valley for Lee's move into Pennsylvania.
June 17	The Loudoun Valley Campaign begins with fighting in Aldie.
June 18–21	Cavalry fighting in Loudoun continues in Middleburg and Upperville.
June 24	Hooker's army begins crossing the Potomac at Edward's Ferry, following Lee into Maryland and Pennsylvania.
June 27	Pennsylvanian George Meade replaces Hooker as commander of the Army of the Potomac.
June 30	The Battle of Gettysburg begins.

treated according to the usages of civilized warfare to which Early only replied that the dispatch needed no answer, and he might have added, no comments. In Mrs. Milroy's trunks was found every article of Mrs. Logan's silver marked with Mrs. Logan's name. Mrs. Milroy had left Winchester a week before to visit her friends, carrying with her twenty trunks loaded with plunder.[24]

We had heard the morning after Hal's return, that a large body of Yankees were at Piedmont[25] and consequently felt most anxious but about twelve o'clock Hal came in bringing Welby Carter[26] with him, and imagine our astonishment at learning from them that Longstreet with his entire corps was at Upperville, General Stuart with his Cavalry on the turnpike, Fitz Lee's brigade actually passing the gate, and the whole army coming on. Knowing it would be needed, I instantly made preparations for entertaining soldiers in and out of the house, and had scarcely dressed myself when Hal came back bringing Fitz Lee with him. I had not seen him since he was a Cadet at West Point. He has changed a good deal and grown stout. He is not handsome, but has an expression of quickness and sagacity and occasionally of sweetness and humor that is decidedly attractive. He was sent for by General Stuart that evening, but returned in the morning very unwell. Having obtained leave, he stayed with us till last night, when he was again sent for by General Stuart. He is in evident bad spirits, from what cause I do not know.[27]

Several skirmishes have taken place on the turnpike above Middleburg,[28] and this morning the cannonading is quite heavy, and we see distinctly the smoke from the guns. We have had constant and violent rains. General Stuart, though nearby several houses, slept on the ground with the rain beating on him in torrents.[29] Of course we have seen all our friends and numbers of calls from soldiers we do not know. Hal has just come in to say our forces are falling back in this direction and the smoke from the cannon is about two miles nearer. A man from Middleburg says the Yankees are in force and have Cavalry, Infantry and Artillery.[30] I dread lest Stuart should fall back past us and then last fall over again will be our fate, with only this difference, that then we had a great deal to lose, and now we are blessed in having nothing to gratify Yankee cupidity. I cannot write any more as I wish to watch the motions of the armies that are just come in sight on a distant hill.[31]

1 o'clock.
Hal is driving off cows, sheep, etc. as even the few we have are worth saving. The last news is that we are still falling back. Fitz Lee wrote Hal a note just now stating that we were falling back in consequence of an infantry reinforcement. We will go back to the mountain Gap.[32]

2 o'clock.
The Confederate batteries are at Number Six, Federals, just below. Hal has ridden to the hill near here where General Stuart is standing to see him about

a guide for Loudoun County, so I suppose they will fall back towards Union. I see a squad of Cavalry coming towards us, and groups on horseback on the adjacent hills, and so exactly is the scene similar to that enacted here last fall that I can scarcely believe six months have passed since then. We have the same forces under the same Commanders, and so have the Yankees, the batteries occupy successively exactly the old positions. It is again Sunday and we have even the same persons with some exceptions staying in the house. Could I think we were to go through the same ordeal of insolence and plunder and destruction, my heart would be heavy as lead, but I must hope for the best and not make bad worse by anticipating evil.

June 22nd [Monday].
By three o'clock yesterday we were busy concealing every thing that we thought the Yankees would take. Soon the batteries were opposite the house and just as they took the position Robert Gray came to the house bringing about two hundred soldiers with him. Mamma was much alarmed for fear a shell would be sent through the house in firing at the soldiers, so she asked them to move on, while I brought in those I knew to get some thing to eat. I heard afterwards that the soldiers were very much offended at Mamma's alarm and hoped the Yankees might get everything we had. I was much distressed that any of our men, however unjustly, should suspect any disloyalty from our forgetfulness and alarm in that hour of confusion; however, I suppose the poor fellows were hungry and tired, and I wish I had thought to take them out what we had in the house.

 About four o'clock the rapid reports of musketry attracted my attention and I went to the balcony to see what was going on. I saw our men drawn up in line of battle on Vineyard Hill in McArtor's[33] field, and the Yankees pouring in in every direction, up the turnpike, through our fields, over Brown's[34] cornfield and from the Green Garden road. The Yankees advanced and our men made a charge, the Yankees fell back a little way and then charged our men. The skirmish was very sharp for about fifteen minutes, in full sight from the balcony. Mamma was alarmed and took the children in the cellar, but I was spell bound on the balcony. The artillery on both sides kept up a constant roaring, while the reports of the small arms, the shouts of the men, the cries of the wounded, and the flash of the firing, made a scene terrible to me, and every now and then a horse with empty saddle ran terrified by the house, telling the sad tale of his rider's fall. Once my blood turned cold at seeing one gallop by dragging a dead man under him.

 Such numbers of Yankees poured in upon our men that they fell back slowly, the firing of small arms still telling us of the continuation of the fighting after they got out of sight. Soon the place was covered with Yankees, begging something to eat, generally civilly and offering to pay, but I heard a noise in the cellar and on going in I found three men stealing Robert's saddle. I ventured to remonstrate, but was answered with a look of such insolence and language so gross from a horrid looking brute that I left them. Instantly they came out and were going to break open the meat house door when I thought it best to open it. The brute [who was] before licentious, walked in and helping himself to a ham, invited the others to do the same. Only one followed him, the others all exclaiming at his rudeness. To my relief he left when he got the ham. They poured in in such numbers that every thing on the place was soon eaten up and still they came. The servants cooked bread for them as I would not give them the little meat we had.

Just at dusk a party came up saying they were sent to search the house and place for rebels. I did not believe them, but could not prevent their going into the meat house upon the pretence. As I suspected, they only wished to steal. Two took as many hams as they could carry, while another went to the kitchen and took all the bread Wilmouth was baking for our supper. The children were crying for something to eat, and I could get them nothing but some milk and half baked bread. My fatigue became so great that together with my involuntary fasting, it produced a violent headache and I had to go to bed.

Before I was dressed this morning three soldiers sent for the meat house key, saying they would break the door down if I did not send it. Knowing that all the meat had been put in the cellar last night except three shoulders, I sent the key and dressed as quickly as I could. I found the meat house door open, and two men inside looking for hams. They said they knew I had them for they had been told so, and then demanded the cellar key. I opened the flour cellar for them to see, knowing there was nothing they could take. Seeing the meat was not there, they demanded the key of the other cellar where the meat was. This I determined they should not have, and so I told them. They talked some time very blusteringly, declaring they would break the door down if I did not open it. I answered them firmly that my mind was made up not to open the door, [and] I hoped they would not commit the outrage of breaking it down, but they would have to do it before they got the meat. One man then walked to the kitchen while another went to get an axe to open the door.

As soon as they turned their backs, I put one hand upon each door side and stood waiting for them. One soon came with an axe and told me to get out of harm's way, he wanted to get in. I did not move, but looking him full in the face I told him to understand me distinctly that I would not move out of that door, that nothing but brute force could get me out and that he had better reflect before he disgraced himself by offering violence to a lady protecting her property. He tried to induce me to move by talking but I saw instantly that he had no intention of using force, notwithstanding his threats.

At last, finding I was firm he told me he would not take the hams but I must give him the meat house key and let him have the shoulders. I was about to answer him when another came up and asked if General Fitz Lee had not stayed here a few nights ago. I told him "Yes." He said, "He was killed yesterday. I saw him taken off his horse and a lady was crying over him." His manner was so assured that I believed him at first, and was so shocked and grieved that I had to grind my teeth to keep the sorrow I did not wish them to see, but I could not have spoken without giving way entirely, so I looked away from them and made no reply to their repeated demands for the shoulders. After a while I controlled my voice sufficiently to ask if the soldier he saw killed was tall or short. He said tall, and I was somewhat relieved, but still very anxious, as he said the citizens told him it was General Lee. They walked off without saying any thing more about the meat.

Another party came. I asked them if Fitzhugh was killed. They did not know. Another came who said one of our Generals, a short stout man was killed. Another said he was mortally wounded and still in Upperville. I could stand it no longer, but sent Robert to Mrs. Stephenson's to inquire into the truth of the story. I wished to go myself but Mamma did not wish me to leave the place and was sure I could not see him, or do any good and then it may not be true.

11 o'clock.
Robert came back saying the Yankees would not let him go to Upperville. I waited a while till seeing large bodies of men moving down the turnpike and the pickets withdrawn from the Vineyard I thought there might be a better chance of his getting in the town, and told him to go around by McArtor's house, and try to flank the soldiers if there were any there. He has not yet come back. I have heard nothing yet from Hal. For the first time since yesterday at three o'clock, there are no Yankees in sight, and my hope is that they have gone back, but the servants say there is a large force on the Paris side of Upperville.

Uncle Joshua and Robert have been to the camp and brought back bags full of blankets, old clothes, etc., and Rozier and May are distracted to go themselves. I cannot pretend to do any usual work today till I know everything is quiet.

12 o'clock.
I was working by an upstairs window and looked out to see if Robert was coming when I saw a squad of soldiers going across the field. They were too far for me to see their uniform, but there was an expression about them that attracted my attention and made me think them "our men." Looking farther back, I saw a large column advance from McArtor's wood. As they approached I saw with indescribable pleasure our own battle flag, but instantly my joy was checked by the thought that Fitz Lee was killed. Column after column advanced till a very large body of Cavalry occupied the fields in front of the

house, all marching steadily after the Yankees. Soon I saw two of our men going across the field by the house, and wanting to hear the news, I walked out to meet them. They told me that our men were considerably worsted in the skirmish yesterday, being driven back, but the Yankees had lost [the] most men. So far from Fitzhugh's being killed, we lost no officers higher than Captain.[35] Robert came back bringing the same news, so I am satisfied. I wish I knew where Hal is, but look for him every moment.

One of the men told me Longstreet's whole Corps of infantry was in pursuit of the Yanks.[36] Hurrah for the grey boys! And down with the Blue Devils.

June 27th [Saturday].
The Yankees have fallen back some distance below Middleburg, and there are none of our troops near us.[37] General Stuart has gone on a grand raid. The whole force passed just in front of our house. It was a grand sight. The Yankees left us poorly off for provisions, 10 hams and no corn for 50 or 60 people and none to buy.

Evening.
General Robertson dined here today. He is very handsome, gentlemanly and attractive. It is said that in a skirmish yesterday General Stuart captured an entire regiment of horses, their riders being dismounted. It is also reported that Major Mosby's command was captured, but as the report came from one of his men who ran away from the fight, I do not believe it.[38]

June 28th [Sunday].
This morning General Robertson and three of his staff took breakfast with us. I like the General more and more. He was camped last night in the Vineyard and his orderly came here to buy milk for his supper. I sent him up some nice bread, butter and milk and received a very nice note of thanks this morning. Mr. Bolling brought Major Borke [sic][39] over to see me this morning. He is a Prussian and on Stuart's staff, and was severely wounded a week ago. It is astonishing to see how he has recovered, though the ball is still in his neck and his left arm is still paralyzed. He has one of the noblest faces I ever saw and a simple gentlemanly manner that is very attractive.

The rumor about Mosby proved false. I heard today of a piece of Yankee outrage so atrocious even for Yankees as to deserve notice. Captain [Bruce] Gibson who commands Hal's old company has lost all his children and his wife since this time last year. His sister's three girls live without any gentleman in his house. On Sunday night, thirty Yankees went to the house and treated the ladies so shamefully that they were forced to go out of doors in the pouring rain and stand while the wretches destroyed every thing they could lay their hands on, broke the furniture, poured out their groceries, sugar, salt, coffee, spices, etc., all over the floor, trampling and utterly destroying them. They took their clothes and bed clothes, also china and spoons and knives and silver and left them perfectly destitute. Yet our Generals know that our men are in Pennsylvania, but will not allow private property to be touched.[40] It is right for our own sakes, but certainly not from any protection we owe to the families of the wretches who have so long devastated our beautiful country.

July

July 5th [Sunday].
Hal started a few days ago for Maryland to try to get some supplies for the family. Nick Carter[41] called by last evening to tell me he had seen him over the river and that the way was clear. Nick is just returning from Pennsylvania where he has been with Mosby.[42] Mosby being independent has done as he pleased and the Pennsylvania women have had good cause to regret the ravages their men have made in our country. Nick says they followed Mosby for miles crying for their cows and horses, but they received no comfort from Mosby. I wonder what they think [of] the "fortunes of war" now the boot is on the other foot. I do not like making war on women and severely as we have suffered from Yankee outrages, would rather go unavenged than have our men playing Yankee in Yankeeland.

My little May has been quite sick with Diphtheria, but thank God is now out of danger. I was exceedingly anxious for her at first.

Rooney Lee has been captured,[43] also one hundred of the wagons taken by Ewell at Winchester in a raid the Yankees made to Hanover Court House.

July 7th [Tuesday].
Last-night about 8 o'clock, hearing steps on the porch, I went out to see who it was. There stood Hal with a side saddle on his arm, rather gloomy looking, very dirty looking, no collar, no gloves, no pistol. To cut a long story short they had been to Hagerstown, made all their purchases, had crossed the river on their return home, and thought all was safe when they were fired on by a party

Timeline of the War	
July 4	Lee begins his retreat from Gettysburg; Vicksburg surrenders to Grant.
July 9	The Confederate garrison at Port Hudson surrenders, giving the Union control of the Mississippi River.
July 13	Lee crosses the rain-swollen Potomac River into Virginia; draft riots begin in New York.

of Yankees sent to destroy our pontoon bridges, were obliged precipitously to leave wagon, horses, harness goods, clothes and all, and take to the woods for their lives, where they hid behind trees till they had the melancholy satisfaction of seeing saucy Yanks taking off all their valuable possessions, including wagon and horses, and they had to walk home, sans everything. So good-bye for the present to all our blissful dreams of white sugar, new shoes, etc. Don't we love those blessed Yankees? And have we not cause to? As an offset to this disaster we hear the armies met at Gettysburg, the enemy being repulsed and driven back with heavy loss, including three Major Generals. Our losses not reported but small comparatively.[44]

July 8th [Wednesday].
Further news from Gettysburg, and such news! The Yankees beaten after the most terrible fighting ever known. The Yankees acknowledge a loss of sixty thousand killed, wounded and missing.[45] We took all their artillery, and captured thirty thousand. This was accomplished by a movement on their rear by Longstreet. Stuart captured one thousand wagons. Already we have a fearful account of our loss, thirteen Generals, and among them Cousin Lewis Armistead,[46] Norbourne Berkley [sic] mortally wounded and all his brothers wounded and captured by the enemy;[47] Alex Grayson captured and wounded[48] and many others. I shall dread each day's news, knowing I shall hear of more friends among the dead, but thank God for the victory. Oh! That it may lead to peace.

July 12th.
Four days have passed since I last wrote and it is still doubtful whether my last entry was truth exaggerated, or down right falsehood. One day reports Lee victorious and another tells of him defeated and retreating. One courier will tell of a terrible battle on Sunday, while another will say there was no fight at all after Friday. It is impossible to know what to believe. This is certain, Stuart captured no thousand wagons, and our success cannot have been what it was first reported or there would be no doubt.

    I fear there is no longer any doubt as to Vicksburg's having fallen.[49] Another New Orleans blow to us, yet even this needs full confirmation, still Washington was illuminated and Lincoln and Seward[50] made congratulatory speeches to the populace. This morning, for the second time since the war, we are without sugar.

July 13th [Monday].
Yesterday our fancied security was unceremoniously disturbed by a Yankee raid. They did not come on the place, but we saw them go up the turnpike to Upperville. A guard that we had at Ashby's Gap drove them back as fast as

they came. We have again the prospect of expecting them every day or two from Manassas.

July 18th [Saturday].
Our hearts are very heavy today for we hear certain information on the fall of Vicksburg and General Lee's disaster at Gettysburg increases in magnitude with every account. We saw Yankees again today, perfectly jubilant over their unusual successes and claiming treble the advantage they really gained. We have had very dark days before, but this is the darkest we have known, still I will not despond for so surely do I believe in the justice of our cause that I know everything will work out right after a while, and we shall yet bless God for His goodness and mercy in giving us our independence, but Oh! Sad, sad is the record of the dead and dying. So many we have known and liked killed, wounded and captured, and many, many whose names have had honorable mention from all who knew them for every noble quality, perished in that hostile land among strangers and enemies, their names alas! in these terrible times too soon to perish with them, and this fearful contest only indefinitely prolonged by these disasters. And only one short month ago, our hopes were so high and our prospects everything we could wish them. But all in God's own time we will have our release.

Hal succeeded in buying eight hundred pounds of bacon in Loudoun, so my mind is relieved in that matter, for having given out to the servants the last we had in the house, the great scarcity made me doubly anxious. He only gave forty cents in Virginia money, equal to eighty cents in Confederate.[51]

Mamma and Kate have gone to bed, and I am sitting up downstairs alone, waiting for Hal. It is after eleven o'clock and I hear very strange noises about the yard. I suppose I ought to have courage to go out and see what is the matter, but I dare not, so shall put off the investigation till Hal comes. The excitement prevailing in the country and the entire derangement of all usual habits, make Hal absent from home much oftener than was ever the case before, which is to me the crowning [evil] of the war, for no society on earth can recompense me for the loss of that of my husband. If I were alone here this would not be the case, for he never leaves us unless he knows I have companionship. I wonder if we will ever be happy again as we were in the blessed days of peace before this horrid war came to mar in some way the happiness of every family in the whole country. But I bless God that none very dear to me were in that awful battle at Gettysburg, and pray for those poor souls whose loved ones are beyond their knowledge, killed, wounded, and captured by such a foe as ours.

July—.
I do not know the day of the month or the day of the week, or any thing else scarcely, so worried and worn out have I been for the last three or four days.

We are completely surrounded by Yankees, the camp being in the field before the house. As the General has issued orders that the men must take every thing, every thing is being taken. All our hogs, our little beeves, and lastly all our milch cows except Pinkey, and we only saved her by running out and driving her in the yard as the soldiers were carrying her by the gate. I suppose she will be taken tonight. Uncle Nathan has lost everything in and out of the house. Colonel Mann[52] and staff have this house as head quarters, which protects the interior, but outside everything is going. We will be left to live on wheat bread and water, but we still hope for better days.

When Ida died in 1897, her journal was divided among her three children. Approximately one third of her account is missing, leaving a large gap between July 1863 and December 1864. No one knows whether she stopped writing or whether the missing pages were lost.

This was a relatively quiet time for upper Fauquier County, except for frequent Union cavalry raids in response to Mosby's increasing activity in northern Virginia. After a brief period in the fall of 1863 when Lee and George Meade, commander of the Army of the Potomac since Gettysburg, tried to outmaneuver one another, the main armies settled into winter quarters on opposite sides of the Rappahannock River. They remained there until the following May, when the Union army crossed over into the Wilderness and began the bloodletting of the Overland Campaign.

By December 1864, which is where Ida's journal picks up again, the war in Virginia had settled into a bloody stalemate in the trenches surrounding Richmond and Petersburg. In July, Jubal Early had chased "Black Dave" Hunter out of the Shenandoah Valley and marched down the valley into Maryland and to the outskirts of Washington itself. That success was followed by disastrous Confederate defeats at Winchester, Cedar Creek, and Fisher's Hill. By December there were few Confederate soldiers left in the Shenandoah Valley.

Mosby and his men continued to threaten the Union supply lines and communications from their base in Loudoun and Fauquier, however, to such an extent that Phil Sheridan, commanding the Valley District, issued orders for what came to be known as the "Burning Raid" late in November 1864 in a vain attempt to drive the Rangers out of the area.

1864

December

1st of December, 1864 [Thursday].
I am too unsettled, and wearied out today to do any sewing, and it has occurred to me to employ the rest of the evening in writing an account of our life and adventures for the last six weeks, as a sort of addenda to my unfinished journal. I only wish my memory could retain all the minutiae of word and deed, as well as the more important events. About six weeks ago we were told that the enemy was rebuilding the Rail Road (Manassas Gap) and day after day they approached more nearly to us till they got from The Plains to Rectortown and from there to Salem. They had a large force under Major Genl. Augur.[1] As a precautionary measure, we sent some of our cows and the young cattle to Oatlands for safety.[2]

For several days we were not troubled. Hal came back from Oatlands riding his fine grey mare, and we began to think we would escape. Josephine and Mittie Stephenson came out to spend the night with us one night. Old Miss Sally Harding was here. We were, I know not why, a little apprehensive of a visit from Yankees before morning. About two o'clock in the night I was waked by the tramp of many horses in the yard. I knew in an instant that the house was surrounded by them, and sure enough the first thing I saw when I went to the window was a party of them catching the mare, while the whole field seemed covered with them. I soon roused Hal. We would not light a candle, but all moved about the house as quietly as possible arranging every thing for their reception. I was the first person dressed and going quietly downstairs in the dark I waited at the front door till they rang the bell.

Hearing no noise and seeing no light, they were some time in the yard before they came to the house, and we were ready for them when they rang. I asked, "Who is there?" when they did ring, as if I did not know. Some one replied, "Open quick." I repeated my question. One of them then said, "Shoot the door," and ordered it to be opened more authoritatively. I then opened it and asked what they wanted. Three or four pushed by me. I said, "Oh, I see you are Yankees and wish to search the house." It was dark in the hall and I

> ### Timeline of the War
>
> December 10   Sherman's army reaches the sea at Savannah, Georgia.
> December 15   John Bell Hood's Army of Tennessee is virtually destroyed at Nashville.
> December 21   Sherman occupies Savannah.

called upstairs, "Hal, some soldiers wish to search the house, please bring a light." He came down directly. By this time the house was full of men looking into every room and pulling things about generally.

An officer called Hal on the porch and asked him for Lieut. Grogan[3] and Lieut. Mosby[4] who had stayed here a few nights before. They told him at what hour of the night they came and when they left, and seemed perfectly acquainted with every thing about the house, showing that they had had some informant that we had trusted entirely. They took a good many things from the house that the Col. made them return, such as pants, saddles, etc., but many useful things were carried off such as my coffee pot, scissors, etc. While Hal watched them downstairs I took them upstairs. An officer, Col. Brown[5] [sic], kept them from doing much harm, and I could not help being amused at the scene in Ma's chamber. Josephine [Stephenson] stood by the door looking very much alarmed. Jenny was opposite the door in her dressing wrapper, her hair down. Mittie in bed between the two little girls, Ma near the bed and Miss Sally Harding, a petticoat around her shoulders and her frizette[6] almost in her nose, seated on the silver to protect that. Every one was just out of bed and looked decidedly so. The search of that room was not very thorough. From there we went to the other rooms, Col. Browne keeping the men in order.

After they had searched, as we were coming downstairs, the Col. asked me if there was no garret about the house that he had overlooked. My heart sank, for there were arms, whiskey and soldiers' clothes in the garret, and they had said they would burn the house if they found an article of soldier's clothes. I was obliged to acknowledge that there was a garret. Fortunately for us no one but the Col. went up there. I felt my face grow rigid with alarm when he started up, for there were all sorts of contraband articles hid about in different places, and I was sure he would find them. He stayed some time and when he came down, I saw by his face that he had seen everything. He said nothing at the time but I saw that he wished for an opportunity to speak alone with me. The soldiers followed us too closely to allow him to do so, but he said at last that he would warn me to be very careful, for everything that occurred at my house was known in their camp in a few hours. He really was as kind as possible, and the next day we found the arms, etc., all piled up in the middle of the garret floor.

We tried hard to get the mare back, but the Col. Commanding, Col. Pansevoor[7] [sic], positively refused to give her up, and they started off finally with her. The next morning we found that they had gotten into the laundry and destroyed or carried off a great many of our clothes—almost every towel. From the kitchen they took many useful utensils, and from the yard every turkey, duck, and chicken.

Patsey and her children and Tolbert went off with them, and they were piloted by two of Uncle Armistead's men. We found out that every servant knew they were coming except Robert. After a day or two I decided to try and get the mare back. I knew they would not give her to Hal or myself, but Hal had given her to Jenny, and I thought I might recover her for her. So I started with Mr. Kidwell for an escort to Rectortown. When I got there, I had some difficulty in getting into the Officer's Quarters, as the soldier at the door said he was ordered not to let any one in. I pushed by him at last and walked in.

The first person I saw was Col. Browne. He introduced me to Col. Gallonpe[8] [sic] who commanded the Post. Col. Gallupe was a large rather pompous looking person, who immediately upon hearing my business broke into violent abuse of Mosby. "I, Madam, am a very different person from Mosby. I am a Federal Officer and a gentleman, while Mosby is a cut throat, a scoundrel, a robber, a murderer, a blackguard, a thief—" He then went on to inform me that he had held his command in readiness for days to start on a march to lay our country waste with fire and sword, to render it utterly uninhabitable to Mosby and his vile men. I listened to all this as long as I had patience, and rising was about to leave when from something he said I found out that Genl. Augur was in the house—I insisted upon seeing him. After many objections he called Genl. Augur down. As soon as the Genl. came in I saw I had a gentleman to deal with, and felt more at my ease. I laid the case before him and after some conversation procured from him a note to Gansevoort ordering the release of the mare.

Gansevoort was at Piedmont, and I had to ride on there to see him. We want as fast as we could and soon were in his Camp. I handed him the note. He called up a private, talked with him a little, and they then told me that the mare had broken away and they supposed has gone home. I thought it was only a trick to keep the mare, and most reluctantly started for home without her.

The next morning early I started for Rectortown again. Genl. Augur was very kind, looked, himself, all over the camp for the mare. She could not be found, and no wonder for when I returned home, I heard she had been picked up on the road and carried off to the top of the mountain. Hal went for her and brought her home. We were quiet again for a day or two. I was in the basement a few days afterwards, cutting up a hog, when I heard several shots fired, and looking out saw some pickets on the Vineyard Hill. I got the hog in the cellar, and ran upstairs to put money, silver, etc., away. Looking out my window, I saw a column of 175 Yankees coming from the turnpike. A moment afterwards I saw 40 of Mosby's [men] come through the gate on the East of the field, and I was shocked beyond expression to see that they intended charging the whole column of Yankees across the open field. The Yankees stood still, reserving their fire till the men got in full range and then pouring a heavy fire from their carbines into them. Our little handful of men were of course scattered in every direction and looking out I saw three of them fall from their horses, and many horses falling and throwing their riders who were of course captured.[9]

I could not distinguish who they were who were shot, and felt more shocked than I have been since the war [began] at the idea of seeing some one I knew and liked shot before my face. Soon our poor fellows were all out of sight, and the Yankees were in the yard. As soon as the firing ceased I went into the yard and met some Yankees bringing one of their wounded men into the house. I told them to bring him in, and I would take care of him. One of those who brought him said, "You will if you know what's good for you. We will burn your house if you do not." I told him I would do it for humanity's sake but not for his threat. The poor wounded wretch cursed most horribly, and with many oaths swore he would not be left.

A Yankee told me one of our men was badly wounded in the field. I begged some of them to go with me and bring him to the house. None would go. I got some whiskey and a pitcher of water and started out alone. Just as I started a Yankee told me the prisoners wanted to speak to me. I went to the fence and took their names and messages, and then went on to look for the wounded. I met an officer and told him there was a wounded man I wished to get to the house, that I had no one to lift him, and I asked him to help me. He ordered four of his men to dismount and bring him in. I soon found him, and after getting him water and whiskey saw them take him up and then I started to look for others. The grass was so long I could not see any one and after going some distance I called to know if any one was near. Instantly two voices cried imploring help. The one nearest raised his head, covered with gore, from the ground.

He had a hole as large as the end of my thumb through his forehead, and was the most dreadful object I ever beheld. After giving him whiskey and water (the blood ran into the pitcher as he drank) I went to the other. He was shot through the shoulder and lungs. I gave him a drink, and, hearing more firing, went back to the house. I met the Yankees carrying off their wounded man as I entered the yard. They would not go for the men I left in the field. They had laid the man they brought in in the hall. Poor fellow, I soon saw he was dying. They took off Robert and Henson to drive our ox cart with their wounded.

After they left, our own men came on the place and they soon brought in the two wounded men. I sent off at once for Doctors, and while waiting for them Mamma and I washed the wounds to have them ready for examination. Poor Atkins,[10] the first one brought in, suffered terribly. His wound was at once pronounced mortal, and he was let alone. I sat by his side holding his hand. He was a minister's son from Ireland. He said not long before his death, "My mother, my poor mother." His last words were "Jesus, Master, have mercy upon my soul." His dead body lay all night near the other two wounded men. The next morning their friends came and carried away the bodies of Atkins and Gulick[11] (a man who was found dead on the field). And the brother of Davis,[12] one of the wounded men, took him away. Shaw,[13] the other wounded man, was left here. The floor of the Hall was covered with blood, and there were pools of blood about the yard and porches.

We were so troubled at losing the oxen that I decided to go to the Camp for them. Taking Mr. Kidwell again as an escort, I started for Rectortown supposing the Yankees were still there. To my dismay I found Genl. Augur had gone to The Plains, and my oxen had gone with him. I saw Robert who had escaped and said he was going home that night. I told him to tell Hal where I was, and I started at once for The Plains. I was riding a mean horse, and it was already late, but I calculated and found we could get to the camp before dark. I whipped the horse till my arm was sore, but it was to some purpose for I reached The Plains just as the sun set. The Pickets stopped me a quarter of a mile from the village. They would not let me go in till they carried in my name. They soon returned with a staff officer, who conducted me to a Col. Albright,[14] who was I believe second in command to Genl. Augur. The Genl. was unwell and had retired for the night. I represented that the oxen were our only means of getting wood for a large family, and that I wished to recover them. The Col. told me they were at Salem but he supposed the Genl. would give me an order for them in the morning. I applied then for a pass to go to Kinloch and return in the morning, which was readily given. The same Officer who conducted me in escorted me outside the Pickets, but before I got out of the lines another Staff Officer ran after us and told me that the oxen were in the camp and that I could get them in the morning. This was a great relief.

I felt very uneasy in going to Kinloch for it was quite dark, but I got there safely and astonished them all very much by my untimely arrival. I found that Aunt Sarah had just returned from the Camp looking for her oxen. She had failed to get them and she decided to return with me the next day. We took an early breakfast and got to the Pickets in good time. Aunt Sarah walked and Mr. Kidwell and I rode. Before we got to the Pickets some soldiers halted us, and when we went on they leveled their guns at us with a horrible oath.

When we got to the Genl's Head Quarters, my acquaintance of the evening before, Capt. Slosser (I believe),[15] told [me] he was sorry to say it was decided I could not have my oxen. I asked to see the Genl. At first he said they needed oxen and that he could not make an exception in my favor. After a little talk, however, he told Capt. Slosser to take me over to the Camp and get them for me. Much relieved I started over for them. Mr. Kidwell soon found them. He started home with them and I went back to take leave of Aunt Sarah. I found the Genl. had given her hers too.

I started for home and just as I was going out of the Camp, Henson (Lucinda's free husband) met me accompanied by Genl. Augur. Henson told me that he wished to go home with me and get his family. He tried in the presence of the Genl. to make me bind myself for his safe return with his family [to the Union camp]. This I declined doing, telling him that his family did not belong to me, but to Hal, and that though I did not believe he would prevent their going, I could make no promise about it. Genl. Augur advised me to give them up, saying soldiers would be sent for them if we did not. Henson started off home with us, though I expressly told him I could make him no promises, and refused to make myself responsible for him. Mr. Kidwell and I kept close by the ox cart till we were beyond all danger of Yankees, being then very tired, we whipped up our horses and were soon at home.

We met Hal before we got quite to the house and I told him that Henson was coming for his family. At first, he was angry and said they should not go, but when I told him of Genl. Augur's threat to send for them if we prevented their going he came to the conclusion that it was best not to prevent them. As for me I was only too glad to think that I was to be relieved from the charge of servants, who though they were respectful, were so idle that their work would scarcely have bought them bread in these hard times.

When I told Lucinda Henson was coming for her, she pretended to be much surprised, and declared she never has had any intention of going. Since she has gone we have found out that she was ready to go the day of the fight, and that she knew the Yankees were coming the night they searched the house.

Harriet insisted on going with Lucinda, I rather dissuaded her from it, not that I wished to keep her, but [because] I knew she would never prosper left to herself. At first, I told them they must take old blind Polly with them. Harriet consented, as Aunt Polly was her relation, but Lucinda positively refused to take bed ridden Wilmouth, who was her relation, with her. Before Henson got here, two soldiers rode up and told Hal they had been told by [Henson] in the road that [he] was coming for his family and asked if he did not wish to have him arrested before he got here. Hal decided it was best not to do so. They then told him that he had come to the neighborhood in company with the Yankees who had fought on this place with Mosby's men, that before any fighting began he had gone with them to Mrs. Brown's house, and had been seen trying to get her ox cart, but was prevented from getting the oxen by Southern soldiers being in the field. When he saw them he ran back to the Yankees. They also said there was strong evidence that he had brought the Yankees up on that day to get his family, but the unexpected encounter with

Mosby's men had prevented the success of his plan. When Henson arrived here, he boasted to Mr. Kidwell that such was the fact. Poor creature, his head was so turned by his Yankee protection that he thought any danger to himself was impossible. He insisted on Hal's giving him a pass, saying he was afraid to go without one, knowing the feeling that existed among the [Confederate] soldiers against him. Hal told him it would do him no good, but he was so urgent that at last Hal gave it to him, telling him at the same time that it was not worth any thing. They started off the next morning, and I took Rachel and did the washing they left unfinished.

Before night I heard of their arrest [by the Confederates] as a rumor. The next morning it was confirmed. As soon as they left, Hal walked to Upperville, and when he returned told me there was great indignation at Henson's being allowed to go off to the Yankees. He had been so much trusted by every one that he would be very dangerous in the power of the enemy. He said he believed [Henson and his family] would be arrested. Shortly afterwards, he left for Loudoun to look for servants to take the place of those who had left. I was made exceedingly anxious by hearing the rumor of their arrest confirmed, and expected nothing else but that it would in some way be visited on me, and I was really sorry for the women, having felt no provocation with them for leaving. One went with her husband, and the other with the hope of meeting hers, and I thought it was natural. I did not know then of the course of treachery and deceit of which they were both guilty.

About ten o'clock the morning after they left, there came a report of Yankees coming. I, of course, expected they were coming here and we prepared for them. The poor wounded soldier we had in the house was terribly alarmed lest he should be taken, but I told him to make his case out as bad as possible, and he looked badly enough to make me think his case hopeless. Soon I saw them pouring over the wheat field towards the house. There were from three to four hundred, a flag in the centre. When they got near the house they divided into four parties, and remained stationary opposite the corners of the house. About thirty then rode into the yard. Some went to the kitchen and some walked around the house, while a party took their stand on the steps of the back porch. I was sure they had come to burn the house, and was consulting with Mamma as to the best course to pursue when they came on the back porch. I went in to the west parlor and opening the bay window spoke to the Officer asking him what he wanted. He asked for Mr. Dulany. I told him he was not at home; the Officer, Major Waite,[16] then proceeding to inform me that as the "free negro Henson Willis had not made his appearance at Camp, Genl. Augur considered that Mrs. Dulany had been guilty of a breach of honor, and had sent to arrest Mr. Dulany, or in case of his absence, Mrs. Dulany." My first thought was to be truly grateful that Hal had left home—My next to determine to be perfectly composed.

I told the Major that I would be ready to go with him in a few moments as I had been anticipating something of the sort ever since hearing of the arrest of the servants. I stipulated that I should have a gentleman as an escort and should be put on a gentle horse. They wished to know where my horse was. I told them it was sent away where they would not be likely to find it. They then made arrangements for mounting me. I went upstairs to put on my riding dress, and, calling the children, told them I was going away with the Yankees for a little while but would probably be back before long. Rozier and Becky were not old enough to fear anything beyond what I told them, but [eight-year-old] May, knowing there was a possibility of my not returning, became very much distressed. I persuaded her to control herself as I had a great objection to any scene before the Yankees. I was quite shocked to hear what a vocabulary of abuse she had at her command. Jenny began to cry, but all the rest of us were perfectly composed.

When I came downstairs, they had put my saddle on a horse it took two men to hold, and when it saw my riding dress, those two could scarcely hold it. I refused to get on that one, and they changed the saddle and put it on someone's old plough horse they had most probably picked up on the road. As we did not go out of a walk it made very little matter so [long as] he was not vicious. The Major brought up a soldier and introduced him as Mr. Spencer,[17] my escort, the chaplain of the Regt., he said. He looked gentlemanly, and hearing he was a minister gave me confidence, though when he told me he was a Congregationalist and a warm abolitionist I feared the circumstances causing my arrest would not inspire him with very kind feelings towards me.

I was truly thankful that I left Mamma with the children. Had she been at Oatlands, the oldest female in the house would have been a negro child of twelve years. I must do Mr. Spencer the justice to say he was as polite and gentlemanly as it was possible for any one to be. He was more than polite, even considerate, for when it began to rain as it did very soon after we left home, he was as anxious to protect me from the wet as a friend could have been. An officer rode up to me and taking off his oil cloth insisting on my putting it on, saying he could stand the rain better than I could. Once or twice during the ride the Major rode up and said something to me. His remarks were always unpleasant, such as "Have you seen any pick pockets lately? I believe all the men in your country are pick pockets now." Then [he] would [relate] an anecdote to illustrate what he said. Another time he questioned me about the fight which took place before the house, wishing to know the number of killed and wounded on our side, the number of men Mosby had. Of course I told him the truth, which this finely dressed officer did not hesitate to let me see he doubted, saying of course I was interested in representing our loss as smaller than it really was. When he rode off after that, my escort remarked that he ground his teeth when he heard him speak to me so, but he was his superior officer and he could not help it.

A captain, I think the one who gave me his oil cloth, rode up to Mr. Spencer and remarked that he thought as Major Waite had brought me off from home he might have troubled himself to get me a better horse. All the way along the road at every house we passed, the poor turkeys, geese, pigs, etc., were shrieking and squealing, and once a woman rushed out into the road begging for an officer to protect her property; she wrung her hands and cried. I was provoked to see a Southern woman going on so about some poultry. We went some distance out of the usual road, about twenty miles I think. As it was raining hard all the time, the road seemed very long to me.

When we got to The Plains, Genl. Augur walked a few steps from the house where he was to meet me. He was by no means as polite or gracious as on my previous interviews. I asked him why I was arrested? He said I had bound myself for Henson Willis' return, that he had not come back and he held me responsible for him. I asked if he considered me as instrumental in his arrest. He said he had no doubt of it. I told him that whether he believed it or not, as I was a prisoner in his hands, I felt it due to myself to say that I had not bound myself for Henson to return, but had refused to do so, and that I had been in no way instrumental in his arrest. He said if I had not my husband had, and what was worse had skulked away and left me to bear the brunt of it. His manner as he said this was very rude and I thought it so ungentlemanly in him to speak of my husband so, that I did not wish to prolong the interview. He finished by telling me that if Henson were not in Camp before the next morning I would go to Washington by the train. I told him I could go, and that if Henson's release was the condition of my release I would stay there, I believed, till the war was over.

He offered to send to my house for clothing or anything I wanted. I told him I preferred going to Washington just as I was to subjecting my neighborhood to an invasion from his men. He then ordered me to Major Foster's[18] house where he had his head quarters. When I arrived there I found a houseful of ladies, Miss Peyton,[19] Mrs. Richard Washington,[20] Mrs. Morgan,[21] Mrs. Frazier,[22] and some others. They were all much shocked at my arrest, and one of them was kind enough to take out a note to Hal in which I urged him not to think for a moment of coming anywhere near The Plains to see about me, and not to entertain for a moment the idea of giving himself up for me. I borrowed a skirt from Miss Foster[23] till I dried mine. After drying my hair I ate something and then began to turn in my mind the arrangements I thought it best to make in case I did go to Washington. I determined to write to my Uncles, at the North, and getting one of the officers to mail my letter to trust to Uncle Henry to do what was necessary for me.[24]

I was determined no Yankee should see any sign of alarm or distress about me, so I fixed up as well as I could and when supper was announced I went out with the family. I think Genl. Augur looked surprised at seeing me at the table in apparently good spirits and certainly as much if not more at my ease than he was. The officer who ran after me to tell me the oxen were in camp was at the table. He told me he had not anticipated seeing me so soon again. I told him the meeting was equally unexpected to me and especially the circumstances of it, that in all my anticipations of future evil, I had never looked forward to being held as a hostage for a free negro. I noticed that Genl. Augur never raised his eyes to my face when I was looking towards him, but I detected him watching me closely when he thought I was not observing him. I conversed with the family and sometimes with the officers as cheerfully as if I had been entertaining them at my own table.

That night I could not sleep, tormented by the fear that Hal would come and deliver himself up in my place. I think, had my mind been easy on that point, I could have rested very quietly.

The next morning, the first thing Genl. Augur said when he took his seat at the breakfast table was "Mrs. Dulany you are released, I have taken other measures to obtain the release of the negro." It at once occurred to me that they had sent to arrest Hal. I asked Genl. Augur if such was the case. He would not tell me. I told him I preferred remaining myself as a hostage to his sending for my husband. He said he should do as he pleased.

When he left the room an officer told me they were expecting Mr. Dulany every moment; that a party had been sent into Loudoun by Middleburg to get him. From that I feared they had gone to Oatlands and would give George trouble if they did not find Hal. Altogether I felt most anxious to get home. I told Genl. Augur I had no way of getting home and asked if he did not intend providing me with some way. He said it was impossible, that when they left The Plains as they would sometime during the morning he had no doubt I would have plenty of friends who would see me safe home. I could do nothing better than to wait about two hours till I saw the last Yankee move off down the railroad, and then I pinned up my riding skirt and after receiving every kindness from the Fosters I started off on foot [several miles] through the mud to Kinloch, accompanied by Mrs. Foster's old man.

I was almost broken down when I got to Kinloch. I met Uncle Ned before I got to the house. He told me I should certainly have a horse to go home on, and if I could wait till his little boys returned from the Yankee camp one of them should accompany me. I was so tired I was obliged to lie down for about half an hour, during which time Uncle Ned saddled my horse. As soon as it was ready I mounted and started towards home, hoping to meet the little boys. I stopped at The Plains to enquire for them but not being able to find them I started home alone.

Just as I left The Plains it began to rain very hard. I went on as fast as I could, but I must confess my heart failed me when I thought of the fifteen miles solitary ride through the rain. Then I was by no means certain that I knew the road. But I pressed on as fast as my horse would carry [me,] hoping to get to my own neighborhood before dark. I knew I had no time to lose, for every moment increased the probability of Hal's coming to see about me, and that was now my only fear.

For some time I was guided by the tracks of the cavalry who had arrested me but I think I must have become distracted and had forgotten to notice the road, for all at once I became conscious that it was getting late and that the road was entirely unfamiliar to me. I could not imagine where I had made the mistake. I think the pouring rain must have confused me. I rode on farther hoping to meet some one but I soon got into a large tract of wood through which the road seemed to wind interminably. I could not even tell the points of the compass. At last I met a little boy driving a cow. I asked him what road I was on. He did not know, but he told me there was a house near by where I could find out. I followed his directions and soon found the house. The owner gave me poor comfort, telling me I was about seven miles out of the way, and was then going right back to The Plains, having ridden almost around a circle. He told me which road to take, but his directions were not very explicit or my mind was hopelessly confused on the road question, for after riding about a mile further, I was as much mystified as ever. I thought the woods would never end.

It was becoming quite dark and the rain still poured. At last I came to a small white house and a man and boy stood by the door. I asked if they could direct me towards Upperville. The man at once asked if I were not Mrs. Dulany, as indeed did the man at whose house I had stopped just before. I found my arrest was very generally known. They told me I was near Mr. Hathaway's house, and the only road to Upperville ran just by his door. The little boy offered most kindly to get [up] behind me and show me the way. I gladly accepted his offer, and just at dark I arrived at Mr. Hathaway's. I hoped there might be some soldier I knew at the house who would accompany me home, as the idea of going any farther alone had become almost intolerable. Unfortunately, no one was at the house but Mr. Hathaway's son, who seemed to be about fourteen years old.[25] He pressed me to stay all night, but if I would not stay, offered most kindly to go home with me. I could not bear to take a boy of his age out in such weather, and yet I dreaded the consequences of my not getting home that night. I went in the house.

Mrs. Hathaway was very kind but I saw she felt uneasy at her son's going out, so I decided to stay with them all night, but my anxiety was such that for the first time since my arrest I found great difficulty in preserving my self-command. All at once it occurred to me to offer a reward to the little boy who brought me to Mr. Hathaway's if he would take a note for me to Dawson's mill. I knew Mr. Dawson[26] would send it to Oakley. The boy at once consented to take my horse and go. I was greatly relieved, and being completely broken down, I got to bed as soon as possible and slept most soundly. Early the next morning little Miss Hathaway[27] brought me a note from Ma saying Hal was safe. I started home after breakfast with a light heart, little Mr. Hathaway kindly volunteered as my escort.

To find myself at home once more, and to know that Hal was safe, was such cause for gratitude that I soon forgot the annoyance and anxiety I had been subjected to.

Hal's friends had with great difficulty dissuaded him from going at once to Genl. Augur and giving himself up in my place. Every day after that, we would hear that the Yankees were moving further and further down the Railroad, till at last they were entirely gone and we heard nothing more from them in that direction. We, with difficulty, persuaded Hal to leave home. I was sure Genl. Augur would make an effort to get him into his power, but Hal thought it so absurd that he could hold him responsible for Henson's arrest that he most reluctantly consented to go away. At last, however, he left, but would come back every now and then to see about us. Having no horse, and thinking he might have to run from Yankees and would want a horse he could rely on, he gave $60.00 for a very fine one. The country had been quiet for a week or two, and I had begun to think our troubles were over for a time, when one morning Hal rode out with his gun and dog for a hunt. I was looking out of my window when I saw him with some one else riding very rapidly across the field towards the Rectortown road. Looking towards Upperville, I saw about twelve men pursuing him. I at once knew the Yankees were about. We instantly prepared for them, after I had seen them give up their pursuit of Hal.

We saw them posting their pickets and evidently preparing to spend the night in our neighborhood. I began to hope we would have no visitors from among them that evening, but soon I saw three of Mosby's men ride from behind our house and go towards the picket post. They went up within fifty yards of them and taking off their hats waved them and calling to the Yankees dared them to follow them. About thirty started in pursuit, the three men ran back behind our house towards the stable, the Yankees only pursued as far as our house. Several of them came into the house, all into the yard. They wanted bread. I went to get some for them. They followed me into the store room and took all the butter I had, but nothing else except the bread. From the kitchen they took every thing the cook was preparing, and continued to do so till the children were almost starved before I could get anything for them to eat.

While I was trying to manage some privates out in the yard, two of Genl. Merit's[28] [sic] Staff Officers rode up to enquire who the men were who rode away from near the house. They told me that Genl. Merritt with a division of cavalry had been sent to our neighborhood to lay it waste with fire and sword, to render it utterly uninhabitable for Mosby's guerrillas. They were, they said, ordered to burn all forage, all grain, every mill, stable and barn, and to take off every head of stock they saw.[29] I asked, if they did not intend leaving milk cows to the families. They said not one.

They soon rode off, and as soon as it became dark I had my cows driven back to have them ready to start for some hiding place by light in the morning. We slept most uncomfortably expecting the house to be broken into every moment, but though they were camped very near, Mosby's men were about all night and the Yankees kept very close [to camp]. I arose before light and dressed as rapidly as possible, and even then the Yankees were here before I was ready for them. I went down as soon as possible, and was just in time to meet some officers on the front porch who turned out to be a Dr. Richards[30] whom I had met before when Col. Mann had his head quarters here. I never fancied either his manners or appearance and was by no means very cordial in my recognition. The other officer was also a Surgeon. While they were talking on the porch, about 200 men rode towards the corn field. I feared they intended to burn it, but they did not attempt it. About 30 left the field and going to the hay stacks soon had them burning. Our barn yard is so out of sight that it was some time before I knew that all the buildings in it had been set fire to, but soon the smoke and flames bursting from the granary left no doubt of the fact. Two Yankees stayed by the granary till the flames had made such progress that it was impossible to save it, but the moment they left I took Jenny and calling Uncle Joshua and the three little negro girls, we all ran with every bucket we could find to see if any thing could be done.

When we got to the barn yard the granary was almost entirely burnt, the barn just starting to burn, and the flames were bursting out of the large stable door. Over the stables was an immense hay mow filled with hay. I knew if the fire once reached the hay, it would be impossible to save the stables, so our energies were first bent towards saving that.

All the children brought water while Uncle Joshua went inside and poured it in. I put out the fire in the barn as soon as I had gotten the others wild at work on the stable. After about an hour's hard work the fires were all out except the hay and the granary which were burnt to the ground. We pulled down the fence which had caught fire from the granary. When it was all over I felt truly grateful that we had been able to save so much.

All the time we could mark the progress of the Yankees in every direction by the dense columns of smoke arising one after another from every farm through which they passed. One party went towards The Plains, another towards Bloomfield. At Uncle Nathan's they succeeded in putting out the barn after it had burnt two hours. At Mr. Fletcher's not one building was left on the farm except the dwelling house. At Mr. Bolling's, they saved the barn but had every head of stock driven off and all the hay burnt. At Welbourne the barn was saved but the stable burnt. At Bellefield every outbuilding was burnt, and so on through the country for a circuit of about forty miles. At night we could look out and see the whole country illuminated by immense fires. I saw one which I feared was Oatlands, but they were so fortunate as to escape entirely.

In spite of it all, I could but remark the cheerfulness with which the devastation was borne by all the inhabitants. I did not see one sad face. At night in looking at what my neighbors, many of whom were poor, many widows, many soldiers' families, were suffering, I felt like crying out to God for a just judgment on the wicked minds that contrived and the ruthless hands that wrought such a work. As to our own loss I was only grateful it was no greater.

The next day, we heard they had gone. Hal came home in the morning early, and then rode away to enquire the news. He came back saying some said the Yankees had crossed the river, others that they were approaching us from Bloomfield. I did not believe the last report, for I could see no object in their coming back where they had already wrought such ruin. Still, there were two roads that they had not passed over, the turnpike from Upperville to Middleburg, and the road at the foot of the mountain from the Trappe to Upperville, and we had hoped that a considerable quantity of grain and forage had been left in the country through which these roads ran.

Hal in the evening ordered his horse as usual to spend the night on the mountain. I do not know why but I felt a particular reluctance to his leaving home that night. I did not think of Augur's men, and was sure Sheridan's had all left. So I with some difficulty persuaded him to stay. It occurred to me after I had done so that I might be the means of his being taken. We all went to bed, taking fewer precautions against surprise than usual, Walter Bowie stayed also.[31] About twelve o'clock Jenny knocked at the door of my room and said the Yankees were on the front porch. Hal instantly awoke Mr. Bowie and both of them made an effort to escape, which thank God proved successful.

At first I did not think they were Yankees, for the knocking was not violent. I went to the head of the stair case and called to them to wait till I dressed and I would come down and open the door. The knock then ceased. I arranged the room with Ma's and Jenny's help and put everything out of the way I thought the soldiers would be likely to take, locked every drawer so that if searched I might be by to see nothing was taken, and then went down. I opened the door. An officer and several men entered the hall. I saw at once they were Yankees, some of the faces I thought I had seen before. The Captain asked for Mr. Dulany. I asked who he was. He said they were Augur's men come for Mr. Dulany. I could not tell them Hal was not here, so I said I was glad to be able to tell them that Mr. Dulany stayed at home very little now that the Blue Ridge Mountain was his usual place of resort, and that I thought it would be hard for them to find him there. I have been through many trying scenes since the war, and have sometimes been a good deal frightened, but never in my life have I had such a horrible sensation of apprehension as at that moment. I remembered I had persuaded Hal to stay at home against his own judgment, I remembered at the same time how exasperated Genl. Augur seemed to be against him and against me, I thought of his being dragged away from home, of his being insulted, and imprisoned for an indefinite time, and I thought I would be the cause of it all. The men were talking to me, I think the captain was telling me his name, I did not hear what he said, but when in order to make as much delay as possible I asked his name they all laughed, and told me he had just said he was Captain Sargent.[32]

I remembered then the great necessity of my appearing cool and self possessed and putting a violent restraint upon myself I managed after that to talk with composure and to conceal all marks of agitation, but while talking with them and showing them over the house, my limbs were rigid, and my lips and tongue so stiff that I could scarcely articulate and I would never have recognized my own voice. In the cellar they found Mr. Bowie's saddle and blanket, which of course they took. I told them they belonged to a soldier who had been here that day. They did not take anything from the house, but from the Captain down all behaved with perfect propriety. A private found Hal's boots, and showing them to the Captain, said he must be about somewhere. They searched thoroughly. Every now and then the thought that he might fall into their hands would completely paralyze me. The Captain asked me if I had heard any thing from Henson. I told him I had heard he was in the Libby Prison in Richmond, but I could have no pass to obtain his release. I ought to have written or sent some message to Genl. Augur [about Henson], but I had at the time but one thought and that was a dread of their catching Hal, and it did not occur to me till they had all left.

I shall never forget the intense sense of relief I felt when I saw them go out and shut the door after them. Though even then I did not feel entirely secure, fearing they might remain still and carry the search farther. But I believe they went off directly in a hurry for the Major sent two messages for the Captain to make haste before he completed the search of the house. As soon as I found they had gone entirely off, I went to find Mr. Bowie to tell him of his escape, then Jenny and I wrapped our selves up and went down to the stables to see if Hal's horse had been taken, for I hoped to be able to tell him it was safe, but when we got there, the door was open and the stable empty. It was a heavy loss, and I grieved to think my untimely persuasions should have caused it. Still, it was trifling compared with the blessing of Hal's escape.[33] I could but think as the Yankees went off down the turnpike how utterly wretched I should have been had he been with them. We came back to the house, and I then let Hal know they had all gone. He thought it best to stay where he was for an hour or two longer, but he insisted on my going to bed, which I did. And not till I was perfectly quiet did I feel how terribly alarmed I had been, I shook from head to feet for at least two hours, with a nervous chill, and before morning was so entirely prostrated that I could not dress for breakfast.

By day our neighbors who had heard of the Yankees coming but knew nothing more began to call to enquire for Hal. Oh! how thankful I was that he was here to answer their inquiries in person. He rode away after breakfast to enquire if anything had been heard from Sheridan's men, for large fires in Loudoun the night before, and a dense smoke hanging along the mountain that morning made me uneasy. As soon as I felt strong enough I dressed and went down. Going into the yard for something I saw a large fire over towards Mr. Harrison's. While watching that, on the same road only nearer, I saw another, and soon another, and another, till the mountain side was bright with them. I knew there must be a large force of Yankees approaching us, and at once sent out for the cows and oxen to be driven up.

Before I could get them to the house, Hal came riding rapidly back saying the Yankees were coming towards us very fast. He at once carried off all the stock, and fearing they would burn the building we had succeeded in putting out before, I started all hands to moving every thing out of them that was of any value. I could trace their gradual approach by the columns of smoke. They burnt every stable, every barn and all the forage and grain as they had done on the other roads. While we were in one side of the house watching them one of the children called to tell me they were burning along the turnpike towards Middleburg. Looking in that direction I could see immense fires, for there were many fine barns along that road. I watched where I knew Welbourne was, hoping they would not go there a second time, but before many minutes, an unusually large column of smoke from the very spot told me that the fine buildings in Brother Richard's barn yard that had been extinguished the day before were then being destroyed. He lost that day all his granaries, his two barns, and eleven large wheat stacks, and all his stock. There was but one side of the house where we could look out and not see the fires. We counted two hundred at one time.

The morning opened clear and beautiful, but before noon the whole country was wrapped in a pall of dense smoke, which each hour made denser as the day wore on. The men had all gone out of the way, there was not one single head of stock to be seen in the fields, and the whole country presented a vast picture of desolation and gloom. In Upperville they burnt every thing they could find, and we saw them from our upstairs windows riding about the fields near the village.

We of course expected them every moment, and dreaded them, for entirely worn out by the excitement of the previous night we all felt unable to stand another visitation. A merciful Providence protected us. Though in sight they did not come near the house, and we suffered nothing further from them. That night there came a report that Fitz Lee's Cavalry had come to prevent any further devastation, and though there was no truth in the rumor it had the happy effect of driving off the Yankees.

I have heard it said that they burned two thousand barns and stables, and drove off four thousand head of stock, mostly milch cows.[34] Many of the latter escaped from them and returned to their homes. Since the last of that party crossed the river we have heard nothing more of Yankees; the intense cold has probably procured us this respite. Hal has never spent a night at home since his attempted arrest, but in all this severe weather has slept out. Except for the injury to his eye, he stands it very well. I find it very hard to recover entirely from the effects of my alarm. My nerves have ever since been giving me more trouble than in all the rest of my life put together. Hal received today another warning. So I shall every night expect them till they come. It is no trifle to be as entirely at the mercy of a perfectly unscrupulous enemy as we are.

Dec. 26th [Monday].
It has been my intention to continue this narrative in journal form, as any events worth noticing transpired. These are the days of important events and my only fear is that I shall not be able to procure paper enough to record them as they occur. Several weeks have passed since we were last disturbed and though the Yankees have been at different times near us they paid us the compliment to pass us by. Last week the 8th Illinois, Augur's men, made a raid into Fauquier, and [went to] Kinloch [where] they found Mr. Grogan and Mr. Steele,[35] two of our friends, in the house. They captured Mr. Steele at once but Mr. Grogan fought them. He whipped three (having jumped through the window into the yard) but a fourth fired from behind a tree, and shot him in the leg.[36]

The same party went to Mr. Lake's.[37] Col. Mosby was eating at the table. They fired through the window and shot him through the body. A number of them rushed into the house, the Col. threw himself on the floor and pretended to be dying; they asked his name. He told them Lieut. Johnson. They turned him over and over, got his pocket book, his beautiful new cloak, his boots etc. He acted his part so well that they boasted of having left Lieut. Johnson dead at the house. The Col. is now on his way south, doing very well.

Yesterday, a soldier called to say that a raiding party from the Valley sent by Sheridan to Gordonsville had passed Oak Hill[38] [between Piedmont and Salem], and was coming towards Upperville. Late yesterday evening we heard reports of firearms. Still we saw no Yankees. This morning, Hal rode towards Upperville. In a few moments he came galloping back to say that he had run into Yankees on the Vineyard Hill.

It was so foggy he could form no idea of their numbers. He took the horses he could catch, and went off as rapidly as possible, leaving Mr. Kidwell to get off the cows. Before Mr. Kidwell could do more than drive the cows to the barn yard, while I was beating butter in the cellar, one of the children ran down to say that some soldiers were coming to the house.

I sent the butter into the house and waited till the men rode up. I saw at once they were Yankees. They asked for bread, which I gave them. There were only eight in that party. They rode off, but two returned to tell me if I had any thing of value I had better hide it for a party was approaching the house that took every thing they could lay their hands on. One of them then rode away, but one stayed. He was a rough looking man but had a good face. He said "Old lady, I am sorry for you. I am afraid you are going to fare badly. There is a terrible set of men approaching your house, but I will stay by you and do what I can for you." And so he did, in all the scene that followed he never left my side. He had scarcely stopped speaking when the yard was filled with cavalry.

I have seen rough looking men, but never such as these. Of the hundreds of faces that I have seen today there was not one that could be called tolerably good.[39] They rode straight to the door where I was and dismounted; without any salutation they pushed by me into the cellar till the room was crowded to suffocation. I was penned up in one corner of the room and so crowded I could not move. They demanded the keys to my different locked cellars. I called to them in a loud voice to let me out and I would open the doors. They made an opening for me, but I had just time to open one door when I heard Ma calling loudly to me to come upstairs or they would break every lock. I ran up and found every room full of them. They were more like fiends than any human beings I had ever seen, nothing I said made the least impression upon them.

They would not wait for me to unlock any drawers, but with their heavy boots kicked and broke open my handsome furniture. In the dining room they took every knife, broke the liquor case all to pieces and took every thing they could carry off. In the Library they broke open the oak book case, threw everything out of it over the floor, took the books, paper, etc. In the best parlor they broke the mirrors in the rose wood étagère, and kicked out a panel of one of the doors. They carried off or broke up most of the likenesses of different kinds that we had, and took some of the handsome books from the table. They then started upstairs. I sprang before them, telling them there were children upstairs who would be frightened. They tried to push by me but I pushed some of them back as quietly as was possible under the circumstances. One then seized me by the shoulders and twisted me around out of his way, then they all rushed pell mell by me, and every room was filled with them. Jenny terrified almost out of her sense locked the door of the room she and the children were in, two or three began to kick against it with all their strength. They had almost succeeded in breaking it down when Ma called to her to open it. When it was opened they rushed in.

I followed them to my room. They kicked open the trunks, pulled open the drawers, opened the wardrobes, ransacking every thing, taking what they wanted and throwing every thing else on the floor to be trampled with the filth of hundreds of their feet. All Hal's clothes, all mine, all the children's, the cloth cotton, spools of cotton thread, buttons all winged together. It is impossible to tell what they have taken yet.

They opened all the clothes I had packed away for the winter. I can find scarcely any flannel clothes, and they have taken every article of Hal's clothes of any value. My handsome dresses they trampled and greased with bacon, so I fear they are ruined. They soon found the house linen. Every towel but four, some of the best blankets, my nice counterpanes, almost every pillow case were taken. Hal's beautiful white fur robe, his new overcoat, a very handsome suit he had just bought, every pair of pants but one, taken, and the clothes not carried off so destroyed they are almost useless. In the cellars they took axes and cut all the panels out of the doors, took all the milk, breaking the [stoneware] pans as they emptied them. They took most of the meat, almost all the apples, poured out almost all the vinegar, they took all the molasses, and every dust of flour on the place. Three separate parties sacked the house, one after the other, leaving intervals of about half an hour between their visits. The last party went to my little store room where my few groceries were. I had hoped it would escape. They insisted on my opening the door which I at last did to prevent their breaking it. As I opened [it], my sleeve caught in the door knob, so that I could not pull it away immediately, they would not wait an instant, but rudely pulled open the door, straining my wrist violently as they did so. I managed by seizing things from them to save a little, and finally get them out and locked the door again.

While they were upstairs, I was frightened very much by hearing Jenny and the children shriek. I ran up and found one had seized hold of May frightening her very much, Becky was as white as a sheet, and Jenny in violent hysterics.

One of them had found the silver and was dancing in the passage rattling the forks and spoons in his hands. One horrid looking creature seized some matches and went to the cellar saying he was going to set fire to the house. The young man who went about with me as a protector told me he had seen an officer ride into the yard. I went out to look for him and soon found a Lieut. who came in and called the men out of the house. He pretended to be much annoyed at the ruin they had wrought, and he took a few pictures and some things of no value from them, but did not make them give up any thing of any real value such as blankets, clothing, etc.[40]

Shortly after the last of them had left the house, some of our men rode by. I called them in and carried them through the house. They said as they left that they would take no prisoners from that command. I was thankful Hal was not in the house, and I felt truly sorry to show him his house when he rode home in the evening. He was terribly depressed when he heard of all we have endured. When Augur's men have been to the house, though they have fancied they had cause of especial provocation against us, there have always been with them officers who would try to restrain the men from unnecessary destruction, and even the men though they plundered, seemed to have no disposition wantonly to destroy, but these men like wild beasts drunk with blood, reveled in destruction for destruction's sake. Hal heard the other day that Augur had sworn to have him dead or alive. I do not know if it is true, but I think even his enmity would be satiated if he could have been here today.

I asked one of the Yankee officers who pretended to regret the destruction in the house if he had ever seen any thing of the sort before. He answered very flippantly, "Oh yes I have seen nothing else for the last four or five days." So I suppose I have many fellow sufferers. I have not heard from any of my neighbors but Mrs. Loughborough and Doctor Henry. At Mrs. Loughborough's they did not do quite so much damage as here because there were only a few of them at the house, but those few did all the damage they could. At Doctor Henry's their conduct was so outrageous that the poor old man was perfectly deranged when Hal met him this evening.

Dec. 28th [Wednesday].
We have passed a very uncomfortable night, expecting the Yankees to come for Hal every moment having heard they were in the country looking for him. The constant excitement we have undergone for the past month joined to the unusual bodily fatigue of doing our own work begins to tell on us all. Ma has not been able to leave her bed since the Yankees left and seems completely broken down mind and body. For myself, though I go about the house and am able to perform my usual duties, I feel so weak and badly that I fear I shall break down before long. We have heard from Kinloch and Avenel, and learn that they suffered if anything more than we did, having the burning of their barns added to the destruction indoors. I think I could bear it all very well if it were not for my constant anxiety for Hal. All the property we have in the world seems of but little value compared with one human life that we love. I have written to Katey to come and take Ma to Oatlands for a resting spell. I do not think she can stand the life she leads here.

Dec. 29th [Thursday].
Yesterday Sammy Bolling rode by to tell Hal that the Yankees were coming up the turnpike. [Hal] was at Uncle Nathan's so he went over there to tell him. We expected an invasion and search every moment. I did not go to bed till three o'clock in the morning, not wishing them to find me undressed. They did not come last night, and will I hope pass us altogether, as I hear they have gone behind the farm on the road to Piedmont. They camped at Dawson's Mill, two miles from us last night. Their object is most probably a search for Col. Mosby. Katey came up to Bellefield[41] last evening, and I hope will come over to see us today. Ma is still completely prostrated this morning, while my night watching has given me a headache. No very good preparation for Yankees if they come today.

1865

January

January 29th [Sunday].
Since my last entry, we have had less trouble of any sort than for a long time. Before, owing to the intense cold, no Yankees have been in the neighborhood. We hired for the year two excellent servants who do cheerfully the work that ten women grumbled over before the war. Ma has brought from Kinloch our poor old Grandma, whose physical and mental weakness is such that she occupies Ma's entire time.[1]

During the last month, more than half of Mosby's men have gone to the Northern Neck[2] for the winter. There is also some talk of the emancipation of all slaves by our government.[3] I have not heard one slave holder object to the move. There is also some talk of interference on the part of foreign powers to open our ports and force a peace. I have but little hope of anything of the sort. We get no papers.

General Lee has been made Generalissimo of the whole army.[4]

Timeline of the War

January 15	Fort Fisher, guarding Wilmington, North Carolina, falls, closing the last port open to Confederate blockade runners.
January 19	Sherman begins his march into North Carolina.

Epilogue

> I believe everyone realizes that the doing away with slavery will be an incalculable blessing to our country.
>
> Marietta Turner Powell
> Letter to Mrs. Robert E. Lee, July 3, 1865

Peace came to Virginia at last and with it the bleakness of poverty. Across the Confederacy, Southerners contemplated a desolate future. Ida's mother, Marietta Powell, summed up the Oakley family's feelings in a letter to Mary Custis Lee dated June 4, 1865. She wrote, "the last four years . . . have indeed been to us all, dear Mary, years of sorrow, anxiety and suffering, to end only in the disappointment of our dearest hopes. There is but one single comfort to me in it all, which is that God has ordered it, and therefore all must be right."[1]

The war years took their toll on Ida, who was worn down by hard work and adversity. Her mother went on to say, "Ida is absent from home. She has been very delicate for the last few months, and we have sent her to Welbourne hoping [a] change of air and an entire relief from her house cares may benefit and strengthen her. She has looked so badly for the last few months and seems at times so languid and feeble that I cannot help fearing that her health has been seriously injured by all that she had to endure last winter." A month later, however, Ida had recovered enough to return home and was up to inviting General and Mrs. Lee to stay at Oakley. In her letter to Mary Custis Lee dated July 3, Marietta ended with the invitation, "Ida sends her best love and says that *nothing* would give her so much pleasure [as] to see you and Cousin Robert here."[2]

The war also had a profound effect on Marietta's sons-in-law. Hal's weakness for alcohol was a problem with which he wrestled. His signed promise of abstinence is recorded in the Dulany family Bible. George Carter found himself unable to cope with the burden of running Oatlands with many dependents and little money to pay his workers. In the same letter, Marietta confided, "I never expect to see my children as prosperous as they were before the war because both of my sons-in-law were brought up (as is unfortunately the case with so many of our Southern young men) to too much self-indulgence and ease and find it hard to struggle against the difficulties of these times."[3]

Marietta continued, "You ask me in your letter how we are getting along, and if we are not left sadly impoverished. When the war was ended Henry [Hal] had nothing left but his house and land, most of it unenclosed, some cows and two or three old horses. Not a sheep or feathered thing of any sort had the Yankees left us. We never see anything but salt meat, but with vegetables and fruits this is easy to be borne." A family with fewer resources and connections could easily have died of starvation. There were many much worse off than the Dulanys, among these was Janet Weaver Randolph in nearby Warrenton. She recalled, "We would have starved to death if the Negroes [her family's former slaves] had not shared with us the rations given them by the United States government."[4]

The women of Oakley accepted hardship stoically, and Marietta made an effort to be fair to the enemy, writing to Mary Custis Lee, "I was glad to learn from your letter that the Yankees were evincing a desire to conciliate, and show consideration to the people of Richmond.... I think, dear Mary, we should try to give them the credit they deserve, for it was in their power to have made our lives a perfect burden.... The loss of our cause is to every one so much the greatest trouble that you rarely hear individual losses even alluded to, and I believe every one realizes that the doing away with slavery will be an incalculable blessing to our country."[5]

As Ida and her family lost wealth and future prospects appeared uncertain, the new order transformed an entire segment of society. "Slave women not only confronted distinctive hardships and losses [during the war], but also experienced a promise of freedom that served as a beacon of hope"[6] for the future. Emancipation brought excitement and relief to the enslaved black population, but for many long years it did not bring prosperity, good jobs, education, or civil rights. An encouraging first step, however, was the opening of black schools such as the Second Street School in the Quaker community of Waterford in Loudoun County. Sanctioned by the Freedmen's Bureau[7] in 1865, the school moved to a new building in 1867.[8] For two years before that move, Sarah Steer, a Quaker, had been teaching black children and adults in her own yard in the town of Waterford.

In the Virginia piedmont, going back to the familiar farm and household setting where they had worked as slaves may have been less daunting to some than seeking work in the overcrowded cities of Washington or Baltimore or even farther north where decent housing was difficult to obtain. In the inner city tenements, there would be no garden in which to raise vegetables, no game to hunt, no unpolluted streams to fish. For former slaves these decisions were not easy to make, but at last the choice was theirs. Of her former slave,

Robert Buckner, Marietta wrote in the same July 3, 1865, letter, "Robert is still with me." For the first time he was earning wages. He was so much a part of the life at Oakley that Mrs. Lee sent him a message in her letter, which Marietta acknowledged, "I delivered him your message." Robert, fifty-seven years old at the time of the 1870 Census, continued to live at Oakley, working as butler in charge of the household duties, and Ida still depended on him. In her will dated 1891, Ida bequeathed "to my old servant Robert Buckner an annuity of sixty dollars, payable monthly" during his life. Another former household slave, Lucinda, who was married to freed man Henson Willis, never returned to Oakley. They lived independently at Willisville, a small community near Welbourne, where they owned their own house, which is still standing.

Both the social and economic change was evident in the 1870 Census. Former male and female slaves who were once listed as nameless personal property now were listed as individuals with names, some showing as head of households. The net worth of the slave-owning class had dropped dramatically. In the 1860 Census, Hal Dulany's personal property, which included the slaves, was listed at a worth of $60,820, and in the 1870 Census it was valued at $2,550.

At Oakley farming slowly resumed as some of the freed men chose to work the fields, and some women chose to return to household duties for wages. The stables were gradually rebuilt and the outbuildings repaired. At the house the glass was replaced in the smashed windows and the damaged shutters mended. More important to Ida than broken shutters was her husband's health. In 1871 Margaret Turner of Baltimore wrote to her sister-in-law, Marietta, about Ida, "She really seems to have so many troubles pressing upon her, although she does not seem to look upon them as such. . . . Ida tells me that Henry [Hal] has broken his leg again, I can not help feeling very anxious about them."[9] Over time Hal was able to reestablish his horse-breeding operations. When he was well, he enjoyed the pursuits of a country gentleman, riding, quail hunting, and entertaining his neighbors. One of his great pleasures was the time he spent with the Oakley children. His niece Marietta remembered him fondly, writing, "He had a way of disregarding the doctrine that children should be seen and not heard for he engaged me in conversation during these excursions [trips to the village in the buggy] and appeared profoundly impressed with my opinions. . . . His manner convinced me that the rest of the world had not yet awakened to the importance of little girls."[10] As the years went by, Hal grew more arthritic and often sat in the library in a chair made especially for him. Here he could study the bloodlines of his horses as he worked to improve the well-known Dulany stock. Ida continued her managerial role with diplomacy and tact as his health deteriorated. Time did not change his love for Ida or his respect for her. Hal died at age fifty-four, just before his son Rozier's wedding to Anne Willing Carter in 1888.

The postwar years brought a deep sense of loss and insecurity to the Oakley women. "When the elite women of the Confederate South confronted the new world spawned by war, they struggled to cope with the destruction of a society that had privileged them as white, yet subordinated them as females; they sought to invent new foundations for self-definition and self-worth as the props of whiteness, wealth, gentility, and dependence threatened to disappear."[11] The war changed the Powell sisters, raised to be protected gentlewomen, in different ways. After the hardships of the conflict, Ida coped with the reduced economy with determination and confidence. Although still petite in stature, she was respected as a matriarch. She continued to be active in the Episcopal Church and in the community while entertaining friends and family at Oakley with her limited means. Somehow she always found time to read and to write letters. Marietta Andrews described her aunt Ida as "famous for her charm, beauty and intellect."[12] Her charisma did not diminish with age.

Kate, the belle of Oakley, was now the wife of her devoted suitor, George Carter. Her husband was not tall or handsome, but he was kind and, like Hal Dulany, opened his home to those in need. Jenny Powell Minnigerode and her many children spent months at Oatlands every year. Since George's only assets were a magnificent house and land which he could not afford to cultivate profitably, he relied more and more on Kate's energy and good management skills. To provide a source of income, she cultivated a clientele of genteel boarders who fled the humidity of Baltimore and Washington to enjoy healthy country air and delicious food in a beautiful setting. Among the wealthy guests was Mrs. William Randolph Hearst, who not only gave Kate her friendship, but sent the four Carter children to private schools. In times of desperate need, Kate sold many of the treasured Carter pieces that had been handed down for generations. Even these were not enough to support the large household. Oatlands was finally sold, and Kate spent the rest of her days at Little Oatlands, the eighteenth-century tenant house that the Carters expanded into a comfortable home. She died at age sixty-four, and George lived on without his great love, to die at the age of eighty-eight. Oatlands is now an important National Trust property open to visitors.

In 1868 pretty little Jenny, so petite and vulnerable at age eighteen, married Maj. Charles Minnigerode (1845–1888), who had served with distinction on the staff of Gen. Fitzhugh Lee. Of the three men, he stood out as the dashing war hero who enlisted at age sixteen at the beginning of the war and fought all the way to Appomattox, where he was shot through the lung and left for dead on the last battlefield.[13] Unlike the fathers of Hal and George, his father was not part of the old Virginia landed aristocracy, although he was descended from the German feudal nobility. He had no expectations of inheriting substantially from the Reverend Frederic E. Minnigerode, rector of St. Paul's Episcopal Church in Richmond, "the Church of the Confederacy," where President

Jefferson Davis and Gen. Robert E. Lee both worshipped. In a letter to Marietta asking for Jenny's hand in marriage, Charles wrote, "The little property that my father possessed in this Country was almost entirely lost by the war and his investments in Europe were well nigh rendered worthless by the late contest between Austria and Prussia. Independent of this he has a large family and I would be unwilling to take from the other children what I can hope to gain by my own exertions. I have to rely altogether on my own efforts for my success."[14] He was brilliant, charming, and erratic, and it was soon evident that he was unable to support his growing family. He fathered ten children, losing one in infancy, and in January 1888, a few months before his wife gave birth once again, he quietly loaded his gun and committed suicide in the upstairs bedroom of their house in Alexandria, Virginia. Jenny, now penniless, was left alone with a family of nine to support. She had to rely on Ida and Kate and other family members to survive. She died in 1899 at age fifty. The children were able to overcome the tragedy and poverty of their early years.[15]

The three Dulany children grew up at Oakley. Rozier, like many of his peers, went off to the University of Virginia. Ida knew the value of a college education for her son, and she wanted the girls to know more than the usual domestic skills. In time, May married Henry Shroeder Belt, a scion of an old Maryland family, and moved to Baltimore. Rebecca married her cousin John Hill Carter Beverley of the Avenel and Blandfield family and moved to a large farm, Kendale, in Essex County, Virginia. In 1908 they returned to Fauquier County, closer to their childhood homes, and built a house on the farm they called Selby, near The Plains. Rozier, the Oakley heir, and his wife, Anne Willing Carter,[16] inherited Oakley where they bred race horses with success. His career was in real estate and banking in Washington. Ida's children loved and admired her and often returned to Oakley for visits. They passed on to their families the stories of the fires, the Federal invasions of Oakley, their father's narrow escape to the attic when he was caught at home, and the "abduction" of Ida. Their grandmother Marietta wrote, "I feel at times that the dreadful scenes we have passed through cannot be a reality, but must be a troubled dream."[17] For Ida's children the troubled dream had faded into the memory of distant adventure and nostalgia for the "Lost Cause."[18]

Ida Powell Dulany, at the age of sixty-one, died on October 28, 1897, and was buried next to Hal in the cemetery in Middleburg near The Hill, her childhood home. Throughout the countryside many touched by her kindness and charmed by her intelligence mourned her death. In her modesty she died unaware that she would live on in her journal.

Appendix A

Statement of John Peyton Dulany

I, John Peyton Dulany of the county of Loudoun in the State of Virginia, make the following statement which I wish to be considered as if made upon oath. I am upwards of seventy years of age, and have lived in the county of Loudoun for the last forty years. My family now consists of five grandchildren, the oldest twelve years old, their teacher, Mr. Weidmayer, a citizen of Switzerland, two nieces, Miss Herbert and Miss Evans, and the servants.

I have an only son, Richard Henry Dulany, who is forty years old and is now with the Confederate Army. I have never in any way taken part in the present war, never in any way approved of secession and did not vote for the secession of the State of Virginia.

About the last of March, Col. Geary of the United States army occupied the town of Upperville with his command (about four miles from my residence).

A short time after my house was surrounded about twelve o'clock at night by a body of armed soldiers. I suppose some thirty or forty. I got out of bed, went to the door and asked what was wanted; one of the persons spoke and announced himself as Captain Gallier of Col. Geary's command, sent to search my home for my son Richard H. Dulany. I assured him my son was not in the house or so far as I had any reason to believe in the neighborhood. He expressed his regret notwithstanding my assurance at having to search the house, but he must obey orders. I told him certainly, I knew that.

Capt. Gallier then came in, and went through the house. I am glad to state that throughout Capt. Gallier behaved like a gentleman and an officer. I offered to have some supper prepared for him and his men, he said the men would like something to eat, which was accordingly prepared for them.

On or about the sixteenth of April, Col. Geary having removed his camp as I am told to Rectortown about seven or eight miles from my house, another armed party of soldiers came to my house with two officers, who announced themselves as Capt. McCabe [and] Lieut. Laws, that they were acting under the orders of Col. Geary, and came to take horses. I asked to see their authority; they would not show any but said if I chose I could go and see Col. Geary and ask him.

They then went to the stables, took my riding mare, a very valuable animal and my two carriage horses that cost me seven hundred dollars; returned to the house and talked a good deal. On their leaving I told them that I protested against their taking my property and that I considered it robbery. On leaving the farm the carriage horses got away from the men and returned.

On or about the twenty fourth of April Capt. McCabe and Lieut. Laws with another officer, who I was told was a Major in Col. Geary's command (but whose name I have forgotten) came again to my house with an armed force. Capt. McCabe, however, seemed to act as if in command, stationed a guard around the house, commanding that no one should leave it. He and the Lieutenant and Major went to the stables and servants' house and again took my two carriage horses and carriage harness. As Captain McCabe rode off he said he would visit me again.

On or about the twenty eighth of April Capt. McCabe and Lieut. Laws came to my house with an armed body of soldiers, stationed a guard around the house, placed me and the teacher, Mr. Weidmayer, the only two white male adults in the house, under arrest; went to my store room, broke open the lock, took out nearly all the tea, coffee, sugar, wine, whiskey, etc., that I had for my family's use, and when approached by my niece, Miss Herbert, and told that the key for the store room would be sent for if wanted, Capt. McCabe in a most insolent manner told her he would not wait for the key and broke the lock.

Capt. McCabe and Lieut. Laws then went upstairs and as I am informed by Miss Herbert and Mrs. Evans and verily believe, searched the rooms upstairs to the garret, opening trunks and wardrobes, where there was nothing but clothes and ladies dresses, and when requested by Miss Herbert not to open a particular trunk, she telling them it contained nothing but some articles and clothes, which had belonged to Mrs. Dulany before her death, they refused her request, opened the trunk and scattered the contents about.

During the whole of this scene, I am assured by my niece Miss Herbert, Capt. McCabe's language and gestures were most insolent and threatening to her; at one time telling her she should be arrested and sent to Washington, at another time crying out to the man below to fire the house, etc.

Capt. McCabe went to my gardener (who is a white man), and I am told by him and verily believe, cursed and abused him with my servants, drew his sword, threatening if he did not tell him where I had put my bacon he would cut his head off. He then had the house where I had put the bacon broken open, took what he wanted, I do not know how much, but a large quantity, not leaving me enough for my family's use, and then ordered dinner for his men.

He called them into my dining room where the men dined, after which they left, Capt. McCabe taking with them in a wagon and horsecart, my bacon, four or five demi-johns of whiskey, a trunk with the clothes of one of my granddaughters, a gold snuff box, a silver tumbler and the keys of the wardrobes and rooms upstairs. During this scene Lieutenant Laws commanded me to give up my letters and private correspondence, I told him that I had none, but if I had I would not give them. [Written in pencil on this statement is the following list, presumably of items taken from the house.]

    Madeira wine
    — barrel of whiskey
    — barrel of brown sugar
    6 loaves white sugar
    2 chests of tea
    3 saddles
    2 bridles
    1 silver spoon
    3 silver handled knives
    2 guns
    3 horses

Source: deButts Family Papers, 1784–1962, Virginia Historical Society, Richmond.

Appendix B

THE CONFISCATION ACT

A PROCLAMATION.
BY THE PRESIDENT OF THE UNITED STATES OF AMERICA.

IN pursuance of the sixth section of the act of Congress entitled "An Act to suppress Insurrection, to punish Treason and Rebellion, to seize and confiscate the Property of Rebels, and for other Purposes," approved July 17, 1862, and which act, and the joint resolution explanatory thereof, are herewith published, I, Abraham Lincoln, President of the United States, do hereby proclaim to and warn all persons within the contemplation of said sixth section to cease participating in, aiding, countenancing, or abetting the existing rebellion, or any rebellion, against the Government of the United States, and to return to their proper allegiance to the United States, on pain of the forfeitures and seizures as within and by said sixth section provided.

In testimony whereof I have hereunto set my hand and caused the seal of the United States to be affixed.

Done at the City of Washington, this 25th day of July, in the year of our Lord one thousand eight hundred and sixty-two, and of the Independence of the United States the eighty-seventh.
ABRAHAM LINCOLN.
By the President—
WILLIAM H. SEWARD,
Secretary of State.

THE SIXTH SECTION.
Annexed is the sixth section of the Confiscation act referred to by the President in the above proclamation:

Sec. 6. And be it further enacted, That if any person within any State or Territory of the United States, other than those named as aforesaid, after the passage of this act, being engaged in armed rebellion against the Government of the United States, or aiding or abetting such rebellion, shall not, within sixty days after public warning and proclamation duly given and made by the President of the United States, cease to aid, countenance, and abet such rebellion, and return to his allegiance to the United States, all the estate and property, moneys, stocks, and credits of such person shall be liable to seizure as aforesaid, and it shall be the duty of the President to seize and use them as aforesaid, or the proceeds thereof. And all sales, transfers, or conveyances of any such property after the expiration of the said sixty days from the date of such warning and proclamation shall be null and void; and it shall be a sufficient bar to any suit brought by such person for the possession or the use of such property, or any of it, to allege and prove that he is one of the persons described in this section.

DOMESTIC INTELLIGENCE.
NEW INSTRUCTIONS TO GENERALS.
WAR DEPARTMENT, WASHINGTON, July 22, 1862.

First—Ordered, that military commanders within the States of Virginia, South Carolina, Georgia, Florida, Alabama, Mississippi, Louisiana, Texas, and Arkansas, in an orderly manner, seize and use any property, real or personal, which may be necessary or convenient for their several commands, for supplies, or for other military purposes; and that while property may be destroyed for proper military objects, none shall be destroyed in wantonness nor malice.

Second—That military and naval commanders shall employ as laborers, within and from said States, so many persons of African descent as can be advantageously used for military or naval purposes, giving them reasonable wages for their labor.
PRESIDENT.
EDWIN M. STANTON, Secretary of War.

Source: *Harper's Weekly,* August 9, 1862

Appendix C

MAJOR GENERAL JOHN POPE'S GENERAL ORDERS NOS. 5, 7, 11, AND 19

GENERAL ORDERS NO. 5
HEADQUARTERS ARMY OF VIRGINIA
July 18, 1862, *Washington,*

Hereafter, as far as practicable, the troops of this command will subsist upon the country in which their operations are carried on. In all cases supplies for this purpose will be taken by the officers to whose department they properly belong under the orders of the commanding officer of the troops for whose use they are intended. Vouchers will be given to the owners, stating on their face that they will be payable at the conclusion of the war, upon sufficient testimony being furnished that such owners have been loyal citizens of the United States since the date of the vouchers. Whenever it is known that supplies can be furnished in any district of the country where the troops are to operate the use of trains for carrying subsistence will be dispensed with as far as possible.

By command of Major-General Pope:
GEO. D. RUGGLES,
Colonel, Assistant Adjutant-General, and Chief of Staff.

Source: *The War of the Rebellion: A Compilation of the Official Records of the Union and Confederate Armies,* 128 vols. (Washington, DC: Government Printing Office, 1880–1901), ser. 1, vol. 16: 50. Abbreviated below as *OR*.

GENERAL ORDERS No. 7.
HEADQUARTERS ARMY OF VIRGINIA,
Washington, July 10 [?], 1862.

The people of the valley of the Shenandoah and throughout the region of operations of this army living along the lines of railroad and telegraph and along the routes of travel in rear of the United States forces are notified that they will be held responsible for any injury done to the track, line, or road, or for any attacks upon trains or straggling soldiers by bands of guerrillas in their neighborhood. No privileges and immunities of warfare apply to lawless bands of individuals not forming part of the organized forces of the enemy nor wearing the garb of soldiers, who, seeking and obtaining safety on pretext of being peaceful citizens, steal out in rear of the army, attack and murder straggling soldiers, molest trains of supplies, destroy railroads, telegraph lines, and bridges, and commit outrages disgraceful to civilized people and revolting to humanity. Evil-disposed persons in rear of our armies who do not themselves engage directly in these lawless acts encourage them by refusing to interfere or to give any information by which such acts can be prevented or the perpetrators punished.

Safety of life and property of all persons living in rear of our advancing armies depends upon the maintenance of peace and quiet among themselves and upon the unmolested movements through their midst of all pertaining to the military service. They are to understand distinctly that this security of travel is their only warrant of personal safety.

It is therefore ordered that wherever a railroad, wagon road, or telegraph is injured by parties of guerrillas the citizens living within 5 miles of the spot shall be turned out in mass to repair the damage, and shall, beside, pay to the United States in money or in property, to be levied by military force, the full amount of the pay and subsistence of the whole force necessary to coerce the performance of the work during the time occupied in completing it.

If a soldier or legitimate follower of the army be fired upon from any house the house shall be razed to the ground, and the inhabitants sent prisoners to the headquarters of this army. If such an outrage occur at any place distant from settlements, the people within 5 miles around shall be held accountable and made to pay an indemnity sufficient for the case.

Any persons detected in such outrages, either during the act or at any time afterward, shall be shot, without awaiting civil process. No such acts can influence the result of this war, and they can only lead to heavy afflictions to the population to no purpose.

It is therefore enjoined upon all persons, both for the security of their property and the safety of their own persons, that they act vigorously and cordially together to prevent the perpetration of such outrages.

Whilst it is the wish of the general commanding this army that all peaceably disposed persons who remain at their homes and pursue their accustomed avocations shall be subjected to no improper burden of war, yet their own safety must of necessity depend upon the strict preservation of peace and order among themselves; and they are to understand that nothing will deter him from enforcing promptly and to the full extent every provision of this order.

By command of Major-General Pope:
GEO. D. RUGGLES,
Colonel, Assistant Adjutant-General, and Chief-of-Staff.

Source: *OR*, ser. 1, vol. 16: 51.

GENERAL ORDERS No. 11.
HEADQUARTERS ARMY OF VIRGINIA,
Washington, July 23, 1862.

Commanders of army corps, divisions, brigades, and detached commands will proceed immediately to arrest all disloyal male citizens within their lines or within their reach in rear of their respective stations.

Such as are willing to take the oath of allegiance to the United States and will furnish sufficient security for its observance shall be permitted to remain at their homes and pursue in good faith their accustomed avocations. Those who refuse shall be conducted South beyond the extreme pickets of this army, and be notified that if found again anywhere within our lines or at any point in rear they will be considered spies, and subjected to the extreme rigor of military law.

If any person, having taken the oath of allegiance as above specified, be found to have violated it, he shall be shot, and his property seized and applied to the public use.

All communication with any person whatever living within the lines of the enemy is positively prohibited, except through the military authorities and in the manner specified by military law; and any person concerned in writing or in carrying letters or messages in any other way will be considered and treated as a spy within the lines of the United States Army.

By command of Major-General Pope:
GEO. D. RUGGLES,
Colonel, Assistant Adjutant-General, and Chief of Staff.

Source: *OR*, ser. 1, vol. 16: 52.

GENERAL ORDERS, No. 19.
HEADQUARTERS ARMY OF VIRGINIA,
Near Cedar Mountain, Va., August 14, 1862.

The major-general commanding discovers with great dissatisfaction that General Orders, No. 5, requiring that the troops of this command be subsisted on the country in which their operations are conducted, has either been entirely misinterpreted or grossly abused by many of the officers and soldiers of this command. It is to be distinctly under stood that neither officer nor soldier has any right whatever, under the provisions of that order, to enter the house, molest the persons, or disturb the property of any citizen whatsoever.

Whenever it is necessary or convenient for the subsistence of the troops, provisions, forage, and such other articles as may be required will be taken possession of and used, but every seizure must be made solely by the order of the commanding officer of the troops then present and by the officer of the department through which the issues are made. Any officer or soldier who shall be found to have entered the house or molested the property of any citizen will be severely punished. Such acts of pillage and outrage are disgraceful to the army, and have neither been contemplated nor authorized by any orders whatsoever; the perpetrators of them, whether officers or soldiers, will be visited with a punishment which they will have reason to remember; and any officer or soldier absent from the limits of his camp found in any house whatever, without a written pass from his division or brigade commander, will be considered a pillager and treated accordingly. Army corps commanders will immediately establish mounted patrols, under charge of commissioned officers, which shall scour the whole country for 5 miles around their camps at least once every day, and at different hours, to bring into their respective commands all persons absent without proper authority, or who are engaged in any interruption of citizens living in the country; and commanding officers of regiments, or smaller separate commands, will be held responsible that neither officers nor men shall be absent from camp without proper authority.

By command of Major-General Pope:
R. O. SELFRIDGE,
Assistant Adjutant-General.

Source: *OR*, ser. 1, vol. 12, pt. 3: 573.

Appendix D

The Death of "Kinloch Tom" Turner

By his father, Edward Carter Turner

On Saturday, the 25th of April (1863), my dear son and four others of Mosby's men were sent from the neighborhood of Upperville to the vicinity of Warrenton on a scout. At eight o'clock P.M. they arrived at the house of a Mr. Chas. H. Utterback, three miles from Warrenton. A party of from twenty to thirty Yankees, concealed in a body of pines saw them approach and when engaged in conversation with Mr. Utterback, and suspecting no harm, the little party were stolen upon by the Yankees under the cover of night who approached within ten steps of them before they were discovered, and fired on them exclaiming simultaneously, "Surrender you g-d scoundrels."

My poor son was shot near the shoulder of the left side and the ball entered his lungs where it was supposed it lodged. His horse ran off and he fell from his back about twenty steps from the spot where he was shot and about fifty from Mr. Utterback's door. The rest of the party except one made their escape. A young man named Frankland was captured and taken off a prisoner. His murderers approached my son lying on the ground in a state of insensibility and supposing he was dying took him into Mr. Utterback's house and left a note of which what follows is an exact copy:

"Private Thos. Turner, son of Edward Turner, was shot by me. You are to take charge of his effects and hand them over to his father. "Signed E. I. Farnsworth, Capt., 8th Ill. Cal. After taking him to the house the Yankees left hastily, taking with them his pistol and saber. My son's horse ran off and was not captured and was brought to this place on Sunday.

At half-past one A.M. on Sunday morning I was waked out of a sweet sleep by a loud rap at my door, and a note was handed me by a servant sent from Mr. Skinkers to inform me of the sad event. The note was short, merely stating that my son was mortally wounded. Never shall I forget the pain occasioned by this awful announcement, inexpressibly bitter to myself and still more so to my poor wife. I dressed myself in all haste and started to find my dear boy hoping as I rode through the darkness and praying earnestly that it might not prove as bad as it had been represented.

I reached my good friend's Mr. Skinker about daybreak, and he rode with me to the house of Mr. Utterback, where I arrived at sunrise. I found my son alive but suffering severely. His mind was perfect but his body below the wound was entirely paralyzed. He spoke cheerfully and affectionately and was delighted to see me. Dr. Moss who had been sent for came soon after my arrival. He examined and probed the wound, and that the examination might be made we were obliged to cut the clothes from his back. The doctor stated that the ball had entered his lung. My dear son then asked him to be frank with him, and if he thought the wound mortal to tell him so plainly. The doctor told him he thought it a very dangerous wound and Tom listened with composure to the announcement. The doctor subsequently told me that he thought then there was no hope for him.

A litter was procured and at 3 o'clock P.M. he was placed upon it and carried by the neighboring people (who most kindly turned out for the purpose) to Mr. Skinker's on the way to his own loved home. He had borne well his removal and was to all appearance better. Indeed he was suffering but little when taken from the litter and placed on a bed in Mr. Skinker's parlor. He rested tolerably during the night, taking forty drops of laudanum every six hrs. In the morning he was free from pain and his throat which had been obstructed, sometimes painfully obstructed by coagulated blood and matter from the lungs, so as to render respiration difficult, was comparatively clear. Indeed he seemed better and but for the paralysis in which there was no apparent change, we had every reason to be hopeful of his recovery. The doctor thought him well enough to continue his journey homeward, and after breakfast his friends and neighbors gathered in to bear him forward, on his litter.

The morning was warm, but the force was good, for Tom was a great favorite and many friends came to assist him, and the litter moved steadily on, the men spelling each other at intervals and stopping occasionally to bathe his face and hands and otherwise to refresh him. The laudanum administered to him on starting kept him quiet and free from pain and he slept sweetly most of the time.

We reached Kinloch at about one o'clock P.M. He seemed little exhausted when transferred from the litter to the bed from which, poor fellow, he never rose again. Tuesday morning he spoke cheerfully and said he was quite well. He sometimes fancied that sensation was returning to the parts paralyzed, said he thought he could move his legs and complained of their feeling cold. He also thought he could feel when they were touched. This was imaginary, for in order to test their sensibility I pinched his legs without causing him to complain of pain.

Late in the afternoon the Federal cavalry appeared in force on the hills around "The Plains." About the same time Mosby's company of 120 men advancing on the road from Hopewell to "The Plains" halted in sight of the Yankees about opposite to our ice pond. Here they stood for some time eyeing their enemies who at the same time kept an eye on them. They were a little over half a mile apart and their . . . approached to within a few hundred yards of each other. The number of Federals greatly exceeded Mosby's number. The odds were too great to risk a battle and Mosby retreated rapidly toward Mt. Garrison where he got into the mountains. He was not pursued.

After Mosby had gone out of sight, the Yankees began to dash about the neighborhood visiting the different houses and plundering the people of such articles as they valued, meat, horses, corn, poultry, etc. A party dashed up to this house about six o'clock and asked if soldiers were not in the house. They were told that no soldiers were here but one who was badly wounded. For the first time in my life I kept myself out of their sight, fearing they would arrest and take me away from the bedside of my dying son. On hearing there was a wounded soldier in the house, they rushed in and demanded to be shown to his room. My wife entreated them most earnestly not to disturb her dying son. Assured them that his wound was considered mortal and a visit from them would probably lead to the worst results. Nothing that she could say, though she said and did everything short of falling on her knees before them, moved them and they rushed madly into the room with cocked pistols in their hands.

The Capt. of the party, a rough and unfeeling man, suspected my son and family of duplicity. He said my son was a healthy looking man and would not believe that he was wounded unless he could see the wound himself. My wife assured him as did my daughter and our cousin Miss M. Randolph that he was desperately wounded and all entreated him with tears in their eyes not to disturb him with an examination of the wound which could not be done without causing much pain. Their entreaties and tears were of no avail and though they showed him blood on his shirt he would not be satisfied until he had rolled him over in bed and looked at the wound with his own eyes. After asking many questions and addressing to him many unfeeling and insulting remarks, he left the room and with his company rode away.

In a short time they were seen returning to the house at full speed. Again they dismounted and rudely entered my son's chamber, the same rough Capt. leading the way. This time they were attended by a surgeon who said he had been sent by the General to make an examination of the wound with a view of his removal if practicable. My poor wife and daughter again besought them not to arouse and excite my son, reminded them that he had been examined and begged that no further investigation should be made. To their entreaties the surgeon replied that he had no discretion, his orders were peremptory and must be obeyed. 'Tis just to the surgeon to say he did his duty with humanity, handling him gently and giving no unnecessary pain. He apologized for what he did and repeated that the general's order had imposed the unpleasant duty. He pronounced him too ill to be removed, advised my wife to keep him as quiet as possible, and the party mounted their horses and rode away.

When I returned to the house from my place of concealment I found my son calm but visibly weaker. Night came on and the doctor (Cochran) did not return. He had fallen in with Mosby who informed him that the Yankees were in this neighborhood, and he was afraid to venture forward. I must not omit to relate that while the officers of the party were in my house engaged in the examination of my son, the privates were prying into every hole and corner on the premises seeking what they might steal. They with false keys tried the meat house door. Demanded of the servants the whereabouts of my son's horse; broke into one barn by splitting to pieces the door; into another by forcing out a glass window. Fortunately for us their keys did not fit the meat house lock and nothing of value had been left in the barns that was portable to men on horseback. So they got nothing and had to content themselves with wantonly tearing the canvas curtains from the top of a new wagon they found in one of the barns.

I take great pleasure in recording the fidelity of my servants on this occasion. The boys ran with the horses to the woods. The young women and girls were vigilant to protect such small articles of value about the house as might be pocketed. The old servants replied gruffly and unsatisfactorily to their impudent questions. And Wilhelmina [Edmunds], the best and most faithful of servants, the kindest and most affectionate of friends, with characteristic solicitude was everywhere that her presence was required. She boldly confronted them to keep them out of the house. She presented herself to them alongside of her mistress to prevent their entering the chamber of our wounded son, and as she could find opportunity she visited my retreat to keep me posted on their presence and their proceedings, and when they had finally gone 'twas she who came and apprised me of the fact. Indeed to her alone it was known where I had hid myself for she suggested the place of concealment.

My son's saddle and bridle were hid and Dr. Cochran, whose last horse had been taken a short time before, was riding his horse and thus they were foiled in what they greatly desired, getting the wounded soldier's horse and accoutrements. As the night advanced, our poor son became more restless; so distressing to us and so painful to him was this disquietude that in the absence of the physician I ventured to administer an additional dose of laudanum. The opiate caused him to doze, but there was no rest or comfort in his sleep. He was frequently disturbed by unpleasant dreams, would start from his slumbers, ask for some water and fall asleep again. Thus he continued until near day, when he awoke and asked excitedly where he was. I replied "You are at Kinloch" and asked him if he did not know that he was at Kinloch. His memory seemed to revive and he answered: "*Yes, this is Kinloch.*" Suspecting that his mind was failing, I asked him if he knew me. He answered "Yes, you are Henry Dulany." His mother at that moment approached the bedside and I asked him if he knew who she was. He replied "Aunt Maryetta." His mother then said "Tom don't you know me?" He replied "Oh yes, Mamma that is you."

His breathing had become difficult, but it had been more or less so all the while from the accumulation of matter in his throat which from time to time he expectorated and though he was gasping for breath we hoped that he would presently clear his throat as he had constantly done before and were not particularly alarmed at this symptom. After daylight I left him with his mother and went to my office to dress myself. While thus engaged a servant came with a message from my wife to come immediately to Tom. On reaching his bedside I was struck with the change in his condition. He was gasping most painfully and throwing his hands wildly about. He attempted to speak but could not articulate. He was dying, and surrounded by his weeping friends, his spirit in a few moments took its flight. His death occurred at quarter past six o'clock on the morning of the 29th day of April. He lacked only nine days of being twenty years of age. He was born on the eighth day of May, 1843. Thus had fallen another victim to this most unholy, unnecessary war; a young man of the purest character and the finest promise. Oh! Unhappy, victimized, ruined Virginia, how hast thou suffered in the loss of the flower of thy youth, in the destruction of the cream and essence of thy population.

Led blindly into a war from which under the most favorable circumstances thou hadst nothing to expect but ruin, thy people butchered, thy property squandered, thy territory wasted, thy altars profaned, history must necessarily record the folly, and thy children yet unborn read the humiliating fact that thou allowed thyself to be made a cats paw of others who to save themselves, plotted and accomplished thy ruin. . . .

Source: Turner Family Papers, 1740–1927, Virginia Historical Society, Richmond.

Appendix E

Accounts of Mosby's Rangers and Engagement at Oakley

The Fight at Oakley

Saturday, October 29.—A strong detachment of the Eight Illinois Cavalry was sent from Rectortown on a scout towards Upperville. Capt. Walter E. Frankland, with about 100 men, struck their trail and followed, finding them at Hatcher's Mill, dismounted and feeding their horses. He waited in the woods until they had resumed their march, when he again started on their track. Meanwhile he had been joined by Colonel Mosby, Harry Hatcher, and a number of others who had also been watching the Federal cavalry. Mosby ordered Frankland to intercept them on their return—to get between them and their camp.

"I want you to make it a second Dranesville," said Mosby. "I will do the scouting and will keep you informed of the enemy's movements."

From Upperville the Eight Illinois struck across a level stretch of land in the direction of Rectortown. As they drew near the house of Henry Dulaney [sic], about a mile from Upperville, Frankland determined to attack them in the open field. Dividing his force between Lieut. Albert Wrenn and Lieutenant Grogan, he, with Lieutenant Wrenn and the larger portion, was to attack in front, while Grogan was to march off to the right and strike on their flank.

The Federals formed in three squadrons. Frankland in his charge broke and drove back the first squadron, but the other two remained firm and poured their fire into his party and also into Grogan's men, who now charged on their left. Between Grogan and the Eighth Illinois was a ditch and also a high rail fence. In the charge he was compelled to take his men through a gate in this fence, which not only delayed but also confused their movements, and in consequence Frankland was beaten off before Grogan could unite with him. The squadron in front of Dulaney's house showed signs of wavering, but the Federals on the right of the gate sat quietly on their horses and poured a steady fire into Grogan's flank.

Though our loss was severe, it is surprising that it was no greater. Had the Federals charged us when crowded in passing through the gateway, or cut us off in the inner field, many more would have been lost.

Luther Carrington and George Gulick were killed; John Atkins and Edgar Davis mortally wounded, both dying soon after the fight. Thos. Adams, Geo. Turberville, Maddux and Shaw, wounded. James Chancellor, John Munson, J. J. Williams, C.H. McIntosh and Dennis Darden were taken prisoners.

The Eighth Illinois lost but few, yet they pressed into service a wagon and ox-cart to carry off their dead and wounded.[1]

John Atkins was an Irish gentleman, who, having heard of Mosby's exploits, left home and country to join his fortune with ours. He was brave, generous, of good education, agreeable in his manner, and had in the short time he was with us made many friends. Poor fellow, he suffered greatly, but when death came it was not that grim monster usually pictured, but a kindly spirit, which transported him in his last moments from scenes of blood and carnage back to home and friends; and as he murmured faintly the words, "Oh, my poor mother!" he sank to rest. He was buried in the little cemetery at Paris.

At one time when Atkins was in Richmond on leave of absence, an alarm was sounded that the enemy was about making an attack on the city. Guards were placed on the streets and the provost guard picked up all officers and soldiers absent from their commands, sending them out to the trenches to check any advance. Atkins was arrested and taken to the Soldiers' Home and handed a musket. This was too much for his good nature, even. "Let me go back to my command," said he; "when I am at home I have my horse to ride and boots up to my middle, and I am not going out to the trenches to shovel dirt." He was released on the following day, through the good offices of Capt. Ed. Hudson, of General Elzey's staff.

Edgar Davis was thought to be but slightly wounded, but from the first he persisted in saying he would die. He lingered a few days. His horse was shot, as was also the horse of his brother William. Davis was a very quiet, unassuming man and his loss was much regretted.

Lieut. John N. Murphy of Co. G was, with a few others, at the house of Captain Richards near Upperville. He had just reached there from the Northern Neck—had not taken off his saddle—when the word came: "There are the Yankees!" He and his companions mounted and quickly rode out to the turnpike just as the fight commenced. Murphy had been a captain in the regular service before joining our command, but this was his first experience in our mode of fighting. Seeing the men scattered over the field in every direction, he was confused. He recognized Lieut. Harry Hatcher dashing across the field at full speed, and being well mounted, on a daughter of the famous old race horse Bailey Peyton, Murphy spurred on and overtook him. "Which are our men and which are the Yankees?" asked Murphy.

Harry's reply was: "Damn the difference! Go right in!" Then, turning his head toward Murphy, he said: "There's a Yankee, right by you now!" As Murphy turned towards him, the man wheeled his horse, threw back his hand and fired, the ball from his revolver striking the ground a few feet from Murphy's horse. He then dashed off and rejoined the men of his squadron near Dulaney's house.

Source: James J. Williamson, *Mosby's Rangers: A Record of the Operations of the Forty-Third Battalion of Virginia Cavalry from Its Organization to the Surrender, from the Diary of a Private, Supplemented and Verified with Official Reports of Federal Officers and Also of Mosby* (New York: R. B. Kenyon, 1896), 284–87.

Captured at Oakley

A newly appointed Captain, chosen by Mosby from what he used to call his blue hen's chickens, because of their unfailing excellence, had a chance to win his spurs in a fight that was due to come off near Upperville. A detachment from the Eighth Illinois Cavalry was on a short raid from their camp near Rectortown, to Upperville, and Colonel Mosby ordered them attacked. The officer to whom I refer had been with Mosby since the very inception of the Partisan Rangers and, as an individual fighting man, had no superior in the Command, his promotion from the ranks being a just reward for a continuous record of brilliant service. His waving plume was ever at the head of the column when here was fighting to be done, and everybody in the Command loved Walter Frankland.

Captain Frankland's plan was to divide his Command for the purpose of charging a stone-wall of Federal cavalry in front and flank simultaneously. It did not work if my memory serves me right, as the enemy had our first detachment whipped before Lieutenant Grogan with his flanking party reached the scene. Grogan had no idea that Frankland had been disposed of, until the Federals turned their attention to his little squad, and discomfited him at the same handy pace.

They poured a deadly carbine fire into us as we rushed on. We were charging in fours, and I was at the front, and did not know that our men had wavered and turned off from the hopeless attack until it was too late to follow them. When I discovered my predicament I believe it would have been a safe thing for me to have headed my horse straight at their line and trusted to my breaking my way through by the impetus of the charge. It takes a good strong horse to withstand the charge of another one, head on. What I should have done, and what I did, are two widely different things. Luck, too, was against me. I only realized that I was up against it, and must try to get away. When I headed my mare for a high and forbidding stone fence the animal refused to take the leap. For an instant, as she approached the ugly barrier, I thought she would go over, but that short, firm step that a jumper makes just before rising failed, and a wave of anxiety passed through me as she hesitated. I tried to lift her with the movement that the rider involuntarily makes, and touched her with my spur. She trembled, gave a frightened little neigh, and fell back on her haunches.

It looked bad for me. I jumped from her back, scrambled over the wall on my own hook, and was breaking the world's record in a fine two hundred yard dash for some timber on the other side. At one time I thought I would actually get away, but the Yankees found a gap in the wall I had overlooked and got on my trail at once. My mare jumped the wall after me like a deer, and with head and tail up defiantly, though really as badly scared as I, dashed away across the field and was found the next day riderless, miles away from the scene of my troubles. I fancied, as I saw her fading from me, that she looked back pityingly, but I could fancy any old thing just then.

Before I got a hundred yards from the wall they pounced on me and made the most complete capture of a rebel ever witnessed. About twenty men made as many passes at me, and the baubles and splendors of guerrilla life disappeared. They got my hat and plumes, my gloves and pistols, my watch and belt, and all my personal belongings. Before I had time to make the slightest protest, one fellow sat me down abruptly, put his foot on me, and relieved me of my boots in a most startling and finished manner. Talk about Mosby's men going through a man! There was not a man in our Command who could swoop down and capture a pair of boots like the man who took mine! It was my initial touch at the game of retaliation, and the Yankees trimmed me well.

Source: John W. Munson, *Reminiscences of a Mosby Guerrilla* (New York: Yard and Co., 1906), 168–70.

Notes

Introduction

1. Brenda E. Stevenson, *Life in Black and White: Family and Community in the Slave South* (New York: Oxford Univ. Press, 1996), 38.

2. Lt. Col. Leven Powell served with the 16th Virginia Regiment at White Marsh and Valley Forge, as recorded on his 1937 memorial tablet in the Episcopal Church of Middleburg. Powell genealogy and Leven Powell memorial, Middleburg, Va.

3. Stevenson, *Life in Black and White,* 34.

4. George Cuthbert Powell, 1775–1849. Among his many accomplishments, he served as mayor of Alexandria, a member of the Virginia legislature, a member of the U.S. Congress, and a justice of the peace for Loudoun.

5. Rosalie Noland Ball, *The Family Tree of Col. Leven Powell's Line of the Powells of Virginia* (Richmond: privately printed, 1938), 14.

6. Marietta Minnigerode Andrews, *Memoirs of a Poor Relation: Being the Story of a Post-War Southern Girl and Her Battle with Destiny* (New York: E. P. Dutton, 1927), 32.

7. Eliza Carter Randolph Turner, 1782–1866, was the daughter of Elizabeth Hill Carter of Shirley, a half sister of Anne Hill Carter, Robert E. Lee's mother. Eliza's father, Col. Robert Randolph of Eastern View, near Warrenton, was one of the men named in Charles Carter's will to serve as trustee for the property left in trust to Anne Carter Lee. These men and their heirs were designated to take care of Anne Lee and her children.

8. Colonel Randolph provided a school for family members at Eastern View that included the Turners and young Robert Lee. John T. Toler, "The Turner Family of Kinloch," *News and Notes from the Fauquier County Historical Society* 12, no. 4 (1990): 3.

9. Mary Anne Randolph Custis, 1808–1873, was the only child of Mary Lee Fitzhugh and George Washington Parke Custis, the adopted son and great admirer of George Washington. Her home, Arlington, was filled with Washington memorabilia.

10. Marietta Fauntleroy Turner Powell, 1812–1894.

11. Thomas Turner, 1807–1881, one of Lee's closest childhood companions, chose to stay in the U.S. Navy and retired a rear admiral at the end of the war. He was married to Fanny Palmer.

12. Mary Custis Lee's last letter to Marietta was dated Sept. 22, 1873.

13. Letter from Mildred Lee to Marietta Turner Powell, Dec. 17, 1873. The letters addressed to Marietta Tuner Powell quoted in this book are in the possession of her descendants, the Mackall and Sasscer families.

14. The Powell children were Robert Randolph, Conrad, Mary Eliza (Ida), Thomas, George Cuthbert (died in infancy), Katherine and Virginia.

15. Andrews, *Memoirs of a Poor Relation*, 83.

16. Letter from Mary E. "Ida" Powell to Marietta F. T. Powell, Aug. 14, 1846.

17. Hal's mother was Fanny Addison Carter of Sabine Hall, a direct descendant of Robert "King" Carter. His father, Henry Rozier Dulany of Shuter's Hill, Alexandria, was descended from Daniel Dulany of Maryland, the brilliant barrister and statesman. Both parents had died by 1839, when Hal was five.

18. From colonial times the Dulany men traditionally married well-connected women of wealth. For example, Benjamin Dulany of Alexandria wed the heiress Eliza French, the ward of George Washington and George Mason.

19. Col. Richard Henry Dulany, 1820–1906, the son of Hal's great-uncle, John Peyton Dulany.

20. Hal and Ida Powell Dulany's children were Marietta "May" Randolph, 1856–1926, Henry Rozier, 1857–1940, Rebecca Anne, 1859–1948

21. Katherine Whiting Powell, 1839–1903, and Virginia Cuthbert Powell, 1849–1899.

22. "The Upperville Union Club for the Improvement of Horses," *Southern Planter* 17 (Aug. 1857): 508.

23. Some of the slaves may have belonged to Marietta Turner Powell.

24. At a young age, Rebecca Dulany, 1828–1858, inherited a vast fortune from her childless great-aunt Rebecca, Lady Hunter, of London, married to Sir Richard Hunter, the queen's physician. Lady Hunter was the heir of her wealthy uncle, Daniel Dulany III, a Tory who moved to London after the Revolution and pursued a brilliant legal career in the family tradition. An interesting provision of her will required Rebecca's husband to take the name Dulany in order to inherit, so it was fortunate that Rebecca married her close cousin Richard Dulany, who retained his own name.

25. Stevenson, *Life in Black and White*, 51.

26. Ida's daughter, Rebecca, continued the Oakley tradition of wine making on her own farm near The Plains well into the twentieth century.

27. Stevenson, *Life in Black and White*, x.

28. Letter from Henry G. Dulany dated Feb. 24, 1856. The letters from Hal to Ida quoted in this book are in the possession of their descendants, the Mackall and Sasscer families.

29. Paul C. Nagel, *The Lees of Virginia: Seven Generations of an American Family* (New York: Oxford Univ. Press, 1990), 268.

30. The home of William Fitzhugh, the only brother of Mrs. George Washington Parke Custis, and Ida's cousin.

31. Walker K. Armistead, Jr., and his nephew, Walker K. Armistead, both served in Company A.

32. Journal of Ida Powell Dulany, Dec. 18, 1861.

33. His sister Rebecca died of tuberculosis.

34. Richard Dulany's father, John Peyton Dulany (1787-1878) of Welbourne.

35. Hal was referring to the salted pork that was kept in large supply for use during the year.

36. John Armistead Carter of Crednal, the farm across the road from Welbourne.

37. The entrance to Oakley was on the public highway. The house itself was located almost a mile back from the road, surrounded by fields.

38. Now Route 50.

39. Katherine Whiting Powell's diary is now in the possession of Oatlands Plantation, a National Trust site.

40. Dr. A. W. Thompson. Record Division, Rebel Archives. War Department.

41. Journal of Ida Powell Dulany, July 31, 1862.

42. Margaret Ann Vogtsberger, *The Dulanys of Welbourne: A Family in Mosby's Confederacy* (Berryville, Va: Rockbridge Pub. Co., 1995), 232.

43. Journal of Ida Powell Dulany, June 6, 1862.

44. Journal of Ida Powell Dulany, Nov. 30, 1861.

45. Journal of Ida Powell Dulany, Aug. 10, 1862.

46. Journal of Ida Powell Dulany, Dec. 1, 1864.

1861

1. Daniel Burr Conrad (1829–1898) of Winchester, formerly in the U.S. Navy, enlisted as a surgeon on June 8, 1861, but was serving on the staff of the 2nd Virginia Infantry. He was the son of Elizabeth Whiting Powell and Robert Young Conrad of Winchester. The Conrad brothers, Daniel, Powell, Holmes, and Charles and their sisters, Kate and Sallie, were Ida's first cousins.

2. Joseph Eggleston Johnston (1807–1891), whose name Ida consistently misspelled, was the highest ranking army officer to resign and offer his services to the new Confederate States Army. When Ida began her diary, he was commander of the Army of the Shenandoah, headquartered in Winchester, Virginia. On receiving word that Union general Irwin McDowell was moving his army toward Manassas, Johnston hurried the bulk of his army across the Blue Ridge Mountains to reinforce the Confederate army there.

3. Lawson Botts, 2nd Virginia Infantry, a prominent Virginia attorney who had served as lead defense counsel in the trial of John Brown. He was promoted to lieutenant colonel September 1, 1861 and colonel June 27, 1862. Shot through the cheek and mouth at Second Manassas on August 28, 1862, Botts died in Middletown, Virginia, on September 16, 1862.

4. Piedmont, now known as Delaplane, was a small railroad station village near both Upperville and Salem (now Marshall).

5. Pierre Gustave Toutant de Beauregard (1818–1893), commanding the Confederate Army of the Potomac. Beauregard's first assignment in Confederate service had

been the command of the forces in Charleston, South Carolina. On April 12, 1861, his men there fired the first shots of the war when they began the bombardment of Fort Sumter.

6. John, son of the wealthy planter Robert B. Bolling of Bollingbrook near Upperville. His younger sister, Anna Dade Bolling, was a friend of Ida's youngest sister, Jenny, and a frequent visitor at Oakley. The other Bolling children were William, Stewart, Bartlett, Samuel, and Monroe.

7. Skirmish at Blackburn's Ford on Bull Run Creek, where Confederates repulsed a Union reconnaissance in force on July 18, 1861. Despite Ida's inflated description, eighty-three Union and sixty-eight Confederate men were killed, wounded, or captured.

8. Capt. William H. Dulany, Co. D, 17th Virginia Infantry, son of Hal's cousin Daniel French Dulany, was wounded at Blackburn's Ford. The wound did not prove to be mortal, though it was serious enough to end his military career.

9. Jesse Richards of Green Garden, just east of Upperville. Two of his sons, Adolphus ("Dolly") and William, later joined John Mosby's 43rd Battalion, Virginia Partisan Rangers.

10. "McDonald's Rangers," a cavalry company formed by Col. Angus McDonald. The Rangers formed the nucleus of the 7th Virginia Cavalry, which in turn grew into the Laurel Brigade. Because MacDonald was in his sixties when the war started, he did not long exercise field command of his regiment. In the spring of 1862, he turned it over to Col. Ashby and assumed command of the defenses of Winchester.

11. Trinity Episcopal Church, Upperville, built in 1842. The present church building, a gift of philanthropist Paul Mellon, was constructed in 1960 in the style of a French country church of the twelfth century.

12. Turner Ashby (1828–1862) of Markham, Virginia, a popular cavalryman known as "The Black Knight of the Confederacy."

13. Richard Ashby died July 3, 1861, several days after being bayoneted repeatedly by Union soldiers who attacked him as he already lay wounded. He was killed near Harpers Ferry, not Romney (West Virginia) as Ida reported.

14. The chaplain of McDonald's regiment was John Battle Averitt. Born in Onlsow County, North Carolina, he had practiced law in Alabama and North Carolina before attending theological seminary in Staunton, Virginia. He was the founder of the Dunbar Female Institute in Winchester.

15. Manassas Junction.

16. Better known as First Manassas (Bull Run), the first major battle of the war and an unqualified Confederate victory.

17. Holmes Addison Conrad and his brother Henry Tucker Conrad, Co. D, 2nd Virginia Infantry. The only sons of the Martinsburg Conrads, both were killed at First Manassas. They were first cousins to the Winchester Conrads, Ida's family.

18. Captain William N. Nelson, Co. C, 2nd Virginia Infantry, was badly wounded in the left breast. He never fully recovered and was discharged from the service in May 1862.

19. Ida's cousin Lloyd F. Powell, Co. F, 2nd Virginia Infantry, son of Selina Lloyd of Alexandria and Charles Leven Powell, killed in action.

20. Robert B. Bolling of Bollingbrook near Upperville, and his two youngest children, Anna Dade, thirteen, and Monroe, ten.

21. William A. Wilson of Middleburg, Co. H, 1st Virginia Cavalry, captured at First Manassas and confined in Fort Monroe on the James River peninsula. Wilson was Ida's cousin Burr Powell Noland's brother-in-law.

22. Sgt. Maj. T. Fitzhugh Grayson, 8th Virginia Infantry, captured at First Manassas.

23. John F. Kidwell, overseer of the Oakley farm, lived on the farm with his wife and six children.

24. James Bishop, a farmer living near Salem (now Marshall).

25. Welbourne, the home between Middleburg and Upperville of Hal's brother-in-law Richard H. Dulany.

26. Sarah Powell Conrad (1811–1863), daughter of Ida's great-uncle Alfred Harrison Powell and Mary Elizabeth Tidball.

27. The community of Ashland, located some fifteen miles north of Richmond, was developed by the railroad as a mineral spring spa in the 1840s. The abundance of water and easy access to transportation and supply made it an ideal location for a camp of instruction for the Confederate cavalry.

28. A physician practicing in Upperville and Hal's first cousin, Dr. Eliason entered the army as captain and assistant surgeon in the 6th Virginia Cavalry. In June 1863 he was promoted to colonel and given a position as surgeon on the staff of Gen. J. E. B. Stuart.

29. Mary Landon Carter Eliason, widowed mother of Talcott, William, and Rutledge "Rutty" Eliason, the sister of Hal's mother, Frances Addison Carter Dulany. Both sisters were Carters of Sabine Hall, the Carter plantation in Warsaw, Virginia.

30. William Eliason, younger brother of Dr. Talcott Eliason.

31. He was mistaken. Total casualties for the battle were approximately 4,700 Union and 1,750 Confederate. Most of the Union loss was in prisoners.

32. One of the slaves living at Oakley, he was the dining room butler. "Uncle" was a term used for older men.

33. Ida's cousin Holmes Y. Conrad (1840–1916) of Winchester. Educated at Virginia Military Institute, he served on the staff of Maj. Gen. Thomas L. Rosser. After the war he taught law at Georgetown University.

34. Ben, Dan, and Simon were slaves at Oakley.

35. Confederate forces in Missouri celebrated their first victory in the state on July 5, 1861, when Governor Claiborne Jackson and four thousand militiamen chased Col. Franz Sigel and his one thousand men out of the town of Carthage.

36. Robert Randolph Powell (1832–1883), five years older than Ida, was living in St. Louis in 1861.

37. C. E. Weidmayer, a Swiss citizen who lived at Welbourne, where he was employed as tutor to the Dulany children. Because he was a foreigner and allowed to pass through the lines, he served the family well as the war progressed and vital supplies became scarce in the Confederacy.

38. Ida's cousin, William Hall Turner (1841–1864), was the son of William Fitzhugh Turner of Kinloch and Jane Hall of Baltimore. While serving as one of Mosby's Rangers, he was mortally wounded in a fight on the Loudoun Heights above Harpers Ferry.

39. John Peyton Dulany (1787–1878) of Welbourne, father of Richard Henry Dulany.

40. John Armistead Carter (1807–1890) of Crednal, Hal's mother's brother, was a veteran of the Virginia legislature, having served in the House of Delegates from 1842 to 1844 and the State Senate from 1859 to 1861. He was one of two delegates elected to represent Loudoun County at the secession convention in April 1861. A slaveholder who favored the Union, he voted against secession in both the initial vote of April 4 and the post–Fort Sumter vote of April 17.

41. John Armistead Carter's only son, Richard Welby "Web" Carter (1837–1889), captain, Co. H, 1st Virginia Cavalry. The regiment was under fire most of the day at First Manassas, finally making several charges on the enemy infantry that helped turn the tide and begin the Union rout late in the battle.

42. Of Carter's part in the battle, cavalry commander J. E. B. Stuart wrote: "Captain Carter's company, on which the heaviest of the action fell, lost 9 men killed or mortally wounded, and — wounded, and 18 horses killed. Captain Carter's horse was shot dead as he was gallantly leading his company in to the enemy. Of the gallantry of those engaged I cannot speak in too high terms. The regiment charged was the Fire Zouaves, and I am informed by prisoners subsequently taken that their repulse by the cavalry began the panic so fearful afterwards in the enemy's ranks." *The War of the Rebellion: A Compilation of the Official Records of the Union and Confederate Armies*, 128 vols. (Washington, DC: Government Printing Office, 1880–1901), ser. 1, vol. 2: 483. This source is abbreviated hereinafter as *OR*.

43. George Emory Plaster, a thirty-five-year-old physician who later served as captain of Co. H.

44. To satisfy the needs of the ill-equipped Confederate armies, the Congress in Richmond authorized the "impressment," or mandatory purchase of horses, wagons, and food from civilians at prices set by the government.

45. The Dulany children's "mammy."

46. O. A. Kinsolving, minister of the Episcopal Church in Upperville. In 1870 he became rector of the Episcopal Church in Springfield, Illinois, the same church in which Abraham Lincoln married Mary Todd in 1842.

47. Ida's cousins Holmes and Powell Conrad (1833–1862) of Winchester.

48. Probably Charles Marshall Barton (1835–1862) of Winchester, Powell Conrad's close friend.

49. Holmes Boyd of Winchester, son of Rev. A. A. H. Boyd, a Presbyterian minister. These young men had all grown up together in Winchester.

50. One of the Oakley slaves.

51. One of the Dulany house slaves; wife of free black Henson (Hanson) Willis, for whom the Loudoun County village of Willisville is named.

52. Eliza French Hall Carter, a distant cousin of the Dulany family, wife of Hal's cousin Robert Carter, a lieutenant in Co. A, 6th Virginia Cavalry.

53. Mary Carter Dulany, age twelve, the eldest of Richard and Rebecca Dulany's five children. "Fanny" was Frances Addison Carter Dulany, age ten, the second child in the family. Their other children were John Peyton, Henry "Hal" Grafton, and Richard "Dick" Hunter Dulany.

54. Brig. Gen. Ben McCulloch, CSA, who died in the Battle of Pea Ridge in March 1862.

55. Brig. Gen. Nathaniel Lyon (1818–1861), U.S. His death at Wilson's Creek made him a military hero in the North.

56. The Battle of Wilson's Creek, Missouri, fought August 10, 1861, gave Confederates control of southwestern Missouri and allowed Maj. Gen. Sterling Price to advance as far as Lexington. Ida's rumor was just that; the battle had not yet been fought when she made this entry.

57. Margaret Patterson Turner of Baltimore, wife of Ida's late uncle Charles Cocke Turner (1803–1861) of Kinloch. She was related to Betsy Patterson, who was briefly married to Napoleon's brother, Jerome Bonaparte. Baltimore was considered enemy territory once Virginia withdrew from the Union.

58. The Union naval blockade of Confederate ports began in April 1861.

59. William Herbert (1825–1901), a Dulany cousin. His sister, Elizabeth D. "Mittie" Herbert, lived at Welbourne, having moved in to help raise Richard's five children after the untimely death of Rebecca Dulany.

60. Elizabeth Carter Randolph Turner (1782–1866), wife of Thomas Turner IV of Kinloch.

61. Rebecca Beverley Henderson (1823–1897), sister of Robert Beverley of Avenel and Sarah Jane Beverley, the wife of Ida's uncle Edward Carter Turner of Kinloch. She and her husband, Thomas Henderson, lived at Roland, a nearby farm. Ida called her "aunt" as a courtesy, though they were not directly related.

62. Sophie Calhoun Turner, daughter of William Fitzhugh Turner and Jane Hall of Baltimore, was Ida's cousin. She was staying with her aunt, Rebecca Henderson.

63. Julia Mary Hunt Turner (1822–1900), wife of Ida's uncle Maj. Henry Smith Turner of Kinloch, then living in St. Louis, Missouri.

64. These were railroad cars from the Alexandria, Loudoun, and Hampshire Railroad. The authorities in Richmond ordered them burned, but Col. Eppa Hunton, commander of the forces in Leesburg, decided to move them cross-country on huge sledges to the Manassas Gap Railroad. He even managed to move one of the three AL&H engines; although the other two fell into Union hands because they were in Alexandria when the Union army crossed the Potomac on May 24, 1861. *Autobiography of Eppa Hunton* (Richmond, Va.: William Byrd P, 1933), 27.

65. Maj. Gen. Nathaniel Prentiss Banks (1816–1894), governor of Massachusetts from 1858 to 1860. Lincoln considered Banks for a cabinet post, but he eventually appointed him major general of volunteers. Banks first commanded at Annapolis, Maryland, suppressing support for the Confederacy there. He was sent to command

Union troops on the upper Potomac when Brig. Gen. Robert Patterson displayed timidity and a lack of aggression in that command.

66. It was a mistake. The first skirmish in Kentucky was not fought until September 19, 1861.

67. Col. Richard Dulany wrote to his daughter Mary on August 10, "I saw a letter from your Aunt Ida that there had been some foolish report about my horse having thrown and hurt me. You must never believe anything you hear about me unless I write it to you myself. I have never had better health in my life." From a letter in the possession of Nathaniel Morison, present owner of Welbourne and a descendant of Colonel Dulany.

68. The fires in Hampton were set by order of Confederate brigadier general John Bankhead Magruder, who had heard the town was to be used to house escaped slaves fleeing to General Butler's lines at Fort Monroe.

69. Hal raised pointers and setters.

70. Elizabeth Stanley Armistead, Hal's great-aunt by marriage, the widow of Gen. Walker K. Armistead and mother of Lewis Addison, Walker Keith, and Bowles E. Armistead.

71. Margaret Hereford, a sixty-one-year-old widow, lived in Upperville with her daughter, Fanny Graham, and her six-year-old grandson, Eugene Graham.

72. Nineteen-year-old second son of Robert and Sarah Minge Bolling.

73. Tom was one of the slaves Ida hired out to local businessmen. Eben Taylor Laws ran a hotel in Upperville.

74. Twenty-seven-year-old John M. Scott, an Upperville farmer. On September 1, Scott enlisted in Co. I, 2nd Virginia Cavalry, and served until the end of the war.

75. Captain, Co. H, 17th Virginia Infantry, brother of William and Mittie Herbert.

76. Robert Bolling's first wife had died in 1854, and he was divorced from his second wife, so there were no female relatives in the house.

77. The Battle of Wilson's Creek, fought August 10, 1861.

78. In May 1861 Capt. Nathaniel Lyon, 2nd U.S. Infantry, captured and imprisoned Missouri militia who had been called out for state defense by prosecessionist Governor Claiborne Jackson. In the ensuing rioting in Springfield, a number of civilians were killed when Lyon ordered his men to fire on the mob. Jackson then declared the state was no longer part of the Union and petitioned to join the Southern Confederacy. Over the next several months, he and Lyon conducted a stumbling campaign in southwestern Missouri that finally resulted in a Confederate victory at Wilson's Creek, where Lyon was killed, in August.

79. The Union army lost 1,235 men, and the Confederates 1,095.

80. Fauquier County village formerly known as "White Plains."

81. Ida's cousin Charles Frederick Conrad (1844–1912), eighteen-year-old son of Robert Young Conrad and Elizabeth Whiting Powell of Winchester.

82. Robert Buckner was one of Marietta Powell's slaves. Later in the war, when Uncle Billy ran away, he became the Oakley butler. Wilmouth did not belong to the Dulany family but was hired from another owner for her skills as a domestic.

83. William Carrere, a Baltimore native, lived in Richmond prior to the war. At this time he was volunteer aide-de-camp to Gen. Isaac Trimble.

84. Marion Turner Carrere, Sophie's late sister and daughter of Jane Hall and William Fitzhugh Turner of Baltimore.

85. She refers to the First Manassas battlefield. The smell came from rotting corpses of unburied horses and from the bodies of men buried in shallow graves.

86. Hal's cousin and brother of Talcott Eliason, Rutledge "Rutty" was a member of Hal and Richard's Co. A, 6th Virginia Cavalry.

87. Alexander Homer, Co. A, 6th Virginia Cavalry.

88. Lt. Robert Carter, Cousin Eliza's husband, Co. A, 6th Virginia Cavalry.

89. Thomas "Goody" Carter, Co. A, 6th Virginia Cavalry.

90. Possibly a relative of Ida's grandmother, Catherine Brooke Powell.

91. One of the Oakley slaves Hal took into the service with him as his personal attendant.

92. Nancy Jackson was the Dulany children's "mammy."

93. Ida's cousin Richard William Noble Noland (1822–1886), son of Lloyd and Nancy Whiting Powell Noland of Glen Ora near Middleburg. He was a widower with several children.

94. Ida and Hal's niece, Marietta Minnigerode Andrews, noted in her book *Memoirs of a Poor Relation*, 98, "The family at Oakley were great readers."

95. Marietta Andrews described the dairy at Oakley, "The dairies were exclusively for the milk, with rows of big gray and blue crocks in which the milk was held. The skimming of the cream was a matter of great moment, always supervised by the mistress, and so sweet, and done in a manner so spotless as to put modern sanitary methods to the blush—at least, as it was conducted by my Aunt Ida." *Memoirs of a Poor Relation*, 124.

96. Col. Charles W. Field, commanded the 6th Virginia Cavalry from September 1861 through March 1862, when he left the cavalry to take command of a brigade of Virginia Infantry.

97. William Hall Turner of Baltimore, brother of Sophie and Marion, Willie Carrere's late wife.

98. The Spottswood on Main St. was one of Richmond's most fashionable hotels and a popular stopping place for Confederate officers throughout the war.

99. Dr. Randolph Fitzhugh Mason (1823–1862), great-great-grandson of George Mason, was a surgeon in the Confederate navy. His mother, Lucy Bolling Randolph Mason, was Ida's grandmother's sister.

100. George Washington Custis Lee (1832–1913), eldest son of Robert E. Lee, whose mother was a Carter.

101. Daniel Lee Powell (1826–1871), son of Lucy Lee and William Alexander Powell of Leesburg.

102. Dr. Llewellyn Powell (1802–1870) was the eldest son of Ida's great-uncle George Cuthbert Powell.

103. Thomas Theodore Turner (1841–1897) of St. Louis, Mo., known as "St. Louis Tom" Turner to distinguish him from his cousins, "Kinloch Tom," and "Baltimore Tom" Turner, served as an aide to Gen. Richard S. Ewell. His brother, Wilson Price Hunt Turner (1844–1862), age sixteen, had just left VMI to serve in the 1st Stuart Horse Artillery. They were the sons of Ida's uncle Henry Smith Turner.

104. On August 28, 1861, the Union Navy began a bombardment of the Hatteras Inlet forts while Maj. Gen. Benjamin Butler landed two thousand New York soldiers to attack the nine hundred-man Confederate garrison from the rear. The next day Confederate colonel William F. Martin, having lost nearly one hundred men to combined naval and army gunfire, surrendered almost seven hundred survivors in Forts Hatteras and Clark. Union losses were one man killed and two wounded.

105. Brig. Gen. John B. Floyd, C.S.A. (1804–1863), secretary of war under President James Buchanan.

106. Col. Erastus Barnard Tyler (1822–1891), 7th Ohio Infantry.

107. Battle of Kessler's Cross Lanes, fought August 26, 1861. Floyd, commanding Confederate forces in the Kanawha Valley, surprised and routed Col. Erastus Tyler's 7th Ohio Regiment. Tyler lost 245 men to Floyd's 40 casualties.

108. Ida's aunt, Lavinia Beverley Turner of Kinloch (1814–1892), wife of Confederate surgeon John Foushee Fauntleroy (1809–1884).

109. Ida's cousin Elizabeth Randolph Fauntleroy (1843–1909).

110. Probably skirmishing around Munson's Hill near Falls Church. The casualty figures are exaggerated, as newspapers were prone to do in both North and South.

111. This Anna Bolling, age nineteen, was a daughter of Martha Stith and George Washington Bolling of Petersburg and a niece of Robert Bolling of Bollingbrook. "Little Anna" was Anna Dade Bolling, the thirteen-year-old daughter of Robert Bolling.

112. Probably "Mick" Powell. In her diary for August 27, Kate comments, "Nick [sic] Powell left us yesterday after a visit of a few days." Kate's diary is now in the possession of Oatlands Plantation, a National Trust site.

113. Col. Robert Beverley (1822–1901) of Avenel was married to Ida's cousin Jane Carter (1821–1915). His sister, Sarah Beverley, was married to Ida's uncle Edward Carter Turner of Kinloch.

114. Cutting a rooster's comb was said to be a way to make him stop crowing.

115. Shirley Carter Turner (1806–1868) of Kinloch, older brother of Ida's mother, was married to Sarah Levering Bascom and living in Charleston, South Carolina, in 1861. A former naval officer, he was captain of a passenger ship, the *United States*, when, en route from Liverpool to New York, it struck an iceberg on April 6, 1836, very near the spot where the *Titanic* would sink seventy-six years later. Despite severe damage to the vessel, Capt. Turner brought his ship and passengers safely to port amid much public acclaim.

116. Mary D. Stephenson, wife of William A. Stephenson, a native of Ireland farming near Upperville. Their children often visited Oakley.

117. Elizabeth Whiting Powell Conrad (1809–1872), Ida's father's younger sister.

118. George Carter, Jr., (1838–1928) of Oatlands, who would marry Ida's younger sister, Katherine, in October 1863.

119. The Battle of Cheat Mountain was fought September 12–15, 1861, when Confederate forces led by Gen. Robert E. Lee and Col. Albert Rust attempted to force Brig. Gen. Joseph Reynolds out of his entrenchments at the summit of Cheat Mountain and in the Tygart Valley. Against stubborn Union resistance, poorly coordinated Confederate attacks failed, and Lee was forced to withdraw, having lost ninety men as opposed to eighty Union casualties.

120. Martha L. Stephenson, twenty-three-year-old daughter of William and Mary Stephenson of Upperville.

121. Ida's first cousin Thomas Baynton Turner (1843–1863), known as "Kinloch Tom" to distinguish him from other cousins of the same name, was the son of Sarah Jane Beverley and Edward Carter Turner of Kinloch.

122. This was Union artillery fire from the north side of the Potomac at Edwards Ferry. There was no other military action reported in the area of Leesburg on this date.

123. Lily D. Dandridge, age fifteen, daughter of Philip Pendleton Dandridge of Winchester, a distant cousin of the Dulany family.

124. Generals John B. Floyd, C.S. Army, and William S. Rosecrans, U.S Army. She may have gotten her spelling from the newspapers; but Ida consistently spelled these names incorrectly. The engagement to which she refers is the Battle of Carnifex Ferry, fought on September 10, 1861. On learning of Tyler's defeat at Kessler's Cross Lanes, Rosecrans moved three Union brigades south from Clarksburg to attack Floyd's camps at the ferry. Although darkness forced an end to the fighting with no clear victor, Floyd retreated during the night, blaming his defeat on former Virginia governor Brig. Gen. Henry Wise.

125. The Alexandria Riflemen were a militia company organized in 1856, originally under the name "Alexandria Sharp Shooters." The name was changed when the men of the company realized how it would look to have the unit's initials painted on their knapsacks. In May 1861, shortly after Virginia Ordinance of Secession was passed, the riflemen became Co. A, 17th Virginia Infantry.

126. Col. John Augustine Washington of Waveland near Salem, Virginia, owned Mount Vernon until 1858. One of two staff officers who accompanied Lee to western Virginia, he was killed while scouting possible routes along the Tygart River to attack Federal camps at Elkwater.

127. Ida's cousin Katherine Brooke Powell Conrad (1836–1902) was the daughter of Elizabeth Whiting Powell Conrad of Winchester.

128. Rev. Kinloch Fauntleroy (1837–1907), later a major in the Confederate army, was the son of Lavinia Turner and Dr. John F. Fauntleroy.

129. Bowles Edgar Armistead (1836–1916), son of Gen. Walker Keith Armistead and brother of Gen. Lewis A. Armistead, served as corporal, Co. A, 6th Virginia Cavalry. He was wounded three times and left the army as a lieutenant when Lee surrendered at Appomattox.

130. Isaac Ridgeway Trimble, who was promoted to brigadier general in August 1861 and assigned command of a brigade in Maj. Gen. Richard Ewell's division.

131. Elizabeth Graham, daughter of Margaret Hereford and wife of James Graham, an Upperville neighbor.

132. Joseph E. Johnston was one of five men advanced to the grade of full general in the Confederate armies. Because he was the highest-ranking officer to leave the "Old Army" for Confederate service, he felt he should have been ranked first rather than fourth behind Samuel Cooper, Albert Sidney Johnston, and Robert E. Lee (only Beauregard was lower on the list). The perceived slight led to lasting enmity between Johnston and President Jefferson Davis.

133. Throughout her life Ida suffered from the migraines common to her family.

134. Bruce Gibson of Upperville at this time was a sergeant in Hal's Co. A, 6th Virginia Cavalry. He was eventually promoted to captain and was captured in the Battle of Yellow Tavern, where J. E. B. Stuart was mortally wounded, in May 1864. He later became one of the "Immortal 600" Confederate prisoners used as human shields by Union forces in Charleston Harbor, South Carolina.

135. Hal's cousin, son of Mary L. Carter and William B. Eliason.

136. George H. Dawson, a farmer and mill owner in northeastern Fauquier County.

137. The Rev. A. M. Randolph, an Episcopal clergyman.

138. Probably Jesse F. Murrell, Co. B, 9th Virginia Infantry.

139. Lt. William Carroll, Co. B, 9th Virginia Infantry.

140. George M. Hughes, Co. B, 9th Virginia Infantry

141. Mary Catherine "Cat" Powell Cochran (1814–1895), daughter of Nancy Whiting Powell and Lloyd Noland of Glen Ora, was married to Dr. William B. Cochran and living in Middleburg.

142. Susan Wilson Noland (1827–1872) of Middleburg. She was married to Burr Powell Noland, son of Ida's eldest aunt, and was Catherine Cochran's sister-in-law.

143. The John Harrison home was near Paris, Virginia.

144. Maj. Gen. Sterling Price laid siege to the fortified Union position at Lexington, Missouri, on September 13, 1861. One week later, following successful Confederate assaults on the works (the "Battle of the Hemp Bales"), Col. James Mulligan surrendered his remaining men, having suffered 1,774 casualties. Price had only one hundred men killed or wounded.

145. Fanny Berkeley Cochran Dudley (1839–1865), Cousin Cat's daughter, was married to Thomas Underwood Dudley, who became mayor of Middleburg in 1865 and later Episcopal bishop of Kentucky.

146. Richard Dulany's eight-year-old son, John Peyton Dulany II.

147. Sarah Melville Bolling, age twenty-one, and Mary Tabb Bolling, fifteen, were daughters of Martha Stith and George Washington Bolling of Petersburg and nieces of Robert Bolling of Bollingbrook. Their sister was the Anna Bolling identified in note 111 above. "Little Anna" refers to Anna Dade Bolling, daughter of Robert Bolling.

148. Bettie F. Armistead, daughter of Aunt Armistead.

149. Robert Taylor Scott (1834–1897), a twenty-six-year-old attorney living near Upperville with his wife, Fanny, and their two-year-old son, Richard. Fanny was the daughter of Maj. Richard Henry Carter of Glen Welby. Scott was serving as a captain in the 8th Virginia Infantry. He later served on the staff of General George Pickett and after the war was elected attorney general of the Commonwealth of Virginia.

150. Hal's cousin Walker Keith Armistead, Jr. (1835–1906), second son of Elizabeth Armistead. Walker and his nephew, also named Walker K. Armistead, both served in the 6th Virginia Cavalry.

151. One of the Oakley slaves.

152. She is probably talking about a male sheep or goat for breeding. Ladies could discuss crops but not breeding.

153. A type of parasitic worm.

154. Dr. Francis Whiting Powell (1811–1874) of Middleburg was the younger brother of Ida's father.

155. On the night of October 5, Rosecrans abandoned his camp on Sewell Mountain (western Virginia). Ineffectual pursuit by Lee and Gen. William Wing Loring (1818–1886) was still seen by Southern papers as a victory.

156. A cousin living with the Richard Henry Carter family at Glen Welby, Edith was the same age as Sophie.

157. Sophia deButts Carter, who wed Richard Welby Carter of Crednal in 1866.

158. Like the several "Tom Turners" in Ida's family, the locations of their homes were used to distinguish the two girls named Anna Bolling.

159. Sophie's sister, Eliza Turner, daughter of William Hall Turner.

160. Probably Richard Tavenner, a Hillsborough merchant.

161. Tabb Bolling (1846–1924) married William Henry Fitzhugh "Rooney" Lee, the second son of Gen. Robert E. Lee, in 1867. Rooney's first wife, Charlotte Wickham, and their two children died while he was a prisoner at Fortress Monroe during the war.

162. One of several sons of Col. Angus McDonald; probably William N., who was then between assignments in the Confederate army and who joined McDonald's Company of the 7th Virginia Cavalry the following spring.

163. James M. Mason and John Slidell, Confederate commissioners to London and Paris, respectively, were aboard the British mail packet *Trent* when it was stopped near the Bahamas by Captain Charles Wilkes, commanding the U.S.S. *San Jacinto*. The commissioners and their secretaries were removed from the ship, taken to Boston, and imprisoned in Fort Warren. While Wilkes was hailed as a hero in the North, his action was greeted with outrage in England. For a brief time, it appeared the British would declare war over the issue; but cooler heads prevailed, and the Southerners were released and allowed to complete their journey to Europe in January 1862.

164. Second wife of the Rev. O. A. Kinsolving and daughter of Gen. Asa Rogers of Middleburg. She died six months after this visit, shortly after giving birth to her second child. The Rogers home, Vine Hill, is now the headquarters of the *Chronicle of the Horse*, a periodical dedicated to equestrian sports. It is also the site of an unusual memorial, a bronze statue of a riderless horse commissioned by Paul Mellon in honor of the 1.5 million horses and mules lost to wounds and disease during the war.

165. Alex Grayson, Co. F, 8th Virginia Infantry.

166. Nathan Loughborough, owner of the Rokeby Farm, married Ida's aunt Elizabeth Carter Randolph Turner ("Lattie") of Kinloch in 1842. She died two years later, leaving no children. Loughborough remarried and fathered a large family.

167. Possibly Robert Conrad Powell.

168. Mrs. Ludwell Knapp, a Southern fugitive from Washington, DC, living in Middleburg.

169. Hog killing is done in cool weather to reduce the chance the meat will spoil before it can be preserved. Marietta Andrews later described hog killing at Oakley in her book *Memoirs of a Poor Relation:* "[The hog] is stuck in the throat and left to bleed until thoroughly drained... then the carcass is scalded in an immense pot of boiling water.... Next it is scraped, then hung up head down" (118–20). After it is cut and drawn, the hog hangs to chill for about twenty-four hours. It is carved into various cuts of meat such as hams and shoulders, which are rubbed and covered with saltpeter and finally smoked. The lard comes from fat around the ribs. Everything is used, including the intestines for chitterlings and the head, feet, and tail. The ribs are not cured, however, but eaten fresh.

170. In the prewar years in Northern Virginia, hiring out slaves became a common practice as the demand for slave labor in the Deep South raised the cost of buying slaves. They were usually hired out in January for one year, with contracts specifying the responsibilities of the renter. It was a profitable business for slave owners.

171. Both armies used reconnaissance balloons early in the war. Ida is referring to one of the balloons flown by Union aeronaut Thaddeus S. C. Lowe. In all, Lowe built and flew seven of them: *Union, Intrepid, Constitution, United States, Washington, Eagle,* and *Excelsior.* Once Gen. George McClellan lost command of the Army of the Potomac, aerial observation fell into disfavor; and the balloon corps was disbanded in August 1863.

172. Ida's cousin Thomas Shirley Turner (1837–1865). He was known as "Baltimore Tom" to distinguish him from his cousins, "Kinloch Tom" and "St. Louis Tom" Turner. The son of William Fitzhugh Turner, he was the brother of Willie, Sophie, and Lizzie. "Baltimore Tom" served as a member of the cavalry escort for Gen. Richard S. Ewell before taking command of Co. A, 39th Virginia Cavalry, the headquarters escort for Gen. Robert E. Lee.

173. Ida must have picked this word up from the newspapers. In the antebellum South, slaves were most often referred to as "servants" or "darkies." The word "contraband" was first applied to them by Union general Benjamin Butler, who justified his refusal to return escaped slaves to their masters by designating them "contraband of war," subject to seizure to impair the Confederate war effort.

174. Nickname of St. Mary's of Bethlehem Hospital, the notorious London insane asylum.

175. The village of White Post on the west side of the Blue Ridge Mountains.

176. Virginia Powell, Ida's thirteen-year-old sister.

177. The wagon returned to Oakley after delivering provisions to Hal's company.

178. William Moss, a farmer living near Paris, Virginia. His son, Herbert (Hubert) was serving in Co. B, 8th Virginia Infantry.

179. Small group of officers pitching in together to purchase food, which their servants cooked and served them each evening.

180. On December 11, 1861, Charleston experienced the worst fire in its history, which destroyed more than 575 homes and businesses.

181. The Battle of Dranesville, fought December 20, 1861, was a chance meeting of foraging parties commanded by J. E. B. Stuart on the Confederate side and Brig. Gen. E. O. C. Ord on the Union side. As Ida expected, both sides claimed victory in an indecisive and strategically meaningless fight often called the "Battle of the Hay Wagons." Ord suffered 68 casualties, and Stuart 194.

182. Julia Lunceford, wife of Upperville farmer Harrison Lunceford.

183. Brig. Gen. Milledge L. Bonham (1813–1890) of South Carolina, commanding the 1st Brigade in the Confederate Army of the Potomac. He resigned his commission in January 1862 to take a seat in the Confederate Congress, and he served as governor of South Carolina from December 1862 until December 1864. He rejoined the army as a brigadier general of cavalry in February 1865 and served the rest of the war.

184. Mottrom Dulany Ball of Fairfax, son of Mary Dulany and Spencer Mottrom Ball, was a grandson of Daniel French Dulany.

185. John C. Fremont's occupation of Springfield in October 1861 was the only Union victory over Confederate general Sterling Price in southwest Missouri that year. When Fremont was sacked and replaced by Maj. Gen. David Hunter, the Union army withdrew from Springfield to Rolla and Sedalia, only to return early in 1862 to hold the town for the rest of the war.

186. Catherine Huntington Noland (1849–1871), twelve-year-old daughter of Burr Powell Noland and his wife, Susan Wilson Noland, of Middleburg.

1862

1. T. N. Latham, an attorney living at the W. G. Yerby boardinghouse in Upperville.

2. One of the unrecorded deeds was the deed to Oakley, which Hal had purchased from Richard in 1857. At the time no law required that the deeds be recorded at the court house to be valid; but the sale was finally recorded in Warrenton on January 27, 1862.

3. Archibald McGill Fauntleroy (1836–1886), a surgeon serving on Gen. Johnston's staff. After the war he married Sallie Harrison Conrad, Powell's youngest sister.

4. Fanny Chichester, a seventy-year-old widow living with her two spinster daughters.

5. Samuel Newlan, an Upperville merchant.

6. Rebecca Rogers deButts Pinkney, wife of Captain Robert F. Pinkney, U.S. Navy.

7. "Out hands" were the slaves who worked the fields, as opposed to the house servants, who worked mostly inside the Dulany residence.

8. Prince Albert of Saxe-Coburg and Gotha married his first cousin, Victoria, in 1840, two years after she became queen of England. The cause of Albert's death on December 14, 1861, was diagnosed at the time as typhus. A number of modern

physicians, however, believe the prince's symptoms are consistent with stomach cancer. The queen spent the rest of her long reign in mourning for him.

9. Probably Sgt. Elijah J. Hotchkiss, Co. A, 6th Virginia Cavalry.

10. Ida is referring to the skirmish at Port Royal Ferry, South Carolina, on January 1, 1862. The papers were mistaken, Union brigadier general Isaac I. Stevens achieved his objective at the ferry, then withdrew his troops back to Hilton Head, per Gen. W. T. Sherman's orders.

11. Probably the widow of Allen Pettit, 2nd Virginia Infantry, who died of disease in Winchester in December 1861.

12. Stonewall Jackson left Winchester on January 1, intending to attack and capture Romney (now in West Virginia). To do this, he first needed to occupy Bath (now Berkeley Springs) and Hancock. He reached Bath on January 4, only to find the enemy had fled. He caught up with them in Hancock, where he fought the first skirmish of the campaign. This and another skirmish at Hanging Rock undoubtedly constitute the fighting to which Ida refers.

13. Possibly David Waldhauer, 1st Lt., Co. E, 6th Virginia Cavalry.

14. Typhus, a parasite-borne disease characterized by severe headache, chills, high fever, stupor, and rash. In the days before antibiotics, it was often fatal.

15. Dr. Joseph W. Bronaugh of Lovettsville, Virginia

16. Possibly Lieutenant Robert Gray, Co. F, 8th Virginia Infantry.

17. Commissioned second lieutenant of Co. F, 8th Virginia Infantry, April 26, 1862.

18. In mid-January 1862 approximately one hundred Federal ships set sail for the North Carolina coast. The combined Union naval and land forces under the command of Gen. Ambrose E. Burnside scored easy victories over the Confederates at Roanoke Island, New Bern, Washington, and Plymouth. The expedition ground to a halt in late March when Gen. McClellan recalled a large number of Burnside's troops to take part in the upcoming Peninsula Campaign.

19. The Evansport Battery was on the site of the present-day Marine base at Quantico, Virginia.

20. Better known as the Battle of Mill Spring, or Logan's Crossroad, fought on January 19, 1862. Confederate brigadier general Felix Kirk Zollicoffer was killed and his men driven all the way back to Murfreesboro, Tennessee, ending Southern control of central Kentucky.

21. Capt. O. Jennings Wise, the son of former Virginia governor Henry A. Wise, commanded the Richmond Light Infantry Blues of the 46th Virginia at the Battle of Roanoke Island. He was shot in the wrist early in the battle but continued to lead his men. Late in the conflict he was shot in the chest and was being carried to the rear when he was hit three more times. Mortally wounded, Wise had been put in a boat to be taken to Nags Head when soldiers of the Hawkins Zouaves fired on the party and struck him again. He died in the hands of Union surgeons.

22. Fort Henry on the Tennessee River surrendered to Union gunboats on February 6, 1862. Brig. Gen. Lloyd Tilghman surrendered after sending most of his troops to Fort Donelson.

23. The Confederate government realized that it would soon lose the experienced soldiers who enlisted for one year of service in the spring of 1861. Beginning December 11, 1861, they offered a fifty-dollar bounty and furlough of up to sixty days to any man who reenlisted for the duration of the war. Even this was not enough to keep all the men in the ranks. In April the Congress extended the term of service of all men in the field to three years or the duration of the war.

24. The twelve-thousand-man garrison of Fort Donelson, ten miles from Fort Henry on the Cumberland River in Tennessee, surrendered to a combined army-navy assault force on February 16, 1862, after three days of fighting.

25. Prior to this date, Davis had been presiding over a provisional government. Elections were held in November 1861, and the "permanent" government took office in February 1862.

26. Confederate losses actually totaled 15,067 killed, wounded, or captured.

27. Both rumors were false.

28. The Confederate Army of the Potomac was not renamed the Army of Northern Virginia until March 14, 1862.

29. The army was falling back on Richmond to defend the capital against the army of Maj. Gen. George McClellan, who was then landing on the James River peninsula.

30. The Confederate army abandoned Leesburg on March 6, 1862. The town was quickly occupied by Pennsylvanians commanded by Col. John White Geary.

31. Soldiers of the 28th Pennsylvania Infantry, commanded by Col. John White Geary, commander of the Military District of the Upper Potomac.

32. The Oakley butler at this time. The day after Ida made this entry, "Uncle Billy" left Oakley and Robert became the new butler.

33. According to Ida's sister, Kate, who also recorded the incident in her own diary, young Richard had been working as a cook for the Union army. Finding the work more than he bargained for, he returned home, bringing two federal soldiers with him. The sight of additional Yankees in her kitchen was more than Ida could abide.

34. John White Geary knew Loudoun County well, having run the Potomac Iron Company before the war. Wounded five times in the Mexican War, he had served as San Francisco's first postmaster and later as the first mayor of the city before accepting an appointment as territorial governor of Kansas. He was an ardent abolitionist and Republican, with little sympathy for Southern slaveholders.

35. The skirmishing on March 18 was at Middletown, south of Winchester.

36. George Brown owned the farm adjacent to Oakley.

37. There were eleven people in the Loughborough household at this time, eight of them younger than twelve years of age.

38. Lt. Edward Ratchford Geary, Knap's Battery E, Pennsylvania Light Artillery.

39. Robert continued to serve the Dulany family for years after the war.

40. The Battle of Pea Ridge (Elkhorn Tavern), Arkansas, March 7–8, 1862, appeared to be a Confederate victory at the end of the first day of fighting. The second day, however, saw the Union victorious, and two Confederate generals, Benjamin McCulloch and James M. McIntosh, dead along with 4,600 killed, wounded, or

captured Confederate soldiers. The Union forces lost 1,349 men. It was the largest battle fought west of the Mississippi River.

41 New Bern, North Carolina, fell on March 14, 1862. The Evansport Battery was abandoned by Confederate forces falling back on Richmond.

42. Trinity Episcopal Church in Upperville.

43. A village on the Ashby's Gap Turnpike east of Middleburg.

44. Now called Bluemont.

45. "Mittie" Herbert, niece of John Peyton Dulany, as previously mentioned, lived at Welbourne to help care for Richard Dulany's motherless children.

46. Stonewall Jackson fought and lost the Battle of Kernstown on March 23, 1862. Despite his defeat his presence in the Shenandoah Valley unnerved the authorities in Washington, causing them to send several thousand troops to the valley who would otherwise have reinforced McClellan's army near Richmond.

47. Edward Carter "Ned" Turner of Kinloch (1816–1891), youngest son of Ida's grandfather Col. Thomas Turner, inherited Kinloch in 1839. His first wife, Sarah Jane Beverley, with whom he had nine children, was the sister of Robert Beverley of Avenel. Although Turner was opposed to secession, two of his sons, Bradshaw and Tom, fought for the Confederacy.

48. Actual Union casualties were 590 killed, wounded, or missing, while Jackson lost 718 men.

49. Berry's Ferry crossed the Shenandoah River a few miles south of Berryville.

50. Joseph H. Armstrong, of Warrenton, 44th Virginia Infantry, who died in Chimborazo Hospital in Richmond on May 11, 1862.

51. Resident of Markham and neighbor of the Ashby brothers.

52. Complication of liver disease attributable to alcohol abuse.

53. Col. Thomas T. Munford, 2nd Virginia Cavalry.

54. Turner Ashby's artillery was Capt. Roger Preston Chew's battery of horse artillery. Chew was a native of Loudoun County, born near Snickersville, who grew up in Jefferson County (now West Virginia).

55. Elijah V. White, Poolesville, Maryland native, who lived in Loudoun County before the war, was raising a cavalry company in northern Loudoun "for service on the border." White's company became the 35th Virginia Cavalry, later known as "White's Comanches."

56. The Mustang Liniment note was a small, colorful card advertising a medicinal rub "suitable for man and beast."

57. Sixty-year-old Asa Rogers was a general in the prewar Virginia Militia.

58. Ida's cousin Olivia Clagett Powell, eighteen-year-old daughter of Dr. Francis Whiting Powell of Middleburg.

59. Lucien Powell, fifteen-year-old son of John and Maria Powell, whose farm was between Middleburg and Snickersville.

60. Pennsylvania troops, many of whom were recent immigrants, often spoke English poorly, if at all. Whether they were of Dutch or German extraction, they were commonly known as "Dutchmen" to the people of both North and South.

61. Kate Powell wrote in her diary on April 11, "I never saw Ida calmer in my life. She asked them over and over again, 'Do you call yourselves men and force yourselves into a house where there are none but unprotected ladies? Have you no sisters, no mothers and would you like to see them treated as you are treating us now?'"

62. The Battle of Shiloh was fought April 6–7, 1862, when Gen. Albert Sidney Johnston made a surprise attack on Grant's camps near Pittsburg Landing on the Tennessee River, driving them nearly into the river. Johnston was killed, and command of the Confederate army passed to Gen. P. G. T. Beauregard. During the night Grant was reinforced by another army led by Maj. Gen. Don Carlos Buell. Beauregard, now outnumbered, was forced to retreat to Corinth, Mississippi, after hard fighting the next day.

63. The Battle of Valverde (Fort Craig), New Mexico, was fought on February 21, 1862. Despite the Confederates' victory and their subsequent occupation of Santa Fe, they were forced to leave New Mexico within four months.

64. Henry Smith Turner (1811–1881) of St. Louis, Missouri, brother of Edward Carter Turner. A West Point graduate and career army officer, he was sent to France to study French cavalry tactics. He retired from the army in 1848 and subsequently had a successful career in banking. He and his wife, Julia Mary Hunt, were the parents of Wilson Turner of the Stuart Horse Artillery and "St. Louis" Tom Turner, aide-de-camp to Gen. Ewell.

65. The C.S.S. *Virginia*, the Confederacy's first ironclad naval vessel, was built in the Gosport Navy Yard in 1861. On March 8, 1862, she ventured into Hampton Roads and destroyed the Union frigates *Congress* and *Cumberland*. The next day she engaged in the famous battle with the U.S.S. *Monitor* from which neither ship emerged clearly victorious. She was scuttled on May 11, 1862, to keep her out of Union hands. The news that *Virginia* had "captured six more vessels" was just a rumor with no basis in fact.

66. Rokeby, later the home of philanthropist and horse breeder Paul Mellon.

67. Brig. Gen. Louis Blenker, formerly colonel of the 8th New York Infantry (also known as the First German Rifles), came to America from Germany in 1849.

68. Addison Carter, who lived near Welbourne, was a distant cousin of Hal's.

69. The Harrisons owned Windsor, a large home north of Upperville.

70. Robert Wheat, an Alexandria merchant.

71. J. Alexander Carter, who lived at Meadow Grove, near Salem (Marshall) and later served in the Confederate navy.

72. Twenty-three-year-old Elizabeth Grayson, sister of Alexander Grayson.

73. There had been no fighting yet at Corinth. The Union army, now under the personal command of Gen. Henry W. Halleck, slowly followed Beauregard from Shiloh to Corinth, Mississippi, and laid siege to the town, which the Confederates abandoned on May 29, 1862, without a serious fight.

74. Samuel Hutchinson, age sixty-four, postmaster of Upperville. Hutchinson had a longstanding feud with Henry T. Dixon, known as the only man in Fauquier County to vote for Abraham Lincoln. Dixon is said to have provoked the incident that resulted in Hutchinson's death. There is no report on the killing in the *OR*.

75. Ransel Johnson of Rectortown.

76. Capt. George F. McCabe, 28th Pennsylvania Infantry. See appendix A for John Peyton Dulany's description of this incident.

77. Robert Eden Scott (1808–1863), a prominent Warrenton attorney, had been a member of Virginia state house of delegates, delegate to the Virginia state Constitutional Convention, delegate to the Virginia secession convention, and delegate from Virginia to the Confederate Provisional Congress. Abraham Lincoln invited Scott to join his first cabinet as Secretary of the Navy. He was killed in a skirmish with Union deserters on May 3, 1862. Since he was the father-in-law of Hal's cousin Fanny Carter, Ida was deeply concerned about his death.

78. Sarah Harrison Conrad (1843–1908), daughter of Robert Y. Conrad of Winchester.

79. Kernstown. The Union forces suffered 590 casualties, and Jackson 718.

80. Ann Rebecca Holmes Boyd Powell (1807–1895), widow of Ida's uncle, Humphrey B. Powell. The deceased daughter was her eldest, Louisa. While she was in Richmond, her home was occupied by Union soldiers and five women, who stole "all of her cut glass, china and everything that was left in the house," according to Kate Powell's diary entry for May 6.

81. The Confederates abandoned their entrenchments around Yorktown on May 3, after delaying McClellan's advance up the James River peninsula for more than a month. While Northern papers claimed a great victory had been won, the only fighting in this stage of the campaign was skirmishing and a rearguard action that took place on May 4 near Williamsburg.

82. John Matthews, a carpenter from Brandywine, Virginia.

83. The killings took place on Frank Smith's farm near Salem. The Union soldier who killed the two men, H. H. Bayard, Co. A, 7th Wisconsin Volunteer Infantry, later showed up in Gen. Geary's camp at Rectortown, claiming to have escaped from Confederate scouts who had captured him and his companion, William C. Franklin, who died. Bayard said he and Franklin were only trying to return to their command when they were attacked by the citizen posse; but Geary concluded, "It appears . . . that they had been guilty of marauding in the section through which they passed."

84. The first major battle of the Peninsula Campaign, the action at Williamsburg involved nearly 41,000 Union troops and 32,000 Confederate. It was a clash between Gen. George McClellan's advance forces and Gen. James Longstreet's rearguard of the Army of Northern Virginia. The fighting cost McClellan 2,283 men and Longstreet 1,560. The Confederates continued their withdrawal into the defenses of Richmond without further molestation.

85. Richard Hunter Dulany (1856–1917), youngest son of "Brother Richard" and Rebecca Ann Dulany.

86. Maj. Gen. Richard Stoddert Ewell (1817–1872), a native of Washington, DC, who grew up in Virginia.

87. James H. Credeler, a butcher from Leesburg.

88. On May 15, 1862, a party of Geary's 28th Pennsylvania Infantry was attacked at Linden Station on the Manassas Gap Railroad by several companies of the 6th Virginia Cavalry, including Richard Dulany's Co. A. The Pennsylvanians lost one man killed, three wounded, and fourteen captured. The Confederates reported no casualties.

89. George S. Ayre, owner of Ayreshire, a farm on Trappe Road, north of Upperville.

90. Co. A, 17th Virginia Infantry; son of Albert B. Fairfax of Warrenton.

91. Winston Carter, Second Lieutenant, Co. F, 17th Virginia Infantry.

92. Richard Henry Carter of Glen Welby, Captain, Co. B, 8th Virginia Infantry.

93. Joseph Gibson, father of Lt. Bruce Gibson of Co. A.

94. Richard deButts, who was married to Sarah Hall, lived near Linden.

95. Geary was promoted to brigadier general on April 25, 1862.

96. On May 15, 1862, the Union ironclads *Monitor* and *Galena*, and accompanied by gunboats *Port Royal*, *Aroostook*, and *Naugatuck* steamed up the James River from Fort Monroe to test the defenses of Richmond. The five gunboats encountered submerged obstacles and deadly accurate fire from the batteries of Fort Darling at Drewry's Bluff, which inflicted severe damage on the *Galena*. The Union vessels turned back after suffering at least fourteen dead and thirteen wounded.

97. Twenty-two-year-old daughter of William A. Stephenson.

98. Ida is keeping the man's name a secret in case her journal should fall into Union hands. Anyone caught carrying mail between Confederate forces and territory occupied by the Union army could be imprisoned for disloyalty or hanged as a spy. It was probably Robert McArtor, who had been Upperville's mail carrier prior to the war.

99. This was the Battle of First Winchester (Bower's Hill), in which Stonewall Jackson, having already beaten Banks at Strasburg and Guard Hill, drove down the valley and beat him again at Winchester, which is less than twenty miles from Ida's home near Upperville.

100. Anna Wilson Noland (b. 1847), daughter of Susan and Burr Powell Noland and granddaughter of Nancy Whiting Powell Noland, Ida's father's sister. In 1867 Anna married author Virginius Dabney.

101. Brig. Gen. Edward "Allegheny" Johnson defeated two Union brigades commanded by Brig. Gen. Jacob D. Cox in three days of fighting in Mercer County, western Virginia (May 15–17). Rosecrans was no longer in western Virginia, having been transferred to the Army of the Mississippi earlier in the year.

102. Capt. John W. Fletcher, Co. A, 7th Virginia Cavalry, killed while leading a charge at Buckton Station, midway between Front Royal and Strasburg, on May 23.

103. Sixty-year-old Catherine Brooks of Bristersburg, Virginia

104. Maj. Arthur Herbert, 17th Virginia Infantry, brother of William and "Mittie" Herbert.

105. Brig. Gen. Robert Milroy and Brig. Gen. Robert Schenck, beaten by Jackson in the Battle of McDowell on May 8, the first Confederate victory in Jackson's Valley Campaign.

106. Probably William Fletcher of Upperville.

107. Mr. Bolling was mistaken. Brig. Gen. Edmund Kirby Smith was transferred from the Shenandoah Valley to the Department of East Tennessee in March 1862.

108. Maj. Charles Case, 3rd Indiana Cavalry.

109. Because the 6th Virginia Cavalry made a successful surprise attack on the 28th Pennsylvania on May 15, Richard Dulany was well known to and hated by the men of the regiment.

110. Powell Conrad was twenty-seven years old when he died May 23, 1862, in the Battle of Front Royal.

111. Charles Marsall Barton, 1st Stuart Horse Artillery, was killed in the fighting at Bower's Hill near his parents' home in Winchester.

112. Lucy Kinsolving died two weeks after giving birth to her last child.

113. Col. Scott Carter, 3rd Indiana Cavalry.

114. The firing was from skirmishing at Strasburg and Woodstock as Jackson hurried back up the valley toward Harrisonburg to avoid being encircled by three Union armies.

115. The Battle of Seven Pines (Fair Oaks), May 31 and June 1.

116. Also known as Shiloh.

117. Possibly Capt. Freeman Orme, 6th New York Cavalry. As part of the cavalry division in the Military District of Washington, the regiment frequently scouted through Loudoun and Fauquier counties.

118. The Confiscation Act, officially entitled "An Act to suppress Insurrection, to punish Treason and Rebellion, to seize and confiscate the Property of Rebels, and for other Purposes," was passed by the U.S. Congress on July 17, 1862. See appendix B for the *Harper's Weekly* article on its passage and provisions.

119. Dr. William Presley Gunnell was living in Upperville at this time.

120. Margaret was probably suffering from tuberculosis, known at the time as "consumption," which was the leading cause of death in antebellum America.

121. The series of battles known as the Seven Days formed one of the bloodiest campaigns of the entire Civil War. Lee's Army of Northern Virginia suffered about 20,000 casualties (3,286 killed, 15,909 wounded, and 946 captured or missing) out of a total of more than 90,000 soldiers. McClellan reported casualties of about 16,000 (1,734 killed, 8,062 wounded, and 6,053 captured or missing) out of a total of 105,445.

122. Mary Lee and her daughters were visiting Charlotte Wickham Lee, Rooney's wife, at her home, the White House on the Pamunkey, which Rooney Lee inherited from his grandfather George Washington Parke Custis, when McClellan began his move up the James River peninsula toward Richmond. They were only briefly detained when they left the house after pinning a note to the door that read, "Northern soldiers who profess to reverence Washington, forbear to desecrate the home of his first married life, the property of his wife, now owned by her descendants." Initially the house was protected, but on June 27, in the confusion following McClellan's defeat at Gaines' Mill, someone burned it to the ground.

123. Richard Dulany was shot in the right thigh in a skirmish near Strasburg on June 1, 1862. The wound was serious enough to put him out of action for several months.

124. Co. A, 17th Virginia Infantry, killed at Seven Pines (Fair Oaks) May 31, 1862.

125. The day after Johnston was wounded, command of the Army of Northern Virginia passed to Gen. Robert E. Lee, who had been serving as military adviser to Jefferson Davis.

126. John Peyton Dulany's personal body servant.

127. Clarence C. Whiting (1844–1939), Co. I, 6th Virginia Cavalry, was not killed, but he was captured at Fair Oaks on May 31 while serving as a courier for Gen. Stuart. He was exchanged from Fort Delaware on August 5, 1862, and returned to his regiment. Whiting was the grandson of John Peyton Dulany.

128. Mr. Kidwell had a wife and six children to feed.

129. Turner Ashby was killed near Harrisonburg on June 6, 1862.

130. John Haley, overseer at Welbourne.

131. Arthur Rogers, Co. D, 8th Virginia Infantry, was the son of Gen. Asa Rogers and brother of Lucy Kinsolving. The report of his death was a mistake. He survived the war and became a prominent attorney in Middleburg.

132. Brig. Gen. James Shields, commanding a division in the Union Army of the Shenandoah. The battle Ida describes is the Battle of Port Republic, fought June 9, 1862.

133. Fourteen-year-old Mary Doughty, who lived with the Bollings at Bollingbrook.

134. Fifteen-year-old Samuel Bolling, younger son of Robert B. Bolling.

135. William, another son of Robert Bolling, was serving in the Rockbridge Artillery.

136. Maj. Gen. John C. Fremont, commanding the new Mountain Department. He resigned his commission later in 1862, when his command was made subordinate to Maj. Gen. John Pope.

137. Jackson actually beat Fremont at Cross Keys on June 8 and Shields at Port Republic the following day. Their retreat left him in control of the middle and upper Shenandoah Valley and cleared the way for him to move his army to Richmond to reinforce Lee for the Seven Days Campaign.

138. Col. Henry Anisansel, 1st West Virginia Cavalry.

139. Rebecca Dulany later recalled that a typical supper at Oakley consisted of thin sliced ham cured on the property, salad or perhaps asparagus from the garden, hot rolls or spoon bread, and strawberries, peaches, or other fruit in its season, always served with heavy cream.

140. Robert Randolph Powell married Anna Lucas Hunt of St. Louis, Missouri.

141. Turner Ashby was originally buried in the University of Virginia Cemetery in Charlottesville. In 1869 his body was moved to the Stonewall Cemetery in Winchester, where he now shares a grave with his brother, Richard.

142. A slave at Glen Welby.

143. Wife of Richard Henry Carter of Glen Welby.

144. Jackson and his men actually left the Shenandoah Valley on June 17 to join Lee's army near Richmond for what would become known as the Seven Days Campaign. That the Union soldiers did not realize he was gone is a testimony to the effectiveness of the small force he left behind to screen his movements.

145. Brig. Gen. Beverly H. Robertson (1827–1910). In September 1862 Robertson was sent to North Carolina to recruit and train new cavalry regiments, W. E. Jones was promoted to brigade command, and Richard Dulany transferred from the 6th to the 7th Virginia Cavalry to become its new lieutenant colonel.

146. Lt. Robert Carter was married to Elizabeth French Hall, who nursed Col. Dulany during his recovery at her brother's home.

147. Brig. Gen. Richard Taylor (1826–1879), son of former president Zachary Taylor, commanded the Louisiana Brigade during Jackson's Valley Campaign of 1862. Although he had no formal military training, many considered him one of the best Confederate generals of the war.

148. Actually there were five. Taylor's attack at the Coaling turned the Union left flank and forced their withdrawal from the battlefield.

149. Mr. Fletcher's son, William H. Fletcher, was serving with the 39th Virginia Cavalry, the Provost Guard of the Army of Northern Virginia, attached to Lee's headquarters.

150. John Mason Harrison, younger brother of Burr William Harrison. Ida was related to the Harrisons through her paternal great-grandmother, Sarah Harrison.

151. Probably George Bitzer, a farmer from Middleburg.

152. George Carter, coming to court Kate Powell.

153. Benjamin C. Carter, son of Henry H. Carter of Salem (Marshall), lieutenant, 8th Virginia Infantry. Some records indicate he never returned to the service after being wounded at Ball's Bluff in October 1861.

154. Probably James William McCarty, 1st lieutenant and adjutant, 7th Virginia Cavalry.

155. Newstead.

156. Home of George Carter's widowed mother. She had left her husband's property, Oatlands, in 1861.

157. Newstead Farm is on Greengarden Road, east of Upperville.

158. Windsor Farm is on Trappe Road, north of Upperville

159. John M. and Susan Harrison.

160. Capt. Thomas W. Higgins, Co. B, 73rd Ohio Volunteer Infantry.

161. It would have been improper for Ida to accept a valuable gift from a gentleman who was not a relative.

162. Elizabeth Grayson Carter, mother of George and Benjamin Carter, owned Bellefield and Oatlands in Loudoun County. George, youngest of her two sons, moved into Oatlands when he married Kate Powell in 1863 and inherited the property when his mother died in 1885.

163. Robert F. Gray of Loudoun County, who later became a lieutenant in Mosby's Co. B, 43rd Battalion, Virginia Partisan Rangers.

164. Henry Arthur Hall, son of Edward Hall and Louisa French Dulany, was married to Susan Grayson. His sister, Eliza French Hall, was married to Robert Carter of Co. A, 6th Virginia Cavalry.

165. Both the Fort Darling (Drewry's Bluff) and Charleston actions involved the repulse of Union gunboats by Confederate artillerymen.

166. The Seven Days Campaign to drive McClellan away from Richmond started on June 25 with the Battle of Oak Grove. It ended July 1 in the Battle of Malvern Hill. The battle to which Ida refers was Gaines Mill, fought on June 27.

167. Turner H. Gallaher of Union (now Unison), in Loudoun County.

168. Aquilla Glasscock of Rockburn, near Rector's Crossroads.

169. Sickles's Brigade, also known as the Excelsior Brigade, was commanded by a former congressman from New York, Brig. Gen. Daniel Edgar Sickles. In 1859, he had made legal history by successfully pleading temporary insanity for shooting his wife's lover, Philip Barton Key, the son of Francis Scott Key, in Lafayette Park across from the White House.

170. On June 16, 1862, Brig. Gen. Nathan "Shanks" Evans, the hero of Balls Bluff, defeated a Union attempt by Brig. Gen. Henry Benham to take control of Fort Lamar and the town of Secessionville near Charleston. The Union lost 685 men, and the Confederates 204.

171. Maj. Gen. Benjamin F. Butler's General Orders No. 28 read: "As the officers and soldiers of the United States have been subjected to repeated insults from the women (calling themselves ladies) of New Orleans, in return for the most scrupulous noninterference and courtesy on our part, it is ordered that hereafter when any female shall, by word, gesture, or movement, insult or show contempt for any officer or soldier of the United States, she shall be regarded and held liable to be treated as a woman of the town plying her avocation."

172. Brig. Gen. Richard H. Anderson (1821–1879) commanded a brigade in Longstreet's Corps.

173. Brig. Gen. Lawrence O'Bryan Branch (1820–1862), commander of a North Carolina brigade in Hill's Light Division. Branch would be killed at Antietam only a few months later.

174. The Seven Days battles cost the Confederate Army of Northern Virginia 20,614 men, while the Union Army of the Potomac lost 15,849.

175. It is not clear what general Ida had in mind here. There was no General Bonham in the Union army. General Henry Bohlen commanded a brigade under two inept division commanders, Blenker and Schurz; but he personally performed well at the Battle of Cross Keys on June 8. The fact that Ida has attached a nonexistent name to this account speaks loudly as to the level of rumor mongering on the home front.

176. Susan Kidwell, wife of Oakley overseer John F. Kidwell.

177. A family near Upperville.

178. Only four Union generals became casualties in the Seven Days battles. Three (Sumner, Sedgwick and Casey) were wounded, and one (McCall) captured.

179. Asa Rogers was taken prisoner along with thirty other citizens to be held hostage for Union sympathizers imprisoned by Confederate authorities. Most were exchanged quickly; but Gen. Rogers was held for several months in Fort Delaware. He was Rev. Kinsolving's father-in-law.

180. Rev. William Tudor, D.D., a Methodist minister in Paris, Virginia.

181. Craig Woodrow McDonald, killed in the fighting along the Chickahominy.

182. Adie and Grayson, both serving in Co. C, 17th Virginia Infantry, were killed at Frazier's Farm.

183. Brig. Gen. Richard Griffith, commanding the Mississippi Brigade, was mortally wounded at Savage Station.

184. Brig. Gen. Arnold Elzey survived a serious head wound at Gaines' Mill on June 27, 1862, and actually returned to duty in command of the Department of Richmond the following December.

185. "Dirge for Ashby" by Margaret Junkin Preston (1820–1897). Preston was the sister-in-law of "Stonewall" Jackson.

186. John Wornal, who kept a store in Upperville.

187. Richard Dulany was promoted to lieutenant colonel of the 7th Virginia Cavalry on June 20, 1862.

188. In her book *Scraps of Paper* (New York: E. P. Dutton, 1929), 45, Marietta Minnigerode Andrews, daughter of Virginia Powell, noted: "Captain Dulany, my Uncle Hal, had lost one eye entirely in his childhood, owing to an accident." Hal was offered Richard's old position as captain of Co. A, 6th Virginia Cavalry, but resigned on July 6, 1862, slightly more than a year after he enlisted for one year's service.

189. Probably John Thomas Dowdell of Leesburg, discharged from Hal's company on May 1 because of heart disease.

190. One of the young Welbourne slaves.

191. On the morning of June 17, 1862, four Union gunboats, *Mound City*, *St. Louis*, *Lexington*, and *Conestoga*, steamed up White River toward Saint Charles, attempting to resupply Maj. Gen. Samuel R. Curtis's army near Jacksonport, Arkansas. While engaging Confederate batteries on Saint Charles Bluff, *Mound City* was hit and her steam drum exploded, scalding most of the crew to death. An attack by the 46th Indiana Infantry, hurriedly landed from accompanying transport vessels, ended the firing from the batteries and left Saint Charles open to Federal occupation.

192. By July 1862 Confederate cavalry under the command of Brig. Gen. Nathan Bedford Forrest (1821–1877) and Col. John Hunt Morgan (1825–1864) made separate cavalry raids into middle Tennessee and Kentucky. Perhaps the most dramatic event of the campaign was Forrest's capture of approximately nine hundred men of the Union garrison at Murfreesboro, Tennessee, on July 13, 1862. The Confederates destroyed Union supplies and tore up railroad track in the area, but the main result of the raid was the diversion of Union forces from a drive on Chattanooga. This raid, along with Morgan's raid into Kentucky, made possible Bragg's concentration of forces at Chattanooga and his early September invasion of Kentucky.

193. Maj. Gen. John Pope (1822–1892) was appointed commander of the newly formed Army of Virginia (Union) June 26, 1862. See appendix C for the text of his general orders concerning the treatment of civilians and their property.

194. C.S.S. *Arkansas*, an ironclad partially built in Memphis, was completed in Yazoo City, Mississippi, and crewed by volunteers from the Missouri militia. On the morning

of July 17, 1862, it set course for Vicksburg. To get there, it had to pass through a blockading force that consisted of at least ten ships of war, six ironclads, and seven rams. In the ensuing action U.S.S. *Carondolet*, an ironclad, was severely damaged, while several other Union vessels sustained lesser damage. The *Arkansas* was so badly damaged by shots through its smokestack that it was barely able to maintain a one-knot speed by the time it reached the protection of Vicksburg's forts. After this defeat the Federal commanders had no choice but to end the blockade of Vicksburg, with the lower fleet heading south toward New Orleans and the upper fleet back toward St. Louis. The Union navy did not reappear in front of Vicksburg for four welcome months, after the *Arkansas* had gone.

195. Capt. Samuel C. Means was a Waterford miller given special authority by U.S. Secretary of War Stanton to raise a regiment of cavalry among Loudoun County's Unionist population. He began recruiting for his Independent Loudoun Rangers on June 20, 1862. The unit never reached full regimental strength because most of Loudoun's Unionists were Quaker, Brethren, and German Reformed Church pacifists.

196. Walter R. Leigh, Co. A, 5th Virginia Cavalry.

197. Brig. Gen. John Porter Hatch (1822–1901) commanded the cavalry of the V Corps.

198. David Glasgow Farragut (1801–1870), who married a Virginian, remained loyal to the Union when that state seceded in 1861. He became a national hero in the North when he led the fleet that captured New Orleans.

199. Unable to identify. Prior to Lt. Gen. John C. Pemberton's arrival, the commander of the Vicksburg garrison was Col. James L. Autry. The commander of the Department of Mississippi and East Louisiana was Maj. Gen. Earl Van Dorn.

200. Co. I, 4th Virginia Cavalry, killed at Malvern Hill July 24, 1862. He was the son of Thomas Nelson Carter of Shirley.

201. When Congress outlawed the importation of foreign slaves in 1808, an extensive domestic trade opened between the older slave states such as Virginia and Maryland and cotton-growing Gulf States. Because of the hard labor and malarial climate on the Gulf coast, being "sold south" was seen as the worst possible punishment for slaves in the mid-Atlantic region.

202. The only wartime "pestilence" in Richmond was a scarlet fever epidemic that swept through the city in December 1861 and January 1862.

203. Brig. Gen. Robertson commanded a brigade of cavalry under Maj. Gen. J. E. B. Stuart during the Second Manassas Campaign.

204. The newspapers possibly referred to Brig. Gen. Meriwether Jeff Thompson, a cavalry commander in Missouri who became known as "The Swamp Fox of the Confederacy." If so, they were mistaken about his having been defeated. Thompson did not begin his active campaign against the Union forces in the southeastern portion of the state until October 1862. The Confederate defeat mentioned in the paper was probably the defeat of Confederate colonel John C. Porter in Kirksville on August 6.

205. Probably Isaac Throckmorton of Summit Point, Virginia. His son, William W. Throckmorton, was captured at Boonsboro, Maryland, during the Antietam Campaign and remained a prisoner until February 1865.

206. The Battle of Cedar Mountain on August 9, 1862, involved roughly 17,000 men of Stonewall Jackson's corps against slightly more than 8,000 under the command of Nathaniel Banks. It signaled a shift of military action from Richmond and the James River peninsula to northern Virginia. The battle cost Banks 1,400 men as opposed to 1,307 Confederate casualties.

207. Brig. Gen. Charles Sidney Winder, a Marylander by birth, was killed while commanding the Stonewall Brigade.

208. Geary was seriously wounded in the arm and leg at Cedar Mountain but did not lose either limb.

209. Probably Willie Hall, age nine, John Peyton Dulany's great-nephew.

210. Brig. Gen. George W. Morgan held Cumberland Gap for the Union from June 18 to September 17, 1862, despite harassment from John Hunt Morgan's Raiders. Finally, cut off from supplies and completely surrounded, Morgan and his nine thousand men successfully retreated to Camp Dennison, Ohio.

211. Gen. Van Dorn ordered the *Arkansas* to support a land attack at Baton Rouge. The ship departed under the command of her first officer, Lt. H. K. Stevens. The ship was scuttled when its finicky engine broke down near Baton Rouge.

212. Davis instructed Lee to notify Union officials that Pope and certain of his officers would not be granted the status or rights of prisoners of war if they should fall into Confederate hands but would instead be treated as "robbers and murderers."

213. Sixteen-year-old Jane Peter Turner, eldest daughter of Edward ("Ned") and Sarah Beverley Turner.

214. Sarah Beverley Turner was the mother of nine children, seven of whom were still living at home.

215. The Battle of Cedar Mountain (Slaughter Mountain), August 9, 1862.

216. Dr. Thomas C. Williams.

217. John Carr, a farmer who was the son of Joseph Carr, the founder of Upperville.

218. Twenty-four-year-old Joseph Gibson, an Upperville merchant.

219. Capt. Henry A. Cole's Maryland 1st Potomac Home Brigade Cavalry and Capt. Samuel C. Means's Independent Loudoun Rangers.

220. In a letter to his daughter Mary, dated August 17, Richard H. Dulany wrote, "I received your second letter by your Uncle Hal, who joined me at yr. cousin James Hall's on Sunday last" (August 10). Colonel Dulany had incurred a serious thigh wound on June 1 near Strasburg and spent time recuperating at Buffalo Springs Spa near Amherst, Virginia. The letter is in the possession of Nathaniel Morison of Welbourne.

221. The Union forces under Banks lost twenty-seven hundred men, and the Confederate forces under Jackson thirteen hundred in the fighting at Cedar Mountain. Although Banks fought well, his defeat signaled a shift in the fighting in Virginia from the peninsula to the northern portion of the state and indicated the initiative would belong to Lee for the time being.

222. The firing Ida heard on the twenty-fourth was a demonstration designed to keep Pope in position on the banks of the Rappahannock while Jackson slipped

around his right flank to get to his rear. It worked, and the next night Jackson's hungry men feasted on Pope's supplies at Manassas Junction.

223. General Lee spent the night before Second Manassas at Avenel, home of his cousin Jane Carter Beverley. She later wrote, "The next time I saw General Lee was the night before Second Manassas. Robert [Jane's husband] came in the afternoon and said General Lee and his staff would spend the night. We were very busy getting supper for them all and put down palettes on the floor. At supper I apologized for the warm milk which was just from the cow, the other milk having been drunk up by the soldiers. General Lee declared the milk delightful and said he hoped it was none of his men who had got the other milk, which of course it must have been. At supper he was the life of the whole crowd and kept everyone laughing and in good spirits. That night he slept in the little room and the members of his staff slept in the room at the head of the stairs and in the far room. The servants were up nearly all night cooking breakfast for the staff which of course left early. I did not come out in the morning but from the end of the porch I saw the General mount his gray horse and at the head of his staff ride down the road at the foot of the garden. They told me he had been heard walking the floor until three o'clock in the morning when a courier came with news that Jackson had held his own" Robert Beverley Herbert, *Life on a Virginia Farm* (Warrenton, Va.: Fauquier Democrat, 1968), 86.

224. Son of Otway and Judith Carter.

225. Ida's cousin Bradshaw Beverley Turner (1841–1910), son of Edward Carter Turner of Kinloch, serving in the 9th Virginia Cavalry, was wounded at Second Manassas but recovered only to be wounded again near Richmond in 1864.

226. Maj. Gen. Richard S. Ewell was seriously wounded and lost a leg in the fighting at Groveton, the opening stage of the Battle of Second Manassas on August 29, 1862.

227. Charles L. Powell, Jr., Fredericksburg Light Artillery, killed at Warrenton Springs on August 24, 1862. He was the son of Charles Leven Powell. His only brother, Lloyd, was killed at First Manassas.

228. Randolph Fitzhugh Mason, a surgeon in the Confederate navy, died August 9, 1862.

229. Walker Keith Armistead, Jr., brother of Gen. Lewis A. Armistead. He enlisted in Co. A, 6th Virginia Cavalry on September 15, 1861, but was given medical leave in July 1862.

230. Dr. George C. Carrington of Halifax Court House.

231. On September 18 Edward Carter Turner of Kinloch wrote in his diary, "Gen. Ewell arrives here to dinner on a litter. They are conveying him to the interior for safety." Turner Family Papers, 1740-1927, Virginia Historical Society.

232. Dr. Ira Williams of Fairfax.

233. The Battle of Second Manassas, August 28–30, was followed on September 1 by the Battle of Ox Hill (Chantilly).

234. In her journal entry of September 8, Kate described the situation in Middleburg on September 2, following the fighting at Second Manassas and Chantilly: "Whole trains of wagons filled with wounded were brought into town. Every church

was taken for hospitals [and] yards [filled with] wounded in every possible manner. From the time we were dressed in the morning till we went to bed, we were busy. The married ladies went into the hospitals. We worked at home or carried food to those under the trees."

235. Wilson Turner, brother of "St. Louis" Tom Turner.

236. From Edward Carter Turner's diary, September 1, 1862: "I learn this morning that my nephew Wilson was killed on Friday and buried on the field of battle.... [His comrades] gave him all that under the circumstances they were capable of giving, a decent burial in a soldier's grave. I go to the battle field in quest of his grave, search all day, but do not find it.... Ground literally covered in many places with dead men and horses...." On September 2, Turner continued, "I return in company with William Turner of Baltimore ... to renew my search for poor Wilson's grave. We find it on the farm of Mr. Thomas Leachman who kindly undertakes to protect it until the body can be removed." Turner Family Papers.

237. The battles of South Mountain and Antietam (Sharpsburg).

238. Ida does not mention Jackson's capture of Harpers Ferry and its eleven thousand–man garrison. Had she known about that, she might not have considered the Maryland Campaign such a disaster.

239. Sadly the planks Ida mentioned almost all disappeared during the war. After the war most of those men were reburied in mass graves of unknown war dead such as the one in Sharon Cemetery in Middleburg. In 1866 a monument was erected over their graves inscribed, "To the Unknown Dead." It was the first such monument in the country.

240. The Battle of Perryville, Kentucky, was fought on October 8, 1862, as Confederate general Braxton Bragg withdrew from the outskirts of Louisville and Cincinnati, the high-water mark of his invasion of Northern territory. Maj. Gen. Don Carlos Buell's Union forces were driven back all along the line; but Bragg left the field to them because he lacked reinforcements and supplies. He continued his retreat through the Cumberland Gap into East Tennessee.

241. The battle was fought October 3–4, 1862, between a combined Confederate army comprising Sterling Price's Army of the West and Earl van Dorn's Army of West Tennessee, against William S. Rosecrans's Army of the Mississippi. The Confederates tried and failed to seize the vital railroad junction at Corinth, Mississippi, in preparation for an advance into middle Tennessee.

242. Brig. Gen. James A. Walker.

243. Maj. Gen. Daniel Harvey Hill, "Stonewall" Jackson's brother-in-law.

244. Mostly men of Cos. I, L and M, 1st Rhode Island Cavalry, ambushed by Stuart near Mountville on October 29.

245. This duel was between Pelham's Battery of the Stuart Horse Artillery and a portion of Battery C, 3rd U.S. Artillery, commanded by Capt. Horatio G. Gibson.

246. Now the site of Pelham, a home Richard Dulany built for his daughter, Mary Dulany Neville, when she married after the war. She and her husband named the home after the young commander of J. E. B. Stuart's horse artillery battalion, Maj. John Pelham.

247. Asa Rogers, Jr., Co. H, 1st Virginia Cavalry.

248. Number Six was a parcel of land between Oakley and Upperville owned by "Brother Richard" Dulany.

249. On April 19, 1861, Union troops attempting to pass through Baltimore on their way to Washington, D.C., were attacked by prosecessionist civilians. Panicked soldiers fired into the crowds, killing twelve and injuring dozens more. The next month, Northern troops occupied the city and placed it under martial law. The incident was immortalized in the song "Maryland, My Maryland," which includes a line saying, "Avenge the patriotic gore / That flecked the streets of Baltimore."

250. George Henry Chapman, 3rd Indiana Cavalry.

251. Brig. Gen. Orlando Wilcox, commanding 1st Division, IX Corps.

252. Possibly Chaplain John H. Van Ingen, 8th New York Cavalry.

253. Cavalry from the defenses of Washington crossed the Blue Ridge at Snicker's Gap and attacked Confederate pickets from "Grumble" Jones's brigade on the west side of Castleman's Ferry. They advanced as far as Elijah White's camp near Berryville, which they destroyed, before returning to Loudoun County.

254. The Battle of Barbee's Crossroads, fought November 5, 1862, was the first time the Union and Confederate cavalry in Virginia met and fought in brigade strength on both sides. It was not fought in Chester's Gap, as Ida was told, but in that general direction from Oakley.

255. Flora V. Fletcher, wife of William Fletcher. His death left her responsible for three of her own children and five of his from an earlier marriage.

256. Undoubtedly not her real name. "Miss Chaste" is a sarcastic dig at the General's mistress.

257. Crackers.

258. Dr. John W. McIlhaney of Warrenton.

259. Jane Carter Beverley (1821–1915), daughter of Susan Baynton Turner and John Hill Carter of Faulkland. She was married to Robert Beverley.

260. Jane Peter Beverley, the widow of James Bradshaw Beverley of Blandfield. They lived at Acrolophos, now called Dumbarton Oaks, in Georgetown (Washington, DC), before moving to Avenel.

261. Edward Carter Turner wrote in his diary of November 15, 1862: "Myself and son Thomas are arrested without charges and taken to the Thoroughfare and released at 8 PM without a question being asked us to return through the dark (my son on foot) home."

262. Maj. Gen. Ambrose E. Burnside replaced Maj. Gen. George McClellan as commander of the Army of the Potomac on November 7, 1862.

263. Eliza Randolph Beverley, eighteen, daughter of Jane and Robert Beverley.

264. Virginia Cuthbert Powell, Ida's youngest sister.

265. Amanda Virginia "Tee" Edmonds gives a slightly different version of this episode in her diary entry for November 29, 1862: "Further particulars of the unfortunate affair of Cornelia (Triplett) and Kate (Sarah Catherine Brown).... They were riding between Upperville and Paris when a troop of horse rode furiously around them, and

turned to screen themselves behind a stone fence, and fire at ours. Poor girls, their horse became frightened and reared, and dashed right for the firing. It was shot, and fell on Kate, breaking her leg."

266. Horace McKinster of Upperville.

267. A sutler was a civilian merchant who supplied provisions to an army post.

268. Fort McHenry, in Baltimore, was used as a military prison during the war. Carter, who had been captured while serving with the 4th Virginia Cavalry, was home on furlough looking for a new horse. According to regimental records, he returned to duty December 15, 1862.

269. Margaret Patterson Turner (1816–1873) of Baltimore was the widow of Capt. Charles Cocke Turner, U.S. Navy. She was related to Betsy Patterson, who was briefly married to Jerome Bonaparte, Napoleon's brother.

270. Maj. Gen. Benjamin F. Butler earned the nickname "The Beast" for his treatment of the people of New Orleans after that city fell under Union control in April 1862. By the time Ida made this note, Butler's military incompetence and his continued insults to representatives of European nations had become so blatant that the Lincoln administration could no longer ignore them. After the mid-term elections, Butler, an influential War Democrat, was relieved of his command on November 12, 1862, by Gen. Nathaniel Banks.

271. The Battle of Fredericksburg, fought December 11–15, 1862, cost the Army of the Potomac thirteen thousand men in exchange for forty-five hundred Confederate casualties. At its conclusion, Burnside pulled his army back north of the Rappahannock River and went into winter quarters.

272. On December 17, Brig. Gen. John G. Foster, leading a Union expedition to destroy the Wilmington and Weldon Railroad at Goldsboro, began a rapid retreat back to his base at New Bern after encountering increasing Confederate resistance.

273. Brig. Gen. John Hunt Morgan began another cavalry raid on Union supply lines in Tennessee as Rosecrans withdrew his army into Nashville, apparently going into winter quarters.

274. Lincoln's cabinet was not dissolved, although there was a good deal of discord after he issued his Emancipation Proclamation in September.

275. On December 24, 1862, Jefferson Davis issued his General Orders No. 111, which said, in part, "That all commissioned officers in the command of said Benjamin F. Butler be declared not entitled to be considered as soldiers engaged in honorable warfare but as robbers and criminals deserving death, and that they and each of them be whenever captured reserved for execution."

1863

1. Normally, in spring and summer, the curtains were taken down and the carpets rolled up and stored to make the house cooler.

2. Brig. Gen. Fitzhugh Lee (1835–1905), a nephew of Gen. Robert E. Lee, commanded a brigade of cavalry under Maj. Gen. J. E. B. Stuart.

3. Mosby began his independent operations in January with nine men borrowed from the 1st Virginia Cavalry. He instructed them to board at the homes of local citizens loyal to the Confederacy, no more than two men to a single dwelling.

4. Jon Horace Barnes, formerly of Co. D, 17th Virginia Infantry.

5. As previously mentioned, Henson Willis was a free black man married to one of the Oakley slave women, Lucinda. Shortly after Lucinda came to Oakley in 1859, Marietta wrote to Ida: "I am very glad to hear that Lucinda is to do so well. I should think it would be a great convenience to you to have so useful a person as Henson brought so much about you. He will always be in reach when you want to employ him." The letter from Marietta Powell to Ida dated August 3, 18— (last two digits illegible) is in the possession of the Mackall and the Sasscer families.

6. "Kinloch Tom" was shot by Capt. Elon Farnsworth, 8th Illinois Cavalry, at the home of Charles Utterback, approximately three miles from Warrenton. See appendix D for his father's account of his death.

7. This episode actually happened at Warrenton Junction, not Dranesville, on May 3. After capturing a number of men of the 1st Virginia (Federal) Cavalry, Mosby and his men were attacked by a much larger party of 5th New York and 1st Vermont cavalrymen. In one of his worst defeats of the war, Mosby lost between twenty and thirty men. The Federals had two men killed and five officers and ten privates wounded.

8. John Charles Buchanan, of Martinsburg, Virginia (now West Virginia), one of the original fifteen men detailed to Mosby from the 1st Virginia Cavalry.

9. Ida was mistaken in the location. Sixteen-year-old John W. Turner was the son of William T. Turner of Waterloo, Virginia.

10. Buchanan was wounded in Mosby's attack on Union pickets at Blakely Grove, near Upperville, on May 6, 1863.

11. George Brown, whose farm was between Oakley and Upperville.

12. Robert F. Gray of Loudoun County had only recently been released from Old Capitol Prison in Washington after being captured while riding with Mosby at Middleburg in January.

13. William Elzey of Loudoun lost several teeth in the Blakely Grove fight when he was hit in the face by a Union cavalryman.

14. The Battle of Chancellorsville, April 30–May 6, 1863.

15. Union losses were fourteen thousand killed, wounded, or captured. The Confederates lost ten thousand, including Jackson, whose left arm was amputated. The general died a few days later.

16. French phrase meaning "We shall see."

17. "There's many a slip twixt the cup and the lip" is a modern variation of an ancient Greek proverb first quoted in English by Richard H. Barham in *The Ingoldsby Legends* (London: Richard Bentley, 1840).

18. The battle of Black River Bridge on May 17, 1863, marked Lt. Gen. John C. Pemberton's last attempt to save Vicksburg. A forty-seven-day siege of that city followed this battle.

19. The buyer was Gustavus Lesner.

20. Lt. Hill W. Carter, 57th Virginia Infantry, was wounded during the siege of Suffolk, Virginia, in May, but he did not die until July 24, 1863.

21. Stuart's cavalry corps clashed with Union cavalry under Alfred Pleasonton near Brandy Station on June 9, 1863, in one of the largest cavalry battles ever fought on American soil.

22. Ewell drove Brig. Gen. Robert Milroy out of Winchester in a three-day battle June 13–15, 1863, killing and capturing 4,443 of Milroy's 7,000 men with a loss of only 266 of his own.

23. Jubal Anderson Early (1816–1894), West Point Class of 1837.

24. Milroy made his headquarters in the home of Lloyd Logan, a tobacco merchant, on the corner of Piccadilly and Braddock Streets in Winchester. The building still stands opposite the Handley Library.

25. Brig. Gen. Julius Stahel's brigade from the defenses of Washington rode into Fauquier County in search of the Army of Northern Virginia, which had slipped away from its camps along the Rappahannock and was moving west toward the Shenandoah Valley.

26. Then serving as lieutenant colonel, 1st Virginia Cavalry.

27. Brig. Gen Fitzhugh Lee was ill at the time and had just turned over temporary command of his brigade to Col. Thomas T. Munford, 2nd Virginia Cavalry.

28. Fighting in the Loudoun Valley took place June 17–21 with battles at Aldie (June 17), Middleburg (June 18–19), and Upperville (June 21) and skirmishes at Pothouse (Leithtown), Snickersville (Bluemont), and along Millville Road.

29. Stuart spent the night in the yard of the Caleb Rector home in Rector's Crossroads (now Atoka).

30. The Union infantry involved in the Loudoun Valley fighting was Brig. Gen. Strong Vincent's brigade of V Corps, Army of the Potomac. The cavalry was Maj. Gen. Alfred Pleasonton's entire Cavalry Corps of the Army of the Potomac, with its horse artillery attached.

31. Ida was on her upper balcony, a spectacular vantage point.

32. Ashby's Gap, where modern Route 50 crosses the Blue Ridge. Stuart had to keep the Union cavalry out of this gap to hide the movements of Lee's army in the Shenandoah Valley.

33. Robert C. McArtor, an Upperville tanner and mail carrier prior to the war.

34. George Brown.

35. Actually Col. Peter G. Evans of the 5th North Carolina Cavalry was killed in the Upperville fighting and Lt. Col. O. O. Funsten of the 11th Virginia Cavalry seriously wounded.

36. A portion of Longstreet's Corps crossed the Shenandoah River and moved into Ashby's Gap on the twenty-first but did not get involved in the fighting. When the Union cavalry returned to Aldie the next day, only Stuart's cavalry followed them.

37. Having driven Stuart's cavalry all the way back to Ashby's Gap, Pleasonton still had not succeeded in his mission of finding the Army of Northern Virginia. For

some unknown reason, poised on the brink of success, he withdrew all the way back to Aldie on June 22 and from there started the march to the Potomac River two days later.

38. Mosby sustained no losses in the Loudoun Valley fighting. The extent of his involvement was the capture of Union couriers and signal officers on the evening of June 17.

39. Maj. Heros von Borcke, a Prussian volunteer serving on Stuart's staff, was shot in the throat during the fighting in Middleburg on June 19. He was taken to Dr. Eliason's home in Upperville, where his wound was pronounced mortal. He survived, although he never returned to active service in the Confederate army.

40. On June 22, 1863, Gen. Lee issued General Orders no. 72, which forbade the destruction of private property. The ANV quartermaster corps was in charge of appropriating goods for the army's use, for which they paid in Confederate money.

41. Loughborough "Nick" Carter was the son of John Hill Carter of Falkland and Jane Loughborough. Called "Nick" as a child because of his devilish temperament, he grew up to be handsome, cruel, a heavy drinker, a crack shot and a fine horseman, the source of both amazement and embarrassment to his family. After the war, he allegedly fled to Mexico with a price on his head. Herbert, *Life on a Virginia Farm*, 102–3.

42. After the war Mosby denied that Nick Carter had ever been a member of his command, although he was a participant in the Mercersburg, Pennsylvania, raid on June 28, 1863. Carter often went on unsanctioned raids with Charles McDonough and Charles Hall. In his *Reminiscences of a Mosby Guerrilla*, John Munson called Carter and McDonough "brevet outlaws" (New York: Moffat, Yard, and Co., 1906), 78.

43. Lee was captured at Hickory Hill, home of the Wickham family, where he had gone to recuperate from a serious wound he received in the Battle of Brandy Station. He was held prisoner for nearly ten months before being exchanged in March 1864.

44. Seven Union generals were either killed or mortally wounded in the three-day Battle of Gettysburg: Maj. Gens. John Reynolds and S. K. Zook and Brig. Gens. Stephen Weed, A. VanHorn Ellis, George H. Ward, Paul Joseph Revere, and Louis R. Francine. Lee's army lost five generals: Maj. Gen. William D. Pender and Brig. Gens. William Barksdale, Lewis Armistead, Richard B. Garnett, and Paul J. Semmes.

45. Gettysburg was definitely one of the costliest battles of the war for both sides. Meade's Army of the Potomac suffered approximately twenty-three thousand casualties, while Lee's Army of Northern Virginia lost twenty-eight thousand men killed, wounded, or captured.

46. Armistead was wounded during Longstreet's assault on July 3 and died in a Federal field hospital.

47. All four Berkeley brothers from Aldie served in the 8th Virginia Infantry. Norborne and William were wounded and captured at Gettysburg, and Charles captured there. Only Edmund escaped the battle unscathed and still with the regiment.

48. Capt. Alexander Grayson, Co. F, 8th Virginia Infantry, was in fact killed at Gettysburg. He had been Anna Bolling's suitor.

49. Vicksburg's beleaguered garrison surrendered on July 4, 1863.

50. Secretary of State William Henry Seward (1801–1872).

51. The Confederate constitution guaranteed each state the right to print its own money along with currency issued by the Confederate States government.

52. Col. William D'Alton Mann, 7th Michigan Cavalry.

1864

1. Maj. Gen. Christopher C. Augur (1821–1898) commanded the Department of Washington from October 1863 until the end of the war.

2. Ida's younger sister, Kate, had married George Carter in October 1863 and was now living at Oatlands.

3. 2nd Lt. Charles E. Grogan, Co. D, 43rd Battalion, Virginia Partisan Rangers. Grogan joined Mosby after escaping from the infamous prison camp at Johnson's Island, Ohio, where he was sent after being captured at Gettysburg.

4. Lt. William Mosby, Co. A, 43rd Battalion, Virginia Partisan Rangers, younger brother of Col. John S. Mosby.

5. Lt. Col. Joseph Browne, 5th Pennsylvania Heavy Artillery.

6. An artificial fringe of bangs or curls worn on the forehead.

7. Col. Henry S. Gansevoort, 13th New York Cavalry.

8. Col. George Shields Gallupe, 5th Pennsylvania Heavy Artillery, commanding a brigade in the XXII Corps, District of Washington.

9. The fight at Oakley between Mosby's men and the 8th Illinois Cavalry took place on October 29, 1864. See appendix E for James Williamson's description of the action and John Munson's account of his capture.

10. John Atkins, Co. D, 43rd Battalion, Virginia Partisan Rangers, was an Irishman who came to America specifically to join Mosby.

11. George Milton Gulick of Aldie, Co. A, 43rd Battalion, Virginia Partisan Rangers.

12. 3rd Sgt. Edgar F. Davis of Fairfax, Co. E, 43rd Battalion, Virginia Partisan Rangers. His wound was declared not serious by the doctors, but Davis insisted he was going to die, which he did only a few days later.

13. Christopher Columbus Shaw, Co. A, 43rd Battalion, Virginia Partisan Rangers, had served in the 1st Virginia Cavalry prior to joining Mosby in December 1863.

14. Col. Charles A. Albright, 202nd Pennsylvania Volunteer Infantry.

15. Most likely Capt. Christian Ross, Battery G, 5th Pennsylvania Heavy Artillery. No Capt. Slosser can be located among Gen. Augur's headquarters staff.

16. Maj. John M. Waite, 8th Illinois Cavalry.

17. Chaplain William A. Spencer, 8th Illinois Cavalry.

18. Thomas R. Foster.

19. Margaret Peyton of Gordon's Dale.

20. Christian Washington of Jefferson County (now West Virginia), near Charles Town.

21. Ann Morgan, wife of William J. Morgan of Salem.

22. Elizabeth Frazier, wife of James H. Frazier of Charles Town (now West Virginia).

23. Either Thomas and Mary Foster's twenty-two-year-old daughter, Kate, or her eighteen-year-old sister, Cornelia.

24. Henry Smith Turner, a retired U.S. Army officer, lived in St. Louis. His brother, Thomas Turner, lived in Philadelphia and was an admiral on active duty in the U.S. Navy.

25. James and Elizabeth Hathaway of Western View, a safe house for Mosby, had three sons: Henry Clay (age twenty-four in 1864), James A. (sixteen), and George G. (fourteen).

26. George H. Dawson of Rectortown.

27. Mary, age eleven.

28. Brig. Gen. Wesley Merritt (1834–1910), commanding the Reserve Brigade, Army of the Potomac Cavalry Corps.

29. This operation, known in Loudoun and Fauquier counties as the "Great Burning Raid," began on November 28 and lasted for the next five days. The only exceptions to Merritt's orders to burn and/or destroy everything in the two counties were no private homes were to be burned, nor any violence offered toward citizens.

30. Alva Richards, assistant surgeon of the 126th Ohio Volunteer Infantry.

31. Walter Bowie served in the 1st Virginia Light Artillery, 11th Virginia Infantry and 9th Virginia Cavalry before joining Mosby.

32. Capt. Daniel F. Sargent, Co. G, 1st Maine Cavalry.

33. Ida's daughter Rebecca later recalled a secret hiding place in the garret behind the large lead-lined water tank.

34. Gen. Merritt's preliminary report, made on December 3, stated that Sheridan's orders were "literally" complied with, and "from 5000–6000 head of cattle, 3000–4000 head of sheep, and 500–700 horses had been driven off, while 1000 head of fatted hogs had been slaughtered." The Reserve Brigade was the only one to give a detailed report of the operations, which indicated that that brigade alone burned 230 barns, 8 mills, 1 distillery, 10,000 tons of hay, and 25,000 bushels of grain.

35. Billings Steele of Maryland, Co. D, 43rd Battalion, Virginia Partisan Rangers, was sent first to Old Capitol Prison in Washington and then to Fort Warren in Boston, where he spent the rest of the war. Although a Union surgeon declared Grogan unfit for further service, he recovered and later returned to active duty.

36. Grogan was taken to Glen Welby, near Rectortown, to recover from his wound.

37. Ludwell Lake of Lakeland Farm.

38. Home of Chief Justice John Marshall near Salem (Marshall). When his grandson, Col. Thomas Marshall, was killed in 1864, the house was sold at public auction.

39. The Union troopers involved in this incident were from Maj. Gen. A. T. A. Torbert's command, scouring the area around Rectortown looking for the wounded Mosby.

40. In the bitterly cold weather of that winter, these items were more important than silver. John Peyton Dulany wrote of that month, "I do not think I have ever known

so severe a December as this has been—the very elements seem to be against us." Vogtsberger, *The Dulanys of Welbourne*, 247.

41. She was visiting her mother-in-law, Elizabeth Carter.

1865

1. Eliza Carter Randolph Turner died in July 1866, having outlived her husband, Maj. Thomas Turner IV, by twenty-seven years. Of her fourteen children, only six were still living at the time of her death.

2. The land between the Potomac and Rappahannock Rivers east of Fredericksburg, where the people were better able to feed the Rangers and their horses.

3. By late 1864 a desperate shortage of manpower in the South led the Confederate Congress to consider long-resisted proposals to free blacks in return for their service in the army. A watered-down version—finally passed in February 1865—permitted the recruitment of free blacks and others whose owners offered their services but specifically prohibited the conscription of slaves.

4. By an act of the Confederate Congress, Lee was confirmed as commander in chief of the Armies of the Confederate States on January 23, 1865. Since 1862 he had commanded only the Army of Northern Virginia.

Epilogue

1. Letter from Marietta Powell to Mary Custis Lee, June 4, 1865. The Virginia Historical Society.

2. Letter from Marietta Powell to Mary Custis Lee, July 3, 1865. The Virginia Historical Society.

3. Letter from Powell to Lee, July 3, 1865.

4. Janet Randolph was a founder of the Richmond Chapter of the United Daughters of the Confederacy and other memorial organizations. Edward D. C. Campbell, Jr., and Kym S. Rice, eds., *A Woman's War: Southern Women, Civil War, and the Confederate Legacy* (Richmond: Museum of the Confederacy, and Charlottesville: Univ. Press of Virginia, 1996), 143.

5. Letter from Powell to Lee, July 3, 1865.

6. Campbell and Rice, eds., *A Woman's War*, 1.

7. The U.S. Bureau of Refugees, Freedmen, and Abandoned Lands, better known as the Freedmen's Bureau, was established by Congress in 1865 to help former slaves adjust to a free society.

8. In July 1866, "the Colored people of Waterford and vicinity," with help from the Quaker community and under the auspices of the Freedmen's Bureau, bought a lot on Second Street in Waterford and erected a building to be used as both a school and a church. By 1868, there were sixty-three students enrolled, twenty-eight of whom were older than sixteen. Miss Sarah Ann Steer was the first teacher. http://www.waterford history.org/history/second-street-school.htm (accessed May 24, 2007).

9. Letter from Margaret Patterson Turner to Marietta Turner Powell, March 7, 1871.

10. Andrews, *Memoirs of a Poor Relation*, 104.

11. Drew Gilpin Faust, *Mothers of Invention: Women of the Slaveholding South in the American Civil War* (Chapel Hill: Univ. of North Carolina Press, 1996), 7.

12. Andrews, *Memoirs of a Poor Relation*, 33.

13. Because he was too badly wounded to move, Gen. Fitzhugh Lee pinned a note to his young aide's jacket asking the rapidly advancing Union soldiers to notify his father of his death. Union surgeons saved his life. Andrews, *Memoirs of a Poor Relation*, 27.

14. Letter from Charles Minnigerode to Marietta Turner Powell, September 11, 1867.

15. In ways unimaginable to the prewar generation, two of Jenny's daughters had notable careers outside of the home. Marietta Fauntleroy Minnigerode, 1869–1930, was a successful artist and writer. She married Eliphalet Fraser Andrews, curator of the Corcoran Art Museum in Washington. Lucy Minnigerode, 1871–1935, served as the director of nursing for the U.S. Public Health Service in Washington.

16. She was the daughter of Col. Thomas H. Carter of Pampatike in King William County, a physician who served as chief of artillery, 2nd Corps, Army of Northern Virginia.

17. Letter from Powell to Lee, July 3, 1865.

18. This romantic vision of the past blurred reality and made it easier to accept the crushing defeat and poverty.

Appendix E

1. Augur to Halleck, October 30: "A portion of the Eighth Illinois had a brush with Mosby yesterday near Upperville, and whipped him badly, killing 7 or 8, and capturing 9. The track will be taken up half way between this [place] and Rectortown to-day. They are getting on very slowly—as fast, however, as they possibly can. I go to White Plains this morning." *OR*, ser. 1, vol. 43, pt. 1: 646.

Index

Adams, Thomas, 218
Adie, George, 121, 246
Albright, Col. Charles A., 177, 256
Aldie, Va., xxvi, 5, 76, 77, 254–56
Alexandria, Va., xviii, xx, xxvi, 3, 26, 92, 97, 109, 125, 132, 199, 221, 222, 224, 227, 231, 239
Anderson, Gen. Richard H., 119, 245
Andrews, Marietta Fauntleroy Minnigerode, 197, 198, 259, 221, 222, 229, 234, 246, 259
Anisansel, Col. Henry, 108, 109, 111, 114–17, 126, 130, 243
Antietam, Battle of, xxvi, 139, 245, 247, 250
Arlington, Va., 3, 21
Arlington House, xix, 221
Armistead, Bettie F., 30, 232
Armistead, Bowles Edward, 27, 28, 29, 32, 228, 231
Armistead, Elizabeth Stanley ("Aunt Armistead"), 15, 27, 28, 30, 32, 228, 232, 233
Armistead, Gen. Lewis A. ("Cousin Lewis"), 136, 170, 228, 231, 249, 255
Armistead, Gen. Walker Keith (father of Lewis A. and Walker K. Armistead), 228, 231
Armistead, Walker Keith, Jr. (brother of Lewis Armistead), xxiv, 32, 44, 61, 77, 136, 137, 222, 228, 231, 233, 249
Armistead, Walker Keith (son of Lewis Armistead), xxiv, 138, 222, 233
Armstrong, Joseph H., 78, 79, 238
Army of the Potomac (CSA), 68, 69, 223, 235, 237
Army of the Potomac (USA), 139, 150, 172, 234, 245, 251, 252, 254, 255, 257

Arthur, Henry. *See* Henry Arthur Hall
Ashby, Richard, 5, 78, 79, 224, 238
Ashby, Turner, 5, 13, 79, 104, 107–10, 116, 122, 224, 238, 243, 246
Ashby's Gap and Turnpike, xxvi, 170, 238, 254
Ashland, Va., xvii, xxiv, 7, 10–21, 24, 27, 225
Atkins, John, 177, 218, 256
Augur, Gen. Christopher C., 173, 175, 177–79, 181–82, 184, 186, 187, 189, 191, 192, 256, 259
Avenel, 27, 35, 146, 192, 199, 227, 230, 238, 249, 251
Avenel Slave
  Edmunds, Wilhelmina, 214
Averitt, John Battle, 5, 224
Ayre, George S., 103, 105, 110, 114, 126, 241
Ayreshire, 241

Ball, Mottrom Dulany, 45, 58, 184
Baltimore, Md., 27, 42, 57, 59, 66, 91, 95, 132, 138, 142, 149, 158, 196–99, 226, 227, 229, 230, 234, 250–52
"Baltimore Tom". *See* Thomas Shirley Turner
Banks, Gen. Nathaniel P., 13, 78, 92–95, 101, 131, 227, 241, 248, 252
Barbee's Crossroads, Battle of, 145, 251
Barnes, John H., 157, 159–61, 253
Barton, Charles Marshall, 11, 99, 226, 242
Barton, David R., 58
Baton Rouge, La., 132, 133, 248
Beauregard, Gen. Pierre G.T., xxiv, 5, 59, 86, 96, 101, 119, 223, 232, 239
Bellefield, 114, 116, 185, 192, 244

Belt, Henry Shroeder, 199
Belt, Marietta Dulany. *See* Marietta Randolph Dulany
Berkeley Springs (Bath), W.V., 60, 61, 236
Berkeley, Norborne, 170, 255
Beverley, Elizabeth Randolph, 147, 251
Beverley, James Bradshaw, 251
Beverley, Jane Carter, 146, 249, 251
Beverley, Jane Peter, 146, 251
Beverley, John Hill Carter, 199
Beverley, Robert ("Cousin Robert"), 23, 147, 227, 230, 238, 251
Bishop, James, 7, 73, 225
Bitzer, Harmond, 112, 244
Blackburn's Ford, Skirmish at, 5, 224
Blakeley, Charles, 120, 245
Blandfield, 199, 251
Blenker, Gen. Louis, 85, 239, 246
Bloomfield, Va., 185, 186
Bolling, "Bollingbrook Anna", 6, 16, 23, 30, 35, 41, 42, 60, 81, 85, 107, 120, 124, 135, 224, 225, 230, 233
Bolling, "Petersburg Anna", 23, 25, 30, 39–43, 45, 230, 232, 233, 255
Bolling, Anna Dade. *See* "Bollingbrook Anna"
Bolling, Bartlett, 120, 121, 124, 125, 224
Bolling, George Washington, 230, 232
Bolling, George, Jr., 33
Bolling, John, 5, 224
Bolling, Martha Stith, 230, 232
Bolling, Mary Tabb, 30, 35, 232, 233
Bolling, Monroe ("Munzy"), 6, 72, 224, 225
Bolling, Robert B., 6, 7, 9, 13, 15, 29, 30, 31, 33, 35, 41, 44, 60, 71, 73, 76, 78, 81, 84, 85, 88, 96, 98, 103, 107–9, 111, 116, 117, 119, 120, 127, 131, 132, 135, 138, 147, 162, 168, 224, 225, 228, 230, 232, 241
Bolling, Robert and Sarah Minge, 228
Bolling, Samuel, 107, 111, 192, 224, 243
Bolling, Sarah Melville, 30, 35, 232
Bolling, Stewart, 15, 72, 124, 130, 133, 224
Bolling, William ("Willie"), 21, 107, 224, 243
Bollingbrook, 7, 25, 30, 35, 45, 71, 72, 85, 111, 162, 224, 230, 243
Bollings, The, 125, 243
Bonham, Gen. [Unknown], 120, 245
Bonham, Gen. Milledge L., 45, 235
Botts, Lawson, 5, 223

Bowie, Walter, 186, 187, 257
Boyd, Rev. A.H., 226
Boyd, Holmes, 11, 226
Bragg, Gen. Braxton, 140, 246, 250
Brandy Station, Battle of, 163 254, 255
Bronaugh, Dr. Joseph W., 61, 236
Brooke, Leina and Nannie, 19
Brooks, Catherine, 95, 241
Brown, Ann, 178
Brown, George, 73, 149, 159, 165, 237, 253, 254
Brown, John, 223
Brown, Sarah Catherine, 148, 251, 252
Browne, Col. Joseph, 174, 175, 256
Bruin, Mr., 132
Buchanan, President James, 230
Buchanan, John Charles, 159, 160, 161, 162, 253
Burnside, Gen. Ambrose E., 61, 62, 147, 150, 236, 251, 252
Butler, Gen. Benjamin F. ("The Beast"), 118, 149, 228, 230, 234, 245, 252

Carnifex Ferry, Battle of, 26, 231
Carr, Edward, 105, 110, 243
Carr, John, 133, 248
Carrere, Marion Turner, 17, 20, 229
Carrere, William ("Willie"), 17, 20, 27, 46, 57, 61, 85, 95, 138, 229
Carrington, Dr. George C., 136, 249
Carrington, Luther, 218
Carroll, William, 29, 232
Carter, Addison, 85, 135, 239
Carter, Anne Hill. *See* Anne Hill Carter Lee
Carter, Anne Willing, 197, 199
Carter, Benjamin C., 114, 244
Carter, Charles, 221
Carter, Edith, 35, 233
Carter, Eliza French Hall ("Cousin Eliza"), 11, 13, 14, 29, 31, 33, 111, 227
Carter, Elizabeth Grayson, 115, 116, 122, 244
Carter, Elizabeth Hill. *See* Elizabeth Hill Carter Randolph
Carter, Frances Addison. *See* Frances Addison Carter Dulany
Carter, George, 25, 36, 43, 45, 61, 65, 113, 114, 116, 122, 131, 149, 158, 182, 195, 198, 230, 244, 252, 256

Carter, Henry H., 244
Carter, Hill W., 162, 254
Carter, J. Alexander ("Alick"), 85, 239
Carter, John Armistead ("Uncle Armistead"), xxiii, xxv, 9, 13, 14, 15, 17, 31, 45, 46, 47, 175, 223, 226
Carter, John Hill, 251, 255
Carter, Judith, 249
Carter, Julian, 127
Carter, Katherine Whiting Powell ("Kate"), xix, xx, xxiii, xxvii, 5, 8, 9, 11, 20, 27, 29, 30, 34, 44, 58, 61, 65, 72, 77, 85, 89, 90, 92, 95, 101, 104, 107, 109, 111–14, 121, 131, 137, 144, 158, 160, 171, 192, 199, 223, 230, 237, 239, 240, 244, 249, 256
Carter, Loughborough ("Nick"), 169, 255
Carter, Mary Welby, 109, 243
Carter, Otway, 249
Carter, Richard Henry, 92, 232, 233, 239, 241, 243
Carter, Richard Welby ("Web"), 9, 37, 120, 164, 226, 233
Carter, Robert, 29, 69, 101, 111, 117, 142, 227, 229, 244
Carter, Robert ("King"), 222
Carter, Sarah, 31, 109
Carter, Col. Scott, 100, 103, 242
Carter, Sophia deButts ("Sophie"), 35, 36, 85, 104, 233
Carter, Thomas Goode ("Tom Goody"), 19, 31, 34, 63, 229
Carter, Thomas H., 259
Carter, Thomas Nelson, 247
Carter, Winston, 92, 241
Case, Maj. Charles, 97, 241
Cedar Mountain (Slaughter Mountain), Battle of, 134, 248
Centreville, Va., 36, 37, 41, 42, 44, 45, 57, 67, 69, 75
Chancellorsville, Battle of, 159, 253
Chapman, George H., 142, 251
Charleston, S.C., 44, 117, 224, 230, 232, 235, 245
Charles Town, W.V., 13, 256, 257
Charlottesville, Va., 109, 131, 243, 258
Cheat Mountain, Battle of, 25, 231
Chew, Roger Preston, 79, 238
Chancellor, James, 218
Chichester, Fanny, 57, 235
Cincinnati, Oh., 125, 250

Cochran, Catherine Powell ("Cousin Cat"), 29, 30, 136, 232
Cochran, Dr. William B., 214, 232
Cole, Capt. Henry A, 133, 248
Conrad, Charles Frederick, 16, 23, 223, 228
Conrad, Daniel Burr, 4, 22, 34, 223
Conrad, Elizabeth Whiting Powell ("Aunt Betty"), 25, 28, 29, 228, 230, 231
Conrad, Henry Tucker, 6, 224
Conrad, Holmes Addison, 6, 224
Conrad, Holmes Y., 8, 11, 95, 225, 226
Conrad, Katherine Brooke Powell ("Kate"), 29, 30, 34, 223, 231
Conrad, Powell, 11, 57, 99, 223, 226, 235, 242
Conrad, Robert Young, 223, 228, 240
Conrad, Sallie Harrison, 89, 223, 235, 240
Conrad, Sarah Powell, 7, 225
Corinth, Battle of, 86, 95, 250
Corinth, Miss., 101, 140, 239
Credeler, James H., 91, 240
Crednal, 37, 145, 223, 226, 233
Cross Keys, Battle of, 107, 243, 245
Crowe, Edward, 105
CSS Arkansas, 126, 132, 194, 246
CSS Virginia, 83, 239
Culpeper Courthouse, Va., 78, 131, 132
Curtis, Gen. Samuel R., 125, 246
Custis, George Washington Parke, 221
Custis, Mary Anne Randolph. See Mary Anne Randolph Custis Lee
Custis, Mary Lee Fitzhugh, 221

Dandridge, Lily, 26, 231
Dandridge, Philip Pendleton, 231
Darden, Dennis, 218
Davis, Edgar F., 177, 218, 256
Davis, President Jefferson, 31, 38, 66, 91, 132, 149, 199, 232, 237, 243, 248, 252
Dawson, George H., 29, 61, 183, 232, 257
deButts, Richard, 241
"Dirge for Ashby," 122, 246
Doughty, Mary, 25, 243
Dowdell, Thomas, 124, 246
Dranesville, Battle of, 45, 65
Dranesville, Va., 158, 217
Dudley, Fanny Cochran, 30, 32, 36, 232
Dudley, Thomas Underwood, 232
Dulany, Benjamin, 222

Dulany, Daniel (of Maryland), 222
Dulany, Daniel French, 224, 235
Dulany, Elizabeth French, 222
Dulany, Frances Addison Carter (Hal's mother), 222, 225
Dulany, Frances Addison Carter ("Fanny"), 11, 17, 18, 20, 30, 36, 120, 149, 225, 227
Dulany, Henry Grafton ("Hal"), xvii, xxviii, xix–xxix4–10, 12,–17, 19–36, 38–46, 57–59, 61–69, 72, 77,–79, 81–82, 85–87, 89–93, 95, 98, 101, 103, 105, 107–8, 110–12, 114, 116–17, 119, 121, 124–34, 136, 138, 141–47, 159–61, 163–64, 167–69, 171, 173–75, 177–79, 181–84, 186–92, 195–99, 217, 219, 222, 227–29, 235, 246, 248
Dulany, Henry Grafton (Richard's son), 227
Dulany, Henry Rozier of Shuter's Hill, xx, 222
Dulany, Henry Rozier, xx, 7, 9, 10, 12, 14, 28, 39, 58, 62, 66, 133, 136, 145, 162, 167, 180, 197, 199, 222
Dulany, John Peyton ("Uncle John"), xxv, xxviii, 9, 13, 14, 24, 25, 27, 31, 33, 60, 69, 83, 85, 90, 92, 104, 105, 111, 120, 121, 124, 131, 162, 202, 222, 223, 226, 238, 240, 243, 248, 257
Dulany, John Peyton ("Johnny"), 30, 120, 227, 232
Dulany, Marietta Randolph ("May"), xx, 8, 12, 39, 58, 62, 66, 82, 92, 124, 162, 167, 169, 180, 191, 199, 222
Dulany, Mary Carter, 11, 17–20, 22, 36, 120, 149, 227, 250
Dulany, Rebecca Ann ("Sister"), xx, xxi, 44, 87, 222, 227, 240
Dulany, Rebecca Anne ("Little Becca"), xx, 8, 9, 14, 39, 41, 46, 91–93, 199, 222, 243, 257
Dulany, Richard Henry ("Brother Richard"), xx, xxi, xxv, xxvii, 4, 11–14, 19, 34, 44, 46, 47, 57, 64, 68, 83, 85, 87, 90, 92, 93, 102, 105, 107, 110, 111, 121, 124, 131, 137, 138, 141, 146, 202, 222, 223, 225–28, 232, 238, 242, 244, 246, 248, 250, 251
Dulany, Richard Hunter ("Dicky"), 91, 227, 240
Dulany, William H., 5, 224
Dulany's Lost Company, 10

Eliason slave: Harriet, 77
Eliason, Armistead, 28, 232
Eliason, Mary Landon Carter ("Aunt Mary"), 7, 15, 17, 23, 25, 26, 27, 43, 61, 77, 95, 101, 225, 232
Eliason, Rutledge ("Rutty"), 19, 82, 133, 134, 142, 225, 229
Eliason, Dr. Talcott, 7, 36, 42, 82, 146, 225, 229, 255
Eliason, William, 7, 37, 43, 225
Eliason, William B., 232
Elmwood, 30
Elzey, Gen. Arnold, 122, 218, 246
Elzey, William, 159, 161, 253
Evansport, 59, 61, 76, 236, 238
Ewell, Gen. Richard S., 63, 68, 91, 95, 101, 120, 131, 136, 163, 169, 230, 231, 234, 239, 240, 249, 254

Fairfax, Albert B., 241
Fairfax Courthouse, Va., 28, 104, 150, 235, 249, 256
Fairfax Station, 29, 31, 34
Fairfax, Eugene, 92, 241
Farnsworth, Capt. Elon, 211, 253
Farragut, Adm. David G., 127, 247
Faulkland, 251, 255
Fauntleroy, Archibald M., 57, 235
Fauntleroy, Elizabeth Randolph ("Lizzie"), 21, 230
Fauntleroy, Dr. John Foushee ("Uncle John"), 70, 230, 231
Fauntleroy, Kinloch, 27, 231
Fauntleroy, Lavinia Beverley Turner ("Aunt Bena"), 21, 23, 28, 70, 133, 230
First Manassas, Battle of, xxiv, xxvi, 6, 224–26, 229, 249
First Winchester (Bower's Hill), Battle of, 94, 241
Fletcher, Flora, 145, 146, 251
Fletcher, John W., 95, 107, 241
Fletcher, William, 241, 251
Fletcher, William H., 96, 109, 111, 141, 142, 185, 244
Floyd, Gen. John B., xxix, 21, 26, 230, 231
Fort Darling (Drewry's Bluff), 93, 117, 241, 245
Fort Donelson, Tennessee, 64–66, 236, 237
Fort Henry, Tennessee, 62, 65, 236, 237

Fort McHenry, 149, 252
Fort Sumter, xxiii, 224, 226
Foster, Gen. John G., 252
Foster, Kate or Cornelia, 181, 257
Foster, Mary A., 182, 257
Foster, Thomas R., 181, 182, 256
Frankland, Capt. Walter, 211, 217, 219
Frazier, Elizabeth, 181, 257
Frazier's Farm, Battle of, 246
Frazier, James H, 257
Fredericksburg, Battle of, 149, 252
Fredericksburg, Va., 10, 11, 19, 81, 82, 92, 258
Fremont, Gen. John C., 107, 112, 235, 243
French, Mary, 202
Front Royal, Va., 70, 94, 99, 101, 116, 241, 110

Gallaher, Turner H., 117, 245
Gallupe, Col. George S., 175, 256
Gansevoort, Col. Henry S., 175, 256
Geams, Polly, 80
Geary, Gen. John W., 72–74, 76, 78, 79, 81, 83, 84, 91–95, 98, 100, 103, 108, 111–17, 120, 131, 147, 202, 237, 240, 241, 248
Gettysburg, Battle of, xxvi, 170, 171, 233, 255, 256
Gibson, Bruce, xxv, 28, 36, 38, 46, 69, 77, 95, 145, 168, 232, 241
Gibson, Horatio G., 250
Gibson, Joseph, 93, 133, 241
Gibson, Joseph (24–year–old merchant), 248
Glasscock, Aquila, 118, 245
Glen Welby 104, 232, 233, 241, 243, 257
Goody, Thomas. *See* Thomas Goode Carter
Gordon's Dale, 256
Gordonsville, Va., 76, 88, 189
Graham, Elizabeth, 28, 231
Graham, Eugene, 228
Graham, Fanny, 228
Graham, James, 231
Grant, Gen. Ulysses S., 86, 150, 239
Gray, Cecil, 141
Gray, Robert F., 61, 159, 161, 165, 244, 236, 253
Gray, Willie, 105, 242

Grayson, Alexander ("Alex"), 39, 40–42, 46, 114, 170, 233, 239, 255
Grayson, Elizabeth ("Nannie"), 86, 239
Grayson, Richard, 61, 121, 246
Grayson, T. Fitzhugh, 6, 45, 225
Griffith, Gen. Richard, 122, 246
Grogan, Charles E., 174, 189, 217, 218, 219, 256, 257
Gulick, George Milton, 177, 218, 256
Gunnell, Dr. W. P., xxvii, 104, 117, 118, 119, 133, 160, 242

Haley, John, 107, 243
Hall, Charles, 255
Hall, Edward, 244
Hall, Henry Arthur, 31, 69, 117, 244
Hall, James, 111, 248
Hall, Jane, 226, 227
Hall, William ("Willy"), 248
Harding, Sally, 173, 174
Harpers Ferry, W.V., 66, 101, 113, 158, 163, 224, 226, 250
Harrison, Burr William, 244
Harrison, George W., 30, 35, 45, 85, 115, 188
Harrison, Jenny, 30, 135, 149
Harrison, John M., 30, 35, 45, 85, 115, 188, 239, 244
Harrison, John Mason ("Cousin John"), 29, 112, 232, 244
Harrison, Sarah, 244
Harrison, Susan, 115, 239, 244
Harrisonburg, Va., 121, 122, 242, 243
Hatch, Gen. John P., 127, 247
Hatcher, Harry, 217–19
Hatcher's Mill, 217
Hathaway, Elizabeth, 183, 257
Hathaway, James H., 183, 184, 257
Hathaway, Mary, 183, 257
Hearst, Mrs. William Randolph, 198
Hemp Bales, Battle of, 29, 232
Henderson, Rebecca Beverley ("Aunt Becca"), 13, 17, 227
Herbert, Arthur, 15, 228, 241
Herbert, Elizabeth D. ("Cousin Mittie"), 77, 88, 116, 136, 201, 202, 227, 228, 238
Herbert, William, 12, 227, 228
Hereford, Miss Margaret, 15, 25, 28, 61, 77, 228, 231
Hill, Gen. Ambrose Powell, 140, 141

Hill, Gen. Daniel Harvey, 119, 250
Hill, The, xviii, 199
Homer, Alexander, 19, 229
Hooker, Gen. Joseph, 150, 157, 159
Hopwell, Va., 213
Hotchkiss, Elijah J., 59, 236
Hudson, Capt. Edward, 218
Hughes, George M., 29, 232
Hunter, Rebecca (Lady), 222
Hutchinson, Samuel, 86, 239

Independence, Mo., 132

Jackson, "A man named", 122
Jackson, Claiborne (Gov. of Missouri), 225, 228
Jackson, Gen. Henry, 28
Jackson, Nancy, 19, 229
Jackson, Gen. Thomas J. "Stonewall", xxiv, 58, 61, 73, 77–79, 89, 93, 94, 100, 101, 103, 104, 107, 110, 111, 112, 119, 120, 121,123, 130, 131, 132, 135, 136, 138, 145, 148, 160, 236, 238, 240–44, 246, 248–50, 253
James Island, Battle of, 118, 245
Jennings, Mr., 132
Johnson, "A man named", 148
Johnson, Gen. Edward "Allegheny", 95, 241
Johnson, Ransel, 86, 239
Johnson's Island, Oh., 256
Johnston, Gen. Albert Sidney, 119, 232, 239
Johnston, Gen. Joseph E., xxiv, xxix, 5, 28, 82, 85, 105, 162, 223, 232, 235, 243
Jones, Gen. William E. "Grumble", xxvii, 244, 251

Kendale, 199
Kernstown, Battle of, 77, 78, 89,238, 240
Key, Francis Scott, 245
Key, Old Mr., 19
Key, Philip Barton, 245
Kidwell, John F., xx, 7, 8, 15,–17, 23–27, 29, 31–36, 41–43, 45, 57, 60, 70–72, 75–77, 81, 83, 86, 91, 96–98, 100, 102, 104–6, 109, 113, 114, 116, 117, 119, 120, 122, 128, 131, 135, 144, 175, 177–79, 189, 225, 243, 245

Kidwell, Susan, 120, 245
Kinloch, xviii, 132, 138, 146, 147, 158, 161, 177, 182, 189, 192, 193, 222, 226, 227, 230, 231, 233, 238, 249
Kinloch slave, Wilhelmina Edmunds, 214
"Kinloch Tom". *See* Thomas Baynton Turner
Kinsolving, Lucy, 39, 95, 99, 233, 242, 243
Kinsolving, Rev. O.A., xix, 11, 16, 25, 32, 40, 41, 43, 59, 60, 77, 78, 99, 121, 226, 233, 245
Knapp, Mrs. Ludwell, 40, 234

Lake, Ludwell, 189, 257
Lakeland Farm, 257
Latham, T. N., 47, 235
Lee, Anne Hill Carter, 221
Lee, Charlotte Wickham, 233, 242
Lee, Gen. Fitzhugh, 150, 157, 164, 166, 167, 188, 198, 252, 254, 259
Lee, Gen. George Washington Custis, 20, 229
Lee, Henry, "General Light Horse Harry", xviii
Lee, Lucy, 229
Lee, Mary Anne Randolph Custis ("Cousin Mary"), xviii, 104, 195, 196, 197, 221, 242, 258, 259
Lee, Mildred, xix, 222
Lee, Gen. Robert E., xviii, xxiii, xxvi, 26, 28, 91, 119, 134, 135, 138, 140, 159, 161, 163, 170–72, 193, 195, 199, 221, 229, 231–33, 242–44, 248, 249, 252, 254, 255, 258
Lee, Gen. William Henry Fitzhugh ("Rooney"), 169, 233, 242, 255
Leesburg, Va., 13, 26, 33, 36, 69, 70, 85, 91, 103, 104, 129, 227, 229, 231, 237, 240, 246
Leigh, Walter, 127, 247
Lesner (Lursnes), Gustavus, 162, 254
Lexington, Mo., 29, 227, 232
Lincoln, President Arbaham, xxviii, 3, 6, 12, 36, 43, 58, 112, 126, 138, 140, 149, 150, 170, 205, 226, 227, 239, 240, 252
Little Oatlands, 198
Llangollen, xviii
Logan, Mr. and Mrs. Lloyd, 164, 254
Longstreet, Gen. James, 119, 136, 164, 168, 170, 240, 245, 254, 255
Loring, Gen. William W., 34, 233

Loughborough, Anna, 143, 146, 192
Loughborough, Elizabeth Carter Randolph Turner, 233
Loughborough, Nathan ("Uncle Nathan"), 31, 39, 70, 73, 74, 84, 85, 93, 103, 112, 116, 117, 135, 138, 141, 143, 147, 172, 185, 192, 233, 237
Lowe, Mrs., 19
Lowe, Thaddeus S.C., 234
Lunceford, Harrison, 235
Lunceford, Julia, 45, 235
Lyon, Gen. Nathaniel, 12, 16, 227, 228

Maddux, Henry Cabell, 218
Manassas Gap Railroad, 173, 227, 240
Manassas Junction, 5, 9, 11, 18, 23–25, 27, 135, 136, 224
Manassas, Va., xxiv, xxv, 3, 7, 9, 21–24, 27–29, 37, 68, 94, 121, 135, 137, 171, 223–26, 229, 247, 249
Mann, Col. William D'Alton, 172, 185, 256
Marshal, Ashton, 79
Marshall, Anne Kinloch Lee, xxiii
Marshall, Chief Justice John, xviii, 257
Marshall, Lucy Bolling Randolph, 229
Marshall, Col. Thomas, 257
Marshall, Va. *See* Salem, Va.
Mason and Slidell, 43, 46, 58, 59, 233
Mason, George, 222, 229
Mason, Randolph Fitzhugh, 20, 136, 229, 249
Matthews, John, 90, 240
McArtor, Robert C., 165, 167, 241, 254
McCabe, Capt. George F., 87, 98, 102, 202, 203, 240
McClellan, Gen. George B., 59, 85, 91, 103, 119–22, 125, 130, 134, 139, 140, 145, 234, 236–38, 240, 242, 245, 251
McCulloch, Gen. Ben, 12, 76, 227, 237
McDonald, Angus, 5, 13, 224, 233
McDonald, Craig Woodrow, 121, 246
McDonald, William N., 36, 233
McDowell, Va., Battle of, 241
McDowell, Irvin, xxiv, 223
McIlhaney, Dr. John, 146, 251
McIntosh, Charles R., 218
McIntosh, Gen. James M., 237
Means, Capt. Samuel C., 126, 133, 247, 248
Memphis, Tenn., 64, 246

Merritt, Gen. Wesley, 184, 257
Middleburg, Va., xxvi, 17, 30, 40, 78, 80, 81, 90, 95, 96, 109, 121, 131, 132, 136–39, 157, 161, 164, 168, 182, 186, 188, 199, 222, 225, 229, 232–35, 238, 243, 244, 249, 250, 253–55
Mill Springs (Somerset), Battle of, 62, 236
Millwood, Va., 125
Milroy, Mary, 164
Milroy, Gen. Robert, 95, 163, 241, 254
Minnigerode, Maj. Charles, 198, 259
Minnigerode, Rev. Frederic E., 198
Minnigerode, Lucy, 259
Minnigerode, Virginia. *See* Virginia Cuthbert Powell
Morgan, Ann, 181, 256
Morgan, Gen. George W., 132, 248
Morgan, Gen. John Hunt, 125, 127, 246, 248, 252
Morgan, William, 256
Mosby, Col. John S., xxvi, xxvii, 150, 158, 168, 169, 172, 175, 176, 178–80, 184, 185, 189, 192, 193, 211, 213, 214, 217, 219, 220, 224, 226, 244, 253, 255–57, 259
Mosby, William, 174, 256
Moss, William, 43, 234
Mount Garrison, 213
Munford, Col. Thomas T., 79, 238, 254
Munson, John, 218, 220, 255, 256
Munson's Hill, 230
Murfreesborough, Tenn., 125, 236, 246
Murphy, John N., 218, 219
Murrell, Jesse F., 29, 232

Nashville, Tenn., 64, 66, 125, 252
Nelson, William N., 6, 224
New Bern, N.C., 76, 236, 238, 252
New Orleans, La., 118, 119, 126, 127, 170, 245, 247, 252
Newlan, Samuel, 58, 235
Newstead, 115, 244
Noland, Anna, 94, 124, 241
Noland, Burr Powell, 80, 138, 225, 232, 235, 241
Noland, Catherine Huntington, 46, 235
Noland, Lena, 148
Noland, Lloyd, 229, 232
Noland, Nancy Whiting Powell, 229, 232, 241

Noland, Richard William ("Cousin Dick"), 19, 32, 46, 229
Noland, Susan ("Cousin Sue"), 29, 30, 232, 235, 241

Oak Grove, Battle of, 117, 245
Oak Hill, 189, 257
Oakley, xvii, xix–xxii, xxiv, xxvi, xxvii, xxx, 4, 20, 39, 44, 67, 118, 133, 183, 196–99, 218, 219, 222–26, 228–30, 234, 235, 237, 243, 245, 251, 253, 256
Oakley slaves
—Aunt Louise, 92, 121
—Aunt Polly, xxix, 28, 105, 178
—Beck, 60, 117, 118, 132
—Ben, 8, 24, 29, 31, 33, 42, 45–47, 70, 93, 113, 116, 120, 127, 225
—Dan, 8, 61, 78, 225
—Davy, 35, 36, 70
—George, 112
—Harriet, 11, 30, 92, 121, 143, 178
—Horace, 91
—Johnny (husband of Mary), 19, 31, 32, 61, 62
—Letty, 45
—Lucinda Willis, 11, 28, 30, 33, 75, 121, 178, 197, 253
—Margaret, 104, 118, 132, 133, 242
—Maria, 60, 116, 117, 118, 128, 132
—Mary (wife of Johnny), 28, 31, 113, 116, 128, 133
—Mimi, 72, 85, 120
—Otway, 70, 71
—Patsey, 28, 30, 58, 105, 117, 118, 149, 175
—Rachel ("Mammy"), 10, 12, 30, 46, 57, 58, 121, 179, 226
—Ralph, 70
—Richard (Uncle Billy's son), 70, 71, 112, 237
—Robert Buckner, xxii, 17, 28, 75, 84, 110, 114, 116, 117, 146, 159, 165, 167, 168, 175–77, 197, 228, 237
—Rosetta, 97, 117, 118
—Selina, 120, 127
—Simon, xxix, 8, 104, 116, 127, 225
—Talbot, 17
—Tolbert, 119, 121, 175
—Tom, 15, 228
—Uncle Billy (father of Richard), 8, 11, 33, 40–42, 45, 57, 69–71, 97, 225, 228, 237
—Uncle Dan, 58, 110, 117, 118, 132, 142, 161, 170
—Uncle Joshua, 75, 110, 112, 117, 133, 137, 167, 185
—Uncle Reed, 117, 118
—Wilmouth, 17, 24, 118, 166, 178, 228
Oatlands, 36, 173, 180, 182, 185, 192, 198, 223, 230, 244, 256

Paris, Va., 5, 41, 145, 167, 232–34, 246, 251
Pea Ridge, Battle of, 76, 227, 237
Pelham, John, 150, 250
Perryville, Battle of, 140, 250
Pettit, Mrs. Allen, 60, 236
Peyton, Margaret, 181, 256
Piedmont Hunt, xxi
Piedmont (Delaplane), Va., 5, 13, 35, 83, 89, 97, 141, 142, 148, 164, 175, 189, 192, 223
Pinkney, Rebecca Rogers deButts, 58, 235
Pinkney, Capt, Robert F., 235
Plains (White Plains), Va., The, xviii, 16, 18, 23, 24, 78, 115, 135, 145, 159, 173, 177, 181–83, 185, 199, 213, 222, 245
Plaster, George Emory, xxv, 10, 11, 44, 46, 226
Pope, Gen. John, xxviii, 125, 126, 130–34, 207–9, 243, 246, 248, 249
Porter, Col. John C., 247
Port Republic, Battle of, 107, 111, 243
Powell, Alfred Harrison, 225
Powell, Ann Rebecca Holmes Boyd ("Aunt Ann"), 89, 240
Powell, Anna Lucas Hunt ("Annie"), 125, 243
Powell, Catherine Brooke, 229
Powell, Charles Leven, 136, 224, 249
Powell, Conrad, xix
Powell, Daniel Lee ("Cousin Lee"), 20, 229
Powell, Fannie, 124
Powell, Dr. Francis Whiting ("Uncle Frank"), 33, 71, 233, 238
Powell, George Cuthbert (Ida's father), xviii, xix
Powell, George Cuthbert (Ida's great-uncle), xviii, 221, 229
Powell, Humphrey B., 240
Powell, John and Maria, 238
Powell, Katherine Whiting ("Kate"). *See* Katherine Whiting Powell Carter

Powell, Lt. Col. Leven, xviii, 221
Powell, Lizzie, 141
Powell, Dr. Llewellyn, 20, 229
Powell, Lloyd F., 6, 224, 249
Powell, Lucien ("Buddy"), 81, 238
Powell, Lucy Lee, 229
Powell, Marietta Fauntleroy Turner ("Mamma"), xvii, xviii, xix, xx, xxi, xxiv, 7, 8, 12, 13, 15, 20–22, 25, 29, 30, 34, 40–44, 46, 58, 60, 61, 71, 72, 82, 85, 90, 92, 93, 95, 96, 99, 101–4, 107, 109, 113, 121, 124, 131, 132, 141, 161, 165, 167, 171, 174, 177, 179, 180, 183, 190, 192, 193, 195–99, 221, 222, 228, 253, 258, 259
Powell, "Mick", 23, 230
Powell, Olivia Claggett ("Lilly"), 81, 89, 238
Powell, Robert Randolph ("Brother"), 13, 44, 225, 243
Powell, Robert Conrad, 40, 234
Powell, Thomas, xix, 222
Powell, Virginia Cuthbert ("Jenny"), xviii, xx, 43, 46, 80, 81, 94, 120, 148, 174, 175, 180, 185, 186, 187, 190, 191, 198, 199, 224, 234, 246, 251, 259
Powell, William Alexander, 229
Preston, Margaret Junkin, 123, 246
Price, Gen. Sterling, 46, 64, 227, 232, 235, 250
Prince Albert of England, 58, 235

Queen Victoria, 58, 119, 235

Randolph, Allan, 44
Randolph, Rev. A.M., 29, 232
Randolph, Eliza Carter. *See* Eliza Carter Randolph Turner
Randolph, Elizabeth Hill Carter, 221
Randolph, Janet Weaver, 196, 258
Randolph, Miss M., 213
Randolph, Col. Robert, 221
Ravensworth, xxiv, xxv
Rectortown, Va., 83, 91, 93, 94, 103, 173, 175, 177, 184, 201, 217, 239, 240, 257, 259
Richards, Capt. Adolphus ("Dolly"), 218, 224
Richards, Dr. Alva, 185, 257
Richards, Jesse, 5, 224
Richards, William, 224

Richmond, Va., xxiii, xxiv, 3, 6, 7, 17–20, 27, 62, 66, 93, 101, 103–5, 107, 108, 118–22, 125, 127, 129, 130, 160, 162, 172, 187, 225, 227, 229, 236–38, 240–43, 245–49, 258
Roanoke Island, 62, 64, 65, 236
Robertson, Gen. Beverly H., xxix, 110, 129, 168, 244, 247
Rogers, Arthur, 107, 108, 243
Rogers, Asa Jr., 142, 251
Rogers, Gen. Asa, 80, 121, 233, 238, 243, 245
Rogers, Mrs. John, 80
Roland, 227
Romney, W.V., 5, 58, 61, 224, 236
Rosecrans, Gen. William S., xxix, 26, 34, 95, 231, 233, 241, 250, 252
Ross, Capt. Christian, 177, 178, 256
Ruggles, Col. George D., 207, 209

Salem (Marshall), Va., 23, 81, 82, 135, 136, 173, 177, 189, 223, 225, 231, 239, 240, 244, 256, 257
Savannah, Ga., 66
Schenck, Gen. Robert, 95, 241
Scott, Betsy, 147
Scott, Fanny Carter, 17, 30, 85, 232, 240
Scott, John M., 15, 16, 17–19, 31, 228
Scott, Robert Eden, 89, 90, 147, 240
Scott, Robert Taylor, 32, 41, 76, 91, 92, 232
Second Manassas, 137, 223, 247, 249
Selby, 199
Seward, Sec. of State William, 138, 170, 205, 255
Sharpsburg. *See* Antietam
Shaw, Christopher C., 177, 218, 256
Shenandoah Valley (the Valley), xxvi, 4, 67, 101, 104, 107, 119, 125, 139, 140, 163, 172, 189, 208, 238, 241, 243, 254
Sheridan, Gen. Philip, 172, 186, 188, 189, 257
Shields, Gen. James, 107, 243
Shiloh, Battle of, 83, 101, 239, 242
Shirley, 162, 221, 247
Sickles, Gen. Daniel, 118, 245
Skinker, Samuel L., 211, 212
Smith, Capt. Boyd, 64, 68
Smith, Gen. Edmund Kirby, 96, 241
Smith, Frank, 240
Snickersville (Bluemont), Va., 76, 116, 120, 160, 238, 254

INDEX 269

South Mountain, Battle of, 139, 250
Spencer, William A., 180, 181, 256
St. Louis, Mo., 16, 20, 22, 44, 63, 64, 83, 95, 131, 225, 227, 230, 234, 239, 243, 247, 257
"St. Louis Tom". *See* Thomas Theodore Turner
Stanton, U.S. Sec. of War Edwin, 206, 247
Staunton, Va., 122, 224
Steele, Billings, 189, 257
Steer, Sarah Ann, 196, 258
Stephenson, Johnny, 129
Stephenson, Josephine, 24, 93, 113, 129, 173, 174
Stephenson, Martha L. ("Mittie"), 25, 43, 74, 75, 101, 173, 174, 231
Stephenson, Mary D., 25, 74, 95, 167, 230, 231
Stephenson, Nannie G., 74, 113
Stephenson, William A., 27, 36, 73, 74, 86, 121, 230, 231, 241
Stephensons, The, 29, 30, 74, 85, 92, 111, 125, 160
Stone Bridge. *See* First Manassas
Strasburg, Va., 73, 93, 101, 103
Stuart, Gen. J. E. B., xxiv, 63, 133, 139, 141, 144, 150, 161, 163, 164, 168, 170, 225, 226, 232, 235, 243, 247, 250, 252, 254, 255

Tavenner, Richard, 35, 233
Taylor, Agnes, 25
Taylor, Katey, 141
Taylor, Nannie, 124
Taylor, Gen. Richard, 111, 244
Taylor, Pres. Zachary, 244
Thompson, Gen. Meriwether Jeff, 129, 247
Throckmorton, Isaac, 130, 247
Throckmorton, William W., 247
Trimble, Gen. Isaac, 27, 229, 231
Tudor, Rev. William, 121, 246
Turberville, George, 218
Turner, Bradshaw Beverley, 135, 137, 238, 249
Turner, Edward Carter ("Uncle Ned"), xxiii, 78, 83, 121, 132, 138, 147, 162, 182, 211, 227, 230, 231, 238, 239, 249–51
Turner, Elizabeth Carter ("Lizzie"), 21, 27, 35, 57, 234

Turner, Eliza Carter Randolph ("Grandmother,""Grandma"), xx, 12, 21, 62, 70, 72, 78, 90, 113, 125, 132, 193, 221, 258
Turner, Fanny Palmer, 221
Turner, Henry Smith ("Uncle Henry"), 83, 181, 227, 230, 239, 257
Turner, Jane P. ("Janey"), 132, 248
Turner, John W., 159, 253
Turner, Julia Mary Hunt ("Aunt Julia"), 13, 227, 239
Turner, Margaret Patterson ("Aunt Margaret"), 12, 58, 149, 197, 227, 252, 259
Turner, Sarah Beverley ("Aunt Sarah"), 132, 177, 178, 227, 230, 231, 238, 248
Turner, Shirley Carter ("Uncle Shirley"), xix, 44, 230
Turner, Sophie Calhoun, 17, 20, 27, 57, 227, 229, 233, 234
Turner, Adm. Thomas, xix, 221
Turner, Maj. Thomas IV, xviii, 258
Turner, Thomas Baynton ("Kinloch Tom"), 26, 27, 37, 40, 41, 57, 99, 135, 138, 147, 158, 211–15, 230, 231, 234, 238, 253
Turner, Thomas Shirley ("Baltimore Tom"), 42, 43, 57, 230, 234
Turner, Thomas Theodore ("St. Louis Tom"), 20, 22, 95, 121, 131, 136, 138, 139, 230, 234, 239, 250
Turner, William Fitzhugh, 226, 234
Turner, William Hall ("Willie"), 9, 20, 22, 27, 35, 46, 57, 61, 95, 135, 138, 139, 226, 229, 233, 234
Turner, Wilson Price Hunt, 20, 22, 35, 95, 136, 138, 230, 239, 250

Union (Unison), Va., 120, 141, 159, 165
Upperville, Va., xvii–xx, xxv, xxvi, 5, 8, 9, 14–17, 21, 24–26, 28, 35, 40, 41, 43, 47, 57, 61, 68, 70, 71, 73, 77, 78, 82, 85, 87, 89, 92 95–97, 110, 112, 116, 118, 119, 121, 126, 128, 129, 133, 136, 137, 139, 141, 142, 146, 148, 157, 159, 161, 162, 164, 167, 170, 179, 183, 184, 186, 188, 189, 201, 217, 219, 222–26, 228, 230–32, 235, 238, 239, 241, 242, 244, 246, 248, 251–55, 259
Utterback, Charles, 211, 212

Valverde (Fort Craig), N.M., Battle of, 83, 239
Van Dorn, Gen. Earl, 140, 247, 248, 250
Van Ingen (Van Dryen), John H., 144, 251
Vicksburg, Miss., 126, 127, 129, 150, 162, 170, 171, 247, 253, 255
von Borcke, Maj. Heros, 168, 255

Waite, Maj. John M., 179, 181, 256
Waldhauer (Waldhoem), David, 61, 236
Walker, Gen. James A., 140, 250
Warrenton, Va., 47, 61, 70, 77, 81, 133, 221, 235, 238, 240, 241, 249, 251, 253
Washington, Christian (Mrs. Richard), 181, 256
Washington, D.C., xvii, xxiv, xxvi, 8, 16, 21, 22, 83, 88, 92, 97, 117, 120, 129, 138, 145, 149, 170, 172, 181, 196, 198, 234, 238, 240, 242, 251, 253, 254, 256, 257, 259
Washington, George, xviii, 221, 222, 242
Washington, John Augustine, 26, 231
Washington, N.C., 236
Weidmayer, C.E., 8, 9, 11, 13, 14, 30, 35, 71–73, 75–77, 85, 87, 97, 105, 107, 108, 110, 111, 114, 115, 116, 120, 128, 130, 138, 202, 225
Welbourne, 7, 11–13, 24, 27, 28, 31–33, 44, 58, 71, 85, 87, 90–92, 94, 102, 104, 110, 114, 116–18, 131, 136, 141, 145, 185, 188, 197, 223, 225–28, 238, 239, 243, 246, 248
Welbourne slaves: Jackson, Nancy, 19, 229; Lewis, 124, 246

Wheat, Robert, 85, 92, 239
White House, Va., 119, 242
White Post (The Post), Va., 43, 46, 70, 234
White, Elijah V., 80, 81, 238, 251
White's Ford, 139
Whiting, Clarence, 105, 107, 108, 136, 243
Wilcox, Gen. Orlando, 143, 251
Williams, Dr. Ira, 137, 249
Williams, John J., 218
Williams, Dr. Thomas C., 133, 248
Williamsburg, Battle of, 91, 92, 95, 101, 240
Williamson, James, 256
Willis, Henson or Hanson (husband of Lucinda), 158, 176, 178, 179, 181, 184, 187, 197, 226, 253
Willisville, 197, 226
Wilson, William A., 6, 61, 138, 225
Winchester, Va., xxvi, 5, 7, 8, 23, 25, 26, 34, 59, 61, 66, 67, 69, 76, 78, 88, 89, 94, 95, 101, 107, 110, 122, 125, 163, 164, 169, 172, 223–26, 228, 231, 236, 237, 240–43, 254
Winder, Gen. Charles S., 131, 132, 248
Windsor Farm, 115, 239, 244
Wise, Gen. Henry A., 62, 231, 236
Wise, O. Jennings, 62, 236
Wornal (Wurnel), John, 124, 127, 246
Wrenn, Lt. Albert, 217

Yerby, W. G., 132, 235
Yorktown, Va., 83, 85, 86, 88, 89, 91, 240

Zouaves, 18, 226, 236

In the Shadow of the Enemy was designed and typeset on a Macintosh OS 10.4 computer system using InDesign software. The body text is set in 10/13 Palatino and display type is set in Palatino Oldstyle. This book was designed and typeset by Stephanie Thompson.

www.ingramcontent.com/pod-product-compliance
Lightning Source LLC
Chambersburg PA
CBHW030306080526
44584CB00012B/460